Individuality and the Group

Contributor Affiliations

Gamze Baray, University of Exeter

B. Ann Bettencourt, University of Missouri

Nyla R. Branscombe, University of Kansas

Bertjan Doosje, University of Amsterdam

Naomi Ellemers, Leiden University

Michael J. Halloran, La Trobe University

S. Alexander Haslam, University of Exeter

Matthew J. Hornsey, University of Queensland

Jolanda Jetten, University of Exeter

Emiko S. Kashima, The University of Melbourne

Geoffrey J. Leonardelli, University of Toronto

Fabio Lorenzi-Cioldi, University of Geneva

Fathali M. Moghaddam, Georgetown University

Lisa Molix, University of Missouri

Thomas A. Morton, University of Exeter

Cynthia L. Pickett, University of California

Tom Postmes, University of Exter

Deborah Prentice, Princeton University

Stephen Reicher, University of St Andrews

Katherine J. Reynolds, Australian National University

Kennon M. Sheldon, University of Missouri

Russell Spears, Cardiff University

Roderick I. Swaab, Northwestern University

Amelia E. Talley, University of Missouri

John C. Turner, Australian National University

Kristine E. Veenstra, Australian National University

Individuality and the Group

Advances in Social Identity

Edited by

Tom Postmes
and
Jolanda Jetten

SAGE Publications
London ● Thousand Oaks ● New Delhi

Chapter 1 © Jolanda Jetten and Tom
Postmes 2006
Chapter 2 © John C. Turner, Katherine J.
Reynolds, S. Alexander Haslam, and Kristine
E. Veenstra 2006
Chapter 3 © Deborah Prentice 2006
Chapter 4 © Cynthia L. Pickett and Geoffrey
J. Leonardelli 2006
Chapter 5 © Matthew J. Hornsey 2006
Chapter 6 © Fabio Lorenzi-Cioldi 2006
Chapter 7 © Jolanda Jetten and Tom
Postmes 2006
Chapter 8 © Michael J. Halloran and Emiko
S. Kashima 2006

Chapter 9 © Fathali M. Moghaddam 2006
Chapter 10 © Russell Spears, Naomi Ellemers,
Bertjan Doosje, and Nyla R. Branscombe
2006
Chapter 11 © B. Ann Bettencourt, Lisa
Molix, Amelia E. Talley, and Kennon
M. Sheldon 2006
Chapter 12 © Tom Postmes, Gamze Baray,
S. Alexander Haslam, Thomas A. Morton,
and Roderick I. Swaab 2006
Chapter 13 © Stephen Reicher and S.
Alexander Haslam 2006
Chapter 14 © Tom Postmes and Jolanda
Jetten 2006

First published 2006

SAGE Publications Ltd
1 Oliver's Yard
55 City Road
London EC1Y 1SP

SAGE Publications Inc.
2455 Teller Road
Thousand Oaks, California 91320

SAGE Publications India Pvt Ltd
B-42, Panchsheel Enclave
Post Box 4109
New Delhi 110 017

British Library Cataloguing in Publication data

A catalogue record for this book is available
from the British Library

ISBN-10 1-4129-0320-3   ISBN-13 978-1-4129-0320-2
ISBN-10 1-4129-0321-3 (pbk)   ISBN-13 978-1-4129-0321-9

Library of Congress Control Number: 2005905985

Typeset by C&M Digitals (P) Ltd., Chennai, India
Printed in India by Gopsons Papers Ltd., Noida
Printed on paper from sustainable resources

Contents

1

Introduction: The Puzzle of Individuality and the Group

Jolanda Jetten and Tom Postmes

> How can we combine that degree of individual initiative which is necessary for
> progress with the degree of social cohesion that is necessary for survival?
> (Russell, 1949, p. 11)

The start of Bertrand Russell's 1949 book *Authority and the individual*
(the text of the first BBC Reith Lecture) is a familiar question. Russell
was certainly not the first to ponder about the relationship between the
individual and the collective, and his question reflects a classic dichotomy
that runs through the social sciences: the distinction between individual
and collective interest. Before Russell, many philosophers struggled with
this issue, and many had taken the view (like him) that there is a fundamental tension between the two; they appear to stand in opposition. For
instance, Hobbes (1650/1931) concluded that the relationship between
the individual and the collective is fundamentally conflictual.

More recently, historians and sociologists have identified that self-
interested values and morals are – in most eras and in particular in the
twentieth century – opposite and contradictory to those that would benefit
society at large (e.g., Baumeister, 1991; Putnam, 2000). Some theorizing
portrays the group as perverting the performance and wellbeing of individuals; and conversely many have argued that the individual may undermine
group cohesion and unity. For instance, Janis' (1982) archival research into
groupthink suggested that cohesion suppressed individual voice and his
model argued that disastrous decision-making outcomes were the result of
a lack of individuality in ordinary group members. Individuality has similarly been associated with mental health. For instance, it is argued that self-
actualization is best achieved by focusing on the individual self and turning
away from others and the groups one belongs to (Bellah, Madsen, Sullivan,
Swindler, & Tipton, 1985; Jung, 1971). In sum, there is a pervasive

assumption of antagonism between situations where the self operates individually and autonomously, and situations where self is subsumed in or merged with a group or collective. Moreover, in this antagonistic relationship the individual self is almost invariably seen as supreme – as a more rational, healthier, and authentic self.

This book is concerned with two theories that arose in opposition to such views, social identity theory (SIT) and self-categorization theory (SCT). These theories not only contest the notion that individual self is necessarily inferior, they also undermine the dichotomy between individual and group upon which such evaluative contrasts are based (Turner, Hogg, Oakes, Reicher, & Weatherell, 1987). The key problem in the classical analysis, according to these theories, is that group and individual are not independent and separate, but are intimately connected and fundamentally inseparable. Hence, one cannot celebrate the individual without celebrating the "group", and vice versa.

The core theoretical construct in both theories, social identity, provides a bridge between the individual and the group, by incorporating key group characteristics into "personality" or identity. In this conception, it is social identity that enables the individual to act as a member of their group, even in isolation and on their own. Thus, a core feature of the social identity approach is its interactionist nature – breaching the static distinction between individual and group.

Social identity perspectives and individuality

The perspective on identity provided by the social identity and self-categorization theories has had many consequences, but perhaps the key one has been a rehabilitation of the group. Rather than being treated as the cause of various social ailments, the group is now also seen as part of the solution to faulty decision-making (Postmes, Spears, & Cihangir, 2001), a coping resource in times of organizational challenge (Haslam, 2001; Jetten, O'Brien, & Trindall, 2002), and even as a remedy for intergroup conflict (Gaertner & Dovidio, 2000; Hornsey & Hogg, 2000). These and other concepts and ideas developed within the social identity approach are increasingly part of mainstream social psychology, but they also find broad acceptance outside this field, in areas such as communication, organizational studies, management, political sciences, sociology, and even theology. The idea that groups and intergroup relations play a crucial role in our self-definitions and our responses to others has become widely accepted.

Notwithstanding this growth and enthusiasm, it is fair to say that social identity theory has also been subject to its fair share of criticism. Most of these critiques relate to a perceived mismatch between empirical research findings and hypotheses that were assumed to flow directly from social identity theory's core reasoning (e.g., whether there is a correlation between identification and ingroup bias: Hinkle & Brown, 1990), or discussions of the motivations underlying group behaviour (e.g., self-esteem enhancement, uncertainty reduction, achievement of positive distinctiveness: see Hogg & Abrams, 1990). These issues have been dealt with and have led to refinement of the theorizing and further development of the scope of the theory (e.g., Rubin & Hewstone, 1998; Turner, 1999).

The focus of this book is slightly different in that it is not so much concerned with controversies within social identity theory or with the question of what it has achieved so far. Rather, we set out to deal with the more thorny issue of individuality in the group. The key reason for this is that we believe recent advances in thinking about social identity have afforded a much more active and central role for the individual in social identity processes. The individual has become a central player in both intergroup and intragroup behaviour. For instance, even in the most extreme cases of intergroup behaviour (and perhaps especially in those cases, cf. Tajfel, 1978), individuality (in leadership, initiative, skills etc.) remains a key factor. The role of individuality is even more acute in intragroup processes, where strong intergroup dynamics may not be very important, but where social identity processes nevertheless do play an important role.

This new research on the role of individuality in the group is both refreshing and innovative. For one, it is a response to the common assumption that social identity perspectives have something to say about groups, but nothing about individuals. There is some truth to this assumption – the bulk of social identity research has focused on intergroup relations, and the role of the individual has not always been apparent in it. But, as this volume seeks to underline, this seems to be more a matter of empirical focus than of theoretical impotence – after all, both social identity and self-categorization theories were always intended to speak to the dynamic interplay between the individual and the group. Moreover, and more importantly, it extends social identity perspectives into new territory. As the chapters in this volume underline, exploration of this territory enables us to study phenomena such as personality and the subjective experience of individuality and autonomy, it enables us to study different kinds of groups such as cultures, and it enables us to study a different class of processes such as those observed in small group dynamics.

Reasons for the neglect of individuality in social identity

Why is it that the social identity approach has not dealt in as much detail with individuals and individuality as it has with groups? The causes for this limited attention can be traced to a multitude of factors but the most important probably relates to the fact that social identity theory itself is mainly a theory of intergroup relations. Indeed, as the title of the seminal chapter by Tajfel and Turner (1979) suggests, they proposed "an integrative theory of intergroup conflict" and not a theory of intragroup processes and/or the individual. At the same time, it is fair to say that, as a result of this emphasis, the theorizing about the individual in the group remains rather underdeveloped.

To appreciate the origins of the theory, we need to go back to early formulations of social identity theory and understand the issues the theory originally tried to tackle. In an attempt to counter the prevailing individualism in explaining intergroup relations in his time, Tajfel (1978) proposed a continuum with purely interpersonal behaviour at one extreme, and purely intergroup behaviour at the other. The importance of distinguishing interpersonal behaviour from intergroup behaviour cannot be underestimated and has led to important insights regarding the unique nature of intergroup dynamics. However, it does echo the classic contrast between individual and group to a certain extent, and there has been limited attention for the role of the individual. This is despite the fact that, as already noted, the interpersonal–intergroup continuum does not treat the individual *self* and the group as fundamentally opposed or antagonistic – it was more concerned with the treatment of *others* as individuals or group members. Indeed, in social identity theory, both individual and group behaviour are perceived as equally valid forms of self-expression. Nonetheless, by putting interpersonal and intergroup at opposite ends of a continuum, they have become each other's opposites.

A second reason for the limited attention to the role of the individual in the group relates to the way in which SIT and SCT are interpreted and adopted: social identity is sometimes presented in such a way that these theories, intended to theorize the interaction between individual and group, are turned into socially deterministic ones. For instance, a scant reading of social identity (and especially self-categorization) theory literature would easily give the impression that the influence of social identity is fairly mechanistic: when social identity is salient, people will act according to that identity and individual identities cease to exert their influence. Social identity is treated as an "on/off switch". This may be in part because the literature, which these students have relied on, is somewhat restricted, and in part because warnings in the original writings not to apply the theory mechanistically occasionally got lost along the way. For instance, Tajfel (1978) himself cautioned against this when introducing and discussing the interpersonal–intergroup continuum. With respect to the assertion that all social situations fall between the two extremes, he argued that:

This statement contains its own limitations, and it is important to make them as explicit as possible. There are the extreme outgroup haters who are likely to perceive all (or most) social situations involving the objects of their hatred as being relevant to the relations between the groups involved; but to most people, the simple appearance of members of an outgroup in a social situation does not necessarily classify the situation as being of an intergroup nature and does not therefore necessarily imply that they will engage in the corresponding forms of social behaviour. (p. 43)

In an attempt to do justice to the richness of SIT and SCT, this book aims to open up the discussion about some of these key concepts. In this regard, the reason why an overly mechanistic interpretation of the social identity approach is problematic becomes apparent when one starts applying the theory to a variety of domains. For example, teams and groups do not perform better to the extent that everyone blindly follows company rules or complies with norms. In crowds, the form that collective action takes is not simply "given" by existing social identities, but evolves over time in a dynamic in which intergroup processes and intragroup negotiation play a key role. In intergroup encounters, intragroup processes play a key role in determining a variety of ways in which relevant social identities will be construed, and in influencing a wide range of outcomes. At a more abstract level, any mechanistic interpretation of the social identity approach is challenged by the dynamics of identity change, the heterogeneity of perceptions of social identity, and the ability of individuals to influence the course of group action through communication, negotiation, and strategic and autonomous behaviours.

Aim of this book

The emphasis of the book is firmly on the central theoretical premises of the social identity approach and on exploring the ways in which this approach can take account of both individuality and social structure in its explanation of social behaviour. The book's theme is one of the key questions in the social identity approach: how to account for individual autonomy, disagreement, and disunity within groups that act in terms of a common identity.

We brought together several scholars at the cutting edge of this field, all of whom have a strong background in social identity theorizing. At the same time, although all contributors started from the same theoretical perspective, there is considerable diversity in the proposed solutions and the way they propose we can improve our thinking about individuality and the group. The result of this is that the theoretical solutions to the puzzle of individuality and the group are rich and varied in terms of their level of analysis, their theoretical starting point and the way the issues are studied.

One important way of ensuring this variety from the outset is by including in this book not only those who self-define as social identity researchers, but also those who work from closely related theoretical frameworks on these important issues (e.g., self-determination theory), and asking them to relate their insights to the wider frameworks of social identity theory and self-categorization theory.

Thus, the aim of this book is to represent the diversity in approaches, with the aim of reinvigorating debate about the individual in the group, rather than to offer clear-cut answers or solutions. Aside from this diversity, it is also important to highlight the commonalities in the chapters of this book. Most importantly, what *unites* all contributions is that they all move away from a classic distinction between the individual and the group. This is an important step in theory development and opens up the possibility of exploring the myriad ways in which the individual and the group interact, influence and inform each other. Indeed, a clear sense of curiosity and enthusiasm for the ways in which we can advance our theorizing and better understand social identity processes, at both the group and the individual level, emerges powerfully from all chapters.

Moreover, the purpose of the book is to illustrate the applications of this approach to various domains and a diverse range of group contexts. The question of the individual in the group is addressed in a wide variety of group contexts including family and friendship groups, small decision-making groups and teams, organizations, intergroup relations, social categories, and cultural groups. All contributors describe what the implications of their theoretical analysis are for practice in groups in a wider sense. In this way, the emphasis throughout the book is very much on identifying general principles (derived from social identity perspectives), which are then applied to a range of group contexts.

Structure of the book

The topic of individuality and the group is explored in three parts. The first part, about *expressing and experiencing individuality in the group*, is concerned with the different perspectives on how the interaction between individual and group can be conceptualized. The chapters in this part all propose ways to understand individuality and the group (and their simultaneous occurrence) by focusing on categorization processes and individual needs. Different approaches to studying this issue are sampled to understand categorization and feeling as an individual, individual need satisfaction, and consequences of expressions of individuality in the group.

In their self-categorization analysis of personality, *John Turner, Katherine Reynolds, Alex Haslam,* and *Kris Veenstra* discuss how traditional self-categorization theory concepts can inform our thinking about individuality and personality. With an emphasis on categorization processes, personal identity is seen as intrinsically linked to and interdependent with social identity and, like social identity, contingent on social context and social change.

Following this, the chapter by *Deborah Prentice* addresses the fundamental question of how one can be true to one's individuality and at the same time emerge the self in a group or larger collective. The proposed solution is concerned with the distinction between acting like an individual and feeling like an individual. In this way, Prentice maintains a firm categorical distinction between personal identity and group identity, and describes empirical research showing how people can feel like individuals but act like group members.

Another way to reconcile individual and group identity is put forward by *Cynthia Pickett* and *Geoffrey Leonardelli* and resides in the proposal that individual needs and motives influence identification processes and categorization. Drawing on optimal distinctiveness theory, they focus on two particular core human needs – the need for assimilation and the need for differentiation. These authors present recent empirical evidence to support their proposal that collective identities can be seen as resources which aid in the achievement of optimal distinctiveness.

The final chapter of the first part, by *Matthew Hornsey*, is concerned with the consequences of expressing individuality in the group. The idea that individuality is lost in the group is challenged by the notion that individuals do not always submerge in groups and that individuals can criticize groups and hold them accountable – without being ousted. The emphasis in this chapter is not so much on the motivations of the critic, as on the responses by the group and other group members to the critic. Hornsey discusses when standing out and criticizing the group is tolerated and when criticism is perceived as constructive or damaging to the group.

The second part addresses the issue of *shaping individuality through culture and social identity content*. All four chapters examine attributes of the group that regulate the expression of individuality and play a role in defining individuality within group and cultural contexts. In contrast to the earlier chapters, the emphasis here is predominantly on the *content of identity* in these groups, and how content shapes and structures the nature of individuality within the group. These chapters also discuss studies that suggest that the principles operating within culture can be equally applied to other types of groups (e.g., social categories, organizational settings, small groups).

Fabio Lorenzi-Cioldi starts this part by suggesting that status hierarchies have a crucial impact on social identification processes, and that the socio-structural context and group status affect the degree to which individuality within the group can be expressed. He presents an analysis and research showing that high-status and low-status groups adopt different and often contrasting identities. Whereas high-status group members express personal characteristics, members of low-status groups tend to emphasize perceptual interchangeability between the self and other ingroup members.

One of the conclusions of Lorenzi-Cioldi's analysis – that personal identity is as much a group phenomenon as social identity – chimes well with the second chapter in this part, by *Jolanda Jetten* and *Tom Postmes*. These authors argue that the degree to which individualism is prevalent and guides behaviour in a group may depend on the salience of group norms promoting individualism. It is suggested that when a person defines themselves as an individual this may be the product of social influence, guided by specific group norms of individualism. In this view, intragroup variability, individualism and differentiation are seen not only as compatible with but also as flowing from shared social identity.

These ideas on how the content of identities can represent both individualist and collectivist tendencies is applied to culture by *Michael Halloran* and *Emiko Kashima*. They present empirical research showing how cultural worldviews (and conceptions of the nature and place of the individual in society in particular) are closely bound up with social identities. Their research shows that social identity salience (and not personal identity salience) regulates the relative importance of different conceptions of self, depending on the content of the worldview in question.

The implications of culture for the social identity approach are also elaborated in the final chapter of this part by *Fathali Moghaddam*. He presents an analysis of the way the self is construed in Eastern versus Western cultures and explores the compatibility of social identity theory with cultural perspectives. Specifically, social identity assumptions underlying the concept of the individual are critically examined in the light of different cultures and whether they allow for cultural variations.

The third part examines *the individual–group dynamic*. Whereas the second part focuses on the role of the content of identity in shaping individuality, the emphasis of the chapters in the third part is very much on the interplay between individuality and the group. A theme that unifies the chapters in this part is that they all explore ways in which both the individual informs the group and the group informs the individual. The chapters differ, however, in their theorizing about the processes that are seen as crucial in this process.

Russell Spears, Naomi Ellemers, Bertjan Doosje, and *Nyla Branscombe* start their chapter with the observation, using the concept of respect, that groups shape individuals, but also that individuals shape the group. These authors propose breaking away from dualist thinking about individualism and groups and present research which explores the consequences of group-based respect for perceptions, feelings, and group behaviour, and the group-based nature of respect.

Along these lines, *Ann Bettencourt, Lisa Molix, Amelia Talley*, and *Kennon Sheldon* discuss how social roles allow for individual differentiation within groups. They present research showing how social roles can simultaneously meet needs for authentic self-expression and connectedness. Their research illustrates the value of bringing together and integrating literatures on group memberships, social roles, and motivation. Moreover, it is proposed that social roles can facilitate the mutual satisfaction of needs for autonomy and relatedness, without necessarily presenting a conflict between individual and group motivations.

Tom Postmes, Gamze Baray, Alex Haslam, Thomas Morton, and *Roderick Swaab* address the issue of group formation in their chapter, distinguishing between the influence of intragroup and intergroup processes. Using Durkheim's distinction between mechanical and organic solidarity, they argue that groups can be formed (and social unity achieved) on the basis of diversity as much as on the basis of similarity. The primary concern here is with organizational contexts and small (decision-making) groups, and examples of the application of these ideas in these contexts are provided.

The chapter by *Stephen Reicher* and *Alex Haslam* discusses data from the BBC Prison Study and argues for the interaction between personality and group factors (e.g., status, power). Notably, the authors challenge the notion that, in groups, people become mindless and lose agency. This research is relevant to a variety of group settings – in particular in the organizational and institutional realm – and leads to the consideration of the dynamics of intergroup conflict and (intragroup) leadership.

The final chapter in this book is a discussion chapter by *Tom Postmes* and *Jolanda Jetten*. In this, the key themes emerging from the contributing chapters are identified and discussed. This review makes it clear that the book is unique in the sense that it brings together diverse research on a central issue and provides a marketplace for important theoretical advances. An attempt is made to integrate these novel developments, but the chapter also recognizes the diversity and difference in theoretical solutions to issues at the heart of social identity research: the relation between individuality and the group.

REFERENCES

Baumeister, R. F. (1991). *The meanings of life*. New York: Guilford.

Bellah, R. N., Madsen, R., Sullivan, W. M., Swindler, A., & Tipton, S. M. (1985). *Habits of the heart: Individualism and commitment in American life*. Berkeley: University of California Press.

Gaertner, S. L., & Dovidio, J. F. (2000). *Reducing intergroup bias: The common ingroup identity model*. Philadelphia: Psychology Press.

Haslam, S. A. (2001). *Psychology in organizations: The social identity approach* (1st ed.). London: Sage.

Hinkle, S., & Brown, R. J. (1990). Intergroup comparisons and social identity: Some links and lacunae. In D. Abrams & M. A. Hogg (Eds.), *Social identity theory: Constructive and critical advances* (pp. 48–70). New York: Harvester Wheatsheaf.

Hobbes, T. (1650/1931). *Leviathan*. New York: Dutton (originally published London, 1650).

Hogg, M. A., & Abrams, D. (1990). Social motivation, self-esteem and social identity. In D. Abrams & M. A. Hogg (Eds.), *Social identity theory: Constructive and critical advances* (pp. 28–47). London: Harvester Wheatsheaf.

Hornsey, M. J., & Hogg, M. A. (2000). A comparison of the mutual intergroup differentiation and common ingroup identity models of prejudice reduction. *Personality and Social Psychology Bulletin, 26*, 242–256.

Janis, I. L. (1982). *Groupthink: Psychological studies of policy decisions and fiascos* (2nd ed.). Boston: Houghton Mifflin.

Jetten, J., O'Brien, A., & Trindall, N. (2002). Changing identity: Predicting adjustment to organisational restructure as a function of subgroup and superordinate identification. *British Journal of Social Psychology, 41*, 281–297.

Jung, C. G. (1971). The spiritual problem of modern man. In *The portable Jung*. New York: Viking (original work published 1928).

Postmes, T., Spears, R., & Cihangir, S. (2001). Quality of decision making and group norms. *Journal of Personality and Social Psychology, 80*, 918–930.

Putnam, R. D. (2000). *Bowling alone: The collapse and revival of American community*. New York: Simon & Schuster.

Rubin, M., & Hewstone, M. (1998). Social identity theory's self-esteem hypothesis: A review and some suggestions for clarification. *Personality and Social Psychology Review, 2*, 40–62.

Russell, B. (1949). *Authority and the individual*. London: Allen & Unwin.

Tajfel, H. (Ed.) (1978). *Differentiation between social groups: Studies in the social psychology of intergroup relations*. London: Academic.

Tajfel, H., & Turner, J. C. (1979). An integrative theory of intergroup conflict. In W. G. Austin & S. Worchel (Eds.), *The social psychology of intergroup relations* (pp. 33–47). Monterey, CA: Brooks/Cole.

Turner, J. C. (1999). Some current issues in research on social identity and self-categorization theories. In N. Ellemers, R. Spears, & B. Doosje (Eds.), *Social identity: Context, commitment, content* (pp. 6–34). Oxford: Blackwell.

Turner, J. C., Hogg, M. A., Oakes, P. J., Reicher, S. D., & Wetherell, M. S. (1987). *Rediscovering the social group: A self-categorization theory*. Oxford: Blackwell.

PART 1

Expressing and Experiencing Individuality in the Group

2

Reconceptualizing Personality: Producing Individuality by Defining the Personal Self

John C. Turner, Katherine J. Reynolds, S. Alexander Haslam and Kristine E. Veenstra

Introduction

In this chapter we take a fresh look at personality and individuality by making use of insights from self-categorization theory (SCT). The fact of human individuality is striking. We take for granted that people are characterized by individual differences and, where these are sufficiently stable and consistent and seem related to their underlying psychological make-up, we talk of personality. Explaining personality is one of the major tasks which psychology has attempted over the last hundred years. Every significant psychological perspective, from Freudian psychodynamics to classical and social learning theory to the cognitive perspective, has developed one or more ways of understanding personality. There is also the trait approach, which has been developed for no other purpose.

It is not our aim to review this huge literature, or to deny the importance of the many factors it has explored. Rather we wish to outline a way of thinking about personality which we believe addresses significant gaps and problems in mainstream understanding. We suggest that the implicit model of personality which has taken root in psychology is problematic in significant ways.

The approach to personality taken here builds on an existing and distinguished tradition which gives pre-eminence to the self-process and the self-concept in understanding individuality. A range of important theorists have adopted the view that the key to understanding personality is through a cognitive analysis of the processes and structures of the self-concept (e.g., Bandura, 1997; Epstein, 1973; Markus, 1977; Markus & Wurf, 1987; Mischel, 1973; Mischel & Shoda, 1995; Stryker & Statham, 1985). It is assumed that the way in which an individual perceives, defines and feels about himself or herself determines the way in which he or she will behave in any given situation, and that the self-concept is both a repository of past experience, learning and socialization and a contemporary source of motivation, values, beliefs and knowledge. This tradition provides a way of understanding how individual behaviour can both vary idiosyncratically from situation to situation and at the same time express a continuity of the psychology which an individual brings to each situation.

The present approach differs from the existing tradition in several ways, but most notably in rejecting the idea that *the human self can be reduced solely to phenomena of personality and individuality*. SCT is a theory of the psychological group as well as of individuality. It assumes that both collective and individual behaviour are a function of self-categorizing. By making a distinction between personal and social identity in order to account for the psychological discontinuity between individuality and groupness, it throws new light onto the special character of individuality. By denying that personality is the whole story of the self-concept, by giving much more weight to the group aspects of the self-concept, what emerges, paradoxically, is a much richer and more complex view of personality than is found currently in the literature. Understanding the particularity of personality within the self-concept is not to deny its importance but to enrich the theoretical context within which it must be interpreted. We shall first sketch the basic analysis of personal and social identity provided by SCT and then summarize briefly the key points about individuality which immediately arise.

Personal and social identity

The founding idea of the self-categorization analysis of personality is the concept of personal identity. It is assumed that people display individuality in their behaviour to the degree that they are acting in terms of some salient personal identity, a cognitive definition of self as a unique individual person defined in terms of personal attributes, individual differences and interpersonal relationships. This particular conceptualization of personal identity was put forward by Turner (1982) in the context of a contrast with social identity, the cognitive definition of self in terms of shared social category memberships and associated stereotypes. He proposed that the self-concept, defined as the sum total of the cognitive representations of self available to a perceiver, comprised both personal and social identities and that self-perception tended to vary along a continuum defined solely by personal identity at one extreme and solely by social identity at the other.

It was argued that as a particular personal or social identity became salient (cognitively influential), self-perception tended to become "personalized" or "depersonalized" and that depersonalization produced group behaviour and emergent group processes. From a psychological perspective, "group behaviour" was simply the kind of behaviour that arose where people defined themselves and acted in terms of a shared social identity. Conversely, "individual behaviour", individuality, was simply the kind of behaviour that arose where one defined oneself in terms of an idiosyncratic personal identity, in terms of individual differences from others and distinctive personal attributes.

The idea of the personal–social identity distinction as a bipolar continuum had its problems and tended to create some misunderstanding. Researchers tended to see it as implying an all-or-none contrast between the salience of personal and social identity, and the false inference was drawn that where social identity was salient a monolithic conformity within the group would be the result in which all differences between group members would be eliminated (e.g., Swann, Kwan, Polzer, & Milton, 2003). A further misconception was that SCT had no interest in individual differences and that these were seen as the normal, default condition of social interaction, as if group processes were an aberration from the baseline. These and other issues were resolved by a significant reformulation of the theory in the early 1980s (Turner, 1985).

Levels of self-categorization

To address the problem of the interrelationship of personal and social identity in a way that acknowledged their interdependence as well as their opposition, Turner (1985, 1987a) replaced the bipolar continuum with the idea of different levels of self-categorization and provided a formal analysis of the antecedents and effects of self-categorizing. Summarizing, it is assumed that cognitive representations of self take the form of self-categorizations, in which the self and certain stimuli are cognitively grouped as identical in contrast to some other group of stimuli. Self-categorizations vary in their level of inclusiveness and are organized hierarchically. For example, an individual may categorize himself or herself as an individual person in contrast to other persons within some ingroup, or may categorize self as an ingroup in contrast to some outgroup within some higher-order self-category such as "society". These levels of self-categorization represent personal and social identity respectively, but an infinite number of levels are available in principle. Individuals may define themselves as "humanity" in contrast to other species, or may categorize the self at a level less inclusive than the individual, as the real me compared to the inauthentic me, or the public me in contrast to the private me, and so on (Turner & Onorato, 1999).

It is argued that self-perception is a function of the level or levels of self-categorization which are salient and that salience is a function of an interaction between the perceiver's readiness to use a self-category in a given instance and the fit of that self-category to the apprehended stimulus reality (Oakes, Haslam, & Turner, 1994; Turner, Oakes, Haslam, & McGarty, 1994). Perceiver readiness reflects a person's goals, motives and expectations and fit reflects the match between any self-categorization and the stimulus field being categorized. Two kinds of fit come into play, "normative" and "comparative". Normative fit refers to the degree to which categorizing stimuli makes sense in terms of the perceiver's background theories and knowledge about the world, and comparative fit refers to the degree to which categorized stimuli have a high meta-contrast. Meta-contrast is a unique theoretical principle of SCT which specifies that, all things being equal, stimuli tend to be cognitively grouped into contrasting classes so as to enhance the ratio of the mean perceived difference between stimuli in different classes to the mean perceived difference between stimuli in the same class (i.e., the ratio of interclass to intraclass differences).

Meta-contrast means that self-categories are inherently comparative, relational and flexible. They represent the perceiver in terms of his or her social relational, social contextual properties. Self-categorizing is seen as highly dynamic and fluid, always varying with and relative to a frame of reference (Turner et al., 1994). Variation in the relative salience of different levels of self-categorization is seen as normal and ever present, always shifting with motives, goals, expectations, knowledge and the pool of stimuli being cognized and compared. In this way, the process of self-categories becoming psychologically salient is seen as the same as the process of their formation. They do not exist before they are used and they are created as and when they are needed for use. A person may of course have knowledge of a previous self but this is not the same as a functioning self-category – such knowledge may be used to create a functioning self-category but only where all other conditions are appropriate.

Where a particular self-categorization becomes salient, it is hypothesized that there tends to be a perceptual accentuation of similarities within categories and of differences between categories. This perceptual accentuation at one level reduces the perceived meta-contrasts at other levels and therefore makes alternative levels of categorization less appropriate and perceptible. Thus there is a functional antagonism between different levels of self-categorization such that as one or more levels become salient it becomes harder for the others to become salient. This does not mean, however, that only one level can be salient at one time or that the causes of the salience of one or more levels need be inversely related. On the contrary, there are often perceiver and situational factors making for the salience of different identities at the same time, which will tend to induce an effort to create a coherent and unified self-category for action.[1]

For example, a situation which might tend to increase simultaneously the salience of both personal and social identity could be a highly conflictual negotiation between the leaders of two warring groups in which each leader also disagreed with fellow ingroup members about how the negotiation should be conducted (cf. Stephenson, 1981). Each leader might experience a strong sense of personal identity whenever they thought about the intergroup negotiation, believing that their policy and no other was right for their group, but at the same time feel completely at one with their group when they contemplated the common dangers posed by the enemy and the inadequate policies of their rivals. In this case the bases of the salience of each level of identity are strongly interdependent such that each identity provides the context for evoking the other. The outcome of such simultaneously conflicting and mutually evoking tendencies for self-perception is likely to be a high degree of variability, tension and complexity, reflecting the relative strength of each identity and the degree to which they can be creatively reconciled in particular instances. In all cases salient self-categorization is likely to reflect compromise and conflict between levels rather than simply the forces for the salience of one (cf. Simon, 2004). Thus the idea of functional antagonism does imply that in general the more salient is personal identity the less salient will social identity *tend* to be and vice versa (Turner, 1987a, p. 49), but it does not mean that there cannot be situations which increase the pressure for both to be salient, and nor does it mean that such antagonism is always resolved by a capitulation to one. The whole idea of "levels" is to emphasize the *variability* of self-categorizing as a response to the complexities of the situation within which the person finds himself or herself, not to argue for arbitrary restrictions on such variability, restricting it to the few reified "levels" for which we have easy verbal labels.

Thus personal identity is one level of self-categorization, reflecting an interplay between perceiver factors and situational and stimulus realities. Personal identity will vary with (a) the social and group contexts within which the individual is defined, (b) the theories and knowledge used to make sense of observed intrapersonal and interpersonal differences, and (c) the motives, expectations and goals which shape the readiness to interpret such differences in specific self-categorical terms. It is also affected by the relative salience of other levels such as intrapersonal identity and social identity.

Seven ideas about individuality

This brief summary of SCT leaves many questions unanswered. Some of these will be addressed presently, but it is useful to provide some interim orientation by listing seven distinctive ideas about individuality which flow from the theory.

1. Individuality is a product of personal identity and represents only one level of behaviour, just as personal identity represents only one level of identity. In the same way that a person may act more or less as a group member, so they can act more or less as an individual. By individuality is meant all the psychologically significant ways in which a person behaves, feels, perceives and thinks differently from his or her fellows in particular and across subsets of situations. The tendency to define the self as a unique individual person different from other ingroup members, to accentuate perceived homogeneity and consistency within one's personal self and one's perceived individual differences from others, is assumed to make possible a unique singularity of response, a psychologically meaningful distinctiveness of individual behaviour.[2]

2. Individuality is highly variable in that personal identity can vary in inclusiveness, kind, content and internal structure depending on the interplay between perceiver factors, stimulus realities and the context of judgement. I can define myself as including more or fewer instances of particular personal behaviours, as one kind of individual in one context and as a different kind in another; I can define myself on different content dimensions in different settings; and I can define what is personally typical of me differently depending on the other people I distinguish myself from (just as instances of self-categories at all levels vary in prototypicality with the available meta-contrast: see Turner et al., 1994, and below).

3. Self-categorization in terms of personal identity is a process of reflexive social judgement rather than the activation of a pre-formed, stored cognitive structure (see Turner et al., 1994, for a fuller discussion).

4. Individuality is not one of the basic terms of the person × situation interaction (as if the person were nothing but personality), but one of its *products* like groupness (although these outcomes, individuality or group-ness, can then affect the interpretation of subsequent events, producing personal identity × situation or social identity × situation interactions).

5. Personal identity is *inter alia* a derivation of social identity and group products such as social values, ideologies, theories, beliefs and social structures which shape perceiver readiness and fit. The ways in which one makes sense of one's personal differences from others depends upon the nature of the group identity one shares with those others, the relevance of those differences to that identity, and the values, theories and beliefs anchored in one's group memberships which help one to make sense of them and define their relevance to one's life and goals. Self-categories at any level are always based on comparisons between stimuli defined as similar in terms of a higher-order self-category. The personal self there-fore always reflects differences from ingroup members, just as intraper-sonal identities reflect comparisons within the personal self. Also, just like other categories, self-categories are defined and created by theories which specify complex causal relationships between events (McGarty, Yzerbyt, & Spears, 2002; Murphy & Medin, 1985), and these theories are socially produced. For example, a religious theory of sin is likely to create a self-category of "criminal" which differs in important ways in meaning from a social scientific theory emphasizing social learning. If I see being a criminal as akin to being a sinner, I am likely to see myself differently and act differently in many situations compared to where I see my criminality as a kind of social disadvantage or protest.

6. Personal identity is not a fixed product of past socialization, learning or maturation but a *contemporary* product of social, societal and psycho-logical forces. It depends *inter alia* on *current* group identities, social con-texts and the goals, motives, expectations, beliefs and knowledge which are shaped by social influence and social ideologies. An individual's past experience, individual and social, may certainly affect how he or she reacts to and cognizes the contemporary social world, but present social realities, norms, values and ideologies, and reference group memberships are decisive for producing personal identity. Personal change is made possible by social change which impinges on the factors influencing the creation of personal identities.

7. Individual and group, personal and social identity, personality and collective behaviour, are interdependent. Under certain conditions, indi-viduals acting in terms of their personality can change and redefine group forces and people acting collectively as group members can transform their personalities (see Reicher & Haslam, Chapter 13 in this volume). There are constraints in both directions but there is no Chinese Wall

between the individuality and groupness of people. One cannot be reduced to or subsumed by the other but neither should any false dichotomy be invented to deny the living reality of people in which being an individual and being a group member function collaboratively.

These schematic points can now be made more concrete by presenting three "case studies", where issues which have tended to be addressed in conventional personality terms have been given a different slant by SCT. The studies are presented chronologically, in the order in which the issues first emerged in self-categorization research.

Case study 1: personality and leadership

What is leadership? What determines who is an effective leader? By effective leadership in this context we mean the capacity of one or more individuals in a group to get other group members to follow them, agree, accept their suggestions, orders, commands, to direct the behaviour of the group towards the goals perceived by the leader (Haslam, 2004; Turner, 2005). Leadership is the degree to which group members differ in their capacity to influence each other (French & Snyder, 1959), with more leadership being displayed by those who are more influential.

The dominant tendency in the explanation of leadership has been to individualize it, to assume that there is something special and distinctive about the personal qualities, attitudes, behaviours or behavioural styles of leaders which in some way uniquely determines their rise to leadership and capacity to exert it. The search for such characteristics has been going on forever and has proved largely fruitless (e.g., Stogdill, 1948). In more recent "contingency" theories, it is assumed that effective leaders have specific leadership styles (e.g., being more or less relationship-oriented) which in some way match, fit or are appropriate for the specific situation of the group. Effective leadership is about the individual characteristics of the leader as they interact with the particularities of the situation. The focus is still on the individual and whether the individual is right for the situation.

The self-categorization analysis follows Hollander (1985) in focusing on the nature of the influence process within groups but adopts a different theory of influence, one that sees it as an outcome of shared social identity (Turner, 1982, 1985, 1987b). It rejects the idea that effective leadership is an expression of the personality or other individual attributes of the leader, in isolation or in interaction with the situation, and argues that it is produced by group forces and relationships. An individual becomes a leader to the degree that in any relevant setting they come to be perceived as the embodiment of the group, and this in turn depends upon the intra- and intergroup relationships within a specific social context that define the social identity of the group and the relative prototypicality of its members (Haslam, 2004; Turner, 1987b, 1991; Turner & Haslam, 2001; Turner & Oakes, 1986, 1989).

This hypothesis was originally developed by Turner to explain group polarization (Turner, 1987b; Turner & Oakes, 1986, 1989). He argued that people are influenced by the responses of ingroup members to the degree that the latter are perceived to exemplify an ingroup norm or consensus. The perceived informational validity of responses follows directly from the degree to which they are in line with or exemplify a normative ingroup position. Where individuals define themselves in terms of a shared social identity and see themselves as similar perceivers confronting the same stimulus situation, then they will believe that they ought to agree, to respond in the same way. Where they do so, they will experience subjective validity, confidence that their response is correct, appropriate, objectively demanded by the situation rather than being an expression of bias or error. Where they disagree they will experience uncertainty and seek to resolve such uncertainty.

Thus within the group, where there is disagreement amongst members, where members are trying to persuade each other of the validity of their differing positions, it is those views which already better express the emerging group consensus which will tend to be perceived as valid, as providing evidence about reality, compared to those which are more deviant, less typical of the existing group consensus. By extension, any individual within the group will tend to be perceived as more valid and be more persuasive in influencing group members to the degree that he or she is perceived as exemplary or typical of the group as a whole. The twin assumptions here are that group consensus is not a monolithic absolute but a matter of degree and that even within more or less consensual groups the differing positions, responses, views of group members can be ordered and perceived as more or less typical of the group as a whole.

Turner (1985) employs Rosch's (1978) concept of prototypicality to describe this property of members of being more or less typical of the group as a whole, and defines and operationalizes the relative prototypicality of members by means of the meta-contrast principle. Thus, any member of a category can be defined as more prototypical of the category to the degree that their average differences from other ingroup members are less than their average differences from outgroup members on any relevant dimension or set of dimensions in any given context. It should now be clear that under specifiable theoretical conditions, where there are differences of opinion within a group, there will be a hierarchy of relative influence which will follow the hierarchy of members' perceived relative prototypicality. Since a hierarchy of relative influence is the same as a leadership hierarchy (French & Snyder, 1959; Sherif, 1967), it follows that group members will emerge as leaders to the degree that they are perceived as relatively prototypical of the group as a whole and that the most prototypical person will tend to be recognized as *the* leader where such a role is defined.

It also follows from meta-contrast that group identity varies with the frame of reference within which it is defined. In particular, the internal structure of relative prototypicality of any group varies not only with ingroup positions but also with the positions of the contrasting outgroup. Thus, for example, if a political group contains both left-wing and right-wing members then extreme left-wing members will tend to become more prototypical and be more likely to exert influence and leadership where the salient outgroup is right-wing rather than left-wing, whereas right-wing extremists will tend to become more prototypical and exert more influence where the outgroup is left-wing rather than right-wing. In both cases the groups are moving to the position or person (the leader) who best represents what they have in common as a group in contrast to other relevant groups; they are moving towards each other not as individuals but as group members and the mutual influence process is always mediated by their perceptions of each other in terms of the group as a whole. Group polarization – in which group members shift to a normative position which is more extreme than the average of their initial individual responses – was explained as arising from the fact that people shift to the most prototypical position rather than to the average individual position and that the former tends to be more extreme than the latter where group identity is defined within specific intergroup contexts (Turner & Oakes, 1986).

The general analysis has been applied extensively to the social influence field (e.g., David & Turner, 2001; Haslam, 2004; Haslam & Platow, 2001; Haslam, Turner, Oakes, McGarty, & Reynolds, 1998; Hogg, 2001; McGarty, Turner, Hogg, David, & Wetherell, 1992; Reicher, 1987; Reicher & Hopkins, 1996a, 1996b; Reicher, Hopkins, & Condor, 1997; Turner, 1991; Turner & Haslam, 2001). Leadership in this formulation is an emergent group process which is produced by group forces and relationships. It arises from the nature of social identity and is a universal feature of group life precisely because it follows directly from the psychological processes of self-categorization which create group identity. There are leaders because psychological groups have an internal self-categorical structure of relative prototypicality which is inherent in the meta-contrastive basis upon which they form. It is not the personality traits or individual attributes of any individual which makes them a leader (or not) but their position within a web of intragroup and intergroup relationships. Group identities change with the range and distribution of members included within the group, their psychological resources (e.g., goals, experience, ideologies and knowledge) and the social comparative frame of reference. But, as group identity changes, relative prototypicality gradients and leadership hierarchies change too. The motives and understanding of people in a given situation create the identity that they need to act collectively and effectively and call forth the leadership they need as part of the process of identity construction. This is not meant to be understood as a passive process. Individual members who believe they know what the group needs will often work actively to produce the identity which gives them influence (Reicher & Haslam, Chapter 13 in this volume; Reicher & Hopkins, 1996a, 1996b; Reicher et al., 1997). There is no enduring specific make-up of a person which makes them a leader.

In sum, leadership is not a function of personality but is an emergent group process. Leadership hierarchies are created and change as group identities are created and change. Group identity does not deny individuality or individual differences between members but takes them for granted. A member becomes relatively more prototypical of the group by being different as an individual from other ingroup members in a normative direction. Individual differences do not directly produce leadership, they are combined and transformed by group relationships and forces to become sources of leadership and these differences need not connote what is traditionally regarded as personality.

Furthermore, as collective behaviour is instigated and takes place, shaped by social influence and leadership and guided by normative beliefs and values, so new patterns of group activity (which may include schisms and conflict as well as consensualization and subgroup unification) emerge which in turn make possible new patterns of individuality. As new goals, beliefs, attitudes, roles and actions become normative, members will seek to enact them, differentiating themselves from each other in new ways related to social identity, and will make different judgements of themselves as persons under conditions where intragroup comparisons bring personal identity to the fore. Individuality and groupness are interdependent. People are changed by collective action and the social identities they create (Haslam et al., 1998; Sani & Reicher, 1998; Stott & Drury, 2004; Stott & Reicher, 1998; Reynolds, Oakes, Haslam, Nolan, & Dolnik, 2000; Turner, 2005) and these changes will feed back into their personal identities and individuality under appropriate conditions (e.g., Jetten, Postmes, & McAuliffe, 2002; Lehmiller, Schmitt, & Krauss, 2004; Reicher & Haslam, 2006, 2004b; Reynolds, Turner, Ryan, Veenstra, Burgess, & McKone, 2004a). This view of individuality, construed as in permanent and complex interdependence with group life, moves us away from the standard view of personality as comprising fixed traits stored in psychic isolation.

Case study 2: personality and the self-concept

A close connection between personality and the self-concept has long been recognized. The standard view of the self-concept functions as a theory of personality. Given assumptions that personality embodies the totality of individual behaviour and that it comprises some set of relatively fixed and unique psychological structures acquired from experience, learning and socialization, the result has been a model of the self-concept designed specifically to account for the stability, consistency and distinctiveness of individual behaviour.

Turner and Onorato (1999) refer to this as the personality model of the self-concept. They summarize this model in terms of four major themes found in classic and contemporary accounts of the self:

1 that the self-concept is a representation of one's personal identity; it describes the "I" and the "me" rather than any kind of collective self;
2 that it is a unique or idiosyncratic psychological structure that belongs only to one perceiver and is not shared with others;
3 that it is social in being a "looking-glass" self in the symbolic interactionist sense, a reflection and internalization of one's public self as it is presented and reacted to by others in social interaction; and
4 that it is a relatively enduring, fixed, bounded cognitive structure, an organized system of interrelated self-concepts stored in memory and activated under particular conditions.

From this perspective, the self is the core psychological structure which embodies the individual's personal history, relates the individual to the social situation, shapes cognition and emotion, and acts as a stable anchor for a range of individual motives, needs and goals. It is one's idiosyncratic and relatively stable knowledge structure of one's personal identity and history, reflecting personal experience and the internalized appraisals of others, which gives stability, consistency and individuality to one's behaviour.

Turner and Onorato (1999; see too Onorato & Turner, 2001, 2002, 2004) reject the personality model. Following SCT, they point out that the self is not purely, basically or predominantly personal. The self as "we" and "us" is just as real and important as the personal self and variation in the salience of different levels of self-categorization is normal, arising from the same general principles that govern the salience of personal identity (Turner et al., 1994). Personal identity derives from social identity in the sense that all self–other interpersonal comparisons take place within a psychologically meaningful frame of reference implicitly defined by higher-order self-categories. When I define myself as different from a personal you I do it in terms of the dimensions and values which define what we have in common as, for example, men, Australians, researchers, etc.. Just as depersonalizing on the basis of social identity is a dynamic, flexible process varying with perceiver factors and the situation, so too personalizing, producing individuality in behaviour, is dynamic and flexible. The personal self is not some normal, default, bedrock of individual psychology, it is an example of a more general self-categorizing process at work.

The notion that the self-concept is built up from personal experience and feedback from others is not contentious providing that we grasp that:

1 all personal experience is subject to social reality testing;
2 our experience can be as collective beings as well as individual persons (where we can construct self-categories that do not just belong to one person but that we *share* with others: Haslam et al., 1998); and
3 feedback from others is only likely to be privately accepted where it comes from relevant ingroup members (Turner, 1991).

But, the idea that the self-concept is social primarily because it is a looking-glass self is highly restrictive. The looking-glass self is a public personal self, a "me as perceived by others", but social identity is a subjectively collective self, a self shared with others who are part of that self and act as part of that self. Also, self-categories represent a perceiver in terms of his or her similarities and differences to others, relations to others which vary with the social context of judgement. They are social relational representations of the perceiver, not representations of the individual as some fixed absolute being, somehow adjusted for context, but categorical judgements which derive the identity of the perceiver from his or her relationship to the context. Both perceived individual difference and group similarity express the contextual identity of the perceiver and follow the same principles. Self-categories are social representations of the perceiver and this is just as true at the level of personal identity as it is at the level of social identity. All self-categorizing at whatever level is inherently and intrinsically social, being based on meta-contrast, which is inherently comparative, relational and contextual, and taking place in close interdependence with social reality testing and social influence which affect all components of the perceiver readiness × fit interaction. The looking-glass metaphor is fine as far as it goes, but it is a weak representation of the sociality of self-categorizing even in its cognitive elements. Self-categorizing is fully social psychological at any and all levels.

Finally, the idea of the self-concept as a ready-made cognitive system is implausible if the dynamic, relational, flexible character of self-categorizing is accepted. There is good evidence following the fit hypothesis that the same reported self-category (e.g., "feminist") can vary in meaning and internal structure of relative prototypicality as a function of the self–other comparisons to which it is applied (David & Turner, 1999, 2001). Self-categories are to some degree constructed from the stimulus instances they are designed to represent. If this is so, then how can self-categories be stored in memory as fixed invariant structures prior to their use? Rather than thinking of them as fixed entities waiting to be activated, it is more useful to suppose that they are constructed on the spot as and when they are used, making use of long-term knowledge and theories to create categories that make sense of the immediate realities and reflect perceiver needs, goals and values.

In this view a self-concept is defined as a self-concept not because it is stored as part of some specific cognitive system but because it represents the person doing the perceiving, because it is reflexive. Self-categorizing is a creative process designed to be of use to the perceiver given his or her purposes, needs, values and expectations. It works in the here-and-now to define a person in terms of his or her relations to others within specific social contexts as interpreted by higher-order, more complex theories, knowledge and beliefs about the world. It is a highly functional, adaptive and reality-oriented process. Knowledge from the past is applied to the interpretation of the present but the interpretation is creative, constructive, selective, motivated and social. The apprehended present is by no means merely knowledge of the past activated.

The personality model implies that the self-concept is a fixed thing, a mental homunculus. Having argued for a much more expansive view of the self as a creative process and much more than merely the font of individuality, what follows for a view of personality and individuality? First, what of the consistency, stability and individuality of behaviour? Are there broad stable consistencies of behaviour as the concept of personality trait implies? There are many issues here which have been discussed in more detail elsewhere (Turner, 1999a; Turner et al., 1994; Turner & Onorato, 1999). It is not being argued that individuality is in continual and arbitrary unconstrained empirical flux. A theoretical point is being made that self-categorizing is a dynamic, flexible process, but this does not rule out consistency and stability any more than it rules out inconsistency and instability under specific conditions. Where the factors determining self-categories remain stable and consistent, individuality will be stable and consistent, but equally where such factors change, so can individuality.

The present analysis suggests that there can be both stability and instability, consistency and inconsistency under given conditions. There are many social and psychological conditions which can make for stability and consistency (Turner et al., 1994), but where they are observed there is still no need to posit that individuality is a function of some fixed personality structure. And nothing in this analysis argues for a social constructionist view, as some have suggested, that self-categories are simply constructed in social interaction unconstrained by social realities or internal psychological factors. Self-categorization is not free to vary in any which way, but is always constrained by the motives, goals, values, experience, theories and knowledge the perceiver brings to the situation, as well as by the psychological nature of the categorization process and the social situation within which the perceiver defines himself or herself. These factors are always likely to imply continuity to some degree and at some level, depending on the range of determining conditions that are sampled. Personality traits in the sense of broad stable consistencies of behaviour under specific conditions need not be denied, but they should not be reified into fixed psychological structures. They are there to be explained, not in themselves explanations (Epstein & O'Brien, 1985; Mischel & Shoda, 1995).

Second, what adaptive purpose does this dynamic self-process serve? The variability of self-categorizing enables a more complex, detailed, discriminative and appropriate response to the environment. By providing a self-category that defines the perceiver in terms of his or her relationship to the environment, making use of past experience and knowledge and calibrated to the needs and purposes of the individual, the process enables self-regulation that is highly responsive, reality-oriented and flexible. The variable self makes a high degree of behavioural and cognitive flexibility possible, shaping and fine-tuning its selective perspective on, interpretation of and response to the environment. As the self changes, so the cognitive processing of and behavioural reactions to the world change.

One fundamental example of this is the very fact that self-categorizing links the perceiver to society, providing a representation of the individual which is always socially defined. This immensely enriches the processes and resources available to a perceiver in interacting with the world. SCT makes clear that individuality is created as much as is group identity as perceivers define themselves in terms of their value-laden differences from specific sets of relevant others. It ensures that psychological reactions to the environment are regulated at appropriate times by the specificity and uniqueness of the perceiver, by the singular perspective of the relevant individual. Society checks, coordinates, combines and transforms individual cognition, and individual experience works upon, tests, uses, rejects or accepts, expands, changes, the collective ideas and structures which it confronts. The human individual without the capacity for group life would be a poor thing and hardly human, but group life without individuality would be rigid, inflexible, monotonous, conformist and also hardly human.

The lessons for personality are that it

1   is a dynamic creative process much more than a fixed structure;
2   is a product of contemporary social and psychological forces, not a fixed template acquired in the past and passively activated in the present like some returning ghost; and
3   can and does change under relevant conditions in response to changes in group identities, personal and collective experience, theories, beliefs and ideologies and social realities; it can be stable but it can also change where group activities and social changes in society transform the basis of self-categorizing.

These ideas are all testable and there is a growing body of research which supports them (Jetten et al., 2002; Lehmiller et al., 2004; Onorato & Turner, 2004; Reicher & Haslam, 2006; Reynolds & Oakes, 1999; Reynolds, Turner, Haslam, & Ryan, 2001; Reynolds et al., 2004a; Schmitt, Branscombe, & Kappen, 2003).

Case study 3: the prejudiced personality and social change

The idea of the prejudiced personality is the notion that there are relatively stable personality traits which more or less directly predispose people to prejudice. Examples are classic authoritarianism (the F scale: Adorno, Frenkel-Brunswik, Levinson, & Sanford, 1950), right-wing authoritarianism (RWA: Altemeyer, 1988) and social dominance orientation (SDO: Sidanius & Pratto, 1999). The traits are assumed to be acquired in childhood and adolescence from family and culture through social learning or psychodynamic development. If personality is a product of past life experience, then the possibility of changing it seems moot; and if prejudice is determined by personality, then it is likely to be impervious to social change and social policy. Prejudiced personalities are thus an explanation for why prejudice is irrational and recalcitrant. They are seen as an obstacle to social change.

There are three big problems with this view (Turner, 1999b). First, SCT rejects the idea that one can predict intergroup attitudes from personality traits where people's relevant social identities are salient. Group behaviour is made possible by a psychological transformation of self which stops one from acting as and being a personality. Where people are depersonalized, their attitudes to outgroup members will be a function of their collective understanding of intergroup relations, not individual differences (Reynolds et al., 2001; Verkuyten & Hagendoorn, 1998).

Second, the tendency in this research is to generalize from individual differences observed under restricted conditions to a stable, fixed trait and explain prejudice in terms of it. However, as we have argued, even relatively stable differences need not reflect a fixed psychological structure, but merely indicate relatively stable conditions. This implies that even trait-related behaviour is likely to vary as conditions change. In SCT, personality traits are not causes but descriptive terms summarizing selected individual differences under certain conditions and likely to change under other conditions. Individuality is as much a product of a person × situation interaction as is group behaviour. To postulate a trait as an explanation for an observed difference is a reification which merely redescribes what has to be explained. Studies show in fact that F, RWA and SDO scores can all change across short time spans and in response to social influence (Altemeyer, 1988; Lehmiller et al., 2004; Reynolds et al., 2004a; Schmitt et al., 2003; Siegel & Siegel, 1957). If RWA, for example, is affected by contemporary group influences, then it is hard to see it as a fixed trait laid down in the past by social learning or psychodynamic development. This point can be misunderstood. Personality change in traditional theory is sometimes accepted, but is still assumed to be a product of developmental processes, of social learning but not social influence. We are pointing to changes in trait scores as a function of the normal variability of self-categorization, not changes in underlying psychological structures produced by developmental learning and not surface variation which remains constrained by a person's rank on some supposed trait.

Third, individual differences in RWA or SDO may not be strictly "individual" at all. They may reflect group memberships and beliefs as much as differences in individual psychological make-up. Most of the items are about social groups and intergroup relationships, not about behavioural traits such as "I like going to parties". The items express beliefs about what groups are like, what should be done about them, who should be supported and who opposed. Given the nature of the items it is hardly surprising in the case of RWA (or SDO: Turner & Reynolds, 2003) that scores on the RWA and F scales vary with social and demographic characteristics, social background, occupation, education, political identification, and religion (Altemeyer, 1988; Billig, 1976; Brown, 1965; Pettigrew, 1958). The basic dimension of political thought is radicalism vs conservatism, left-wing vs right-wing, being against or for the status quo, and this dimension is at the heart of RWA. The scale taps right-wing beliefs with a dash of religious fundamentalism. The political nature of the scale is most obvious when it is administered to political activists. There is a definite correlation with people's political views, but if one looks at the people who are definitely interested in politics, who are active in and think about politics, then the correlation is especially strong. The RWA scale measures political-ideological beliefs much more obviously than it measures anything traditionally regarded as personality, and it seems to measure these beliefs more reliably the more that respondents have given some thought to them.

The classic notion of the prejudiced personality implies that personality in an abstract psychological sense leads to an externalizing of hostility as prejudice rationalized as a kind of politics. This is the assumed causal direction. So it has been important to try to find some way in which the scale can measure authoritarianism or something else "psychological" independent of politics. A related issue is that of "cognitive style". Authoritarians are supposed to be rigid in their thinking and intolerant of ambiguity. Cognitive style is ostensibly a psychological variable, empty of political content. If one can show that authoritarians have some such style, then perhaps it is evidence for a psychological characteristic which predisposes them towards extreme politics, and which defines personality prior to the content of their political views. The efforts to validate the Freudian interpretation, or "dogmatism", or "tough-mindedness", or an "authoritarian of the left", or other style variables have been unconvincing (e.g., Altemeyer, 1988; Billig, 1976; Brown, 1965; Perreault & Bourhis, 1999; Reynolds, Turner, Haslam, Ryan, Veenstra, & Wilkinson, 2004b).

Altemeyer writes of RWA being a product of socialization and comprising social attitudes. But he still likes to discuss its dynamics in terms of psychological themes. So right-wing authoritarians, for example, are supposed to have a fear of a dangerous world. They are meant to be particularly anxious, insecure and self-righteous. That is why they get so hostile and touchy, why they are "quick on the trigger". There is a strongly psychological interpretation of what is going on and of what is causing the social and political attitudes. But, of course, the other causal direction actually makes much more sense. To say RWA is a political dimension does not mean it is not telling us about individual differences. It does not mean it does not have psychological aspects and consequences. If someone is absolutely committed to the Bible and the Old Testament, if they think that doing wrong is a matter of sin, it is not surprising that they are sometimes more willing to punish people. But studies of this kind, showing that RWAs are more punitive of law-breakers or people who fail on some task, do not prove that there is a pathological, determining psychology underlying their political beliefs. Such findings make perfect sense if one realizes that RWAs tend to be fundamentalist in religion, to believe in sin and hellfire. Such responses and others like them may well be "psychological" in being associated with feelings, judgements and values, but they are easy to see as psychological reflections of ideology, rather than causes of the ideology. If RWAs see everything from feminism to nudist camps as a threat to the social order and established morality, it is not difficult to see why they might be anxious, insecure and hostile. The psychological follows from the political much more plausibly than the political from the psychological.

This does not mean there are not prejudiced personalities in the sense of individual differences on these dimensions, but it is important to note that, as well as the individual differences, these scales, RWA and SDO, also express group differences. These attitudes and the underlying ideologies are group beliefs, not products of personal idiosyncrasy (Dambrun, Duarte, & Guimond, 2004; Guimond, 2000; Jetten et al., 2002; Lehmiller et al., 2004; Schmitt et al., 2003; Turner & Reynolds, 2003). This does not mean that one cannot use these group beliefs and ideologies to construct one's individuality under specific conditions. On the contrary, one can and does. Personalities are constructed dynamically, in the long term and contemporaneously, out of socially produced theories, ideologies and knowledge, in application to the needs and realities of the individual person in specific settings. But this is a new theory, not the old one. This is not personality as an abstract, content-free psychological structure which leads one to adhere to pre-fascist politics. One's individuality here, psychological and social, is being constructed from group-produced political beliefs; it is directly ideological and political. Social and political change is not prevented by the relevant traits, but can modify and eliminate them, because they are constructed from group beliefs, which are part of specific, contesting political and cultural currents and traditions.

We need to dispense with the classic picture of the prejudiced personality. In SCT, personality is the functioning of personal identities in changing social contexts. Some such self-categories are formed from political and ideological group beliefs which contain analyses of who "we" are and who our friends and enemies are. The "personalities" involved are in this sense directly political and ideological. Their origins in the interplay between the application of group beliefs and the construction of individuality in particular social contexts need to be understood and investigated. What is to be avoided is their abstraction and reification into fixed psychological types and the reduction of historically and collectively produced intergroup attitudes to some inner, purely psychological dynamic. Prejudice flows not from individual psychopathology, but from the implicit political analysis at work in the formation of individual and group differences. It is not generalized, but targeted towards specific outgroups, politically and ideologically defined. The antisemitism and racism of Nazism are inherent in its analysis of humanity, society, life, in its worldview, not in a generalized intrapsychic hostility seeking any kind of expression.

The problem of the prejudiced personality as an obstacle to social change is actually the problem of traditional theory. We need not think of personality as a fixed psychological structure laid down in the past and impervious to political changes. It can be seen as a contemporary product which can be changed by group activities and influences. Political and social change is not prevented by prejudiced personalities, but is needed to get rid of them, to dispute and eliminate their ideological basis. None of this means that the individual is not important. Individuals make up groups and shape group life, and particular individuals can play a special role in so far as they embody group trends and forces. But in understanding the particular origins of intergroup attitudes and the worldview which underlies a scale like RWA, it is necessary to focus on a much wider panorama than merely how individuals differ from each other. It is the similarities amongst the high authoritarians, or amongst the lows, amongst the high social dominators, or amongst the lows, which now assume significance, for this ideological and social homogeneity can be a powerful political force in creating and changing groups and group attitudes in the light of events (Louis, Mavor, & Terry, 2003).

Conclusion: a new look for personality

What points emerge for reconceptualizing personality? Perhaps the most general one is that individuality needs to be understood as the product of a subtle, complex, creative, contemporary and social psychological process rather than of personality as a set of fixed and abstract traits acquired in the past. Personality is part of an active and current process of self-categorization by which people are defined and act in relation to social life and the concrete reality of their specific social location. The conceptual separation of personal from social identity, individuality from groupness, does not impoverish or reduce our view of the former but throws its richness and complexity into sharper relief. In particular, it highlights the social and ideological core of the contents of personality as against a psychologizing vision of abstract, socially meaningless variation between people. It shows how personality is related to and shaped by the social groups and societies of which people are members.

More specifically, we draw the following conclusions.

1. Personality is not all there is to the psychology of the person. People display individual differences under some conditions just as they display collective similarities under others. Individuality is only one level of

self-categorization and behaviour and is a product of the salience of personal identity.

2. Rather than personality being relatively fixed and stable, we suggest that personal identities and individuality are highly variable, at least in principle. Not only does behaviour vary with the person × situation interaction but so too does the determining psychological character of the individual. Personality is not one of the components of the person × situation interaction but one of its outcomes, in terms of the meaning of the constructed personal self-category.

3. Personality is a social psychological process, not a fixed psychological structure. It is an aspect of defining the self in relation to current realities, expressing reflexive social judgement in the here-and-now rather than the activation of a ready-made set of predispositions.

4. Personality is in part derived and constructed from group identities, beliefs and products such as social norms, values, goals, theories and ideologies, as well as from the social structures created through collective action (see Jetten & Postmes, Chapter 7; Postmes, Baray, Haslam, Morton, & Swaab, Chapter 12 in this volume). The meaning of our personal self, the ways we understand how we differ from others and the reality of the situation we are in, are all interpreted through political and social ideologies created in society. In this sense, just as stereotypes express implicit political analyses, so too do personality judgements, and new ideologies make possible new personalities. In general, personality has to be understood as emerging from a unified field in which individual and group are indissolubly linked.

5. Individuality is a contemporary creation; it is being produced through the motivated application of longer-term experience, knowledge and theory to current stimulus realities in light of current purposes. Self-categorizing is adaptive because it orients and defines the perceiver with respect to the contemporary social and physical environment. The idea that self-categories are "habits" understates the creativity of immediate self-experience and action.

6. Empirically, there can be both consistency and inconsistency, stability and instability, continuity and discontinuity in personality, depending on whether the factors determining self-categorizing do or do not change under given conditions. But relevant factors are certainly changeable in principle, not least because collective action and influence, for example, affect people's normative beliefs and group relationships. Political, social and historical change is a normal feature of human society and by definition is about changes in people's interpretative resources and group life. Thus just as social action and change make possible new group identities, so they also make possible personality change. Personality change looks impossible only if one adopts the wrong theory and seeks to modify the

individual in complete isolation from the group, societal and ideological realities within which self-definition takes place.

7. Personality differences and group similarities are interdependent. Groups are made up of and led by individuals and individuals are transformed and given power by groups. One cannot slice them in two and say that one is the sole cause of the other, that one can be reduced to the other. The special form of each depends on the other. Thus human groups are characterized by the capacity for diversity, dissent, leadership and change and human individuals have a capacity for understanding and judgement, for singular, distinctive perspectives, that would be unimaginable but for the products of collective life. New kinds of groups make possible new kinds of personalities and new kinds of people create the groups that they need. Understanding personality requires analysis of the social context within which it was created.

These are relatively large points which need more detailed investigation, but nearly all are spoken to already by relevant data. All are capable of investigation and all open up new avenues for understanding individuality. Anyone who believes that the study of personality should have something useful to say about the pressing political and social issues of modern life cannot but feel that the topic is ripe for a much more social and societal look. Currently it is too much in the sterile grip of reification and psychologism. The present analysis offers an alternative.[3]

NOTES

This chapter was made possible by funding from the Australian Research Council to John Turner and Kate Reynolds (DP0342645). Correspondence to: John C. Turner, School of Psychology, ANU, Canberra, ACT 0200, Australia, John.Turner@anu.edu.au.

1 The effort may not always succeed, since, for example, a person's knowledge, expectations, motives and theoretical resources may not be adequate to deal with or may even conflict with the representation of the instabilities and complexities of the stimulus reality being confronted. This point leads into issues to do with the self-concept and psychopathology which cannot be pursued here.

2 There are of course differences between human individuals which may affect responses which have nothing to do with personal identity or what we normally think of as individuality. Whether there turn out to be individual differences with social psychological significance which are not a function of personal self-categorization is an empirical question, but the hypothesis of this chapter is that all the personality traits, dimensions, factors, etc., of interest to and normally studied by social and personality psychologists are describing or redescribing behavioural variation shaped and produced by personal identity.

3 We reiterate that nothing in this analysis should be interpreted as meaning that personality is unconstrained by biological, psychological or societal factors, being merely an infinitely malleable social construction. We take for granted that human social psychology is a product of biological evolution, that the self-process is a species universal, and that the

flexibility of self-categorizing functions within the limits of human nature and social reality, just as indeed does all social life. We reject simple-minded (i.e., reductionist) biological or genetic determinism, but not the idea that human social and psychological variability reflects our biology and evolution. Similarly, we cannot address here even speculatively the issue of universal, highly general factors of personality difference which may be inherent in our social psychology, routines of social interaction or physiology and how they may relate to this analysis. In general, linking the proposed reconceptualization of personality to existing schemes, exploring convergences and divergences, will require a sustained conceptual and empirical effort in many different areas.

REFERENCES

Adorno, T. W., Frenkel-Brunswik, E., Levinson, D. J., & Sanford, R. N. (1950). *The authoritarian personality*. New York: Harper.

Altemeyer, B. (1988). *Enemies of freedom: Understanding right-wing authoritarianism*. San Francisco: Jossey-Bass.

Bandura, A. (1997). *Self-efficacy: The exercise of control*. New York: Freeman.

Billig, M. (1976). *Social psychology and intergroup relations*. London: Academic.

Brown, R. (1965). *Social psychology*. London: Collier-Macmillan.

Dambrun, M., Duarte, S., & Guimond, S. (2004). Why are men more likely to support group-based dominance than women? The mediating role of gender identification. *British Journal of Social Psychology, 43*, 287–297.

David, B. & Turner, J. C. (1999). Studies in self-categorization and minority conversion: The ingroup minority in intragroup and intergroup contexts. *British Journal of Social Psychology, 38*, 115–134.

David, B. & Turner, J. C. (2001). Self-categorization principles underlying majority and minority influence. In J. P. Forgas & K. D. Williams (Eds.), *Social influence: Direct and indirect processes*. Philadelphia: Psychology Press.

Epstein, S. (1973). The self-concept revisited, or a theory of a theory. *American Psychologist, 28*, 404–416.

Epstein, S. & O'Brien, E. J. (1985). The person–situation debate in historical and current perspective. *Psychological Bulletin, 98*, 513–537.

French, J. R. P. Jr, & Snyder, R. (1959). Leadership and interpersonal power. In D. Cartwright (Ed.), *Studies in social power* (pp. 118–149). Ann Arbor, MI: Institute of Social Research.

Guimond, S. (2000). Group socialization and prejudice: The social transmission of intergroup attitudes and beliefs. *European Journal of Social Psychology, 30*, 335–354.

Haslam, S. A. (2004). *Psychology in organizations: The social identity approach* (2nd ed.). London: Sage.

Haslam, S. A. & Platow, M. J. (2001). The link between leadership and followership: How affirming a social identity translates vision into action. *Personality & Social Psychology Bulletin, 27*, 1469–1479.

Haslam, S. A., Turner, J. C., Oakes, P. J., McGarty, C., & Reynolds, K. J. (1998). The group as a basis for emergent stereotype consensus. *European Review of Social Psychology, 8*, 203–239.

Hogg, M. A. (2001). A social identity theory of leadership. *Personality & Social Psychology Review, 5*, 184–200.

Hollander, E. P. (1985). Leadership and power. In G. Lindzey & E. Aronson (Eds.), *The handbook of social psychology* (vol. 2, 3rd ed.). New York: Random House.

Jetten, J., Postmes, T., & McAuliffe, B. J. (2002). "We're *all* individuals": Group norms and individualism and collectivism, levels of identification and identity threat. *European Journal of Social Psychology, 32,* 189–207.

Lehmiller, J. J., Schmitt, M. T., & Krauss, S. S. (2004). The US, Saddam and the domination of Iraq: Evidence for the context-dependent meanings of social dominance and authoritarianism. Unpublished paper, Purdue University.

Louis, W. R., Mavor, K. I., & Terry, D. J. (2003). Reflections on the statistical analysis of personality and norms in war, peace, and prejudice: Are deviant minorities the problem? *Analyses of Social Issues & Public Policy, 3,* 189–198.

Markus, H. (1977). Self-schemata and processing information about the self. *Journal of Personality & Social Psychology, 35,* 63–78.

Markus, H. & Wurf, E. (1987). The dynamic self-concept: A social psychological perspective. *Annual Review of Psychology, 38,* 299–337.

McGarty, C., Turner, J. C., Hogg, M. A., David, B., & Wetherell, M. S. (1992). Group polarization as conformity to the prototypical group member. *British Journal of Social Psychology, 31,* 1–20.

McGarty, C., Yzerbyt, V. Y., & Spears, R. (2002). *Stereotypes as explanations: The formation of meaningful beliefs about social groups.* Cambridge: Cambridge University Press.

Mischel, W. (1973). Toward a cognitive social learning reconceptualization of personality. *Psychological Review, 80,* 252–283.

Mischel, W. & Shoda, Y. (1995). A cognitive-affective system theory of personality: Reconceptualizing situations, dispositions, dynamics, and invariance in personality structure. *Psychological Review, 102,* 246–268.

Murphy, G. L. & Medin, D. L. (1985). The role of theories in conceptual coherence. *Psychological Review, 92,* 289–316.

Oakes, P. J., Haslam, S. A., & Turner, J. C. (1994). *Stereotyping and social reality.* Oxford: Blackwell.

Onorato, R. & Turner, J. C. (2001). The "I", the "me", and the "us": The psychological group and self-concept maintenance and change. In C. Sedikides & M. B. Brewer (Eds.), *Individual self, relational self, collective self.* Philadelphia: Psychology Press.

Onorato, R. & Turner, J. C. (2002). Challenging the primacy of the personal self: The case for depersonalized self-conception. In Y. Kashima, M. Foddy, & M. J. Platow (Eds.), *Self and identity: Personal, social, and symbolic* (pp. 145–178). London: Erlbaum.

Onorato, R. S. & Turner, J. C. (2004). Fluidity in the self-concept: The shift from personal to social identity. *European Journal of Social Psychology, 34,* 257–278.

Perreault, S. & Bourhis, R. Y. (1999). Ethnocentrism, social identification, and discrimination. *Personality and Social Psychology Bulletin, 25,* 92–103.

Pettigrew, T. F. (1958). Personality and socio-cultural factors in intergroup attitudes: A cross-national comparison. *Journal of Conflict Resolution, 2,* 29–42.

Reicher, S. D. (1987). Crowd behaviour as social action. In J. C. Turner, M. A. Hogg, P. J. Oakes, S. D. Reicher, & M. S. Wetherell, *Rediscovering the social group: A self-categorization theory.* Oxford: Blackwell.

Reicher, S. D. & Haslam, S. A. (2004). Why not everyone is a torturer. BBC News, UK edition, http://news.bbc.co.uk/1/hi/magazine/3700209.stm, 10 May.

Reicher, S. D. & Haslam, S. A. (2006). Rethinking the psychology of tyranny. *British Journal of Psychology,* in press.

Reicher, S. D. & Hopkins, N. (1996a). Seeking influence through characterizing self-categories: An analysis of anti-abortionist rhetoric. *British Journal of Social Psychology, 35,* 297–311.

Reicher, S. D. & Hopkins, N. (1996b). Self-category constructions in political rhetoric: An analysis of Thatcher's and Kinnock's speeches concerning the British Miners' Strike (1984–5). *European Journal of Social Psychology, 26,* 353–372.

Reicher, S. D., Hopkins, N., & Condor, S. (1997). Stereotype construction as a strategy of social influence. In R. Spears, P. J. Oakes, N. Ellemers, & S. A. Haslam (Eds.), *The social psychology of stereotyping and group life* (pp. 94–118). Oxford: Blackwell.

Reynolds, K. J. & Oakes, P. J. (1999). Understanding the impression formation process: A self-categorization theory perspective. In T. Sugiman, M. Karasawa, J. Lui, & C. Ward (Eds.), *Progress in Asian social psychology: Theoretical and empirical contributions* (vol. 2, pp. 213–235). Seoul: Kyoyook-Kwahak-Sa.

Reynolds, K. J., Oakes, P. J., Haslam, S. A., Nolan, M., & Dolnik, L. (2000). Responses to powerlessness: Stereotyping as an instrument of social conflict. *Group Dynamics: Theory, Research and Practice, 4,* 275–290.

Reynolds, K., Turner, J. C., Haslam, S. A., & Ryan, M. (2001). The role of personality and group factors in explaining prejudice. *Journal of Experimental Social Psychology, 37,* 427–434.

Reynolds, K. J., Turner, J. C., Ryan, M. K., Veenstra, K., Burgess, N., & McKone (2004a). Personality, group life and social influence: Explaining change in implicit/explicit prejudice. Australian National University, in submission.

Reynolds, K. J., Turner, J. C., Haslam, S. A., Ryan, M. K., Veenstra, K., & Wilkinson, R. (2004b). The role of personality variables and ingroup identification as motivations for discrimination between minimal groups. Australian National University, in submission.

Rosch, E. (1978). Principles of categorization. In E. Rosch & B. B. Lloyd (Eds.), *Cognition and categorization.* Hillsdale, NJ: Erlbaum.

Sani, F. & Reicher, S. (1998). When consensus fails: An analysis of the schism within the Italian Communist Party. *European Journal of Social Psychology, 28,* 623–645.

Schmitt, M. T., Branscombe, N. R., & Kappen, D. M. (2003). Attitudes to group-based inequality: Social dominance or social identity? *British Journal of Social Psychology, 42,* 161–186.

Sherif, M. (1967). *Group conflict and co-operation: Their social psychology.* London: Routledge and Kegan Paul.

Sidanius, J., & Pratto, F. (1999). *Social dominance: An intergroup theory of social hierarchy and oppression.* Cambridge: Cambridge University Press.

Siegel, A. E. & Siegel, S. (1957). Reference groups, membership groups, and attitude change. *Journal of Abnormal & Social Psychology, 55,* 360–364.

Simon, B. (2004). *Identity in modern society: A social psychological perspective.* Oxford: Blackwell.

Stephenson, G. M. (1981). Intergroup bargaining and negotiation. In J. C. Turner & H. Giles (Eds.), *Intergroup behaviour* (pp. 168–198). Oxford: Blackwell.

Stogdill, R. M. (1948). Personal factors associated with leadership: A survey of the literature. *Journal of Psychology, 25,* 35–71.

Stott, C. & Drury, J. (2004). The importance of social structure and social interaction in stereotype consensus and content: Is the whole greater than the sum of its parts? *European Journal of Social Psychology, 34,* 11–23.

Stott, C. & Reicher, S. D. (1998). Crowd action as intergroup process: Introducing the police perspective. *European Journal of Social Psychology, 28,* 509–530.

Stryker, S. & Statham, A. (1985). Symbolic interaction and role theory. In G. Lindzey & E. Aronson (Eds.), *The handbook of social psychology* (vol. 1, 3rd ed.). New York: Random House.

Swann, W. B. Jr., Kwan, V. S. Y., Polzer, J. T., & Milton, L. P. (2003). Fostering group identification and creativity in diverse groups: The role of individuation and self-verification. *Personality & Social Psychology Bulletin, 29*, 1396–1406.

Turner, J. C. (1982). Towards a cognitive redefinition of the social group. In H. Tajfel (Ed.), *Social identity and intergroup relations* (ch. 1, pp. 15–40). Cambridge: Cambridge University Press. Paris: Maison des Sciences de l'Homme.

Turner, J. C. (1985). Social categorization and the self-concept: A social cognitive theory of group behaviour. In E. J. Lawler (Ed.), *Advances in group processes* (vol. 2, pp. 77–122). Greenwich, CT: JAI.

Turner, J. C. (1987a). A self-categorization theory. In J. C. Turner, M. A. Hogg, P. J. Oakes, S. D. Reicher, & M. S. Wetherell, *Rediscovering the social group: A self-categorization theory*. Oxford: Blackwell.

Turner, J. C. (1987b). The analysis of social influence. In J. C. Turner, M. A. Hogg, P. J. Oakes, S. D. Reicher, & M. S. Wetherell, *Rediscovering the social group: A self-categorization theory*. Oxford: Blackwell.

Turner, J. C. (1991). *Social influence*. Milton Keynes, UK: Open University Press and Pacific Grove, CA: Brooks/Cole.

Turner, J. C. (1999a). Current issues in research on social identity and self-categorization theories. In N. Ellemers, R. Spears, & B. Doosje (Eds.), *Social identity: Context, commitment, content*. Oxford, UK & Cambridge, USA: Blackwell.

Turner, J. C. (1999b). *The Prejudiced personality and social change: A self-categorization perspective*. The Tajfel Memorial Lecture, invited keynote paper presented to 12th General Meeting of the EAESP, Oxford, UK, 6–11 July.

Turner, J. C. (2005). Explaining the nature of power: A three-process theory. *European Journal of Social Psychology, 35*, 1–22.

Turner, J. C. & Haslam, S. A. (2001). Social identity, organizations and leadership. In M. E. Turner (Ed.), *Groups at Work. Advances in theory and research* (pp. 25–65). Hillsdale, NJ: Erlbaum.

Turner, J. C. & Oakes, P. J. (1986). The significance of the social identity concept for social psychology with reference to individualism, interactionsim and social influence. *British Journal of Social Psychology, 25*, 237–252.

Turner, J. C. & Oakes, P. J. (1989). Self-categorization theory and social influence. In P. B. Paulus (Ed.), *The psychology of group influence* (2nd edition, pp. 233–275). Hillsdale, New Jersey: Erlbaum.

Turner, J. C. & Onorato, R. (1999). Social identity, personality and the self-concept: A self-categorization perspecctive. In T. R. Tyler, R. Kramer, & O. John (Eds.), *The psychology of the social self*. Mahwah, NJ: Lawrence Erlbaum Associates.

Turner, J. C. & Reynolds, K. J. (2003). Why social dominance theory has been falsified. *British Journal of Social Psychology, 42*, 199–206.

Turner, J. C. Oakes, P. J., Haslam, S. A., & McGarty, C.A. (1994). Self and collective: Cognition and social context. *Personality and Social Psychology Bulletin, 20, 454–463*. Special issue on The Self and the Collective.

Verkuyten, M. & Hagendoorn, L. (1998). Prejudice and self-categorization: The variable role of authoritarianism and ingroup stereotypes. *Personality and Social Psychology Bulletin, 24*, 99–110.

3

Acting Like an Individual versus Feeling Like an Individual

Deborah Prentice

One of the things that struck Alexis de Tocqueville most forcefully about nineteenth century America was how readily its citizens banded together to form groups. "Americans of all ages, all conditions, and all dispositions constantly form associations. They have not only commercial and manufacturing companies, in which all take part, but associations of a thousand other kinds, religious, moral, serious, futile, general or restricted, enormous or diminutive" (de Tocqueville, 1840/1994, p. 106). Americans formed groups for any and all purposes – political, social, recreational, commercial, intellectual, and moral. "As soon as several of the inhabitants of the United States have taken up an opinion or a feeling which they wish to promote in the world, they look out for mutual assistance; and as soon as they have found one another out, they combine ... Nothing, in my opinion, is more deserving of our attention" (pp. 109–110).

Although more recent observers have noted, and indeed lamented, the decline of civic associations in the United States (Putnam, 2000), de Tocqueville's observations still ring true, in America and throughout Western culture. Western societies are structured around groups and associations, most of them voluntary. Among these are colleges and universities, museums and environmental groups, churches, synagogues, and mosques, corporations and trade unions, charitable organizations and self-help groups, sports leagues and literary societies, sororities and fraternities, parent–teacher associations and day care cooperatives, and residential and professional associations. These groups play a central role in the lives of their members, structuring their everyday experience and defining their place in society. How can we reconcile the importance of these voluntary associations with another central feature of Western life: the powerful strain of individualism that members of Western societies embrace? This question is the focus of the present chapter.

My answer to this question will rest, in brief, on the distinction between acting like an individual and feeling like an individual. One acts like an individual when one's behavior is directed by individualistic goals, motives, and self-definitions. One feels like an individual when one experiences one's actions as autonomous and one's personal qualities as distinctive. I will argue that, in group contexts, Americans sometimes – perhaps often – act like individuals, but they almost always feel like individuals. As a consequence, group experiences typically function to affirm, rather than to threaten, their individuality. An understanding of this seemingly paradoxical outcome requires an analysis of the distinct processes of self-regulation and self-reflection.

Acting like an individual

How does the self regulate behavior in group contexts? Although there are many psychological theories of self-regulation, the ones best suited for answering this particular question find their roots in social identity theory (Tajfel & Turner, 1986) and especially self-categorization theory (Turner, Hogg, Oakes, Reicher, & Wetherell, 1987). Originally focused on the role of the self in group phenomena, self-categorization theory has proven to be equally insightful about the role of the group in self-phenomena. Moreover, it has spawned several related theories that elaborate on its treatment of the pursuit of individualistic motives and self-conceptions in group contexts.

Self-categorization theory

Self-categorization theory proposes that the functioning of the self at any given moment depends on how one categorizes the self – specifically, on which people are seen as similar to self, and which as different. The process of self-categorization determines which aspects of the self become salient guides for behavior. Self-categorization theorists have distinguished broadly between two different levels of self-categorization: the collective level, which highlights similarities among group members, and the individual level, which highlights differences among group members.

The collective level of self-categorization is "based on social similarities and differences between human beings that define one as a member of certain social groups and not others (e.g., 'American,' 'female,' 'black,' 'student,' 'working class')" (Turner et al., 1987, p. 45). People categorize at this level when their membership in a group is made salient, by their own motives and predilections and/or by the context in which they find themselves. When people self-categorize at the collective level, their self becomes depersonalized, in self-categorization theory terminology, and they function as prototypical group members.

The concept of depersonalization is key to understanding collective self-categorization. Turner et al. (1987) described it as follows:

> *Depersonalization* refers to the process of "self-stereotyping" whereby people come to perceive themselves more as the interchangeable exemplars of a social category than as unique personalities defined by their individual differences from others. (p. 50)

They were also clear about what depersonalization is *not*:

> Depersonalization, however, is not a loss of individual identity, nor a loss or submergence of the self in the group (as in the concept of de-individuation), nor any kind of regression to a more primitive or unconscious form of identity. It is the *change* from the personal to the social level of identity, a change in the nature and content of the self-concept corresponding to the functioning of self-perception at a more inclusive level of abstraction. (p. 51)

With this statement, Turner et al. (1987) were distancing themselves from the group mind idea, originally put forward by Le Bon (1896) and McDougall (1921) at the turn of the twentieth century to explain crowd behavior. Turner et al. took pains, in their original theory and elsewhere, to explain that depersonalization is not like a group mind, not an altered state of consciousness, in which the individual is lost and the collective takes over. It is simply a redefinition of identity in more inclusive terms.

The *individual level* of self-categorization is "the subordinate level of personal self-categorizations based on differentiations between oneself as a unique individual and other ingroup members that define one as a specific individual person (e.g., in terms of one's personality or other kinds of individual differences)" (Turner et al., 1987, p. 45). People categorize at this level when their status as a unique individual is made salient, again by their own motives and predilections and/or by the context in which they find themselves. When people self-categorize at the individual level, they think of themselves in terms of the qualities that differentiate them from other ingroup members. They think and act as unique individuals.

The individual level of self-categorization seems reassuringly familiar to most self researchers, especially as compared to the collective level; it reflects how Western psychologists (not to mention laypeople) typically think about self-functioning. However, the formulation offered by self-categorization theory diverges somewhat from the received view. Specifically, categorization at the individual level still involves viewing the self within a social context – that of one particular ingroup. One's relation to that ingroup determines the properties of the self that come to the fore. Therefore, just as one has many collective self-categories, for all the groups to which one belongs, one has many individual self-categories, again for all the groups to which one belongs (Turner, Reynolds, Haslam, & Veenstra, Chapter 2 in this volume).

Recently, Simon and his colleagues (Simon, 1997; Simon & Kampmeier, 2001) proposed an alternative conceptualization of the individual level of self-categorization. Specifically, they argued for a distinction between the individual self and the collective self based on the number of self-aspects that serve as a basis for self-interpretation. Collective self-interpretation is based on a single self-aspect that one shares with others; individual self-interpretation is based on a comprehensive set of non-redundant self-aspects. Thus, the individual and collective selves differ not in whether the attributes that make them up are shared or distinctive, but rather in their complexity. The collective self is simple, defined by a single attribute; the individual self is complex, defined by all of one's attributes. This alternative conceptualization of the individual self has greatly facilitated the study of individuality within a self-categorization framework.

Virtually all of the research inspired by self-categorization theory has focused on self-categorization at the collective and individual levels. However, in its original formulation, the theory included not two but three levels of self-categorization. Turner et al. (1987) defined the third level as "the superordinate level of the self as human being, self-categorizations based on one's identity as a human being, the common features shared with other members of the human species in contrast to other forms of life" (p. 45). This *human level* of self-categorization has received virtually no theoretical or empirical attention since the original formation (although see Wohl & Branscombe, 2005). However, one can speculate that people categorize at this level when their status as a human being is made salient, once again by their own motives and predilections and/or by the context in which they find themselves. Moreover, self-categorization at the human level should lead to depersonalization around the prototype of the human category.

In summary, self-categorization theory holds that behavior in group contexts depends critically on how one categorizes the self in that moment: as an individual or as a group member (or perhaps as a human being). This simple distinction between the self as an individual and the self as a group member has proven to be extremely useful for predicting and analyzing behavior in the laboratory, as well as in the real world. It has also given us some purchase on the relation between individuality and group involvement, at least at a behavioral level.

Individuality

Definitions and conceptualizations of individuality abound. For example, McAdams (1996) highlighted three levels at which individuality is conceptualized: (1) as dispositional traits; (2) as a set of motives; and (3) as a life narrative. Within this framework, self-categorization theory qualifies as a mid-level, motivational approach, in which individuality is defined as an outgrowth of self-categorization at the individual level. As the basis for a program of empirical research, this definition has a couple of very positive features. It is elastic enough to encompass a wide range of individual needs, motives, values, and self-interpretations, all of which can be conceptualized as individual self-categories. In addition, it enables researchers to use the assumptions, concepts, and methodologies of self-categorization research to study the development and expression of individuality within group contexts. This approach has produced a number of major insights.

First, self-categorization theories have provided a new perspective on how individual, group, and cultural differences in individuality develop. Specifically, these theories explain variations in individuality as a by-product of normal self-categorization processes. A person is individualistic or is expressing her individuality when she self-categorizes at the individual level. Some people do this more often than others, either because individual-level self-categories are chronically more salient for them and/or because they often find themselves in ingroup contexts that promote this level of self-categorization (Hogg, 2001; Turner & Onorato, 1999). These differences in the salience of the individual level of self-categorization are responsible for differences across individuals, groups, and cultures in individuality. For example, the high levels of individuality in Western culture derive from the chronic salience of individual-level self-categories promoted by cultural values (Moghaddam, Chapter 9 in this volume). The high levels of individuality among members of majority (compared with minority) groups derive from the fact that majority group members spend most of their time in ingroup settings, which promote this level of self-categorization (Lorenzi-Cioldi, Chapter 6 in this volume). Highly individualistic people frequently self-categorize at the individual level, which promotes the chronic salience of self-categories at this level. And the form that individuality takes depends on how individual self-categories are defined within ingroup contexts. Although this account is better at explaining variations in individuality than at predicting them, it nonetheless specifies a set of mechanisms through which such differences are developed and maintained (Turner et al., Chapter 2 in this volume).

A second insight is that individuality is not unidimensional but instead has two major components: an independence component, which is based on freedom from the restrictions and constraints imposed by group membership, and a differentiation component, which is based on differences from other people (Kampmeier & Simon, 2001; Simon, 1997; Simon & Kampmeier, 2001). This distinction is important to the study of individuality for at least two reasons. First, most researchers have adopted either an independence or a differentiation perspective on individuality; the articulation and empirical validation of a two-component model provide a way of reconciling their disparate findings and perspectives. Second, the two-component model has enabled investigators to make more nuanced and successful predictions about how individuality relates to group functioning.

A third insight to come from the self-categorization approach is that individuality is fully compatible with group membership, at least under some circumstances. For example, building on their two-component model of individuality, Kampmeier and Simon (2001; Simon & Kampmeier, 2001) sought to document some of those circumstances. They reasoned that compatibility between individuality and group membership should depend on which component of individuality is salient, as well as on properties of the group and the comparative context. Specifically, the two components of individuality – independence and differentiation – are compatible with different orientations toward the group. Independence is compatible with group membership when the focus is on ingroup dynamics, because this focus highlights variability within the group; this focus occurs more often for members of majority groups, who interact primarily with ingroup members, than for members of minority groups (see also Lorenzi-Cioldi, Chapter 6 in this volume). Differentiation is compatible with group membership when the focus is on intergroup dynamics, because this focus highlights differentiation from outgroup members; this focus occurs more often for members of minority groups, who interact frequently with outgroup members. The results of several studies supported these predictions, demonstrating that group identification and cohesiveness were stronger when the salience of independence was combined with an ingroup orientation and when the salience of differentiation was combined with an intergroup orientation. It is important to note that in these studies, Kampmeier and Simon (2001) manipulated the salience of independence and differentiation without reference to participants' own standing on those dimensions and observed no effects of the manipulation on participants' ratings of their own independence or differentiation.

Additional evidence that the compatibility of individuality and group membership depends on the type of group in question comes from research by Postmes and his colleagues (Jetten, Postmes, & McAuliffe, 2002; Postmes, Spears, Novak, & Lee, 2004; see Postmes, Haslam, & Swaab, 2005, for a review). One set of studies examined individuality and group identification in groups with individualistic norms (Jetten et al., 2002). The investigators reasoned that membership in this type of group should be compatible with expressions of individuality, given that those expressions are supported and reinforced by group membership. The results of several studies demonstrated that identification with such groups does indeed produce individualistic expressions, though not through self-categorization at the individual level. Instead, individuality results from depersonalization and self-stereotyping in terms of the (individualistic) prototype of the group.

A similar mechanism may operate at the human level of self-categorization to promote individuality in individualistic cultures (Halloran & Kashima, Chapter 8; Jetten & Postmes, Chapter 7; Moghaddam, Chapter 9 in this volume). In the earlier discussion of the human self-categorization, I suggested that it would lead to depersonalization around the prototype of the human category. What is the prototype of the human category? It is the representation of personhood provided by one's culture (D'Andrade, 1992; Sperber, 1985). Culture is a rich source of representations of human nature, representations that often differ across cultures but are consensually shared within a culture. For example, much research in recent years has focused on the sharply different construals of self held by members of North American and East Asian cultures (see Markus & Kitayama, 1991). Underlying these cultural self-construals are divergent representations of personhood, of what it means to be human and what human beings are like; these representations serve as prototypes of the human category. They differ from group prototypes that exist at the collective level primarily in their perceived universality. However, their effects on perception and behavior are similar to those of group prototypes. Thus, in individualistic cultures (e.g., North America, Western Europe), self-categorization at the human level should be a source of individuality: it should lead to depersonalization around an independent human prototype and thereby to individualistic behavior.

A final set of studies by Postmes and his colleagues highlighted another feature of groups that makes them compatible with individuality: the basis for their formation. In these studies, Postmes et al. (2004) examined the relation between individuality and social influence processes – specifically, group polarization – in groups based on individual attachments (common-bond groups) versus those based on group attachments (common-identity groups) (see also Prentice, Miller, & Lightdale, 1994). Much previous research has shown that social influence is dependent on depersonalization, on group members self-categorizing at the collective level (Turner, 1991). Postmes et al. expected to find a very different basis for influence in groups based on interpersonal bonds. Consistent with this expectation, their studies demonstrated that social influence in common-bond groups depended not on depersonalization but on individuation, on making group members identifiable to each other. Additional research suggested that common-bond and common-identity groups had very different dynamics: in the former type of group, influence occurred through diversity of opinion and disagreement, whereas in the latter type of group, influence occurred through coherence and consensus (Sassenberg & Postmes, 2002).

Taken together, the results of these studies begin to document the contingencies that determine whether group membership is compatible or incompatible with expressions of individuality. These contingencies include the norms and dynamics of the group, its relative size, the comparative context, and the component of individuality that is salient. Future research may well identify many more contingencies.

A final and related insight to come from self-categorization research concerns the perceptual and behavioral consequences of individuality. Self-categorization theories are, at their core, models of self-regulation. That is, they all share the premise that salient needs, motives, and self-interpretations guide perception and behavior. In that spirit, several investigations have examined how individualistic needs, motives, and self-interpretations relate to perceptions and behaviors in groups. For example, Brewer and Roccas (2001; Roccas & Brewer, 2002) explored the relation between the salience of the independence component of individuality, and various group-related perceptions and preferences. They assessed the salience of independence-related values using a standard values inventory. In line with Brewer's (1991) optimal distinctiveness theory, they reasoned that individuals who valued independence would have a comparatively low need for differentiation and a high need for inclusion; they would gravitate toward groups that are large in size and would care little about the distinctiveness of the group. Correlational evidence supported these predictions, showing a moderately strong positive relation between group identification and perceived group size and a weaker relation between group identification and perceived group distinctiveness for people with individualistic values. In addition, people with individualistic values held comparatively complex representations of their social identities, in that they represented their ingroups as relatively distinct, with low degrees of similarity and low overlap in membership (Roccas & Brewer, 2002).

In our own research, my colleagues and I examined the behavioral correlates of individuality in everyday life (Prentice, Trail, & Cantor, 2004). We, too, focused on the independence component of individuality, operationalizing it as the extent to which college students placed a high priority on independence values and a low priority on security values. We then examined how these students chose, regulated, and experienced their membership in extracurricular campus groups. Consistent with our predictions, we found that the more students valued independence, the more extracurricular groups they joined, but the less embedded they were in any one group. The more students valued independence, the more stress they experienced when they perceived their membership in a group as getting in the way of their academic commitments or making it difficult for them to manage their time. In addition, the more they valued independence, the less stress they experienced over not having the characteristics that were important for fitting into their group. These results again highlight the fact that individuality is by no means incompatible with group membership. On the contrary, independence-minded people may join more groups as a means of escaping dependence on any one and may interpret their portfolio of diverse group memberships as evidence for their individuality (see also Simon & Kampmeier, 2001).

Summary

In summary, self-categorization approaches have proven fruitful for understanding when and how people act like individuals in group settings. The salience of the independence and differentiation components of individuality, whether manipulated in the laboratory or measured with a values inventory, plays a critical role, predicting the number and type of groups with which people identify, the extent to which they identify, and the conditions under which they identify. The salience of individuality also predicts how people perceive their groups and the relations among these groups. In short, conceptualizing individuality in terms of the individual level of self-categorization tells us a lot about people's perceptions of group membership and their behavior in group contexts.

At the same time, this approach does not capture people's experiences of individuality in group contexts. That is, it does not tell us when and why people feel like individuals in a group. What is clear is that the subjective experience of individuality, and indeed of self, operates on very different principles than those articulated by self-categorization theories. Level of self-categorization may affect behavior, but it does not have the same effect on the interpretation of that behavior. Behavior feels self-authored regardless. This is important in the present context, because it is subjective experience that ultimately determines the compatibility of individuality and group membership. I turn now to an examination of relevant research on the psychology of feeling like an individual.

Feeling like an individual

Compared with the literature on the self-regulation of individuality, the literature on subjective experience lacks nuance. Virtually all studies, from a variety of research traditions, attest to the primacy of the individual level of self-feeling, even in group contexts. People feel like individuals first and foremost, regardless of the forces acting on their behavior. This is not to say that they never feel at one with their fellow group members, but that feeling seems to be much more fleeting. And even when they act as group members – even when they conform to group norms or to direct pressure from group members – they construe that behavior in ways that emphasize their autonomy or uniqueness. Consider the following research findings.

Feeling threatened

People feel threat much more keenly and react to it more strongly when it is directed at them as individuals rather than as group members. Gaertner, Sedikides, and Graetz (1999) delivered positive, neutral, or negative feedback to participants about themselves as individuals (e.g., "you are excessively moody") or about their group (e.g., "women are excessively moody"). Across four investigations, Gaertner et al. found that a threat to the individual was considered more severe, produced a more negative mood and more anger, elicited stronger derogation of the source of the feedback, and produced larger shifts in self-definition than a threat to the group. These effects held even after controlling for the accessibility of the individual and collective selves, for the domain in which feedback was given, for the independence of feedback to the individual and the group, for participants' level of group identification, and for their cultural value orientation. The finding that participants still reacted more strongly to individual-level threats even when their collective identity was salient is especially striking. It suggests that people remain invested in their individuality, even when self-categorizing as a member of a group (see also Sedikides & Gaertner, 2001).

Feeling verified

In a related vein, people seek and profit from validation of their individuality, even when they are contributing to a group effort. Swann, Milton, and Polzer (2000) investigated the effects of self-verification on connection to the group and group performance in small study groups of MBA students. They defined self-verification as the degree to which other group members' appraisals moved closer to a target's initial self-views over time. Their results demonstrated that this process was associated with stronger connections to the study group and better group grades on creative (but not computational) tasks. That is, students felt closer to the group and performed better in the group to the extent that other group members validated their individuality. A second study replicated and extended these results, demonstrating that self-verification depended on the extent to which initial impressions of group members were individuated, which depended, in turn, on the diversity of the group and the positivity of initial impressions (Swann, Kwan, Polzer, & Milton, 2003). Note that it is not clear whether or how initial individuation and self-verification affected the ongoing dynamics of these groups. But what is important, in the present context, is that self-verification would have made group members feel like individuals – it would have validated their individuality – and this feeling could account for why they felt more connected to and identified with their group.

Feeling independent

More direct evidence that people can simultaneously feel like individuals and behave like group members comes from studies that assessed feelings of autonomy in group settings. For example, in an empirical study of membership in campus groups, Sheldon and Bettencourt (2002) asked students to choose one of their groups and to indicate, "How free and choiceful do you feel as you participate in this group?", "How much do you feel wholehearted (as opposed to feeling controlled or pressured) as you do things for this group?", and "To what extent does this group membership allow you to express your authentic self?" The mean response across these three items, on a five-point scale, was 3.67. Moreover, in this investigation, individuals who felt more autonomous also felt better: feelings of autonomy were associated with more positive and less negative affect. However, autonomy did not come at the expense of feelings of inclusion or of attachment to the group – in fact, feelings of autonomy and inclusion were positively associated. In a similar investigation of social roles, Bettencourt and Sheldon (2001) showed that these, too, provide individuals with a sense of autonomy (and of relatedness), especially to the extent that the demands of the roles match individuals' personal characteristics (Bettencourt, Molix, Talley, & Sheldon, Chapter 11 in this volume).

Of course, given considerable evidence that people can choose their groups and regulate their group involvements so as to retain their independence, these high levels of perceived autonomy may come as no surprise. However, additional research suggests that sometimes people *feel* autonomous even when their behavior smacks of conformity. Pronin, Berger, and Molouki (2004) compared how much people attributed their own behavior to conformity and how much they attributed other people's behavior to conformity. Even when the behavior of self and other was manipulated to be identical, participants regarded conformity as a greater influence on others than on the self. When both the self and another person bought the latest style of jeans, the other person was conforming, whereas the self just happened to like the jeans. When both the self and another person voted consistent with their political party, the other person was adopting the party line, whereas the self independently arrived at the same position (see also Cohen, 2003). Given pervasive evidence that people do, in fact, conform under many circumstances, it seems likely that these perceived self–other differences reflect an underestimation of conformity by the self rather than an overestimation of conformity by others.

Feeling unique

Perhaps the most striking examples of the primacy of individual self-experience come from situations in which people recognize they are conforming to group norms but feel unique in the process. Such situations are captured by a phenomenon known as pluralistic ignorance: the belief that one's private thoughts, feelings, and behaviors are different from those of others, even though one's public behavior is identical (Miller & McFarland, 1991). Pluralistic ignorance occurs when people conform to group norms that do not reflect their private beliefs and attitudes: when they drink to excess, even though they prefer more moderate levels of consumption (Prentice & Miller, 1993); when they fail to raise their hand in class, even though they have no idea what is going on (Miller & McFarland, 1987); when they fail to intervene in emergency situations, despite their private concerns for the welfare of the victims (Latané & Darley, 1970); or when they act in line with stereotypes, even though they harbor more egalitarian views (Prentice & Miller, 1996). When most or all of the members of a group exhibit this kind of conformity we find a divergence in the interpretations they give for their own and others' behavior: they recognize that their own behavior is not based on their private beliefs and sentiments, but they assume that all others are behaving more authentically.

One consequence of these divergent interpretations is that victims of pluralistic ignorance end up feeling alienated from each other and from the group. The empirical hallmark of pluralistic ignorance is a gap between ratings of one's own attitudes, beliefs, or sentiments and ratings of the attitudes, beliefs, or sentiments of the average member of the group, the typical member of the group, or most members of the group. Clearly, people interpret themselves to be, at the very least, atypical members of the group. But several additional pieces of evidence suggest that they actually experience this atypicality negatively. In our studies of pluralistic ignorance regarding alcohol use on campus, Dale Miller and I found that students who believed they held different attitudes toward alcohol use than most students felt less attached to the university, holding constant the actual discrepancy between their own and others' attitudes (Prentice & Miller, 1993, Study 4). We also found that male students brought their own attitudes into line with their estimates of their peers' attitudes over the course of a semester on campus (Study 3). And in our study of the consequences of reducing pluralistic ignorance, Christine Schroeder and I found that informing students that others shared their misgivings produced less drinking among students high in fear of negative evaluation and greater comfort among students who did not drink alcohol (Schroeder & Prentice, 1998). All of these findings suggest that the alienation students profess to feel in cases of pluralistic ignorance is both real and painful.

Sources of experienced individuality

This heterogeneous collection of cases highlights a bias in subjective experience toward feelings of individuality, rather than feelings of collectivity. What gives rise to this bias? The psychological literature suggests a number of hypotheses.

First, certain levels of self-awareness highlight the boundaries of the individual. For example, people have an awareness of themselves as active agents in the immediate environment. They experience their own location and movement, what they are doing, and whether an action is their own or not. Neisser (1988) referred to this level of self-awareness as the ecological self, and argued that it is the first and most fundamental form of self-knowledge. As such, it may go some way toward explaining the individualistic bias in self-experience. For one's senses of embodiment and agency extend only to the boundaries of oneself as an individual, and thereby distinguish each person from all others. At this level, self-experience is highly individualizing.

Equally individualizing is the inner world of thoughts, images, sensations, dreams, and feelings. This level of self-awareness probably makes a very important contribution to the individuality bias in self-experience for two reasons: first, people believe themselves to be best defined and most authentically represented by their private thoughts and feelings (Andersen, 1984; Andersen & Ross, 1984); and second, they believe those private thoughts and feelings to differentiate them from other people in many respects. The former belief gives rise to feelings of autonomy and the latter to feelings of uniqueness.

As an illustration of the connection between introspection and feelings of autonomy, consider, once again, Pronin, Berger, and Molouki's (2004) studies of perceived conformity. These studies demonstrated that people saw conformity as less of an influence on their own behavior than on the behavior of their peers. Additional evidence suggested that their comparatively low ratings of their own conformity resulted from their reliance on introspection to determine the causes of their own behavior. For example, when evaluating the extent to which an undergraduate panel influenced their votes on a set of campus policy proposals, participants reflected on introspective information – that is, on what they recalled thinking about the contents of the proposals. Naturally, this self-inference strategy turned up little evidence of conformity. When evaluating the extent to which the panel influenced their peers' votes, they simply looked at the behavioral data – how often did their peers vote with the panel? This behavioral assessment led to much higher ratings of conformity (Pronin, Berger, & Molouki, 2004, Study 3). Pronin, Gilovich, and Ross (2004) have recently argued that this tendency to rely on introspection plays an important part in people's failure to appreciate many of the forces that act on their behavior.

Of course, sometimes people do appreciate the forces that act on their behavior. Sometimes they recognize that they act out of a desire to be part of a group, to forward a group's agenda, or simply to adhere to the reality that a group provides. Sometimes introspection turns up evidence of conformity, not autonomy. In these cases, illusory feelings of individuality result not from people's reliance on introspection to determine the causes of their own behavior but from their faulty assumptions about what underlies other people's similar behavior. Consider, for example, a college student's experiences involving alcohol use on campus. Drinking is a strong norm on this student's campus, and he and his friends go out drinking at the eating clubs every weekend and many weekdays as well. He interprets his friends' behavior as evidence that they love getting drunk, that drinking is their preferred form of social activity. His own feelings about getting drunk are considerably less positive than that, but he goes out anyway in order to be cool, to be part of the group, and to be part of the social scene, such as it is. He recognizes these collectivistic motives in himself, but not in his friends. And as a consequence, when he reflects on his group experience, what stands out is not that everybody behaved similarly, but that he alone felt differently. Experienced individuality, in this case, resides not in a direct inference about the causes of his own behavior, but instead in a perceived difference between the internal states that direct his behavior and those that presumably direct his friends' behavior.

What gives rise to this belief that self and others are guided by different internal states? Dale Miller and I (1994) argued for the importance of two processes, both of which are manifestations of the privileged access people have to their own private thoughts and feelings and the lack of access they have to the thoughts and feelings of others. One, people assume that their private experiences differ from those of others. In their studies of pluralistic ignorance, Miller and McFarland (1987) found that participants believed that they, more than other people, are characterized by traits that have internal referents – traits like sympathetic, self-critical, sensitive, hesitant, bashful, choosy, self-conscious, inhibited, indecisive, and preoccupied, whose recognition requires access to private thoughts and feelings. In other words, people seem to believe that their private worlds are more vivid and more conflicted than the private worlds that othes inhabit (see also McFarland & Miller, 1990). Subsequent studies have suggested that this belief underlies a great many social phenomena, including people's feelings that they, more than others, are inhibited from making a romantic overture by fear of rejection (Vorauer & Ratner, 1997), that they, more than others, refrain from approaching outgroup members because they fear a negative response (Shelton & Richeson, 2005), and that they, more than others, drink alcohol in order to have friends (Schroeder & Prentice, 1998).

If people's access to their own private thoughts and feelings leads them to believe that they have richer internal lives, their lack of access to others' private thoughts and feelings leads them to fall back on implicit theories of human nature and motivation to account for others' behavior. As I noted in an earlier section of this chapter, cultures provide their members with theories and collective representations, including accounts of what motivates people and what ought to motivate people. The representations of American society, for example, emphasize individual agency, rationality, and autonomy: self-determination over social etiquette, self-preservation over social standing. Of course, behavior often violates these representations. People do things they know are wrong at the request of an authority figure. They risk danger to self and others in order to avoid embarrassment. They give social motives primacy. These circumstances are characterized by what Dale Miller and I (1994) termed a *motivational inversion*: a violation of what implicit theories of motivational potency prescribe. As people introspect on the causes of their behavior, they often recognize that they are violating these theories. But they do not generalize from that observation. Instead, they view themselves as a unique case: they assume that other people – others who are behaving similarly – must be acting out of a more appropriate, theory-consistent motivation (Miller & Prentice, 1994). Their momentary insight that they are acting out of social motives, acting as group members, simply leaves them feeling that they are the only ones in the group who are doing so.

Taken together, these results suggest that the tendency to introspect on the causes of behavior leads individuals to experience conformity as, alternately, either autonomy or uniqueness. When introspection turns up attitudes and beliefs that support their behavior, people feel autonomous, even when the behavior in question is common or uniform within the group. When introspection turns up social motives and anxieties that support their behavior, they feel unique, again even when the behavior in question is uniform within the group. Of course, there are no doubt occasions on which introspection turns up evidence of group commitment, group identification, and attachment to group members – true feelings of collectivity. However, this outcome may require that individuals hold implicit theories that support a collectivistic interpretation of their behavior.

Individuality and the self

There is certainly nothing new in claiming a distinction between how the self acts and how it experiences and understands those actions. Many early theories of the self included some version of this distinction. William James (1890/1983), for example, distinguished the empirical self (or me) and the pure ego (or I). The empirical self is the self that directs action moment-to-moment, the one that perceives, thinks, feels, wants, strives, and behaves. This is equivalent to the behaving self that I have analyzed here in terms of self-categorization theories. The pure ego is the self that oversees and reflects on that experience, the one that constructs a concept and narrative of self. This is equivalent to the reflecting self that I have analyzed here in terms of theories of self- and social inference. More recent self theorists have followed in this tradition (e.g., Neisser, 1988).

The important point about these distinctions for the study of individuality is that they define two very different and largely independent, but equally valid, perspectives on the phenomenon. At a behavioral level, individuality is governed by self-categorization processes, which depend on the complex interplay of individual and contextual factors. Research inspired by self-categorization theory (Turner et al., 1987) has given us an increasingly rich and nuanced understanding of how those processes work. At an experiential level, individuality is governed by self- and social inference processes, which tend to promote individualistic feelings of autonomy and uniqueness, regardless of the true sources of behavior. The disjunction between these two sets of processes is most apparent when self-categorization occurs at the collective level, and thus I have focused considerable attention on how people experience the behavior they enact as group members. The fact that that experience is often one of individuality, rather than collectivity, may provide some insight into why American social psychology gravitates toward individualistic theories of self, despite powerful evidence for collective self-definition.

Postscript

For Alexis de Tocqueville, Americans' preoccupation with individualism, on the one hand, and voluntary associations, on the other, was not paradoxical at all. He viewed both of these tendencies as endemic to democracy and, in particular, to equality of condition, which promotes the idea that individuals should think and act for themselves and yet leaves them entirely dependent on one another for validation and effective action (de Tocqueville, 1840/1994). De Tocqueville's analysis is completely (and, indeed, impressively) consistent with current psychological theory. However, what it fails to capture are the psychological dynamics that enable these two apparently conflicting tendencies to coexist within individuals. As researchers continue to probe the distinct processes of self-regulation and self-reflection, an understanding of these psychological dynamics is now within reach.

REFERENCES

Andersen, S. M. (1984). Self-knowledge and social inference: II. The diagnosticity of cognitive/affective and behavioral data. *Journal of Personality and Social Psychology, 46*, 294–307.

Andersen, S. M., & Ross, L. (1984). Self-knowledge and social inference: I. The impact of cognitive/affective and behavioral data. *Journal of Personality and Social Psychology, 46*, 280–293.

Bettencourt, B. A., & Sheldon, K. (2001). Social roles as mechanisms for psychological need satisfaction within social groups. *Journal of Personality and Social Psychology, 81*, 1131–1143.

Brewer, M. B. (1991). The social self: On being the same and different at the same time. *Personality and Social Psychology Bulletin, 117*, 475–482.

Brewer, M. B., & Roccas, S. (2001). Individual values, social identity, and optimal distinctiveness. In C. Sedikides & M. B. Brewer (Eds.), *Individual self, relational self, collective self* (pp. 291–240). Philadelphia: Psychology Press.

Cohen, G. L. (2003). Party over policy: The dominating impact of group influence on political beliefs. *Journal of Personality and Social Psychology, 85*, 808–822.

D'Andrade, R. G. (1992). Schemas and motivation. In R. D'Andrade & C. Strauss (Eds.), *Human motives and cultural models* (pp. 23–44). Cambridge: Cambridge University Press.

De Tocqueville, A. (1840/1994). *Democracy in America.* New York: Knopf.

Gaertner, L., Sedikides, C., & Graetz, K. (1999). In search of self-definition: Motivational primacy of the individual self, motivational primacy of the collective self, or contextual primacy? *Journal of Personality and Social Psychology, 76*, 5–18.

Hogg, M. A. (2001). Social identity and the sovereignty of the group: A psychology of belonging. In C. Sedikides & M. B. Brewer (Eds.), *Individual self, relational self, collective self* (pp. 125–145). Philadelphia: Psychology Press.

James, W. (1890/1983). *The principles of psychology.* Cambridge, MA: Harvard University Press.

Jetten, J., Postmes, T., & McAuliffe, B. (2002). "We're *all* individuals": Group norms of individualism and collectivism, levels of identification, and identity threat. *European Journal of Social Psychology, 32*, 189–207.

Kampmeier, C., & Simon, B. (2001). Individuality and group formation: The role of independence and differentiation. *Journal of Personality and Social Psychology, 81*, 448–462.

Latane, B., & Darley, J. (1970). *The unresponsive bystander: Why doesn't he help?* New York: Appleton-Century-Crofts.

Le Bon, G. (1896). *The crowd: A study of the popular mind.*

Markus, H. R., & Kitayama, S. (1991). Culture and the self: Implications for cognition, emotion, and motivation. *Psychological Review, 98,* 224–253.

McAdams, D. P. (1996). Alternative futures for the study of human individuality. *Journal of Research in Personality, 30,* 374–388.

McDougall, W. (1921). *The group mind.* London: Cambridge University Press.

McFarland , C., & Miller, D. T. (1990). Judgments of self–other similarity: Just like other people, only more so. *Personality and Social Psychology Bulletin, 16,* 475–484.

Miller, D. T., & McFarland, C. (1987). Pluralistic ignorance: When similarity is interpreted as dissimilarity. *Journal of Personality and Social Psychology, 53,* 298–305.

Miller, D. T., & McFarland, C. (1991). When social comparison goes awry: The case of pluralistic ignorance. In J. Suls & T. Wills (Eds.), *Social comparison: Contemporary theory and research* (pp. 287–313). Hillsdale, NJ: Erlbaum.

Miller, D. T., & Prentice, D. A. (1994). Collective errors and errors about the collective. *Personality and Social Psychology Bulletin, 20,* 541–550.

Neisser, U. (1988). Five kinds of self-knowledge. *Philosophical Psychology, 1,* 35–59.

Postmes, T., Haslam, S. A., & Swaab, R. (2005). Social influence in small groups: An interactive model of social identity formation. *European Review of Social Psychology, 16,* 1–42.

Postmes, T., Spears, R., Novak, R., & Lee, T. (2004). Social influence processes in small groups: Inductive and deductive identity and the role of individuality. Unpublished manuscript.

Prentice, D. A., & Miller, D. T. (1993). Pluralistic ignorance and alcohol use on campus: Some consequences of misperceiving the social norm. *Journal of Personality and Social Psychology, 64,* 243–256.

Prentice, D. A., & Miller, D. T. (1996). Pluralistic ignorance and the perpetuation of social norms by unwitting actors. In M. P. Zanna (Ed.), *Advances in experimental social psychology* (vol. 17, pp. 161–209). San Diego: Academic.

Prentice, D. A., Miller, D. T., & Lightdale, J. R. (1994). Asymmetries in attachments to groups and to their members: Distinguishing between common-identity and common-bond groups. *Personality and Social Psychology Bulletin, 20,* 484–493.

Prentice, D. A., Trail, T., & Cantor, N. E. (2004). The pursuit of individuality through group membership: Extracurricular groups in the everyday lives of college students. Unpublished manuscript, Princeton University.

Pronin, E., Berger, J., & Molouki, S. (2004). *Alone in a crowd of sheep: Perceptions of conformity in self versus others.* Unpublished manuscript, Princeton University.

Pronin, E., Gilovich, T., & Ross, E. (2004). Objectivity in the eye of the beholder: Divergent perceptions of bias in self versus others. *Psychological Review, 111,* 781–799.

Putnam, R. D. (2000). *Bowling alone: The collapse and revival of American community.* New York: Simon & Schuster.

Roccas, S., & Brewer, M. B. (2002). Social identity complexity. *Personality and Social Psychology Review, 6,* 88–106.

Sassenberg, K., & Postmes, T. (2002). Cognitive and strategic processes in small groups: Effects of anonymity of the self and anonymity of the group on social influence. *British Journal of Social Psychology, 41,* 463–480.

Schroeder, C. M., & Prentice, D. A. (1998). Exposing pluralistic ignorance to reduce alcohol use among college students. *Journal of Applied Social Psychology, 28,* 2150–2180.

Sedikides, C., & Gaertner, L. (2001). A homecoming to the individual self: Emotional and motivational primacy. In C. Sedikides & M. B. Brewer (Eds.), *Individual self, relational self, collective self* (pp. 7–24). Philadelphia: Psychology Press.

Sheldon, K. M., & Bettencourt, B. A. (2002). Psychological need-satisfaction and subjective well-being within social groups. *British Journal of Social Psychology, 41*, 25–38.

Shelton, J. N., & Richeson, J. (2005). Intergroup contact and pluralistic ignorance. *Journal of Personality and Social Psychology, 88*, 91–107.

Simon, B. (1997). Self and group in modern society: Ten theses on the individual self and the collective self. In R. Spears, P. J. Oakes, N. Ellemers, & S. A. Haslam (Eds.), *The social psychology of stereotyping and group life* (pp. 318–335). Oxford,: Blackwell.

Simon, B., & Kampmeier, C. (2001). Revisiting the individual self: Toward a social psychological theory of the individual self and the collective self. In C. Sedikides & M. B. Brewer (Eds.), *Individual self, relational self, collective self* (pp. 199–218). Philadelphia: Psychology Press.

Sperber, D. (1985). Anthropology and psychology: Towards an epidemiology of representations. *Man, 20*, 73–89.

Swann, W. B., Kwan, V. S. Y., Polzer, J. T., & Milton, L. P. (2003). Fostering group identification and creativity in diverse groups: The role of individuation and self-verification. *Personality and Social Psychology Bulletin, 29*, 1396–1406.

Swann, W. B., Milton, L. P., & Polzer, J. T. (2000). Should we create a niche or fall in line? Identity negotiation and small group effectiveness. *Journal of Personality and Social Psychology, 79*, 238–250.

Tajfel, H., & Turner, J. C. (1986). The social identity theory of intergroup behavior. In S. Worchel & W. G. Austin (Eds.), *Psychology of intergroup relations* (pp. 7–24). Chicago: Nelson-Hall.

Turner, J. C. (1991). *Social influence*. Pacific Grove, CA: Brooks Cole.

Turner, J. C., Hogg, M. A., Oakes, P. J., Reicher, S. D., & Wetherell, M. S. (1987). *Rediscovering the social group: A self-categorization theory*. Oxford: Blackwell.

Turner, J. C., & Onorato, R. S. (1999). Social identity, personality, and the self-concept: A self-categorization perspective. In T. R. Tyler, R. M. Kramer, & O. P. John (Eds.), *The psychology of the self* (pp. 11–46). Mahwah, NJ: Erlbaum.

Vorauer, J. D., & Ratner, R. K. (1997). Who's going to make the first move? Pluralistic ignorance as an impediment to relationship formation. *Journal of Social and Personal Relationships, 13*, 483–506.

Wohl, M. J. A., & Branscombe, N. R. (2005). Forgiveness and collective guilt assignment to historical perpetrator groups depend on level of social category inclusiveness. *Journal of Personality and Social Psychology, 88*, 288–303.

4

Using Collective Identities for Assimilation and Differentiation

Cynthia L. Pickett and Geoffrey J. Leonardelli

Humans are driven by a variety of needs, motives, and goals. Dating back to the early part of the twentieth century, researchers have attempted to understand human behavior by linking behavior to underlying motivations (e.g., Hull, 1943; Spence, 1956). In line with this tradition of examining human behavior within the framework of individual goals and motivations, researchers studying group behavior and intergroup relations from a social identity perspective (e.g., Tajfel & Turner, 1979, 1986) recognized that multiple motives may operate in a group context. Behavior is driven not only by realistic concerns (e.g., conflicts over resources), but also by individuals' desire for positive social identity. In answer to the question of why individuals identify with groups (particularly minimal groups that appear to hold little significance for group members), Turner (1975) argued that "subjects will identify with a social category to the extent that such identification enables them to achieve value significance, to the extent that it is the category most relevant to the desire for positive self-evaluation" (pp. 19–20). Thus, the social identity approach to intergroup relations has always incorporated the concept of needs and motives for understanding intergroup behavior. However, what has been missing to some extent from earlier formulations of social identity theory (SIT: Tajfel & Turner, 1979, 1986; Turner, 1975) and self-categorization theory (SCT: Turner, Hogg, Oakes, Reicher, & Wetherell, 1987) is an integration of the variety of individual needs (beyond positive distinctiveness) that might come into play within group contexts and how these needs might interact with cognitive and structural variables to produce particular patterns of intragroup and intergroup behavior.

The goal of the current chapter is to address the issue of how individual needs and motives influence identification processes and group behavior by focusing on two particular needs – the need for assimilation and the need for differentiation – that have comprised the bulk of our research in this area. We will begin by describing research suggesting that these needs represent core human motivations. We then turn to the subject of how these needs can be satisfied within groups and the implications that these needs have for understanding social identity and group processes. In reviewing our work in this area, we hope to convey that the complexity of intragroup and intergroup behavior requires an understanding of both the external factors (e.g., group status, group size) present in a given context and the internal factors (e.g., personal appraisals, needs, personality) that can vary widely among individuals within that context.

Assimilation and differentiation as fundamental human needs

Most researchers who have attempted to catalog basic human needs have recognized the importance of belonging and social inclusion (e.g., Deci & Ryan, 2000; Maslow, 1943). Humans have a strong desire to feel included in social groups and go to great lengths to maintain and establish inter-personal bonds. In Maslow's (1943) model, love and belonging were placed just after basic physiological needs (e.g., air, water, food) and safety in his need hierarchy, indicating that once these foundational needs have been satisfied, love and belonging become prepotent (i.e., the needs that have the greatest influence over individuals' actions). More recently, Baumeister and Leary (1995) conducted a literature review arguing that the need to belong is a core motivation that drives human thought, action, and emotion (see also Spears, Ellemers, Doosje, & Branscombe, Chapter 10 in this volume). In their review, Baumeister and Leary (1995) pointed to the importance of groups and social bonds for survival and reproduction. Furthermore, a lack of belonging appears to elicit goal-directed action designed to increase social inclusion. For example, Williams, Cheung, and Choi (2000) found that subjects who were ostracized and then subse-quently placed within a new group were more likely to conform to the incorrect judgments of the members of their new group. In sum, the psy-chological literature indicates that belonging represents a core human need and that individuals seek social acceptance and belonging through both interpersonal attachments (Hazan & Shaver, 1994) and social groups (Prentice, Chapter 3; Turner, Reynolds, Haslam, & Veenstra, Chapter 2 in this volume; Smith, Murphy, & Coats, 1999).

In addition to desiring belonging and inclusion, humans (somewhat paradoxically) also devote a lot of effort and resources to achieving dis-tinctiveness. Snyder and Fromkin (1980) argued that humans possess a need for uniqueness and that undistinctiveness is an unpleasant affective state. In an early study, Fromkin (1972) gave subjects bogus test feedback that indicated that they were low, moderate, high, or extreme in uniqueness and then had subjects complete a mood measure. As predicted, mood increased as perceived uniqueness increased. Importantly, Snyder and Fromkin (1980) argued that extreme levels of uniqueness would be undesirable as that degree of uniqueness can lead to feelings of ostracism or rootlessness. Although some have questioned the universality of the desire for distinctiveness (e.g., Kim & Markus, 1999), recent evidence (Tafarodi, Marshall, & Katsura, 2004) suggests that the desire for personal distinctiveness is not limited to just Western cultures. Tafarodi et al. (2004) found that although members of collectivist cultures tended to desire less personal distinctiveness than members of individualistic cultures, collectivists were still more likely to agree than disagree with items such as "I like being different". These researchers concluded that the need for distinctiveness is present in both Eastern and Western cultures, but that the manner in which the need is satisfied may be constrained by cultural norms (see also Halloran & Kashima, Chapter 8; Jetten & Postmes, Chapter 7 in this volume; Vignoles, Chryssochoou, & Breakwell, 2000).

Optimal distinctiveness theory

On the surface, the fact that humans possess strong desires for both inclusion and belonging and distinctiveness from others would appear to be problematic. Joining a group often entails an assimilation process where new group members alter their characteristics and behaviors to fit the norms of the group (Moreland, 1985). According to self-categorization theory (Turner et al., 1987), categorization as a group member involves depersonalization of the self such that aspects of one's personal identity become inhibited when social identity is salient. In sum, group membership (and social identification in particular) is likely to foster a sense of inclusion and belonging but also likely to result in some loss of personal distinctiveness (see Turner & Onorato, 1999). The question that arises then is: how are individuals able to negotiate between these two powerful motives – the desire for inclusion and belonging on the one hand, and the desire for distinctiveness on the other?

In answer to this question, Brewer (1991) developed optimal distinctiveness theory (ODT), which proposed that the need for inclusion and belonging (assimilation) and the need for distinctiveness (differentiation) can be satisfied simultaneously through identification with social groups and subsequent comparisons between one's ingroups and outgroups. An individual's need for assimilation can be met within the group, while the need for differentiation can be met through intergroup comparisons that highlight the distinctiveness of the ingroup. According to ODT, social identification is motivated by the needs for assimilation and differentiation, and group loyalty and satisfaction should be greatest for those identities that optimize the satisfaction of both needs.

One factor that should be taken into account when making predictions from ODT is the social context. An intergroup context is one in which both an ingroup and a relevant outgroup are salient (Tajfel, 1979). In this situation it should be quite easy for a person to achieve assimilation within the ingroup and differentiation via intergroup comparisons. However, in many situations only the ingroup is salient. In this situation, a particular identity might be initially salient, but in order to satisfy the needs for assimilation and differentiation simultaneously, the group member might shift identification to a subgroup of that initial group because doing so differentiates the person from those who do not belong to that subgroup. In summary, although intergroup comparisons are considered an important means through which the need for differentiation can be met (while simultaneously satisfying the need for assimilation), these comparisons can occur between an ingroup and an outgroup or between a subgroup and other subgroups.

As described above, ODT has traditionally posited that differentiation need satisfaction occurs at the intergroup level (Brewer, 1991). The benefit to individuals of this tactic is that satisfaction of the need for differentiation need not come at the expense of the need for assimilation. One can maximize both inclusion and differentiation at the same time. However, this conceptualization has received several challenges. The first is based on the recognition that individuals can define themselves at varying levels of selfhood – personal, relational, and collective (Brewer & Gardner, 1996). And as noted by Brewer and Roccas (2001), the fundamental needs for inclusion and distinctiveness can be expressed at all three levels. An interesting question then is whether individuals are content satisfying the needs for inclusion and distinctiveness at a single level (e.g., at the collective level as proposed by ODT) or whether the ultimate goal is to maintain inclusion and distinctiveness at all levels simultaneously.

Our answer to this question is that individuals are likely to satisfy the needs for inclusion and distinctiveness in reference to the level of self-categorization that is currently cognitively accessible. This argument assumes, consistent with SCT, that personal and social identity salience tend to be antagonistic in terms of their perceptual effects (cf. Jetten & Postmes, Chapter 7; Postmes, Baray, Haslam, Morton, & Swaab, Chapter 12; Turner et al., Chapter 2 in this volume). Thus, a person whose social identity is salient is more likely to behave in line with ODT predictions (i.e., engage in intragroup assimilation and intergroup differentiation) than a person whose personal identity is salient. When personal identity is salient, the needs for inclusion and distinctiveness can be met at the individual level by focusing on interpersonal similarity and differences. For this reason, ODT does not suggest that the needs for inclusion and distinctiveness are necessarily met at the group level. Although collective identities provide a convenient vehicle for simultaneous need satisfaction, how individuals go about meeting the needs for inclusion and distinctiveness will depend on individuals' current level of self-construal.

A second challenge that ODT has confronted is whether (even at the collective level) it is necessary to posit that assimilation needs are always met within the group and differentiation needs met through intergroup comparisons. Hornsey and Jetten (2004) recently proposed several ways in which individuals can achieve both assimilation and differentiation at the intragroup level. For example, perceiving that one embodies the norms and values of a group but that one is more extreme than other group members (the *primus inter pares* or PIP effect) is one way that individuals can feel included within a group while also maintaining individual distinctiveness. From the perspective of ODT, these methods of balancing the need to belong with the need to be different (e.g., role differentiation, identification with an individualistic group: Jetten, Postmes, & McAuliffe, 2002) are certainly feasible and likely to be very useful in particular circumstances. In general, we do not dispute the idea that the needs for assimilation and differentiation can be met through various means. ODT's focus on intragroup assimilation and intergroup differentiation as the means through which optimal distinctiveness is achieved arose out of the recognition that collective identities (by their nature) promote these two processes via self-stereotyping and depersonalization processes (Turner & Onorato, 1999). Thus, collective identities can be seen as a ready-made tool through which optimal distinctiveness can be achieved.

The relationship between ODT, SIT, and SCT

At this point, it might be useful to discuss more explicitly the areas of overlap and distinction between optimal distinctiveness theory and SIT and SCT. First, it is important to note that ODT was built in many ways on the principles previously described in both SIT and SCT. For example, the notions that social categorization involves depersonalization of self-perception and that variation exists in how people categorize themselves are key tenets of SCT (Turner, Oakes, Haslam, & McGarty, 1994) and also assumptions adopted by ODT. In describing the context dependence of self-categorization, Turner and his colleagues (1994) noted that self-categories are not fixed and suggested that aspects of the social context (e.g., perceived intragroup and intergroup differences) and aspects of perceivers (e.g., their perception of the meaning of particular categories) interact to produce social categorization. Thus, at a general level both SCT and ODT are concerned with the issue of social variability of the self. However, where the two theories diverge is in their differing emphases on the processes thought to determine this variability. ODT introduced the idea that social categorization arises from an attempt to reconcile the needs for assimilation and differentiation. People are thought to avoid self-categorization in terms of groups that fail to provide a sense of inclusion and belonging or distinctiveness *vis-à-vis* other groups. In addition, in ODT, group identification, loyalty, and satisfaction are proposed to be greatest for groups that simultaneously satisfy these needs. In sum, ODT differs from SCT in (1) its heavy emphasis on need satisfaction as a key determinant of social categorization, and (2) its attempt to explain variation in identification with those categories as a function of the desire to reconcile countervailing needs for assimilation and differentiation.

Central to SIT is the idea that individuals possess a need for positive social identity, which is "expressed through a desire to create, maintain or enhance the positively valued distinctiveness of ingroups compared to outgroups on relevant dimensions" (Turner, 1999, p. 8). In addition, the self-esteem hypothesis often associated with SIT (e.g., Hogg & Abrams, 1988; 1990) "proposes the existence of a fundamental individual motivation for self-esteem ... which is satisfied in an intergroup context by maximizing the difference between ingroup and outgroup" (1988, p. 23). Although ODT recognizes that individuals possess a panoply of motives (one of which is most certainly self-enhancement and self-esteem), ODT provides an alternative to the idea that social identification and intergroup behavior are driven predominantly by the desire for positive distinctiveness and a positive self-image. ODT proposes that individuals seek distinctiveness *per se* and that distinctiveness for its own sake is valued (see also Mummendey & Schreiber, 1984). Although in many contexts distinctiveness can be achieved through positive intergroup comparisons (and thus the desires for self-enhancement and distinctiveness can be achieved simultaneously), ODT holds open the possibility that individuals might be willing to forgo self-enhancement and opportunities for positive social comparisons in favor of achieving distinctiveness. Thus, a key area in which ODT and SIT diverge is in the degree to which positivity is thought to operate as a key motive in intergroup situations.

A second point of divergence between ODT and SIT is in the extent to which the needs for inclusion and belonging are considered as determinants of identification and intergroup behavior. SIT took as its starting point social categorization. Individuals were thought to recognize or accept that they belong to a particular social category which then leads to the processes of social identity, social comparison, and positive ingroup distinctiveness (Turner, 1999). By contrast, ODT asks the question of why particular social categories are activated over other possible categories, and answers that question by proposing that the degree to which social groups satisfy assimilation and differentiation needs will determine their selection and activation and will shape other subsequent processes (e.g., social identification and social comparison). In summary, ODT and SIT overlap in their recognition that positive social identity is valued by group members, but ODT makes the additional argument that assimilation and differentiation needs are also fundamental human motives that may take precedence over self-enhancement. Furthermore, ODT is more concerned than SIT (at least in its original form) with the individual motivational antecedents of social identification and the motivational processes that give rise to self-categorization.

A growing number of studies have been conducted supporting the basic tenets of optimal distinctiveness theory. In the next sections, we briefly review these studies with the following goals in mind. The first goal is to challenge the assumption that intergroup behavior is largely driven by a desire for positive social identity. Although self-enhancement (i.e., positive self-evaluation) is a powerful motive that drives much of human thought and behavior, ODT has argued that self-enhancement alone cannot adequately account for the patterns of identification and intergroup behavior that have been observed in the literature (Brewer, 1991; see also Rubin & Hewstone, 1998). A second goal is to demonstrate that many of the processes that are often thought to follow somewhat reflexively from self-categorization (e.g., self-stereotyping, accentuation of intergroup differences and intragroup similarity: Turner et al., 1987) are, in fact, moderated by group members' motivational states. A final goal is to briefly touch on how the needs for assimilation and differentiation might influence intergroup behavior.

The role of assimilation and differentiation needs in identity selection and activation

Attempts to demonstrate that the selection and activation of particular social identities are driven by the needs for assimilation and differentiation have typically followed one of three paths: (1) measuring the extent to which particular groups satisfy individuals' needs and correlating these measures of need satisfaction with reported levels of group identification and group commitment; (2) arousing the needs for assimilation and differentiation independently and examining subsequent patterns of identification with groups that vary in their ability to satisfy the needs; and (3) examining relative levels of identification and satisfaction with groups that are more or less optimally distinct (e.g., minority versus majority groups). All three methods have yielded consistent evidence for optimal distinctiveness theory's proposition that assimilation and differentiation needs underlie social identification.

The first approach described above was adopted in a recent study conducted in our lab (Leonardelli & Pickett, 2004). Supporting ODT, results of this study indicated that measures of assimilation and differentiation (i.e., "I feel like I really fit in with this group" and "Being a member of this group distinguishes me from other people") were significant independent predictors of group identification such that identification levels were higher to the extent that assimilation and differentiation were achieved within the group.

In a different set of studies (Pickett, Silver, & Brewer, 2002), we experimentally manipulated levels of assimilation and differentiation need arousal and examined the effects of need arousal on individuals' preferences for groups that varied in level of inclusiveness. According to ODT, level of inclusiveness (i.e., group size) is one determinant of how well a group can meet the needs for assimilation and differentiation. In line with ODT predictions, we found that participants who were randomly assigned to experience a threat to inclusion (assimilation need arousal) exhibited greater identification with larger, more inclusive social categories (Pickett et al., 2002, Experiment 1) and were also more likely to estimate a current ingroup as being larger than it really is (Experiment 2). Participants who were assigned to experience a threat to distinctiveness (differentiation need arousal) exhibited the opposite pattern – lower identification with inclusive social categories and underestimation of ingroup size.

As a third means of testing ODT's proposition that needs for assimilation and differentiation motivate group identification, studies have been conducted that attempt to identify optimally distinct groups within a particular context and demonstrate that identification and satisfaction are greatest for these groups. In a study involving minimal groups (Leonardelli & Brewer, 2001), participants were classified into either a minority group or a majority group. Despite the minimal nature of the group categorization, minority group members exhibited significantly greater group identification than did majority group members (Leonardelli & Brewer, 2001, Experiment 1). This pattern was observed across two additional studies (Experiments 2 and 3) where level of ingroup satisfaction was also measured. Supporting ODT, minority group members were consistently both more identified with their group and more satisfied than were majority group members (see also Simon & Brown, 1987).

Taken together, the research described above is quite consistent with ODT's basic proposition – that social identification is motivated by the desire to satisfy assimilation and differentiation needs and that identification is greatest for those groups that meet both needs simultaneously.

Although SIT always recognized that intergroup distinctiveness is important to group members, the assumption was that social comparisons are motivated by a desire to enhance the positive distinctiveness of the ingroup in order to achieve positive self-evaluation (Turner, 1975). Current research suggests, however, that intergroup distinctiveness *per se* is important to group members and that individuals may select social identities on the basis of their current level of differentiation need and the distinctiveness of salient groups in a given social context. Importantly, the desire for distinctiveness is held in check by the countervailing need for assimilation. What results is an equilibrium state where individuals are typically most identified with groups that are moderately distinctive.

In terms of expanding the social identity approach to take into consideration multiple motivational antecedents to identification, one resolution is to posit a process where individuals' cognitive appraisal of a given context and their motivational states interact to determine self-categorization. According to SCT (Turner et al., 1987), categorization follows from three basic principles: the meta-contrast ratio (the ratio of intracategory similarities to intercategory differences), accessibility (readiness to perceive a category), and normative fit (the match between category norms and observed characteristics). Similar to how motivation has been shown to influence other cognitive processes (e.g., information search, memory retrieval: Kunda, 1990), it is likely that particular motivations can bias self-categorization through their influence on factors such as accessibility, fit, and perceived meta-contrast.

As depicted in Figure 4.1, we propose that within any given social context, individuals will bring with them a set of social motives (examples are listed in the first box of the figure). These motives are not presumed to be equally important, and their relative importance is likely to be quite fluid over time and across different contexts. In line with traditional drive theories (e.g., Hull, 1943; Spence, 1956) we argue that the need (or needs) that are most highly active will drive perception and subsequent categorization. In other words, it is not necessarily the case that group members will try to satisfy all of the needs all of the time. For instance, a person whose self-worth and value has just been affirmed might be quite willing to forgo further self-enhancement in order to satisfy other basic needs (e.g., assimilation or uncertainty reduction).

Also portrayed in Figure 4.1 is the idea that motivations can affect self-categorization via specific cognitive processes. As alluded to above, the desire to achieve a particular outcome can constrain how cognitive processes unfold (Kunda, 1990). A person with a particular motivation (e.g., the need for differentiation) is likely to come into a situation with a set of identities already primed (e.g., distinctive social groups) and those identities should be more likely to be subsequently applied when encountering a

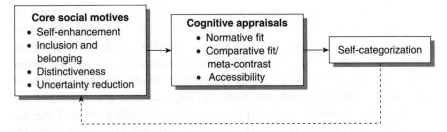

Figure 4.1 Role of social motives and cognitive appraisals is self-categorization

collection of individuals. Similarly, the determination of category fit may be subject to motivational pressures. Fit refers to the match between category content (i.e., norms) and the observed behavior and characteristics of self and others (Turner et al., 1994). Because categories are complex and multi-dimensional, it is possible to imagine that individuals may selectively activate particular aspects of a category when judging fit in order to arrive at a preferred outcome. For example, a person might be motivated to categorize himself as a professor because that categorization confers prestige and satisfies his need for self-enhancement. To achieve this desired outcome, this person might focus (perhaps non-consciously) on the content dimension of professors that best fits the characteristics of the individuals present, and in so doing, ensures a match between the desired category and the instances represented in the situation.

In summary, recent work in our lab and others (e.g., Hogg and Mullin, 1999) points to multiple underlying motivations for social identification. Although we have proposed a basic framework for conceptualizing the interplay between motivation and the cognitive processes presumed to give rise to self-categorization (see Figure 4.1), a goal for future research is to gain a better grasp of when particular motives will be most likely to drive self-categorization and identification and of the mechanisms through which motivational states influence identification. In the following section, we turn to the second goal of this chapter and move beyond the issue of how motivational states affect the selection of particular social identities to how they affect related social identification processes.

Optimal distinctiveness and depersonalization of the self

One of the central tenets of self-categorization theory is that shared social identity depersonalizes individual self-perception and behavior (Turner et al., 1994). This belief is sometimes taken to mean that self-representation ceases to exist once categorization has occurred and personal motives no longer operate, and that this occurs for all individuals. However, this interpretation is unwarranted given an accumulation of studies that point to individual variation in responses to categorization (e.g., Ellemers et al., 2002). Following from optimal distinctiveness theory, we argue that both self-categorization and the outcomes of categorization are influenced by the needs for assimilation and differentiation. According to SCT, depersonalization involves two processes – self-stereotyping (ascribing ingroup traits to the self) and the accentuation of ingroup similarities and between-group differences (Turner et al., 1987). Although both processes have been shown to follow from categorization (e.g., Haslam, Oakes, Reynolds, & Mein, 1999; Hogg and Turner, 1987), relatively little research attention has been paid to variations in the extent to which these processes occur for particular individuals. Our research (Pickett, Bonner, & Coleman, 2002; Pickett & Brewer, 2001) indicates that the motivations to achieve ingroup assimilation and group differentiation can increase depersonalization because depersonalization has the effect of enhancing feelings of ingroup inclusion *and* intergroup distinctiveness.

In one set of studies (Pickett et al., 2002), we experimentally manipulated the needs for assimilation and differentiation by threatening ingroup inclusion and intergroup distinctiveness via false feedback on a personality test. Because self-stereotyping leads to enhanced perceptual identity between the self and the ingroup *and* enhanced perceptual contrast between ingroup and outgroup members, we predicted that experimentally arousing the need for assimilation or the need for differentiation would lead to increased levels of self-stereotyping compared to controls. Results across three different studies (involving different social identities) supported these predictions. It is important to note that in all three experimental conditions (assimilation, differentiation, and control), social identity was made salient through the feedback provided to participants. And in line with SCT, participants considered the stereotype-relevant traits to be more self-descriptive than the stereotype-irrelevant traits, indicating that some degree of depersonalization occurred for all participants. However, self-stereotyping was significantly moderated by participants' need state, which underscores the importance of considering individual motivations in the self-categorization process. It appears that both identity salience and personal motivations impact levels of depersonalization.

Another component of depersonalization is the perceptual enhancement of within-group similarities and between-group differences. Thus, in another line of research (Pickett & Brewer, 2001), we sought to demonstrate the influence of perceiver motivations on perceptions of ingroup and outgroup homogeneity. Based on ODT, it was predicted that arousal of assimilation and differentiation needs (through threats to intragroup standing and intergroup distinctiveness) would lead to heightened perceptions of *both* ingroup and outgroup homogeneity. Because perceived homogeneity enhances both intragroup assimilation and intergroup contrast, such perceptions can serve both the need for increased inclusion within the ingroup and the need for increased distinctiveness between ingroup and outgroup. As predicted, compared to no-arousal controls, participants in the assimilation and differentiation need arousal conditions showed heightened perceptions of ingroup and outgroup homogeneity, greater perceived ingroup stereotypicality, and the tendency to be more restrictive in defining ingroup membership. As was the case with the self-stereotyping studies, this study indicated that individual motivations affected how participants responded to a salient social identity. The process of accentuating ingroup similarities did not occur in a uniform fashion in response to identity salience, but rather salience interacted with motivation to determine the degree of depersonalization.

The research reviewed thus far provides initial evidence for the role of assimilation and differentiation needs in identity selection and activation and related cognitive processes (i.e., depersonalization). It is possible, however, that other motivations might also have an impact on the depersonalization process. For example, individuals who are motivated to reduce uncertainty (Hogg & Mullin, 1999) might be particularly likely to enhance intragroup similarities and intergroup differences as a way of providing more structure in the social environment and reducing feelings of uncertainty. The idea that multiple motives can affect not only the selection of social identities, but also the processes that unfold subsequent to categorization, is depicted in Figure 4.2.

Optimal distinctiveness and intergroup relations

At this point, we would like to move on to the third goal of this chapter and briefly address the implications of optimal distinctiveness theory for intergroup relations. Many of the behaviors that have been the focus of social identity theory (e.g., ingroup bias, outgroup derogation, discrimination) can be thought of as arising out of group members' desire to fulfill basic needs for assimilation and differentiation. A striking similarity is found in the behaviors these needs produce. Along with other possible responses to unmet assimilation and differentiation needs (e.g., altering one's perceptions of the ingroup), we argue that both needs can, under certain circumstances, motivate group members to exhibit ingroup favoritism. However, individuals may exhibit favoritism intent on achieving different outcomes. We hypothesize that those with a need for assimilation

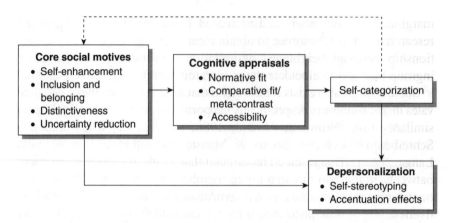

Figure 4.2   Effect of motivations on process following categorization

exhibit ingroup favoritism in an attempt to create a sense of inclusion and acceptance. By contrast, those with a need for differentiation exhibit ingroup favoritism in an attempt to imbue their group (and themselves by extension) with a sense of distinctiveness.

Empirical support (albeit indirect) exists for both claims. Research investigating peripheral membership in groups (e.g., Jetten, Branscombe, & Spears, 2002; Noel, Wann, & Branscombe, 1995) reveals that peripheral ingroup status (current or anticipated) can influence levels of ingroup bias. For example, Noel et al. (1995) found that fraternity and sorority pledges, individuals who see themselves as peripheral members of their pledged fraternity or sorority, were more likely to exhibit outgroup derogation than were active (i.e., core) fraternity and sorority members. Importantly, this effect was only observed in the public condition, where participants' outgroup derogating responses were known to other group members. This suggests then that when the need for assimilation has been activated (e.g., through manipulations of peripheral status), ingroup bias may be more likely to occur when it can be used as a means of signifying to other group members that one is loyal to the group and thus deserves to be included within it. In addition, work by Jetten, Branscombe, and Spears (2002) suggests that for peripheral ingroup status to produce ingroup favoritism, individuals must believe that their atypical status will change. Jetten et al. reported that peripheral group members who believed their peripheral status would improve over time were more likely than peripheral members who did not think their status would improve to exhibit ingroup favoritism. Although these studies did not specifically measure assimilation need arousal, the work does point to a link between conditions where the need for assimilation is likely to be unmet (e.g., being a marginal group member) and increased levels of ingroup bias. Future research is needed, however, to obtain clear empirical support for the relationship between heightened assimilation need arousal and levels of ingroup bias and to elucidate the moderators of this relationship.

Some support also exists for the claim that a need for distinctiveness motivates ingroup favoritism, specifically supported by the research on intergroup similarity (e.g., Brown & Abrams, 1986; Diehl, 1988; Mummendey & Schreiber, 1984; Jetten, Spears & Manstead, 1996, Study 2; White & Langer, 1999). This research has argued that very high levels of similarity between groups can threaten group members' sense of their group's distinctiveness and provoke ingroup favoritism in an effort to restore distinctiveness. Consistent with this, a recent meta-analysis (Jetten, Spears, & Postmes, 2004) found that high intergroup similarity was associated with ingroup favoritism on behavioral measures of discrimination (e.g., reward allocation) among those highly identified with the ingroup (although there was an opposite effect on judgmental measures). In addition, Leonardelli and Brewer (2001) found that when individuals were highly identified members of numerical majority groups, that is, members belonged to groups thought to lack a sense of distinctiveness, they were more likely to exhibit ingroup favoritism as their satisfaction with their group membership decreased. Leonardelli and Brewer (2001) interpreted this effect as support for the idea that a need for distinctiveness motivates ingroup favoritism.

As the above evidence suggests, the needs for assimilation and differentiation may both motivate ingroup favoritism. That is, when individuals are dissatisfied with their sense of ingroup inclusion or intergroup distinctiveness, they may be motivated to favor their group over another group. Implicit in these remarks is that group favoritism is more likely when individual needs are dissatisfied than when they have been met. Although this may be true, members of groups that simultaneously meet the needs for assimilation and differentiation may still exhibit group favoritism, but we think they will do so for reasons other than achieving greater assimilation or distinctiveness. Rather, Leonardelli and Galinsky (2004) argue that individuals are motivated to affirm group memberships that are optimally distinct (that meet both needs simultaneously) and that ingroup favoritism is one way that individuals can satisfy their desire to affirm their group memberships. In short, members of optimally distinct groups are predicted to exhibit ingroup favoritism out of a need for group affirmation. Leonardelli and Galinsky found support for these claims in a series of studies. Their research revealed that members of numerical minority groups, groups thought to be optimally distinct, reported being more satisfied with their group than did members of numerical majorities, and also reported a greater need for group affirmation. In addition, they were more likely to exhibit ingroup favoritism in a variety of contexts as a result of this need for group affirmation.

Summary

The basic assumption of our application of optimal distinctiveness theory to intergroup relations is that group members are motivated to belong to and identify with optimally distinct groups. However, group members often find themselves categorized within groups that fail to satisfy certain needs. In these cases, intergroup behavior is predicted to be driven (at least in part) by group members' motivational state (i.e., whatever needs have been activated), and this is especially so when individuals highly identify with their group and when there is no alternative identity that may better satisfy the group members' needs. We believe that intergroup relations can be better understood by moving the social identity approach toward a broader consideration of the multiple needs that group memberships may serve and how these needs are met within an intergroup context.

Individuality in the group

At its core, the social identity approach is concerned with the relationship between the individual and the group. The goal of this chapter was to address the specific issue of how individual needs and motives influence identification processes and group behavior by focusing on two particular motivations – the need for assimilation and the need for differentiation – derived from optimal distinctiveness theory (Brewer, 1991). Our review focused on three areas: selection and activation of social identities, cognitive processes involved in the social identification process, and intergroup relations. In all three areas, we sought to demonstrate that psychological motives can shape and significantly alter basic social identification processes. For this reason, we believe that the social identity approach might benefit from a greater integration of the variety of needs and motives that individuals possess with social identity and self-categorization principles.

NOTE

Correspondence to: Cynthia Pickett, Department of Psychology, University of California–Davis, One Shields Avenue, Davis, CA 95616, USA, cpickett@ucdavis.edu.

REFERENCES

Baumeister, R. F., & Leary, M. R. (1995). The need to belong: Desire for interpersonal attachments as a fundamental human motivation. *Psychological Bulletin, 117*, 497–529.

Brewer, M. B. (1991). The social self: On being the same and different at the same time. *Personality and Social Psychology Bulletin, 17*, 475–482.

Brewer, M. B., & Gardner, W. (1996). Who is this "we"? Levels of collective identity and self representations. *Journal of Personality and Social Psychology, 71*, 83–93.

Brewer, M. B., & Roccas, S. (2001). Individual values, social identity, and optimal distinctiveness. In C. Sedikides & M. B. Brewer (Eds.), *Individual self, relational self, collective self* (pp. 219–237). Philadelphia: Psychology Press.

Brown, R., & Abrams, D. (1986). The effects of intergroup similarity and goal interdependence on intergroup attitudes and task performance. *Journal of Experimental Social Psychology, 22*, 78–92.

Deci, E. L., & Ryan, R. M. (2000). The "what" and "why" of goal pursuits: Human needs and the self-determination of behavior. *Psychological Inquiry, 11*, 227–268.

Diehl, M. (1988). Social identity and minimal groups: The effects of interpersonal and intergroup attitudinal similarity on intergroup discrimination. *British Journal of Social Psychology, 27*, 289–300.

Ellemers, N., Spears, R., & Doosje, B. (2002). Self and social identity. *Annual Review of Psychology, 53*, 161–186.

Fromkin, H. L. (1972). Feelings of interpersonal undistinctiveness: An unpleasant affective state. *Journal of Experimental Research in Personality, 6*, 178–182.

Haslam, S. A., Oakes, P. J., Reynolds, K. J , & Mein, J. (1999). Rhetorical unity and social division: A longitudinal study of change in Australian self-stereotypes. *Asian Journal of Social Psychology, 2*, 265–280.

Hazan, C., & Shaver, P. R. (1994). Attachment as an organizational framework for research on close relationships. *Psychological Inquiry, 5*, 1–22.

Hogg, M. A., & Abrams, D. (1988). *Social identifications: A social psychology of intergroup relations and group processes.* London: Routledge.

Hogg, M. A., & Abrams, D. (1990). Social motivation, self-esteem, and social identity. In D. Abrams & M. A. Hogg (Eds.), *Social identity theory: Constructive and critical advances.* London: Harvester Wheatsheaf.

Hogg, M. A., & Mullin, B. A. (1999). Joining groups to reduce uncertainty: Subjective uncertainty reduction and group identification. In D. Abrams & M. A. Hogg (Eds.), *Social identity and social cognition* (pp. 249–279). Oxford: Blackwell.

Hogg, M. A., & Turner, J. C. (1987). Intergroup behaviour, self-stereotyping and the salience of social categories. *British Journal of Social Psychology, 26*, 325–340.

Hornsey, M. J., & Jetten, J. (2004). The individual within the group: Balancing the need to belong with the need to be different. *Personality and Social Psychology Review, 8*, 248–264.

Hull, C. L. (1943). *Principles of behavior: An introduction to behavior theory.* New York: Appleton-Century-Crofts.

Jetten, J., Branscombe, N., & Spears, R. (2002). On being peripheral: Effects of identity insecurity on personal and collective self-esteem. *European Journal of Social Psychology, 32*, 105–123.

Jetten, J., Postmes, T., & McAuliffe, B. J. (2002). "We're all individuals": Group norms of individualism and collectivism, levels of identification, and identity threat. *European Journal of Social Psychology, 32*, 189–207.

Jetten, J., Spears, R., & Manstead, A. S. R. (1996). Intergroup norms and intergroup discrimination: Distinctive self-categorization and social identity effects. *Journal of Personality and Social Psychology, 71*, 1222–1233.

Jetten, J., Spears, R., & Postmes, T. (2004). Intergroup distinctiveness and differentiation: A meta-analytic integration. *Journal of Personality and Social Psychology, 86*, 862–879.

Kim, H., & Markus, H. R. (1999). Deviance or uniqueness, harmony or conformity? A cultural analysis. *Journal of Personality and Social Psychology, 77*, 785–800.

Kunda, Z. (1990). The case for motivated reasoning. *Psychological Bulletin, 108*, 480–498.

Leonardelli, G. J., & Brewer, M. B. (2001). Minority and majority discrimination: When and why. *Journal of Experimental Social Psychology, 37*, 468–485.

Leonardelli, G. J., & Galinsky, A. (2004). Optimal distinctiveness and collective self-affirmation: Minority affirmation and ingroup favoritism. Manuscript submitted for publication. Kellogg School of Management, Northwestern University, Evanston, IL.

Leonardelli, G. J., & Pickett, C. L. (2004). A componential approach to assimilation and differentiation need satisfaction within groups. Unpublished manuscript, University of Chicago.

Maslow, A. H. (1943). A theory of human motivation. *Psychological Review, 50*, 370–396.

Moreland, R. L. (1985). Social categorization and the assimilation of "new" group members. *Journal of Personality and Social Psychology, 48*, 1173–1190.

Mummendey, A., & Schreiber, H. J. (1984). Social comparison, similarity and ingroup favouritism: A replication. *European Journal of Social Psychology, 14*, 231–233.

Noel, J. G., Wann, D. L., & Branscombe, N. R. (1995). Peripheral ingroup membership status and public negativity toward outgroups. *Journal of Personality and Social Psychology, 68*, 127–137.

Pickett, C. L., Bonner B. L., & Coleman J. M. (2002). Motivated self-stereotyping: Heightened assimilation and differentiation needs result in increased levels of positive and negative self-stereotyping. *Journal of Personality and Social Psychology, 82*, 543–562.

Pickett, C. L., & Brewer, M. B. (2001). Assimilation and differentiation needs as motivational determinants of perceived ingroup and outgroup homogeneity. *Journal of Experimental Social Psychology, 37*, 341–348.

Pickett, C. L., Silver, M. D., & Brewer, M. B. (2002). The impact of assimilation and differentiation needs on perceived group importance and judgments of ingroup size. *Personality and Social Psychology Bulletin, 28*(4), 546–558.

Rubin, M., & Hewstone, M. (1998). Social identity theory's self-esteem hypothesis: A review and some suggestions for clarification. *Personality and Social Psychology Review, 2*, 40–62.

Simon, B., & Brown, R. (1987). Perceived intragroup homogeneity in minority–majority contexts. *Journal of Personality and Social Psychology, 53*, 703–711.

Smith, E. R., Murphy, J., & Coats, S. (1999). Attachment to groups: Theory and measurement. *Journal of Personality and Social Psychology, 77*, 94–110.

Snyder, C. R., & Fromkin, H. L. (1980). *Uniqueness: The human pursuit of difference.* New York: Plenum.

Spence, K. (1956). *Behavior theory and conditioning.* New Haven, CT: Yale University Press.

Tafarodi, R. W., Marshall, T. C., & Katsura, H. (2004). Standing out in Canada and Japan. *Journal of Personality, 72*, 785–814.

Tajfel, H. (1979). Individuals and groups in social psychology. *British Journal of Social and Clinical Psychology, 18*, 183–190.

Tajfel, H., & Turner, J.C. (1979). An integrated theory of intergroup conflict. In W. G. Austin and S. Worchel (Eds.), *The social psychology of intergroup relations.* Monterey, CA: Brooks-Cole.

Tajfel, H., & Turner, J.C. (1986). The social identity theory of intergroup behaviour. In S. Worchel & W.G. Austin (Eds.), *Psychology of intergroup relations*. Chicago: Nelson-Hall.

Turner, J. C. (1975). Social comparison and social identity: Some prospects for intergroup behaviour. *European Journal of Social Psychology, 5,* 5–34.

Turner, J. C. (1999). Some current issues in social identity and self-categorization theories. In N. Ellemers, R. Spears, & B. Doosje (Eds.), *Social identity: Context, commitment, content*. Oxford: Blackwell.

Turner, J. C., Hogg, M. A., Oakes, P. J., Reicher, S. D., & Wetherell, M. S. (1987). *Rediscovering the social group: A self-categorization theory*. Oxford: Blackwell.

Turner, J. C., Oakes, P.J., Haslam, S.A., & McGarty, C. (1994). Self and collective: Cognition and social context. *Personality and Social Psychology Bulletin, 20,* 454–463.

Turner, J. C., & Onorato, R. S. (1999). Social identity, personality, and the self-concept: A self-categorization perspective. In T. R. Tyler (Ed.), *The psychology of the social self: Applied social research* (pp. 11–46). Mahwah, NJ: Erlbaum.

Vignoles, V. L., Chryssochoou, X., & Breakwell, G. M. (2000). The distinctiveness principle: Identity, meaning and the bounds of cultural relativity. *Personality and Social Psychology Review, 4,* 337–354.

White, J. B., & Langer, E. J. (1999) Horizontal hostility: Relations between similar minority groups, *Journal of Social Issues, 55,* 537–560.

Williams, K. D., Cheung, C. K. T., & Choi, W. (2000). Cyberostracism: Effects of being ignored over the Internet. *Journal of Personality & Social Psychology, 79,* 748–762.

5

Ingroup Critics and Their Influence on Groups

Matthew J. Hornsey

Social psychology has much to say about how groups and systems can shape the attitudes, values, and behaviours of individuals. Furthermore, a cursory glance at an introductory textbook will lead us to believe that the influence is mostly for the worst. For example, Le Bon (1908) spoke of the power of crowds to reduce individuals to barbaric savages acting on instinct and stripped of civilizing influences. Milgram (1974) showed that, when asked to perform an act of cruelty on another person, people were prepared to obey the authority figure even though this caused them (and ostensibly their victims) great distress. Zimbardo showed that group norms can encourage ordinary people to behave in a cruel and abusive way (Haney, Banks, & Zimbardo, 1973). And Asch (1952) showed how the attitudes of others encourage individuals to express attitudes that they know to be untrue. The message is that group influence is to be feared: it compromises individual potential, it distorts people's perceptions of social reality, it intimidates people into cowardly acts, it releases anti-social instincts, it causes people to lose their moral compass. In short, the group is irrational but powerful, and the individual is sane but weak. Even research (such as Asch's conformity studies: Friend, Rafferty, & Bramel, 1990) that originally sought to qualify this view became, over the years, reinterpreted as part of the grand cautionary tale: be wary of groups because they extinguish individuality and, by extension, moral integrity.

According to this portrait, there is little recognition of the notion that the influence can go both ways: the group can shape the individual, but so too can the individual shape the group (see Levine & Moreland, 1985; Moscovici, 1976, for discussions of group socialization and minority influence respectively). There are times (and we can probably all recognize such times in our life) when an individual might feel compelled to stand up and articulate their group's failings and shortcomings. Rather than acting out corrupt or unfair or abusive elements of a group's culture, it is possible for members to police their group and to shape the culture in a way that better approximates the individual's worldview. Indeed, these acts of criticism play a valuable role in group life in terms of promoting positive change and stimulating innovation, creativity, and flexibility in decision-making (Nemeth, 1985; Postmes, Spears, & Cihangir, 2001). Criticism is the cornerstone of protest and political change, and it is difficult to imagine how a group can be reinvigorated, reinvented, or reformed without some process of critical self-reflection.

Having said that, it is clear that criticizing one's own group carries with it enormous social risks. Research on dissent shows that people who do not conform to the "party line" face social censure (Festinger, 1950; Schachter, 1951), and the black sheep literature shows how quick groups are to distance themselves from members who reflect poorly on the group (Marques & Paez, 1994). Furthermore, a mechanistic view of the social identity perspective might lead one to believe that ingroup critics are doomed to face defensiveness because they are attacking a fundamental part of people's self-concept. So what choices are available to a person who no longer approves of the direction their group is taking? Can individuals shape the culture of a group, and if so, who within a group is most able to exert influence? When will legitimate ingroup criticism be accepted and when will it be rejected? These questions are important, not least of all because they comment directly on the dynamic tension that exists between individuality and the group. In this chapter, I review theory and research that strive to answer these questions, and in so doing reflect on the role that the social identity perspective has played in illuminating (and sometimes obscuring) these answers.

The social identity perspective and ingroup criticism

When I first started thinking about group-directed criticism, I sought out a senior social identity theorist and told them that I was interested in looking at how people respond to criticism of the group from one of its own members. The response was that there was no such thing as ingroup criticism; that, by definition, if a person criticizes their group they become an outgroup member (psychologically if not in reality). I don't think this feedback tells us much about the social identity perspective, given that there is nothing in SIT or SCT that precludes ingroup criticism. But it does tell us something about how these theories have traditionally been interpreted: interpretations that have tended to distract attention away from the reality of ingroup criticism.

Although researchers in the social identity tradition have long acknowledged that identities are contested and open to debate (e.g., Reicher, 1996; Reicher & Hopkins, 1996; Sani & Reicher, 1998), they have had little to say on the specific psychological processes surrounding ingroup criticism. The lack of attention paid to ingroup criticism becomes problematic if one extrapolates from already established social identity principles and mechanistically applies them to the domain of group-directed criticism, a process that allows misconceptions to take root. Specifically, naïve readings of the social identity literature can lead to two conclusions about the psychology of ingroup criticism which are incorrect: (1) an ingroup critic is, by definition, a low identifier, and (2) ingroup critics are "black sheep" who will inevitably face social censure and group rejection. I discuss these misconceptions below, before reviewing research that examines the psychological mechanisms that allow some critics to receive an open-minded audience for their arguments while others meet negativity and defensiveness.

Misconception 1: ingroup critics are low identifiers

It is not hard to see why one might draw the conclusion that ingroup critics are low identifiers; indeed, a superficial reading of both the motivational and perceptual arms of the social identity perspective might lead one to this conclusion. The perceptual aspect of the social identity perspective has been articulated most thoroughly by self-categorization theory (Turner, Hogg, Oakes, Reicher, & Wetherell, 1987; see also Turner, Reynolds, Haslam, & Veenstra, Chapter 2 in this volume). A central plank of self-categorization theory is "depersonalization", the notion that the more one identifies with a salient group, the more one's self-definition shifts from the personal to the group, and the more one assimilates to the prototype of the group. Turner et al. (1987), for example, argue that self-categorization in a salient group signals "a shift towards the perception of self as an interchangeable exemplar of some social category and away from the perception of self as a unique person" (p. 50). On first glance the language of depersonalization is startling because it appears to buy into the nightmare scenario painted in the opening paragraph of group influence: of the group as a quasi-fascistic force that eradicates individuality and intragroup dissent. The implication is that only low identifiers could criticize their group, because high identifiers have already cognitively assimilated to the core values and attitudes of the group.

But closer examination reassures us that this was not the theory's intention. Depersonalization provides an acknowledgement of the reality that intragroup interactions take place in the recognition and awareness of shared group membership, but does not necessarily imply that group members have to think and say the same thing (see Prentice, Chapter 3; Spears, Ellemers, Doosje, & Branscombe, Chapter 10; Turner et al., Chapter 2 in this volume). Indeed, embedded in the norms of most groups is an awareness that a certain degree of dissent and critical self-reflection is desirable. In individualistic cultures, for example, many groups normatively prescribe individuality; we are socialized by our cultures and by our group memberships to be ourselves, to march to the beat of our own drum, and to ask tough questions of others if need be (Hornsey & Jetten, 2004; Kim & Markus, 1999; McAuliffe, Jetten, Hornsey, & Hogg, 2003). So whether or not dissent within a group or ingroup criticism is framed as deviant depends largely on the content of the group norm (Hornsey, Jetten, McAuliffe, & Hogg, in press). In university cultures, for example, students are explicitly trained to be critical of the assumptions inherent in the systems and cultures in which they work. To be critical of one's own university group should not just be tolerated, it potentially represents an *outcome* of social influence.

Furthermore, the content of the group norm and the group prototype is not immutable but rather is subject to contest and ongoing negotiation. As Reicher and colleagues have pointed out (e.g., Reicher & Hopkins, 1996), self-categories do not simply materialize as a function of context, they are the subject of extended debate and public disputation (see Haslam, 1997; Turner, 1991, for related arguments about the dynamic nature of social identity processes). Rather than simply existing "under the skull", identities are actively constructed, manipulated and communicated through rhetoric and argument, and are frequently shaped by influential individuals within the group (see also Postmes, Baray, Haslam, Morton, & Swaab, Chapter 12 in this volume). If non-negotiable differences do exist in how the identity is constructed, persuasion, negotiation and discussion might be abandoned, and the group might be vulnerable to schismatic divides (e.g., Sani & Reicher, 1998). Until that point, however, everything is open to contest, and ingroup criticism is an inevitable part of the process. In summary, because there is inevitably some heterogeneity in perceptions of what are the core values and behavioral norms of the group, there is nothing in the notion of depersonalization that necessarily precludes ingroup criticism among high identifiers.

The motivational aspect of the social identity perspective is primarily articulated through social identity theory (Tajfel, 1978; Tajfel & Turner, 1979). For self-esteem reasons we are motivated to see the group through a jaundiced lens; we attend to, process, and remember information in such a way that the group's positive qualities are brought to the fore and the group's negative qualities are minimized. Furthermore, there is an understanding that we work to protect the integrity of the group relative to other groups, and that we loyally participate in the ongoing struggle for intergroup supremacy. On the basis of this, there might be two reasons why one might expect that high identifiers would not criticize their group. First, a high identifier is less likely to notice the negative aspects of their culture, because they see the group through an identity-enhancing lens. Second, even if they were to identify problematic aspects of the group's culture, they would be less likely to articulate these concerns, mindful as they are of maintaining the reputation of the group in the eyes of others.

Neither argument holds up to serious analysis. Social identity theory never intended to argue that people (even high identifiers) are ingroup-serving automatons, mechanistically celebrating everything that the group represents (Turner, 1999). Although there might be a general tendency to have an inflated view of the integrity of one's group, such biases are subject to reality constraints. Sometimes negative aspects of a group are simply unavoidable, and the more the group is wrapped up in one's self-concept the more these negative aspects need to be addressed. One way of addressing these negative qualities is to reframe them or to minimize their impact through the use of social creativity strategies, but there are no doubt limits to the extent one can continue to psychologically wallpaper over problems within the group. Eventually, work needs to be done to correct problems at a more fundamental level. The key point here is that the people who are going to be most *mindful* of the group's problems are likely to be the people for whom the group is most intimately intertwined with their self-concept: the high identifiers.

In a related vein, it does not necessarily follow that high identifiers will hold off from criticizing the group for fear of damaging the group's reputation. This is particularly the case if the failings of the group are openly recognized by outsiders. In this case, the potential for further damage to the group is minimal, and maintaining a front of defiance in the face of problems that exist can only serve to project an image of the group as immature, defensive, and parochial. In contrast, open acknowledgement of shortcomings can project an image that the group is mature, self-assured, and actively seeking positive change (Hornsey, de Bruijn, Creed, Allen, Ariyanto, & Svensson, 2005). The question of reputation becomes more delicate if the flaws of the group are not widely recognized by outsiders. In this case, exposing the flaws does have the potential to cause short-term injury to the reputation of the group, and also potentially leaves the group vulnerable to attacks from enemies. This potential, however, is minimized if one keeps the criticisms "in-house" (see also Elder, Sutton, & Douglas, 2005). Furthermore, concern about the short-term damage to the group's reputation might be counter-balanced by the fact that criticism can provide an opportunity to correct the root causes of the problem, thus protecting the group against damage that might be caused by criticism in the future. It is worthwhile remembering that in most cases the source of the identity threat is not the critic but rather the shortcomings of the group, upon which the critic is merely shining a light.

In summary, there are no compelling reasons to believe that ingroup critics are necessarily low identifiers. Indeed, there is a case for arguing that ingroup criticism is an especially brave act of loyalty and ingroup commitment. To criticize the group carries with it the risk of making enemies and alienating oneself from other group members (including leaders). Some of us no doubt have suspected that their career goals or their standing within a group have been jeopardized by levelling group-directed criticisms, and probably all of us have edited our true feelings about a group so as to avoid negative repercussions. However, it is equally clear that there are times when it is important that flawed, corrupt, immoral or self-defeating aspects of a group's culture are subjected to critical attention. The ingroup critic, then, has to weigh up a choice between their own short-term future and the long-term health of the group. The ingroup critic who risks their own position to advance the long-term goals of the group can hardly be considered to be a traitor or a low identifier; indeed, this is the very essence of loyalty (Zdaniuk & Levine, 2001).

Interestingly, this notion of the committed ingroup critic has long been recognized by social scientists interested in national identification. Shortly after World War II, a debate erupted about the "true" meaning of patriotism. This debate led Adorno and colleagues (Adorno, Frenkel-Brunswik, Levinson, & Sanford, 1950) to make a distinction between two types of patriotism: "genuine" patriotism – defined as "love of country and attachment to national values that is based on critical understanding" (p. 107) – and "pseudo" patriotism, described as "an uncritical allegiance to one's country characterized by rigidity, conformity and rejection of outgroups' (p. 107). Similarly, the upheavals of the Cold War inspired Morray (1959) to contrast a "patriotism of imitation and obedience" with a "patriotism of innovation and disobedience". After the Cuban missile crisis, the philosopher Sommerville (1981) argued the existence of a "patriotism of ignorance and irrationality" and a "patriotism of reason and dissent". More recently, Schatz, Staub, and Lavine (1999) have distinguished between "blind" patriotism – comprising uncritical support for the actions of the group – and "constructive" patriotism, which comprises commitment and loyalty to their country in addition to support for universal human ideals and values. A constructive patriot might oppose their country's actions not only because he or she believes they are morally incorrect or unfair, but because he or she believes that they violate the country's fundamental aspects and are therefore contrary to the country's long-term interests.

Misconception 2: ingroup critics are "black sheep"

One of the most robust phenomena in the social identity literature is the "black sheep effect": the tendency for people who are dislikeable (e.g., Khan & Lambert, 1998; Marques, Yzerbyt, & Leyens, 1988), incompetent (Marques & Yzerbyt, 1988), disloyal (Branscombe, Wann, Noel, & Coleman, 1993), or non-normative (e.g., Abrams, Marques, Bown, & Henson, 2000) to be judged more harshly by members of their own group than by members of outgroups. From a social identity theory perspective (particularly among those who see self-esteem to be a fundamental motivation for group behaviour), this effect makes perfect sense. Group members are motivated to believe that their group is positively distinct from relevant outgroups. Any threat to the integrity of the group is likely to arouse threat, and so ingroup members who damage the standing of the group in the eyes of others – either intentionally or otherwise – are likely to face particularly high levels of ingroup sanction.

Working from this assumption, one might think that ingroup members who criticize the group will be faced with extreme rejection and hostility. It could be argued that the role of the good group member is to support, bolster and defend the group, not to expose its weaknesses and failings. Similar to the dislikeable or incompetent ingroup member traditionally examined in the black sheep research, the ingroup critic is potentially damaging the value and welfare of the group, and so should be dealt with harshly, perhaps even expelled.

There are, however, reasons to believe that this traditional wisdom might not hold for ingroup critics. Yes, the ingroup critic might damage the standing of the group in the short term, and yes, they might antagonize tensions within the group. But it is also possible that internal criticism could be seen by other group members as beneficial in terms of bringing unrecognized problems to light, exposing group members to alternative standpoints and options, and leading to the reassessment of ill-adaptive behaviors, attitudes, and policies. Ingroup critics can be catalysts for positive change, and to the extent that they are recognized as such might be tolerated or even embraced. So group-directed criticism might represent identity threat, but it is a special form of identity threat, tinged as it is with opportunity and the promise of growth. For this reason it is not appropriate to conflate the ingroup critic with the dislikable, disloyal, or incompetent ingroup member typically examined in the black sheep research.

Research on group-directed criticism seems to bear this out: although ingroup critics are not necessarily celebrated, there is little evidence that they are greatly maligned either. For example, Hornsey, Oppes, and Svensson (2002, Experiment 1a) showed that people were just as keen to want to be friends with an Australian who said negative things about Australia as with an Australian who praised Australia. A similar non-effect of comment valence emerged with respect to criticisms of university students (Experiment 1b). Finally, Hornsey and Imani (2004, Experiment 1) obtained ratings of how likable Australians found another Australian to be both before and after discovering that the Australian had criticized their country. Although the target was rated less positively after participants had seen the criticisms, the downgrading of the ingroup critic did not reach conventional levels of statistical significance.

Overall, the data suggest surprisingly high levels of tolerance and generosity with respect to the ingroup critic. This same level of tolerance is not extended, however, to outgroup members. Outgroup members who criticize the group tend to be downgraded more strongly than ingroup members who criticize the group. Furthermore, criticisms articulated by outgroup members tend to arouse more negative emotion and win over less support than when the very same comments are made by an ingroup member (Hornsey & Imani, 2004; Hornsey et al., 2002; O'Dwyer, Berkowitz, & Alfeld-Johnson, 2002). So the group membership of the critic affects not only how appropriate the comments are seen to be, but also how *correct* they are seen to be. The overall message appears to be "It's OK if *we* say it, but *you* can't", a phenomenon dubbed the intergroup sensitivity effect (Hornsey et al., 2002).

When reflecting on the high levels of tolerance found in the face of ingroup criticism, it is worth remembering that the research accesses people's private thoughts and feelings, and that this might not correspond perfectly to the attitudes participants communicate in public. There is a convergence of research showing that when people are visible to an ingroup audience, there is a tendency for them to exaggerate their levels of group loyalty and to "show off" their group credentials (e.g., Jetten, Hornsey, & Adarves-Yorno, in press; Jetten, Hornsey, Spears, Haslam, & Cowell, 2005; Noel, Wann, & Branscombe, 1995). It could be, then, that people will feel the need to condemn the ingroup critic when their reactions are visible to other ingroup members, even if privately they feel supportive. Consistent with this notion, Ford (2004) found that when participants responded privately and anonymously to criticism of their country, defensiveness was lower when the criticisms stemmed from an ingroup member as compared to an outgroup member (the intergroup sensitivity effect). However, when participants were told that their questionnaire responses were visible to other Australians, defensiveness in response to the ingroup critic increased to the point that they aroused as much negativity as did the outgroup critic. If these data can be generalized outside the laboratory, it would suggest that ingroup critics perceive more hostility toward their arguments than exists in reality.

Furthermore, it seems reasonable to expect that this asymmetry in public and private responses might be most dramatic in the context of an intense intergroup conflict, when the norms against ingroup dissent and ingroup criticism are most pronounced. Political scientists (e.g., Kelman, 1995) and social psychologists (Matheson, Cole, & Majka, 2003) have noted a tendency for ingroup dissent to be received more harshly when the dissent is made in the context of competitive intergroup relations. For example, after criticizing American foreign policy in the wake of the 11 September 2001 terrorist attacks, American intellectual Susan Sontag was attacked by conservative columnists as a traitor, an idiot, and a stooge of Saddam Hussein. Many readers sent hate mail and death threats. Yet an absence of internal criticism can be disastrous in terms of leading to inflexible and inappropriate decision-making (Janis, 1982) and quite threatening for those within the country who see freedom of speech and thought as a fundamental way of defending against tyranny. Is it possible, then, that ingroup critics might be granted a quiet respect in times of war even as they are stigmatized publicly? It is interesting to note that, despite her very public vilification, Sontag herself reported that "to this day, and here we are almost two years later, there isn't a day that goes by that someone doesn't come up to me in the street and thank me for my bravery" (cited in Jackson, 2003).

Understanding when and why ingroup critics are tolerated

The research described above is encouraging for the individual who is unhappy with aspects of their group. Criticism from insiders is received in a relatively generous way (at least privately), remarkably so given the mountain of evidence showing the negative attention directed toward ingroup deviants and dissenters (Festinger, 1950; Marques & Paez, 1994; Schachter, 1951). Indeed, ingroup membership seems to help buffer critics against the extremely high level of defensiveness that many outsiders face when criticizing the group. What is it about ingroup membership that appears to give people indemnity from the kind of defensiveness and hostility faced by outgroup critics?

One explanation is that the ingroup critic is simply seen to have more experience of the group than the outsider. If an American criticizes Australia it is very easy for me to dismiss that criticism because I can argue that the American has no experience of my country. What would they know? An Australian citizen, however, has intimate experience with the group that they are criticizing, and as such demands more respect. Although intuitively appealing, this explanation has no support. One striking aspect of the intergroup sensitivity effect is that it survives even when the outsider is attributed extraordinary levels of experience with the target group. For example, foreigners who criticized Australia – and who had spent almost their entire lives in Australia – were received with levels of defensiveness that were statistically indistinguishable from critics who had never been to Australia (Hornsey & Imani, 2004). In other words the intergroup sensitivity effect does not seem to be a rational response to the objective qualifications of the critic, but is rather something deeper and more psychological.

Further investigation has revealed that the intergroup sensitivity effect is in fact underpinned by issues to do with trust. When people hear group-directed criticism, they are entitled to question what is motivating this behavior. Why are they saying this? What are they trying to achieve? In answering these questions, people factor in not just what the critic is saying but also where they come from. When ingroup members criticize their group we assume that they are driven by relatively true and constructive motives; we believe they are trying to improve the group and are making the comments in the best interests of the group. But when outsiders say these same things, we are more suspicious about motive. We are less likely to believe that they are trying to improve the group, and are more likely to believe that the critic has destructive motives for their comments. Across four experiments (Hornsey et al., 2002, Experiment 2; Hornsey & Imani, 2004) it has been shown that this attributional bias fully mediates the intergroup sensitivity effect; insiders are attributed more constructive motives for their criticism than are outgroup members, and this flows on to ratings of likability, negative emotion, and agreement. This tendency to trust the motives of ingroup critics seems to be quite robust, and to hold up even when ingroup members criticize the group to an outgroup audience (Hornsey, de Bruijn et al., in press).

According to this model, group membership (ingroup or outgroup) acts as a powerful heuristic that tells us who can be trusted and who cannot, who is looking out for us and who is not, who cares and who does not. Furthermore, this inherent trust in other group members (and mistrust of outgroup members; see Worchel, 1979) builds up not necessarily through a history of interpersonal exchanges, but rather through self-categorization processes. This is in line with Brewer (1981) who argued that "As a consequence of shifting from the personal to the social group level of identity, the individual can adopt a sort of 'depersonalized trust' based on category membership alone. Within categories the probability of reciprocity is assumed, *a priori*, to be high, while between categories it is presumed to be low" (p. 356). This is also in line with research showing that we expect ingroup members (including ingroup leaders) to treat us preferentially (e.g., Duck & Fielding, 2003; Jetten, Duck, Terry, & O'Brien, 2002;

Moreland & McMinn, 1999; Platow, Hoar, Reid, Harley, & Morrison, 1997) whereas we expect outgroup members to discriminate against us (Insko, Schopler, Hoyle, Dardis, & Graetz, 1990; Vivian & Berkowitz, 1992).

So it is not ingroup membership *per se* that is making the difference, but the relatively positive attributions that flow on from ingroup membership. According to this model, it seems reasonable to expect that this support and trust might be withdrawn depending on the presence or absence of certain other psychological conditions. Specifically, it might be expected that an ingroup critic will only be received more positively than an outgroup critic in so far as the insider is seen to have an ongoing commitment and loyalty to the group. If the commitment and loyalty to the group are questionable, then we might predict that the ingroup critic will face as much defensiveness as the outsider.

There is now a convergence of evidence in favor of this prediction. For example, Hornsey, Trembath, and Gunthorpe (2004) showed that ingroup critics were liked better than outgroup critics, and their comments aroused less negativity and won over more agreement than did the very same comments when made by an outgroup member. But this was only true when participants were given information showing that the critic remained highly identified with the group. When the ingroup critic was described as being a low identifier, they aroused as much defensiveness as did outgroup members. Similarly, critics who used identity-embracing, inclusive language (e.g., "Australians, *we* are not open-minded") were liked more and aroused less negativity than did those who used identity-distancing, exclusive language (e.g., "Australians, *they* are not open-minded"). Furthermore, path analysis of the effects of language revealed a causal path in line with our arguments about identity attachment and trust. Critics who used inclusive language were seen to be more attached to the group than were those who used exclusive language, which in turn led them to be attributed more constructive motives for their comments, which in turn flowed on to various indices of defensiveness. Finally, Hornsey and colleagues (Hornsey, Grice, Jetten, Paulsen, & Callan, 2005) found that allied health professionals at a hospital were more willing to embrace criticism from another allied health professional when the critic had been a member of the group for a long time than when the criticisms came from a newcomer to the group. Indeed, newcomers aroused as much defensiveness as nurses (i.e., outgroup critics). Further analysis revealed that oldtimers were seen to be more attached to their group identity than were newcomers, and this was enough to mediate the effect (see Hollander, 1958, for a related argument). The results of all these studies lead to the same conclusion: it is not the outsider who is going to be able to win over change, or the disinvested insider, but rather the *committed* ingroup member, the one who can stand up and say "I'm making these comments because I love my group and I want it to be the best group possible".

The message here for outsiders and newcomers is quite pessimistic, because it shows that these people are being judged not entirely on the quality of their arguments but on assumptions people make about their underlying attitudes – assumptions rooted in *who they are*. This must be particularly frustrating for newcomers, because sometimes it is the newcomers to a group who can most clearly see the group's qualities (both positive and negative). Oldtimers might have experience, but this experience can mean that they have habituated to the group's flaws, or have been acculturated to the point where they see the group through a jaundiced lens and are unwilling or unable to accept the faults within the group. Newcomers, on the other hand, are in a unique position to appraise the group in a fresh way, because their vision is not dimmed by the film of psychological dust that accumulates on the eyes of those who have habituated to an environment. Furthermore, in many cases, newcomers have recently emerged from another group and can use their experiences in their original group as a frame of reference against which positive and negative qualities of the new group can be contrasted quite clearly. The irony inherent within this research is that the very people who might have most to say about a group culture are the ones who are given least permission to express these attitudes (Gruenfeld & Fan, 1999).

Responses to criticism: an attributional model

In some ways the intergroup sensitivity effect can be seen as an extension of previous research showing how ingroup members tend to exert more influence on us than outgroup members (e.g., Mackie, Worth, & Asuncion, 1990; Turner, 1991). However, a model of how people respond to group-directed criticism would need to take into account the peculiar nature of criticism as a form of persuasion. Unlike the social messages or compliance attempts typically used in the persuasion literature, group-directed criticism directly threatens the (collective) self-concept. When people say negative things about our country, or our gender, or our profession, it is a threatening and emotional experience. Deciding whether to accept or reject these criticisms is not a cold, rational process governed by perceptual or cognitive processes, but rather a decision infused with feelings of threat and self-doubt, wrapped up in basic issues of trust. It is interesting to note that the effects of group membership emerge not when people *praise* the group, but rather when people criticize it (Hornsey et al.,

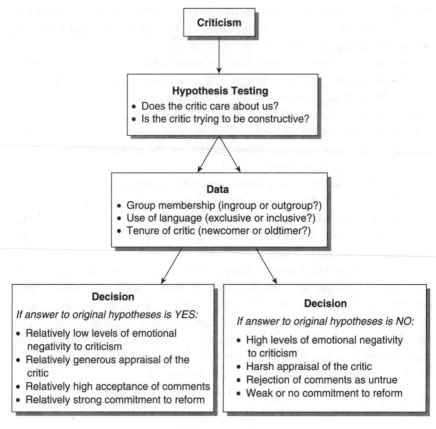

Figure 5.1 Responses to criticism: an attributional model

2002). And the mediating role of constructiveness and identity attachment shows that issues of the heart play a central role.

Although there is still much work to be done, the stories told by the studies presented here are beginning to coalesce around a handful of consistent themes. These themes are summarized in the model presented in Figure 5.1. In this model I argue that, before deciding how to respond to criticism of their group, people engage in a process of hypothesis testing. Why are they saying this? What are their motives? Do they really care about us? Certainly group membership is important in so far as it is a heuristic that helps us make judgments about who can be trusted and who cannot. In the absence of any other information, people assume that ingroup members are more likely than outgroup members to be committed to the group and to have constructive motives for criticizing the group. But if these assumptions are overturned, then so is the intergroup sensitivity effect. For example, if people are told that the ingroup member is not invested in the group psychologically, or they sense from the speaker's language that the speaker is not invested in the group, or if the speaker is a newcomer, then ingroup critics arouse as much defensiveness as outgroup critics.

In all these cases the recipients of group-directed criticism appear to be preoccupied with assumptions about what is going on in the heads and hearts of the critic; they are peering beyond the words to find out what the critic is *really* saying. Rather than simply attending to the presented argument, they are also listening to the *shadow* argument – the assumed motives and implications of the comments. These assumptions about underlying attitudes and motives are wrapped up in issues of trust, which in turn is rooted in relatively superficial cues about who you are (a basic social categorical process). Furthermore, these assumptions appear to overwhelm seemingly more rational considerations (e.g., is the critic experienced with the group?) when determining how people respond.

So when an ingroup member criticizes the group, the struggle between acceptance and defensiveness might be not simply about how successfully one can communicate the integrity of their ideas, but also about how successfully one can communicate ongoing commitment to the group. In turn, the extent to which opponents can succeed in negating criticism might rest on how successfully they can frame the critic as disinvested and uncaring. For example, when Mike Moore released his books and films criticizing American culture and foreign policy, defenders conspicuously (and, I would argue, strategically) used the word "patriot" to describe him. When conservative documentary-maker Mike Wilson released a scathing critique of Moore, the film was titled *Michael Moore Hates America*. Concerned citizen or traitor? Defender of the group or sympathizer with the enemy? It is the struggle to define the critic's underlying attitudes and values – rather than the integrity of the criticisms themselves – that might be most crucial in determining the critic's impact.

Summary

In summary, neither social identity theory nor self-categorization theory precludes the reality of ingroup criticism, but to date this phenomenon has remained undertheorized. Although themes of resistance and social change lie at the forefront of the social identity perspective, the focus has primarily been on groups trying to change the societal status quo rather than on individuals striving to change their groups. With some exceptions (most notably Reicher and colleagues), the restless and dynamic nature of group behavior has been overshadowed by the theoretical and empirical focus on conformity and homogeneity. This, perhaps, has led to certain mechanistic assumptions about ingroup criticism: for example, that ingroup critics are low identifiers, or that people are inherently motivated to quash ingroup criticism.

However, the research we have conducted on ingroup criticism suggests that the picture is more complex (and in many ways more interesting) than this. Group membership operates as a heuristic that decides whether or not critics' motives are seen to be pure, and the success or failure of attempts to change the group's direction can hinge on the extent to which the critic can successfully locate themselves as insiders and communicate their ongoing attachment to the group. Rather than being derogated as "black sheep", ingroup members are actually in a unique position to effect change through criticism, particularly if they have established themselves as trustworthy members of the group. I hope that the research will shine a stronger theoretical light on the reality that social influence works two ways: group cultures influence individuals, and individuals can help shape the group culture through criticism, negotiation and strategic deviance.

NOTE

Correspondence to: Dr Matthew Hornsey, School of Psychology, University of Queensland, St Lucia 4072, Queensland, Australia, m.hornsey@psy.uq.edu.au.

REFERENCES

Abrams, D., Marques, J. M., Bown, N., & Henson, M. (2000). Pro-norm and anti-norm deviance within and between groups. *Journal of Personality and Social Psychology, 78,* 906–912.

Adorno, T. W., Frenkel-Brunswik, E., Levinson, D. J., & Sanford, R. N. (1950). *The authoritarian personality.* New York: Harper & Row.

Asch, S. E. (1952). Effects of group pressures upon the modification and distortion of judgments. In G. E. Swanson, T. M. Newcomb, & E. L. Hartley (Eds.), *Readings in social psychology* (pp. 393–401). New York: Holt, Reinhart & Winston.

Branscombe, N., Wann, D. L., Noel, J. G., & Coleman, J. (1993). In-group or out-group extremity: Importance of the threatened social identity. *Personality and Social Psychology Bulletin, 17,* 381–388.

Brewer, M. B. (1981). Ethnocentrism and its role in interpersonal trust. In M. B. Brewer & B. E. Collins (Eds.), *Scientific inquiry and the social sciences* (pp. 345–360). San Francisco: Jossey-Bass.

Duck, J. M., & Fielding, K. S. (2003). Leaders and their treatment of subgroups: Implications for evaluations of the leader and the superordinate group. *European Journal of Social Psychology, 33,* 387–401.

Elder, T. J., Sutton, R. M., & Douglas, K. M. (2005). Keeping it to ourselves: Effects of audience size and composition on reactions to criticism of the ingroup. Manuscript under review.

Festinger, L. (1950). Informal social communication. *Psychological Review, 57,* 271–282.

Ford, L. (2004). *Public versus private responses to group criticism.* Unpublished honours thesis, University of Queensland.

Friend, R., Rafferty, Y., & Bramel, D. (1990). A puzzling misinterpretation of the Asch "conformity" study. *European Journal of Social Psychology, 20,* 29–44.

Gruenfeld, D. H., & Fan, E. T. (1999). What newcomers see and what oldtimers say: Discontinuities in knowledge exchange. In L. L. Thompson, J. M. Levine, & D. M. Messick (Eds.), *Shared cognition in organizations: The management of knowledge* (pp. 245–265). Hillsdale, NJ: Erlbaum.

Haney, C., Banks, C., & Zimbardo, P. (1973). Interpersonal dynamics in a simulated prison. *International Journal of Criminology and Penology, 1,* 69–97.

Haslam, S. A. (1997). Stereotyping and social influence: Foundations of stereotype consensus. In R. Spears, P. J. Oakes, N. Ellemers, & S. A. Haslam (Eds.), *The social psychology of stereotyping and group life* (pp. 119–143). Oxford: Blackwell.

Hollander, E. P. (1958). Conformity, status, and idiosyncrasy credit. *Psychological Review, 65,* 117–127.

Hornsey, M. J., de Bruijn, P., Creed, J., Allen, J., Ariyanto, A., & Svensson, A. (2005). Keeping it in-house: How audience affects responses to group criticism. *European Journal of Social Psychology, 35,* 291–312.

Hornsey, M. J., Grice, T., Jetten, J., Paulsen, N., & Callan, V. (2005). Group-directed criticisms and recommendations for change: Why newcomers arouse more defensiveness than old-timers. Manuscript under review.

Hornsey, M. J., & Imani, A. (2004). Criticizing groups from the inside and the outside: An identity perspective on the intergroup sensitivity effect. *Personality and Social Psychology Bulletin, 30,* 365–383.

Hornsey, M. J., & Jetten, J. (2004). The individual within the group: Balancing the need to belong with the need to be different. *Personality and Social Psychology Review, 8,* 248–264.

Hornsey, M. J., Jetten, J., McAuliffe, B. J., & Hogg, M. A. (in press). The impact of individualist and collectivist group norms on evaluations of dissenting group members. *Journal of Experimental Social Psychology.*

Hornsey, M. J., Oppes, T., & Svensson, A. (2002). "It's ok if we say it, but you can't": Responses to intergroup and intragroup criticism. *European Journal of Social Psychology, 32,* 293–307.

Hornsey, M. J., Trembath, M., & Gunthorpe, S. (2004). "You can criticize because you care": Identity attachment, constructiveness, and the intergroup sensitivity effect. *European Journal of Social Psychology, 34,* 499–518.

Insko, C. A., Schopler, J., Hoyle, R. H., Dardis, G. J., & Graetz, K. A. (1990). Individual-group discontinuity as a function of fear and greed. *Journal of Personality and Social Psychology, 58,* 68–79.

Jackson, K. (2003). Susan Sontag in the wars. *Weekend Australian,* 22–23 November, p. R4.

Janis, I. L. (1982). *Groupthink: Psychological studies of policy decisions and fiascoes.* Boston: Houghton Mifflin.

Jetten, J., Duck, J., Terry, D. J., & O'Brien, A. (2002). Being attuned to intergroup differences in mergers: The role of aligned leaders and low-status groups. *Personality and Social Psychology Bulletin, 28,* 1194–1201.

Jetten, J., Hornsey, M. J., & Adarves-Yorno, I. (in press). When group members admit to being conformist: The role of relative intragroup status in conformity self-reports. *Personality and Social Psychology Bulletin.*

Jetten, J., Hornsey, M. J., Spears, R., Haslam, S. A., & Cowell, E. (2005). Keeping up appearances: The conditional nature of peripheral group members' loyalty expressions and actions. Revision under review.

Kelman, H. C. (1995). Decision making and public discourse in the Gulf War: An assessment of underlying psychological and moral assumptions. *Peace and Conflict: Journal of Peace Psychology, 1*, 117–130.

Khan, S., & Lambert, A. (1998). Ingroup favoritism versus black sheep effects in observations of informal conversations. *Basic and Applied Social Psychology, 20*, 263–269.

Kim, H., & Markus, H. R. (1999). Deviance or uniqueness, harmony or conformity? A cultural analysis. *Journal of Personality and Social Psychology, 77*, 785–800.

Le Bon, G. (1908). *The crowd: A study of the popular mind*. London: Unwin (original work published 1896).

Levine, J. M., & Moreland, R. L. (1985). Innovation and socialization in small groups. In S. Mocovici, G. Mugny, & E. van Avermaet (Eds.), *Perspectives on minority influence* (pp. 143–169). Cambridge: Cambridge University Press.

Mackie, D. M., Worth, L. T., & Asuncion, A. G. (1990). Processing of persuasive in group messages. *Journal of Personality and Social Psychology, 58*, 812–822.

Marques, J. M., & Paez, D. (1994). The "black sheep effect": Social categorization, rejection of ingroup deviates, and perception of group variability. *European Review of Social Psychology, 5*, 37–68.

Marques, J., & Yzerbyt, V. (1988). The black sheep effect: Judgmental extremity towards ingroup members in inter- and intra-group situations. *European Journal of Social Psychology, 18*, 287–292.

Marques, J., Yzerbyt, V., & Leyens, J. (1988). The black sheep effect: Extremity of judgements towards ingroup members as a function of group identification. *European Journal of Social Psychology, 18*, 1–16.

Matheson, K., Cole, B., and Majka, K. (2003). Dissidence from within: Examining the effects of intergroup context on group members' reactions to attitudinal opposition. *Journal of Experimental Social Psychology, 39,* 161–169.

McAuliffe, B. J., Jetten, J., Hornsey, M. J., & Hogg, M. A. (2003). Individualist and collectivist group norms: When it's OK to go your own way. *European Journal of Social Psychology, 33*, 57–70.

Milgram, S. (1974). *Obedience to authority*. London: Tavistock.

Moreland, R. L., & McMinn, J. G. (1999). Gone but not forgotten: Loyalty and betrayal among ex-members of small groups. *Personality and Social Psychology Bulletin, 25*, 1476–1486.

Morray, J. P. (1959). *Pride of state*. Boston: Beacon.

Moscovici, S. (1976). *Social influence and social change*. London: Academic.

Nemeth, C. J. (1985). Dissent, group process and creativity: The contribution of minority influence. In J. E. Lawler (Ed.), *Advances in group processes* (pp. 57–75). Greenwich, CT: JAI.

Noel, J. G., Wann, D. L., & Branscombe, N. R. (1995). Peripheral ingroup membership status and public negativity toward outgroups. *Journal of Personality and Social Psychology, 68*, 127–137.

O'Dwyer, A., Berkowitz, N. H., & Alfeld-Johnson, D. (2002). Group and person attributions in response to criticism of the in-group. *British Journal of Social Psychology, 41*, 563–588.

Platow, M. J., Hoar, S., Reid, S., Harley, K., & Morrison, D. (1997). Endorsement of distributively fair and unfair leaders in interpersonal and intergroup situations. *European Journal of Social Psychology, 27*, 465–494.

Postmes, T., Spears, R., & Cihangir, S. (2001). Quality of decision making and group norms. *Journal of Personality and Social Psychology*, *80*, 918–930.

Reicher, S. D. (1987). Crowd behaviour as social action. In J. C. Turner, M. A. Hogg, P. J. Oakes, S. D. Reicher, & M. S. Wetherell (Eds.), *Rediscovering the social group: A self-categorisation theory* (pp. 171–202). Oxford: Blackwell.

Reicher, S. (1996). "The Battle of Westminster": Developing the social identity model of crowd behaviour in order to explain the initiation and development of collective conflict. *European Journal of Social Psychology*, *26*, 115–134.

Reicher, S., & Hopkins, N. (1996). Seeking influence through characterizing self-categories: An analysis of anti-abortionist rhetoric. *British Journal of Social Psychology*, *35*, 297–311.

Sani, F., & Reicher, S. D. (1998). When consensus fails: An analysis of the schism within the Italian Communist Party (1991). *European Journal of Social Psychology*, *28*, 623–645.

Schachter, S. (1951). Deviation, rejection, and communication. *Journal of Abnormal and Social Psychology*, *46*, 190–207.

Schatz, R. T., Staub, E., & Lavine, H. (1999). On the varieties of national attachment: Blind versus constructive patriotism. *Political Psychology*, *20*, 151–174.

Sommerville, J. (1981). Patriotism and war. *Ethics*, *91*, 568–578.

Tajfel, H. (Ed.), (1978). *Differentiation between social groups: Studies in the social psychology of intergroup relations*. London: Academic.

Tajfel, H., & Turner, J. C. (1979). An integrative theory of intergroup conflict. In W. G. Austin & S. Worchel (Eds.), *The social psychology of intergroup relations* (pp. 33–47). Monterey, CA: Brooks/Cole.

Turner, J. C. (1991). *Social influence*. Buckingham: Open University Press.

Turner, J. C. (1999). Some current issues in research on social identity and self-categorization theories. In N. Ellemers, R. Spears, & B. Doosje (Eds.), *Social identity: Context, commitment, content* (pp. 6–34). Oxford: Blackwell.

Turner, J. C., Hogg, M. A., Oakes, P. J., Reicher, S. D., & Wetherell, M. S. (1987). *Rediscovering the social group: A self-categorization theory*. New York: Blackwell.

Vivian, J. E., & Berkowitz, N. H. (1992). Anticipated bias from an outgroup: An attributional analysis. *European Journal of Social Psychology*, *22*, 415–424.

Worchel, S. (1979). Trust and distrust. In W. G. Austin & S. Worchel (Eds.), *The social psychology of intergroup relations* (pp. 174–187). Monterey, CA: Brooks/Cole.

Zdaniuk, B., & Levine, J. M. (2001). Group loyalty: Impact of members' identification and contributions. *Journal of Experimental Social Psychology*, *37*, 502–509.

PART 2

Shaping Individuality through Culture and Social Identity Content

6

Group Status and Individual Differentiation

Fabio Lorenzi-Cioldi

The social identity of dominants and subordinates

Group status and personal vs collective self-identification

Does group status influence processes of self-identification? This chapter provides an affirmative answer to this question. The idea that dominant and subordinate groups elicit different social identities is not novel. In documenting the Jewish people's consciousness of belonging to the Jewish group, Lewin (1948), for instance, maintained that subordinates are urged to think about their group membership more often than dominants. Hence, when prompted to describe themselves, they are continuously reminded of their group membership, whereas the dominants are led to disregard the common ingroup's attributes and to invigorate their uniqueness. In a similar vein, Allport (1954, p. 179) asserted that low-status groups are often assigned labels of "primary potency" that are so salient as to prevent alternative classifications or idiosyncratic perceptions of their members.

Interest in relationships between group status and forms of self-identification has declined in contemporary social identity approaches.

Most of these approaches are based on the assumption of a separation, or mutual exclusion, of the personal and the social components of one's identity (Brewer & Gardner, 1996). According to Tajfel and Turner (1979), individuals' self-perceptions and behaviors vary between two theoretical extremes which define a continuum with a self pole (self-conceptions in terms of idiosyncratic attributes and individual differences) and a group pole (self-conceptions in terms of category memberships and collective similarities). Tajfel (1978) reported on this identity continuum by contrasting the *heterogeneous* with the *homogeneous*, the *variable* with the *uniform*, the *individuated* with the *stereotyped*. In so far as they distinguish between ends of a single, continuous dimension, such terms imply that as one pole increases in strength, the other decreases. Individuals must move away from the group pole, or "exit" the ingroup–outgroup relationship, in order to attain a sense of uniqueness.

A more recent account of the distinction between personal and social expressions of one's identity is self-categorization theory (Turner, Hogg, Oakes, Reicher, & Wetherell, 1987). This theory makes an even more radical separation between personal and social. The innovative part of the theory is the assumption that the self can be categorized at different levels of inclusiveness, ranging from the individual to the species level (see also Turner, Reynolds, Haslam, & Veenstra, Chapter 2 in this volume). However, consistent with the original social identity perspective, self-identifications at the personal and the group level show a *functional antagonism*, an *inverse relationship*, an *inevitable conflict*, a *constant competition*. Thus, a greater salience of social identity inhibits, reduces, or precludes personal identity. On the one hand, the personal self "can *only* become salient as a result of intragroup comparisons" (Oakes, Haslam, & Turner, 1994, p. 163), and on the other hand, the depersonalization of self-perception "is the basic process underlying group phenomena" (Turner et al., 1987, p. 50). Depersonalization refers to the process whereby individuals define themselves as similar, equivalent and interchangeable group members rather than as unique personalities defined by their differences from others. They then behave not as distinct persons, but as exemplars of the common characteristics of their group. Social identity and self-categorization theories thus assume a fundamental discontinuity between personal and social identity such that an individual's identity can be represented in only one unique configuration – either personal or collective – in any given situation.

This chapter takes a different approach. It questions the assumption of an antagonistic relationship between the personal and the social, and its major outcome, that groups inescapably depersonalize their members by minimizing the salience of personal identity. This assumption unfortunately obscures the social origin of the personalistic identity which, as will be illustrated, is most pervasively voiced by members of the dominant group. The alternative assumption advanced in this chapter is of a relationship between superior (vs inferior) group status and group members' tendency to stress personal (vs collective) aspects of their self-concept. The logic of this argument implies that personal identity is as much a group phenomenon as social identity is. Indeed, personal identity can develop as a result of intergroup relations. But the groups from which it originates are hardly noticeable, as they lack visibility, concreteness and uniformity.

Collection and aggregate groups

The hypothesis that the personal and the collective components of an individual's identity are group phenomena calls for a reappraisal of the concept of social group. Currently favored conceptions of groups are associated with notions that convey an individual's depersonalization, deindividuation, similarity or interchangeability with other ingroup members. In the present perspective, however, a group may also encompass individual uniqueness, depending on its position in the social hierarchy.

Personal identity prevails in groups located at the top of status hierarchies, and is conducive to *collection* type groups. Members of these groups perceive themselves, and are perceived by others, as endowed with unique attributes. They indulge in expressing an identity that seems to be gained outside their group membership. At best, the group is conceived of as the juxtaposition, with no blending, of its members' characteristics. Collective identity, in turn, predominates at the other pole of the status hierarchy, triggering the formation of *aggregate* type groups. Members of these groups perceive themselves, and are perceived by others, as parts of a relatively undifferentiated entity. Their group is defined by holistic features that distinguish it from other groups. Shared attributes prompt group members' perceptual similarity and interchangeability.

This distinction between collection and aggregate groups has direct implications for identity processes: whether the individual has a personal or collective self-concept, both routes to self-identification are tightly constrained by membership of a group that is favorably, or unfavorably, located in the status hierarchy. Thus, by taking into account status-discrepant group relationships, the often implied antagonism between personal and collective components of an individual's identity fades away. In high-status groups, collective identification leads to feelings of uniqueness, rather than depersonalization. Collections thus impose unity on people who can simultaneously be perceived as distinct persons.

Elsewhere, I have shown how researchers from various disciplines have portrayed dominant and subordinate groups in ways consistent with the above definitions of collections and aggregates, respectively (Lorenzi-Cioldi, 2001; 2002a). High-status groups are depicted as "hazy" (Veblen, 1899) and "vague" (Millett, 1981, p. 68) collectivities, as "fragmented, dispersed, absent" (Guillaumin, 1972) and "hidden" (Hoggart, 1957) groups, or as an "adding up of incomparable and remarkable persons" (Bourdieu & de Saint Martin, 1978). Interestingly, Dahrendorf (1964, p. 262) maintained that *enumeration* is often the only feasible method to provide a definition of the dominant group. Clearly, enumeration alludes to a group whose lack of substance allows the perceivers to make finer differentiations among its members. Conversely, "The bottom of society is evoked as all of a piece" (DeMott, 1990, p. 204). Members of low-status groups are better described as invisible rather than conspicuous individuals, a marker which asserts the lack of recognition of their personal uniqueness (Apfelbaum, 1979). The designation of the poor as "other", and their near invisibility in our societies, exemplify this perceptual minimization of the low-status individual (Lott, 2002). A study by Fiske, Xu, Cuddy, and Glick (1999) illustrates this phenomenon. White students were asked to generate a list of "salient groups in American society". Among the 17 groups most frequently named, only two (*rich people* and *businesswomen*) were indubitably high status. Three other groups indicated status-irrelevant, cultural or geographical, origins (e.g., *northerners*). Most groups were low status (e.g., *housewives*, *migrant workers*, *retarded people*). Apparently, when spontaneously thinking of a "group", people are more attuned to lower than higher positions in the status hierarchy.

The bulk of this chapter will be devoted to advancing reasons for expecting this distinction between collections and aggregates. Five interpretations derived from various research traditions will be considered: *cultural values, oppression, attribution, covariation*, and *ideology*. These interpretations combine with one another to substantiate the view that members of high- and low-status groups uphold distinct, and most often contrasting, self-identities. Let us first consider the way self-identification processes are contingent on values which by and large govern society.

Cultural values

Cultural systems influence the degree to which people define themselves in terms of their group memberships, or in terms of their personal characteristics. It is a common assumption in social psychology that Western societies value the belief in individual separateness (see Moghaddam, Chapter 9 in this volume). Not surprisingly, people confer higher status and prestige on occupations characterized by a high level of self-direction – autonomy, independence, and freedom from supervision – than on occupations in which a person is dependent on others, even if the former are sometimes lower in salary (see Sennett & Cobb, 1972). Western individualism is so compelling that its accounts remain unchallenged even when they are at odds with basic social psychological research findings. As an illustration, consider Triandis' (1994) contention that in Western cultures "social behavior is only somewhat different when the other person is an in-group versus an out-group member", and that "horizontal relations are more important than vertical" (p. 48). These claims convey that intergroup behavior in general, and status disparities in particular, are of lesser significance than interpersonal behavior and equal status relationships.

Individualist values instigate a search for inner potential and excellence, and they value interpersonal diversity. Some proponents of self-categorization theory have speculated that, because of these tendencies, the personal self is the prototype, or default option, of an individual's identity. Simon (1993) advocated an *egocentric categorization* model in which egocentrism, as a motive, operates as an effective counter-force to the depersonalization of self-perception. Accordingly, the ingroup is construed as a more heterogeneous social category than the outgroup, a phenomenon that Simon named a "quasi-intergroup situation". Jetten, Postmes, and McAuliffe (2002) showed that when individuals strongly identify with a group whose norm is individualist rather than collectivist, they value dissent and deviance among ingroup members less negatively. Thus, a greater variability of the group members is a function of group identification, rather than emerging in its absence. The authors commented that in Western cultures people demonstrate collectivism through strong individualism.

However, there is more than shared values in the above phenomena. Although individualism provides a common system of reference in relation to which groups define themselves, group status influences the group members' tendency to linger over individualist values. Those endowed with status and power fit the cultural imperative of uniqueness more closely, and are better equipped to attain it. They thus set the standard of the culturally valued behavior against which others define themselves (Deschamps, 1982). As Guillaumin put it, "The minority cannot define itself in terms of criteria which are internal to it and independent, it must do this starting from points of reference which are offered to it by the majority system" (quoted by Moscovici & Paicheler, 1978, p. 265). Apfelbaum (1979) distinguished between *inner*-normed dominant groups and *outer*-normed subordinate groups in an analogous way. The subordinates define themselves, and are defined by others, as members of an entitative group in reference to the dominants, because the latter are the "cultural default" from which they deviate. The ensuing nebulous if not vanishing high-status group is assigned a positive value, and is contrasted with a more uniform low-status group. This is consistent with findings suggesting that people categorize minority group members more quickly than majority group members (Zàrate & Smith, 1990), and that they search for more explanations of stereotype violations of the former than the latter (Sekaquaptewa & Espinoza, 2004). Interestingly, this tendency pervades social psychological research as well. This is implicit in Fiske's (1998) complaint that "Stereotypes and subtypes about white Anglos are rarely studied, partly because ... the white Anglo person is the cultural default" (p. 379).

It follows from the above that although members of any group strive to define themselves in terms of autonomy and independence (see also Prentice, Chapter 3 in this volume), only members of high-status groups should altogether succeed in this task. Gender provides a likely basis to illustrate this conjecture. The assumption that men have higher status and greater power than women is central to many social psychological analyses of gender stereotypes (e.g., Eagly, 1987). The prediction is that the shared norm of the autonomous person, and the ingroup norm, would coincide for judgments of male targets, but would diverge for judgments of female targets. Initial support for this prediction comes from research on sex-role stereotypes showing that descriptions of "men in general" match closely those of adult, white, healthy persons, whereas descriptions of women comprise more group-specific, i.e., relational and communal, characteristics (see Lorenzi-Cioldi, 1994). Lorenzi-Cioldi (2002b) asked male and female participants to judge various targets, including the self, on normative (e.g., *independent, individualistic*) and counter-normative (*collectivistic, follower*) behaviors. The results showed that "Westerners", "men", and "people in general" were overall attributed behaviors related to an individual's independence. Furthermore, men's self-descriptions paralleled the descriptions of the gender ingroup. In contrast, perceptions of female targets, as well as women's self-descriptions, embodied intermediate levels of both normative and counter-normative behaviors. These findings suggest that in Western societies, only those who have power and status are fully identified with the norm of the self-contained person.

Research on spontaneous self-perception using the *Who am I?* questionnaire shows evidence of similar status effects. People vary in the extent to which they regard their group memberships as crucial to their identities. People in individualist societies, and in particular members of high-status groups in these societies, indulge in ego-autonomy contents such as personality traits and individual preferences. Conversely, people in collectivist societies, as well as members of low-status groups in individualist societies, stick more extensively to their group memberships and social roles. There is support for this trend using various status cues for categorizing participants, such as gender (Lorenzi-Cioldi, 1994), level of education

(Deschamps, Lorenzi-Cioldi, & Meyer, 1982), ethnicity (Smith & Leach, 2004), and professional role (Guillaumin, 1972). Pichevin and Hurtig (1996) and Lorenzi-Cioldi (1991, 1993) provided further demonstrations of this chronic salience of group membership among the disadvantaged. Context parameters, such as the numerical ratio of the gender groups and the dimensions of intergroup comparison, altered the perceptual salience of the male but not of the female sex membership. The latter remained highly accessible and readily available for use in all situations. This indicates that members of low-status groups escape awareness of their group membership with great difficulty, a conclusion that has received extensive support in sociological research. Jackman and Jackman (1973), for instance, examined subjective class identification among whites and blacks in the United States, and found that, for blacks, class identification is insensitive to education and occupational status. They concluded that "The low prestige accruing from ascribed ethnic status is of such overwhelming salience to blacks that additional prestige accruing from universalistic achieved criteria such as education and occupational status cannot make an impact on the ethnic group member's class identification" (p. 578).

To summarize, dominant groups show strong conformity to the norm of the self-contained, autonomous person. They identify with their group and, concomitantly, lay emphasis on their unique qualities and differences from other ingroup members. Conversely, the subordinates' distance from this norm calls attention to their group membership, and leads them to engage in more collective forms of self-identification.

Oppression

The second interpretation for the greater salience of personal identity in high-status groups rests on attentional dynamics. Subordination (LaFrance & Henley, 1994) and outcome dependency (Fiske, 1993) theories provide convergent motivational accounts of people's tendency to produce detailed and individuated representations of high-status, dominant or powerful groups. The basic idea of these theories is that those who possess status and power are a focus of attention for those lacking these attributes. The subordinates' awareness that their fate depends on their adaptation to the dominants motivates them to steer attention towards them. They therefore seek knowledge about outgroup members' attributes, preferences, and behaviors in order to predict their reactions, to respond appropriately and possibly to influence them. Dominants' characteristics thus receive greater thought and elaboration. Accordingly, stable personality attributes rise to prominence for the powerful.

A large body of research has examined this attentional asymmetry in status hierarchies. Members of low-status groups, compared to other people, raise outgroup members to the level of standards for social comparisons (the *I look like them more than they look like me* phenomenon: Hurtig, Pichevin, & Piolat, 1992), possess greater abilities to discern nonverbal cues among outgroup members, particularly facial expression and emotion (Ellyson & Dovidio, 1985), show "normative clear-sightedness" in their interactions (Beauvois, 1994), develop better skills of interpersonal sensitivity and intuition (Snodgrass, 1985), are more mindful of the social parameters that create or sustain group inequalities (Vonk, 1999), and hold less superficial and more accurate views of their opponents (Keltner, Gruenfeld, & Anderson, 2003).

Lorenzi-Cioldi and Doise (1994) tested this attentional asymmetry on gender groups. In an adaptation of Snodgrass' (1985) interpersonal sensitivity paradigm, they asked participants to describe the self and the gender ingroup and outgroup on several gender-related dimensions, according to two instructional sets: on their own behalf, and by predicting the opinions held by a hypothetical outgroup member. Across dimensions, men's judgments of *women in general* were strongly related to women's judgments of *myself, as men see me*, but the reverse judgments (women's judgments of *men in general* and men's *myself, as women see me*) were unrelated. This finding suggests that women are more aware and concerned than men about how others see them. They decode the outgroup's feelings about them as individual persons, while detecting that those feelings are stamped with collective, stereotypical beliefs about women in general. Another, related study testified to the higher sensitivity to the intergroup relationship that is credited to women in the non-verbal domain (Lorenzi-Cioldi, 2002a). Women with inexpressive faces were consensually perceived as *anxious* and *timorous*, whereas when holding a smiling expression they were perceived as *assured* and *relieved*. These characteristics bring women's other-directness to light. For men, the corresponding perceptions comprised more descriptive, ego-oriented characteristics, such as *sad* and *happy*. However, as expected on grounds of oppression theories, gender differences of this kind are largely contingent upon the differential distribution of the sexes in high- and low-status positions: men and women are more similar as long as they share the same positions in a status hierarchy (e.g., Diekman & Eagly, 2000; Moskowitz, Suh, & Desaulniers, 1994; Snodgrass, 1985).

Oppression theories also account for asymmetries in perceptions of intragroup variability. Low-status and minority group members often judge the ingroup as less variable than they judge the higher-status outgroup (see Lorenzi-Cioldi, 1998; Rubin, Hewstone, Crisp, Voci, & Richards, 2004). Advocates of different, competing explanations of group homogeneity phenomena agree on oppression-based interpretations of this deviation from the outgroup effect. Park and Rothbart (1982), for instance, argued that exceptions to the outgroup homogeneity effect "are certainly plausible, since minorities, by virtue of their relative powerlessness, have to know much more about the dominant group than the dominant group needs to know about the minority" (p. 1052). Park, Ryan, and Judd (1992) similarly maintained that it is functional for members of low-status groups to understand the nuances in the high-status group, and thereby to fragment the outgroup into many subtypes. Likewise, the ingroup familiarity advantage in interpreting the outgroup effect may fall short when low-status groups are concerned. For example, members of ethnic minorities interact frequently, incidentally and involuntarily, with members of the majority. Hence, they may not perceive more diversity in their group than in the outgroup (Guinote, 2001).

Extending these interpretations, Lorenzi-Cioldi hypothesized that the tendency to ascribe internal variability to high-status groups is contingent upon the salience of the group status differentials. Experiments using gender (Lorenzi-Cioldi, Eagly, & Stewart, 1995) and years of college education (Lorenzi-Cioldi, Deaux, & Dafflon, 1998) as status cues, as well as minimal status manipulations (Lorenzi-Cioldi, 2005), have consistently shown that the individuation of the high-status group gains robustness with the increase of the perceptual salience of the status hierarchy.

In sum, oppression dynamics account for shifts from categorical and depersonalized perception to more individuated, personalized perception of those endowed with status or power. Members of low-status groups individuate their outgroups as much as, and often more than, they individuate their own groups. Conversely, members of higher-status groups lack the need, motive, or utility to attend to personal idiosyncrasies in a consensually devalued outgroup. Most often, they proceed no further than group membership when thinking of its members.

Social attribution

People display a pervasive tendency to underscore dispositional forces as opposed to situational forces in explaining a target's behaviors (e.g., the *ultimate attribution error*: see Gilbert & Malone, 1995). This tendency downplays the target's collective attributes for his/her unique and disparate qualities, offering the perceivers cues for individuation.

However, there are a number of moderators for this tendency to stress internal explanations. First, it is relatively more pronounced in Western cultures, where people attempt to conform to the prototype of a person who is free from role constraints (Miller, 1984). Second, the use of internal explanations is contingent upon group status. Members of high-status groups attribute personal success and failure to internal factors (ability or inability: Whitley, McHugh, & Frieze, 1986), and favor individualist over structural explanations of social inequality, poverty and wealth (Bullock & Limbert, 2003). Concomitantly, members of these groups, for instance people who earn a high income (Johannesen-Schmidt & Eagly, 2002) and successful schoolchildren (Dubois & Beauvois, 1996), are consensually credited with more positive (e.g., intelligent, skillful) and negative (arrogant, egoistical) dispositions than their counterparts. Lee and Tiedens (2001) further demonstrated that when members of high-status groups make external attributions of undesirable behaviors, they are blamed for violating the expectation that they have personal control over their actions. They thus favor internal causes for their behaviors in order to avoid conveying the impression of powerlessness. Conversely, external causes may have self-protective properties for stigmatized and subordinate people (see Major, Quinton, & McCoy, 2002). Overall, these findings replicate a recurrent pattern of attributions in status relationships: on the one hand, members of high-status groups make more use of dispositional explanations than members of low-status groups (e.g., Beauvois, Gilibert, Pansu, & Abdelaoui, 1998); on the other hand, behaviors enacted by members of high-status groups are often explained by internal and enduring dispositions rather than external factors (Erber & Fiske, 1984; Thibaut & Riecken, 1955).

Attribution of a behavior to internal causes ensues from and emphasizes the target's idiosyncrasies and, eventually, the perceptual variability of the target's membership group. These attributions dwell on personal characteristics, and sustain the belief that individuals matter more than the group. "[The contemporary social psychological] hero", wrote Kitzinger (1992), "is the internally controlled person who attributes individual success or failure to personal merit or demerit, rather than seeking an explanation which derives from social structure or external power" (p. 232). This hero is likely to be the prototypical member of a high-status group.

Covariation of the personal and the collective

It is usually assumed that when identifying with a group, people emphasize similarities with other ingroup members as well as differences between the ingroup and a relevant outgroup (the "meta-contrast" principle: see Turner et al., 1987, pp. 46ff). However, though the literature is replete with demonstrations of the outgroup differentiation process, it lacks compelling support for the supposedly parallel process of ingroup assimilation. For instance,

McAuliffe, Jetten, Hornsey, and Hogg (2004) showed that individuals may display strong acceptance of intragroup diversity without sacrificing group commitment and loyalty (see also Jetten & Postmes, Chapter 7 in this volume). Judd and Park (1988) found that when members of minimal groups anticipate intergroup competition they judge their competitors as a homogeneous entity while displaying better memory for individual competitors. Fiske and Neuberg (1990) showed that participants' attention and memory for individuating attributes of a target are not hampered by increased salience of the target's group membership. In fact, there is a fair amount of evidence for the concomitance of differentiation at the collective and the personal level: people tend to develop an awareness of their membership groups and their own unique qualities in parallel (see Doise, 1988). This concomitance has been documented in a variety of domains, for instance bargaining strategies (Stephenson, 1981), preferences for social change strategies (Elder, 1971), and adolescents' affiliation in peer groups (Palmonari, Rubini, & Graziani, 2003).

This research suggests that personal and collective forms of self-identification do not adequately depict individual behavior when they are understood as alternatives. It thus warrants the prediction that when group members are granted a mark of uniqueness, they do not relinquish intergroup differentiation. A crucial factor of a person's sense of uniqueness is her/his name. Deschamps (1984) created minimal groups in which participants were, or were not, identified by their first name. Participants favored themselves against other ingroup members more in the condition in which they had received this mark of uniqueness. Of particular relevance is that, in this condition, they also engaged in stronger intergroup discrimination. Thus, emphasis on group members' uniqueness did not entail de-emphasis of group behavior. To interpret these results, Deschamps posited a "covariation principle" by which interpersonal differentiation is positively related (and not antagonistic) to intergroup differentiation. Other accounts of this coexistence of the personal and the collective have been proposed, e.g., the *integration* model (Reid & Deaux, 1996), *optimal distinctiveness* theory (Brewer, 1991; also Pickett & Leonardelli, Chapter 4 in this volume), the *egocentric categorization* model (Simon, 1993), and the *primus inter pares* effect (Codol, 1984). However, none of these accounts are aimed at explaining discrepancies in identity configurations as a function of the individuals' location in the social hierarchy. It is the contention here that the concomitance of the personal and the collective typically occurs in the higher strata of society. To illustrate, high-status people tend to draw more distinctions between groups than low-status people – in terms of race, gender, and social class. At the same time, however, they are less likely to conceive of these groups as homogeneous and undifferentiated entities (see Jackman & Senter, 1980).

Commenting on Deschamps' (1984) findings, Lorenzi-Cioldi (1988) speculated that the author's experimental paradigm actually elicited groups of different status: the individuated group typified a collection, whereas the deindividuated group typified an aggregate. This speculation is compatible with Thibaut's (1950) pioneering manipulation of status differentials, in which the members of the low-status group were openly addressed by code numbers instead of by name, and thus were denied a mark of uniqueness. Lorenzi-Cioldi (1988; see also Lorenzi-Cioldi & Doise, 1990) hypothesized that covariation of the personal and the collective would occur only among the higher-status group, i.e., men. In a typical experiment, participants were assigned to an individuated (i.e., collection) or a depersonalized (aggregate) minimal group. They then allocated points to individual ingroup and outgroup members, or to the groups themselves. The results showed that men, but not women, engaged in stronger intergroup differentiation when they had been assigned to an individuated group, and when they were assigning points to individuals. These results support the idea that individuation leads members of the higher-status group to emphasize the collective by increasing intergroup differentiation.

Suggestive evidence for the complicity between a group membership status and the group members' feelings of uniqueness comes from correlational research. Fiske, Haslam, and Fiske (1991) observed that misnaming errors in interpersonal relations are more likely to occur when the person making the error is of higher status than the target person. Zweigenhaft (1970) found that a person's signature size (height multiplied by length), which according to the author varies as a function of people's motivation to assert their uniqueness, is positively related to the person's status (professor vs student vs blue collar worker, in a large university). Taking issue over the typical finding that unusual names have a negative impact on people, Zweigenhaft (1977) further demonstrated that such names may have positive consequences for members of high-status groups. At the top of status hierarchies, he advocated, "an unusually named child might indeed think he is different from the other children with common names, but he also would come to realize that he is different in desirable ways ... In this situation, having an unusual name might simply emphasize one of the advantageous qualities of his life: that he is different from (and, he might assume, 'above') the rest of the herd" (p. 294). To test the hypothesis that high-status people with atypical names might actually be encouraged to do exceptional things, Zweigenhaft randomly selected 2,000 adult male names from a catalogue of the members of the American upper class (*The Social Register*). He then counted how many people with an unusual name (that is, all names that occurred only once in the 2,000), compared to a matched group of common named peers, appeared in the *Who's Who*. The results showed that many more of those with an unusual first name appear in this catalogue of people holding "positions of responsibility" and demonstrating "conspicuous achievement".

Commenting on Codol's (1984) research on the *over-conformity effect* – that members of a group achieve simultaneous assimilation and differentiation from others by competing to conform more than the other group members to the ingroup norm – Tajfel (1982) conceded that "powerful group affiliations or identifications are capable of a robust persistence despite the vagaries of intense likes and dislikes felt towards some or many members of the ingroup" (p. 504). Turner (1999) likewise acknowledged that "in many situations there will be factors making for the salience of both the personal and the social categorical levels of self-definition" (p. 11). It is noteworthy that Hirschman, who coined the distinction between "exit" and "voice" behaviors (1970) which represented a major source for Tajfel's personal–social identity continuum, has ultimately asserted (1995) the possibility that these principles might coexist. In line with the present status argument, however, the concomitance of collective categories of membership and personal characteristics in an individual's identity is more likely to occur at the top end of social hierarchies (Lorenzi-Cioldi, 1998), or in otherwise advantaged groups, such as numerical majorities (e.g., Brewer & Weber, 1994) and powerful groups (Dépret & Fiske, 1999).

Ideology

Members of dominant groups have a vested interest in dismissing their group membership. This neglect of shared, collective attributes may be regarded as the outcome of a strategy to legitimize one's rewards and privileges by advocating that they stem from personal merit (competency, hard work, adherence to moral values) rather than group membership *per se*. A person's social status is most often conceived of as an achieved characteristic, that is the outcome of the person's efforts and actions, not as an ascribed characteristic (Rosenberg & Pearlin, 1978). As a result, the basic unit of the representation of the collective is the person, not the group. Accordingly, the dominants tend to develop a "groupless" perception of themselves.

Furthermore, the dominants strive to interpret this individuated self-perception as evidence of a fluid, classless society. Jackman and Senter (1980) found a general tendency for men, white Americans, and persons with high socioeconomic status to hold a view of the social structure based on individuals' achievements, and a tendency for the respective low-status outgroups to perceive it in more dualistic, categorical terms. Lorenzi-Cioldi and Joye (1988) further demonstrated that people high in occupational status and educational background sort occupations along a continuum with an autonomy pole and a dependence pole (e.g., craftsman vs office worker), whereas low-status people classify occupations in relatively dichotomous and homogeneous classes which uncover status oppositions (low-income vs high-income and blue collar vs white collar occupations). Marques, Lorenzi-Cioldi, and Seixas (2004) provided experimental evidence for the tendency of the dominants to develop a piecemeal representation of the collective. Members of a high-status minimal group (participants with a high level of creativity according to a bogus test) rejected deviant ingroup and outgroup members to an equal extent, whereas members of the low-status group (low in creativity) rejected the deviant ingroup member more strongly than the deviant outgroup member (i.e., the "black sheep effect": see also Hornsey, Chapter 5 in this volume). Hence, advantaged people rely on interpersonal comparisons across group boundaries, whereas the disadvantaged confine themselves to intergroup comparisons. In this process, a more homogeneous low-status than high-status group emerges.

The dominants attempt to transform group-based inequality into psychological, immutable inequality by promoting the concept of a society that is made up of loosely related individuals who are striving for status improvement according to individual merit. Hence, they see the lower position of the outgroup in the status hierarchy as the legitimate consequence of its members' personal deficiencies and inadequacies. In a series of questionnaire studies carried out in organizations, Lorenzi-Cioldi (2002a) showed that managers and supervisors, compared to employees, judged the occupational hierarchy as permeable. Moreover, across the workforce, such an individualist belief was positively related with feelings of the legitimacy and the instability of the occupational hierarchy. These data speak for the pivotal role played by the permeability factor in the legitimization of status inequality. When people assume (realistically or not) that they can improve their individual condition by moving into a higher-status group, they infer that the hierarchy is fair, and that the accumulation of these individual moves will eventually facilitate a change of the status hierarchy itself. This observation is compatible with Lalonde and Silverman's (1994) and Wright, Taylor, and Moghaddam's (1990) findings of an overwhelming preference for individual rather than collective action. It is also compatible with Ellemers' (2001) finding that beliefs in a hierarchy's permeability are conducive to group identification in high-status groups, and to disidentification in low-status groups. The subordinates' prospect of a fluid society, and their awareness that they are attributed, here and there, token positions of high prestige, promote illusions of individual mobility that deemphasize feelings of common fate and common plight, and this reduces commitment to collective action (Augoustinos, 1999; Tajfel & Turner, 1979; Taylor, Wright, Moghaddam, & Lalonde, 1990; Wright, 2001).

There are additional, related arguments for the dominants' tendency to promote feelings of personal uniqueness and to stress intragroup diversity. First, by publicizing a fragmented image of their group, the dominants quell their visibility as a social force. In so far as they behave by means of "a series of uncoordinated though similar individual acts no one of which has more than short-run significance" (Blalock, 1967, p. 160), they protect themselves from the outgroup's attempts to attack or threaten their social position. Second, the dominants' heterogeneity may enhance the credibility of their opinions and secure the group members' attempt to influence the subordinates. "A greater degree of ingroup variability preempts an adversary's discounting the agreement among ingroup members as being due to some common bias" (Mullen & Hu, 1989, p. 234).

As Tajfel (1981) claimed, ideology is one of the most pervasive forces that guide social behavior. As yet, however, empirical support for its role in intergroup dynamics is scant. Nonetheless, the research just mentioned suggests various ways in which ideology intervenes to legitimize the status quo and to perpetuate group status inequalities. By endowing the dominants with an image of themselves as a shapeless collection of unique individuals, each possessing peculiar dispositions and competencies, and by downgrading the subordinates to an aggregate of faceless individuals, ideology sets the standards of distinct pathways to social identification.

Concluding remarks

The judgment that the dominants are hardly known as visible and discernible groups was already expressed by de Tocqueville, who noted that "The poor are strongly and enduringly united among themselves, but the rich are not. Though there are rich men, the class of rich men does not exist; for these rich individuals have no feeling or purposes, no traditions or hopes, in common; there are individuals, therefore, but no definite class" (1835/1986, p. 538). Almost two centuries later, de Tocqueville's allusion to the impact of a group's positioning in the social structure on its internal variability is still topical. This difference between variable and homogeneous groups, I have claimed, is partly contingent on group status. In low-status or aggregate groups, the collective takes precedence over the personal. In high-status or collection groups, the personal predominates over the collective, and allows individuals to mingle with the group without relinquishing their unique qualities and without confusing one another.

This chapter attests to the multiplicity of the causes underlying the differential salience of personal and collective identity among dominants and subordinates. When combined, research on cultural values, oppression, social attribution, covariation, and ideology supports the assumption of a greater salience of personal identity in high-status groups, and implies the opposite phenomenon of a greater depersonalization of self-perception in low-status groups. Each of these interpretations points to a mechanism that contributes to this difference between identification processes in high-status and low-status groups. I have no answer, at this point, as regards to the relative importance of each interpretation. This question is further complicated by the fact that these mechanisms are related to each other in several ways. To illustrate this point, we can think of oppression and ideology dynamics. It is likely that attentional asymmetries ensuing from status discrepancies are boosted when low-status people hold a merito-cratic view of society, which confers at least some degree of permeability to the status structure. In these circumstances, learning about the dominants may indicate anticipatory socialization processes by which lower-status people get ready for mobility attempts.

More generally, the present status model seeks to add to our understanding of social identification processes by calling attention to social structural variables that are too often neglected in current social identity models (see Greenwood, 2004). The two perspectives stress different variables. Within the theoretical tradition of self-categorization, the personal and the collective self are associated with conflicting levels of inclusiveness ("me vs not-me" and "us vs them" categorizations, respectively). This theory then emphasizes shifts in the content of self-perception as a function of the contextual salience of one or the other level. The present status perspective highlights similar differences in the content of self-perception. But it predicts that these differences are a function of a more distal, enduring, and consensually defined property of the social structure, namely group status.

Reference to group status and to the individuals' beliefs about the nature of status differences was unequivocal in early formulations of social identity theory. Tajfel and Turner (1979), for instance, imparted to the continuum they named *social mobility versus social change* a causal role in relation to the personal–social identity discrepancy. Social mobility refers to belief in a flexible and permeable society which allows people to move on an individual basis from one group into another group. As I have pointed out in this chapter, such individualist beliefs are pervasive in society at large, yet even more so among the dominants. In light of this stronger accessibility of the personal self for members of high-status groups, Tajfel's interpersonal–intergroup continuum can be applied not to antagonistic sources of an individual's identity (either the individual or the group), but to qualitatively distinct processes of social identification that are contingent on the positions of the membership groups in the status hierarchy.

Other researchers have raised doubts about how general the depersonalization process proposed by self-categorization theory really is. On the one hand, this notion has been criticized for disregarding motivational, normative, or societal pressures to emphasize individual uniqueness. For instance, Hinkle and Brown (1990) distinguished between groups that are individualist and groups that are collectivist. They maintained that "the kinds of social identity processes conceived of in social identity theory are most readily applicable to collectivist kinds of groups" (p. 66). Dasgupta, Banaji, and Abelson (1999) argued that a cultural preference for individual autonomy, and the conviction that membership in groups inevitably involves the loss of individuality, may lead people to confer more value to variegated than to entitative groups. On the other hand, empirical work has shown that depersonalization is not the only means to social identification. For instance, Hogg (1993) observed that there may be more than one way to construe group prototypes – the representations of the features that best define a group in a salient intergroup context. Consistent with self-categorization theory, group prototypes often consist of undifferentiated ideal types, that is, "a relatively nebulous abstraction of group features" (p. 93). But, as the author contends, they can also consist of individual exemplars, that is, "actual group members who embody the group" (p. 93). Likewise, Prentice, Miller, and Lightdale (1994) distinguished between groups based on interpersonal bonds (e.g., a group of friends), and groups based on members' attachment to a shared, superordinate, symbolic identity (people meeting around a common activity). Such suggestions bear links with the characterization of collection and aggregate types of groups. But the present argument assigns the social structure a position of causal priority in the emergence of these representations of the collective. Low-status, subordinate, minority and stigmatized groups most adequately exemplify the depersonalization of the self. Conversely, high-status groups are more readily judged as an assortment of people, each one possessing his or her own personal characteristics.

For over a decade or so, social psychology has witnessed a growing interest in research that shows the multiplicity of representations of groups, for instance as a function of their entitativity (e.g., Yzerbyt, Judd, & Corneille, 2004), the intimacy of their members' interactions (Prentice, Miller, & Lightdale, 1994), or the prevailing style of relationship among the group members (Fiske, 1992). Likewise, more effort is currently devoted to investigating the dimensionality of the identity concept (Ashmore, Deaux, & McLaughlin-Volpe, 2004) and the diversity of the functions of social identification (Aharpour & Brown, 2002). The ensuing picture is that a person's identity, in so far as it describes the link between the individual and the entire society, follows more complex pathways than a mere bifurcation of the personal and the collective. This chapter has paved the way for a comprehensive theory of identity phenomena, by showing how processes related to identity formation cannot ignore the issue of group status.

NOTE

Correspondence to: Fabio Lorenzi-Cioldi, Faculté de Psychologie et des Sciences de l'Éducation, Uni Mail, 40, Boulevard du Pont d'Arve, CH–1205 Genève, Switzerland, Fabio.Lorenzi-Cioldi@pse.unige.ch.

REFERENCES

Aharpour, S., & Brown, R. (2002). Functions of group identification: An exploratory analysis. *Revue Internationale de Psychologie Sociale*, *15*, 157–186.

Allport, G. W. (1954). *The nature of prejudice*. London: Addison-Wesley.

Apfelbaum, E. (1979). Relations of domination and movements for liberation: An analysis of power between groups. In S. Worchel & W. Austin (Eds.), *The social psychology of intergroup relations* (pp. 188–204). Chicago: Nelson-Hall.

Ashmore, R. D., Deaux, K., & McLaughlin-Volpe, T. (2004). An organizing framework for collective identity: Articulation and significance of multidimensionality. *Psychological Bulletin*, *130*, 80–114.

Augoustinos, M. (1999). Ideology, false consciousness, and psychology. *Theory & Psychology*, *9*, 295–312.

Beauvois, J. -L. (1994). *Traité de la servitude libérale: Analyse de la soumission*. Paris: Dunod.

Beauvois, J. -L., Gilibert, D., Pansu, P., & Abdelaoui, S. (1998). Internality attribution and intergroup relations. *European Journal of Social Psychology*, *28*, 123–140.

Blalock, H. M. (1967). *Toward a theory of minority group relations*. New York: Wiley.

Bourdieu, P., & de Saint Martin, M. (1978). Le patronat. *Actes de la Recherche en Sciences Sociales*, *20–21*, 3–82.

Brewer, M. (1991). The social self: On being the same and different at the same time. *Personality and Social Psychology Bulletin*, *17*, 475–482.

Brewer, M. B., & Gardner, W. (1996). Who is this "we"? Levels of collective identity and self representations. *Journal of Personality and Social Psychology*, *71*, 83–93.

Brewer, M. B., & Weber, J. G. (1994). Self-evaluation effects of interpersonal versus intergroup social comparison. *Journal of Personality and Social Psychology*, *66*, 268–275.

Bullock, H. E., & Limbert, W. M. (2003). Scaling the socioeconomic ladder: Low-income women's perceptions of class status and opportunity. *Journal of Social Issues*, *59*, 693–709.

Codol, J. -P. (1984). Social differentiation and non-differentiation. In H. Tajfel (Ed.), *The social dimension* (vol. 1, pp. 314–337). Cambridge: Cambridge University Press.

Dahrendorf, R. (1964). The education of an elite: Law faculties and the German upper class. In P. Lazarsfeld & T. H. Marshall (Eds.), *Transactions of the Fifth World Congress of Sociology* (pp. 259–274). Louvain: ISA.

Dasgupta, N., Banaji, M. R., & Abelson, R. P. (1999). Group entitativity and group perception: Associations between physical features and psychological judgment. *Journal of Personality and Social Psychology*, *77*, 991–1003.

DeMott, B. (1990). *The imperial middle: Why Americans can't think straight about class*. New York: Morrow.

Dépret, E., & Fiske, S. (1999). Perceiving the powerful: Intriguing individuals versus threatening groups. *Journal of Experimental Social Psychology*, *35*, 461–480.

Deschamps, J. -C. (1982). Social identity and relations of power between groups. In H. Tajfel (Ed.), *Social identity and intergroup relations* (pp. 85–98). Cambridge: Cambridge University Press.

Deschamps, J. -C. (1984). Identité sociale et différenciations catégorielles. *Cahiers de Psychologie Cognitive, 4,* 449–474.

Deschamps, J. -C., Lorenzi-Cioldi, F., & Meyer, G. (1982). *L'échec scolaire [Doing badly at school].* Lausanne: Favre.

De Tocqueville, A. (1835/1986). *De la démocratie en Amérique [Democracy in America].* Paris: Laffont.

Diekman, A. B., & Eagly, A. H. (2000). Stereotypes as dynamic constructs: Women and men of the past, present, and future. *Personality and Social Psychology Bulletin, 26,* 1171–1188.

Doise, W. (1988). Individual and social identities in intergroup relations. *European Journal of Social Psychology, 18,* 99–111.

Dubois, N., & Beauvois, J. L. (1996). Internality, academic status and intergroup attributions. *European Journal of Psychology of Education, 11,* 329–341.

Eagly, A. H. (1987). *Sex differences in social behavior: A social-role interpretation.* Hillsdale, NJ: Erlbaum.

Elder, G. H. (1971). Intergroup attitudes and social ascent among Negro boys. *The American Journal of Sociology, 76,* 673–697.

Ellemers, N. (2001). Individual upward mobility and the perceived legitimacy of intergroup relations. In J. T. Jost & B. Major (Eds.), *The psychology of legitimacy* (pp. 205–222). Cambridge: Cambridge University Press.

Ellyson, S. L., & Dovidio, J. F. (1985). Power, dominance, and nonverbal behavior: Basic concepts and issues. In S. L. Ellyson & J. F. Dovidio (Eds.), *Power, dominance, and nonverbal behavior* (pp. 1–27). New York: Springer.

Erber, R., & Fiske, S. (1984). Outcome dependency and attention to inconsistent information. *Journal of Personality and Social Psychology, 47,* 709–726.

Fiske, A. P. (1992). The four elementary forms of sociality: Framework for a unified theory of social relations. *Psychological Review, 99,* 689–723.

Fiske, A. P., Haslam, N., & Fiske, S. (1991). Confusing one person with another: What errors reveal about the elementary forms of social relations. *Journal of Personality and Social Psychology, 60,* 656–674.

Fiske, S. T. (1993). Controlling other people. The impact of power on stereotyping. *American Psychologist, 48,* 621–628.

Fiske, S. T. (1998). Stereotyping, prejudice and discrimination. In D. T. Gilbert, S. T. Fiske, & G. Lindzey (Eds.), *The handbook of social psychology* (vol. 2, pp. 357–411). New York: Oxford University Press.

Fiske, S. T., & Neuberg, S. L. (1990). A continuum model of impression formation, from category-based to individuating processes: Influence of information and motivation on attention and interpretation. In M. P. Zanna (Ed.), *Advances in experimental social psychology* (vol. 23, pp. 1–74). San Diego: Academic.

Fiske, S. T., Xu, J., Cuddy, A. C., & Glick, P. (1999). (Dis)respecting versus (dis)liking: Status and interdependence predict ambivalent stereotypes of competence and warmth. *Journal of Social Issues, 55,* 473–489.

Gilbert, D. T., & Malone, P. S. (1995). The correspondence bias. *Psychological Bulletin, 117,* 21–38.

Greenwood, J. D. (2004). *The disappearance of the social in American social psychology.* Cambridge: Cambridge University Press.

Guillaumin, C. (1972). *L'idéologie raciste: Genèse et langage actuel [The racist ideology].* Paris: Mouton.

Guinote, A. (2001). The perception of group variability in a non-minority and a minority context: When adaptation leads to outgroup differentiation. *British Journal of Social Psychology, 40,* 117–132.

Hinkle, S., & Brown, R. (1990). Intergroup comparisons and social identity: some links and lacunae. In D. Abrams & M. A. Hogg (Eds.), *Social identity theory: Constructive and critical advances* (pp. 48–70). London: Harvester Wheatsheaf.

Hirschman, A. O. (1970). *Exit, voice, and loyalty: Responses to decline in firms, organizations and states.* London: Harvard University Press.

Hirschman, A. O. (1995). *A propensity to self-subversion.* Harvard: Harvard College.

Hogg, M. A. (1993). Group cohesiveness: A critical review and some new directions. *European Review of Social Psychology, 4,* 85–111.

Hoggart, R. (1957). *The uses of literacy.* London: Chatto & Windus.

Hurtig, M. -C., Pichevin, M. -F., & Piolat, M. (1992). Sex and age as factors of asymmetry in the perceived similarity between two persons: A study designed by J. -P. Codol. In L. Arcuri & C. Serino (Eds.), *Asymmetry phenomena in interpersonal comparison: Cognitive and social issues* (pp. 71–85). Naples: Liguori.

Jackman, M. R., & Jackman, R. W. (1973). An interpretation of the relation between objective and subjective social status. *American Sociological Review, 38,* 569–582.

Jackman, M. R., & Senter, M. S. (1980). Images of social groups: Categorical or qualified? *Public Opinion Quarterly, 44,* 341–361.

Jetten, J., Postmes, T., & McAuliffe, B. J. (2002). "We're *all* individuals": Group norms of individualism and collectivism, levels of identification and identity threat. *European Journal of Social Psychology, 32,* 189–207.

Johannesen-Schmidt, M. C., & Eagly, A. H. (2002). Diminishing returns: The effects of income on the content of stereotypes of wage earners. *Personality and Social Psychology Bulletin, 28,* 1538–1545.

Judd, C. M., & Park, B. (1988). Out-group homogeneity: Judgments of variability at the individual and group levels. *Journal of Personality and Social Psychology, 54,* 778–788.

Keltner, D., Gruenfeld, D. H., & Anderson, C. (2003). Power, approach, and inhibition. *Psychological Review, 110,* 265–284.

Kitzinger, C. (1992). The individuated self concept: A critical analysis of social-constructionist writing on individualism. In G. M. Breakwell (Ed.), *Social psychology of identity and the self-concept* (pp. 221–250). London: Surrey University Press.

LaFrance, M., & Henley, N. M. (1994). On oppressing hypotheses: Or differences in non-verbal sensitivity revisited. In H. L. Radke & H. J. Stam (Eds.), *Power/gender: Social relations in theory and practice* (pp. 287–311). London: Sage.

Lalonde, R. N., and Silverman, R. A. (1994). Behavioral preferences in response to social injustice: The effects of permeability and social identity salience. *Journal of Personality and Social Psychology, 66,* 78–85.

Lee, F., & Tiedens, L. Z. (2001). Who's being served? "Self-serving" attributions in social hierarchies. *Organizational Behavior and Human Decision Processes, 84,* 254–287.

Lewin, K. (1948). *Resolving social conflicts.* New York: Harper.

Lorenzi-Cioldi, F. (1988). *Individus dominants et groupes dominés [Dominant individuals and dominated groups].* Grenoble: Presses Universitaires.

Lorenzi-Cioldi, F. (1991). Self-enhancement and self-stereotyping in gender groups. *European Journal of Social Psychology, 21,* 403–417.

Lorenzi-Cioldi, F. (1993). They all look alike, but so do we, sometimes ... Perception of in-group and out-group homogeneity as a function of gender and context. *British Journal of Social Psychology, 32,* 111–124.

Lorenzi-Cioldi, F. (1994). *Les androgynes [The androgynous person].* Paris: Presses Universitaires de France.

Lorenzi-Cioldi, F. (1998). Group status and perceptions of homogeneity. In W. Stroebe & M. Hewstone (Eds.), *European review of social psychology* (vol. 9, pp. 31–75). Chichester: Wiley.

Lorenzi-Cioldi, F. (2001). The when and the why of how: From mental representations to social representations. In K. Deaux & G. Philogène (Eds.), *Representations of the social: Bridging theoretical traditions* (pp. 217–227). Oxford: Blackwell.

Lorenzi-Cioldi, F. (2002a). *Les représentations des groupes dominants et dominés: Collections et agrégats [Social representations of dominants and subordinates: Collections and aggregates]*. Grenoble: Presses Universitaires.

Lorenzi-Cioldi, F. (2002b). *Expériences sur les groupes dominants et dominés: Les perceptions de l'homogénéité des groupes [Experiments on dominants and subordinates: Perceptions of group homogeneity]*. Bern: Lang.

Lorenzi-Cioldi, F. (2005). Group homogeneity perception in status hierarchies. Submitted for publication.

Lorenzi-Cioldi, F., Deaux, K., & Dafflon, A. (1998). Group homogeneity as a function of relative social status. *Swiss Journal of Psychology*, *57*, 255–273.

Lorenzi-Cioldi, F., & Doise, W. (1990). Levels of analysis and social identity. In D. Abrams & M. A. Hogg (Eds.), *Social identity theory: Constructive and critical advances* (pp. 71–88). London: Harvester/Wheatsheaf.

Lorenzi-Cioldi, F., & Doise, W. (1994). Identité sociale et identité personnelle. In R. Y. Bourhis & J. -Ph. Leyens (Eds.), *Stéréotypes, discrimination et relations entre groupes [Stereotypes, discrimination, and intergroup relations]* (pp. 69–96). Liège: Mardaga.

Lorenzi-Cioldi, F., Eagly, A. H., & Stewart, T. (1995). Homogeneity of gender groups in memory. *Journal of Experimental Social Psychology*, *31*, 193–217.

Lorenzi-Cioldi, F., & Joye, D. (1988). Représentations de catégories socio-profession-nelles: Aspects méthodologiques. *Bulletin de Psychologie*, *40*, 377–390.

Lott, B. (2002). Cognitive and behavioral distancing from the poor. *American Psychologist*, *57*, 100–110.

Major, B., Quinton, W. J., & McCoy, S. K. (2002). Antecedents and consequences of attributions to discrimination: Theoretical and empirical advances. In M. P. Zanna (Ed.), *Advances in experimental social psychology* (pp. 251–330). New York: Academic.

Marques, J., Lorenzi-Cioldi, F., & Seixas, E. (2004). Pouvoir, statut et déviance. Paper presented at the 5ème Congrès International de Psychologie Sociale en Langue Française. University of Lausanne, Switzerland, September.

McAuliffe, B. J., Jetten, J., Hornsey, M. J., & Hogg, M. A. (2004). Differentiation between and within groups: The influence of individualist and collectivist group norms. Submitted for publication.

Miller, J. B. (1984). Culture and the development of everyday explanation. *Journal of Personality and Social Psychology*, *46*, 961–978.

Millett, D. (1981). Defining the "dominant group". *Canadian Ethnic Studies*, *13*, 64–80.

Moscovici, S., & Paicheler, G. (1978). Social comparison and social recognition: Two complementary processes of identification. In H. Tajfel (Ed.), *Differentiation between social groups* (pp. 251–266). London: Academic.

Moskowitz, D. S., Suh, E. J., & Desaulniers, J. (1994). Situational influences on gender differences in agency and communion. *Journal of Personality and Social Psychology*, *66*, 753–761.

Mullen, B., & Hu, L. (1989). Perceptions of ingroup and outgroup variability: A meta-analytic integration. *Basic and Applied Social Psychology*, *10*, 233–252.

Oakes, P. J., Haslam, S. A., & Turner, J. C. (1994). *Stereotyping and social reality*. Oxford: Blackwell.

Palmonari, A., Rubini, M., & Graziani, A. (2003). The perceived importance of group functions in adolescent peer groups. *New Review of Social Psychology, 1*, 60–67.

Park, B., & Rothbart, M. (1982). Perception of out-group homogeneity and levels of social categorization: Memory for the subordinate attributes of in-group and out-group members. *Journal of Personality and Social Psychology, 42*, 1051–1068.

Park, B., Ryan, C. S., & Judd, C. M. (1992). Role of meaningful subgroups in explaining differences in perceived variability for in-groups and out-groups. *Journal of Personality and Social Psychology, 63*, 553–567.

Pichevin, M. -F., & Hurtig, M. -C. (1996). Describing men, describing women: Sex membership salience and numerical distinctiveness. *European Journal of Social Psychology, 26*, 513–522.

Prentice, D. A., Miller, D. T., & Lightdale, J. R. (1994). Asymmetries in attachments to groups and to their members: Distinguishing between common-identity and common-bond groups. *Personality and Social Psychology Bulletin, 20*, 484–493.

Reid, A., & Deaux, K. (1996). Relationship between social and personal identity: Segregation or integration? *Journal of Personality and Social Psychology, 71*, 1084–1091.

Rosenberg, M., & Pearlin, L. I. (1978). Social class and self-esteem among children and adults. *The American Journal of Sociology, 84*, 53–77.

Rubin, M., Hewstone, M., Crisp, R. J., Voci, A., & Richards, Z. (2004). Gender out-group homogeneity: The roles of differential familiarity, gender differences, and group size. In V. Yzerbyt, C. M. Judd, & O. Corneille (Eds.), *The psychology of group perception: Perceived variability, entitativity, and essentialism*. New York: Psychology Press.

Sekaquaptewa, D., & Espinoza, P. (2004). Biased processing of stereotype-incongruency is greater for low than high status groups. *Journal of Experimental Social Psychology, 40*, 128–135.

Sennett, R., & Cobb, J. (1972). *The hidden injuries of class*. New York: Norton.

Simon, B. (1993). On the asymmetry in the cognitive construal of ingroup and outgroup: A model of egocentric social categorization. *European Journal of Social Psychology, 23*, 131–147.

Smith, H. J., & Leach, C. W. (2004). Group membership and everyday social comparison experiences. *European Journal of Social Psychology, 34*, 297–308.

Snodgrass, S. E. (1985). Women's intuition: The effect of subordinate role on interpersonal sensitivity. *Journal of Personality and Social Psychology, 49*, 146–155.

Stephenson, G. M. (1981). Intergroup bargaining and negotiation. In J. -C. Turner & H. Giles (Eds.), *Intergroup behavior* (pp. 168–198). Oxford: Blackwell.

Tajfel, H. (Ed.) (1978). *Differentiation between social groups*. New York: Academic.

Tajfel, H. (1981). *Human groups and social categories*. Cambridge: Cambridge University Press.

Tajfel, H. (1982). Instrumentality, identity and social comparison. In H. Tajfel (Ed.), *Social identity and intergroup relations* (pp. 483–507). Cambridge: Cambridge University Press. Paris: Maison des Sciences l'Homme.

Tajfel, H., & Turner, J. C. (1979). The social identity theory of intergroup behavior. In S. Worchel & W. G. Austin (Eds.), *The social psychology of intergroup relations* (pp. 7–24). Chicago: Nelson-Hall.

Taylor, D. M., Wright, S. C., Moghaddam, F. M., & Lalonde, R. N. (1990). The personal/group discrimination discrepancy: Perceiving my group, but not myself, to be a target of discrimination. *Personality and Social Psychology Bulletin, 16*, 254–262.

Thibaut, J. (1950). An experimental study of the cohesiveness of underprivileged groups. *Human Relations, 3*, 251–278.

Thibaut, J., & Riecken, H. W. (1955). Some determinants and consequences of the perception of social causality. *Journal of Personality, 24*, 272–302.

Triandis, H. C. (1994). Theoretical and methodological approaches to the study of collectivism and individualism. In U. Kim, H. C. Triandis, C. Kâgitçibasi, S. -C. Choi, & G. Yoon (Eds.), *Individualism and collectivism* (pp. 41–51). London: Sage.

Turner, J. C. (1999). Some current issues in research on social identity and self-categorization theories. In N. Ellemers, R. Spears, & B. Doosje (Eds.), *Social identity: Context, commitment, content* (pp. 6–34). Oxford: Blackwell.

Turner, J. C., Hogg, M. A., Oakes, P. J., Reicher, S. D., & Wetherell, M. S. (1987). *Rediscovering the social group.* Oxford: Blackwell.

Veblen, T. (1899). *The theory of the leisure class.* New York: Viking.

Vonk, R. (1999). Effects of outcome dependency on correspondence bias. *Personality and Social Psychology Bulletin, 25,* 382–389.

Whitley, B. E., McHugh, M. C., & Frieze, I. H. (1986). Assessing the theoretical models for sex differences in causal attributions of success and failure. In J. S. Hyde & M. C. Lynn (Eds.), *The psychology of gender* (pp. 102–135). Baltimore: Johns Hopkins University Press.

Wright, S. C. (2001). Strategic collective action: Social psychology and social change. In R. Brown & S. Gaertner (Eds.), *Intergroup processes* (pp. 409–430). Oxford: Blackwell.

Wright, S. C., Taylor, D. M., & Moghaddam, F. M. (1990). Responding to membership in a disadvantaged group: From acceptance to collective protest. *Journal of Personality and Social Psychology, 58,* 994–1003.

Yzerbyt, V., Judd, C. M., & Corneille, O. (Eds.) (2004). *The psychology of group perception: Perceived variability, entitativity and essentialism.* New York: Psychology Press.

Zàrate, M. A., & Smith, E. R. (1990). Person categorization and stereotyping. *Social Cognition, 8,* 161–165.

Zweigenhaft, R. L. (1970). Signature size: A key to status awareness. *Journal of Social Psychology, 81,* 49–54.

Zweigenhaft, R. L. (1977). The other side of unusual first names. *Journal of Social Psychology, 103,* 291–302.

7

"I Did It My Way": Collective Expressions of Individualism

Jolanda Jetten and Tom Postmes

En leur reigle n'estoit que ceste clause: Fay ce que vouldras (In their rules there was only one clause: Do what you will). (François Rabelais, 1553, p. 57)

Group life has traditionally been associated with pressure for uniformity and intragroup homogeneity in beliefs, attitudes and behaviour (e.g., Cartwright & Zander, 1953). For instance, Asch (1951) describes how group formation inevitably leads to a shared understanding among group members, which enhances cohesion and reduces differentiation between individual group members. He notes:

> The individual comes to experience a world that he shares with others. He perceives that the surroundings include him, as well as the others, and that he is in the same relations to the surroundings as the others. He notes that he, as well as the other, is converging upon the same object and responding to its identical properties. Joint action and mutual understanding require the relations of intelligibility and structural simplicity. In these terms the "pull" toward the group becomes understandable. (p. 484)

Over the last decades a psychology of groups has emerged that assumes these processes introduce a fundamental tension between the individual self and the collective or social self (see Brown & Turner, 1981; Kampmeier & Simon, 2001; Lois, 1999, for a similar argument). In these perspectives, the need to be true to one's individual self at the same time as one's social self has been described as "a life-long dilemma" (Worchel, 1998, p. 54). Hewitt (1989) notes that the self is construed through pragmatic compromises whereby sometimes personal interests precede and, at other times, collective interests are given priority. It is a small and relatively easy step from this view to the dualist notion that group membership is the key to the collective self whereas the individual self operates and becomes salient in the absence of social influence.

However, it is not only traditional approaches to group processes that propose that there is a "pull towards the group" at the expense of the individual self when social identities become salient. In some cases, readings of social identity theory and self-categorization theory (Tajfel & Turner, 1979; Turner, Hogg, Oakes, Reicher, & Wetherell, 1987) have led researchers to draw similar conclusions. For instance, some researchers suggest that the salience of group identity will necessarily lead to depersonalization and interchangeability of individual group members and to increased perceptions of cohesion. This idea is implicit in the interpersonal–intergroup continuum, a central tenet of social identity theory, which treats personal identity and social identity as polar opposites (Tajfel, 1978). From this, it might appear at first sight that, within a group context, expressions of individuality cannot flow from identity salience.

In this chapter, we challenge this notion and explore the ways in which individualist behaviour within a group can be compatible with, and indeed can be an expression of, a salient group identity. As the quotation by Rabelais suggests, group rules can encourage a person to be independent, and individualism (or even anarchy) can therefore be a form of conformity.[1] Likewise, invitations to be true to one's individual self can be predicated upon social identity and social influence – as they were when Polonius advised his son Laertes "to thine own self be true", the caveat being that this should be within strict parameters established by his father. Similarly, when Frank Sinatra sings "I did it my way", it is clear that cultural values and norms (e.g., relating to the American dream), and social influence, sanction and shape not only the type of individual achievements that are sought out, but also their interpretation and evaluation by others.

In short, we propose that it is the *content* of the identity and the norms attached to this identity that determine the way in which group members express themselves. Just as collectivism, uniformity and interchangeability can flow from identity salience, so too can individual behaviour, deviance within groups and possibly even personal identity salience be the result of conformity to salient group norms. This reasoning is in our view not incompatible with social identity and self-categorization theory, but follows directly from these theories' focus on the context and content of identity (see also Hutchison, Jetten, Christian, & Haycraft, 2005; Reicher, 1996). If we assume that the difference between individual and collective self does not necessarily map onto the individual–group distinction, we can explore how the individual self and collective self can result from identical processes and consider the consequences of this possibility.

This chapter starts with a brief overview of previous attempts of social psychological theories to reconcile the individual and the group. We will then focus on the importance of the content of identity and on norms prescribing group members to be individuals. We start by outlining our theoretical reasoning and by reviewing some empirical support for our ideas before considering the implications and consequences of individualist norms for group processes. In an attempt to elaborate upon the specific implications of self-categorization and social identity theory in this domain, we will present a model of the relation between identity salience and conformity, taking into account the content of group norms. In the remainder of the chapter, we explore (a) the implications and consequences of these ideas for the relationship between the content of norms and well-being, (b) the importance of norms at various stages of group socialization, and (c) the way in which the content of norms can affect the interaction between personal and social identity.

The individual self within the group

The idea that people not only have a fundamental need to belong (Baumeister & Leary, 1995; Manstead, 1997) but also seek individuation has been put forward by a number of researchers (e.g., Breakwell, 1987; Brewer, 1991; Codol, 1984; Snyder & Fromkin, 1980; Vignoles, Chryssochoou, & Breakwell, 2000; Ziller, 1964; see also Hornsey, Chapter 5; Pickett & Leonardelli, Chapter 4 in this volume). Various models have been proposed to explain how people reconcile these two seemingly opposite needs (see Hornsey & Jetten, 2004, for a recent overview). Some models propose that these needs cannot be met at the same level of abstraction. For instance, optimal distinctiveness theory (ODT) proposes that the need for belonging-ness and assimilation is satisfied by adherence to the group whereas the need for distinctiveness is best satisfied by intergroup comparisons and by distancing the ingroup from relevant outgroups (Pickett & Brewer, 2001; cf. Pickett & Leonardelli, Chapter 4 in this volume).

Hornsey and Jetten (2004) identify alternative strategies through which group members can marry salience of the individual self with a sense of strong group identification. First, group members can achieve this if they emphasize the roles that allow them to differentiate themselves from others within categories or a larger social structure (Bettencourt & Sheldon, 2001; see Bettencourt et al., Chapter 11 in this volume). Second, group members may also attempt to act more normatively than other group members do – the *primus inter pares* (PIP) effect described by Codol (1975, 1984; see also Lorenzi-Cioldi, Chapter 6 in this volume). In that way, standing out as an individual is perfectly compatible with strong alignment with group goals. Third, a particular form of the PIP effect occurs when group members empha-size individualization on one dimension and conformity to group norms on another dimension. For example, Hornsey and Jetten (2005) showed that group members may selectively adhere more to cultural or group norms that prescribe independence or non-conformity than to others which prescribe dependence and conformity. In this vein, when comparing self–other discrepancies in people from individualist and collectivist cultures, it was found that members of individualist cultures tend to self-enhance on independence dimensions whereas members of collectivist cultures self-enhance on loyalty dimensions (see also Sedikides, Campbell, Reeder, & Elliot, 2002; Sedikides, Gaertner, & Toguchi, 2003; Sedikides, Gaertner, & Vevea, 2005). Finally, as will be discussed in greater detail below, group identification and salience of the individual self can go hand-in-hand when group norms prescribe group members to give priority to the individual self over the collective self.

Hornsey and Jetten (2004) acknowledge that this list is by no means exhaustive. Moreover, the idea that people can do justice to individualist self-definitions at a collective level is perfectly compatible with social identity theory. It does, however, require greater openness to the idea that it is the *content* of identities that defines and delineates the expression of both personal and social identities (see also Haslam, 2004). When an identity is salient, group members are more likely to act in accordance with the content of the norms and goals attached to that identity, even if the content of those norms appears to violate some fundamental assumptions of what group life involves (Hutchison et al., 2005; Jetten, Postmes, & McAuliffe, 2002). A group norm may encompass behaviours that are compatible with "doing what is good for the group", but at other times they may, at first instance, appear to contradict this (e.g., being critical of the group, deviating and dissenting behaviours: Postmes, Spears, & Cihangir, 2001; see also Hornsey, Chapter 5 in this volume).

Individualism and collectivism as group norms

Following from these ideas, we examined whether the motivation to be a unique individual and the need for belongingness can both be satisfied at the group level by adhering to specific ingroup norms (Jetten et al., 2002). If this were the case, we argued, we could compellingly show that salience of a group identity and individualist self-definition can be compatible and are not mutually exclusive. Following self-categorization theory we reasoned that when a shared social identity becomes salient as a function of comparative fit and accessibility, individuals' self-perceptions become depersonalized (Turner et al., 1987). Hence, differences between self and other ingroup members become less relevant and group members perceive themselves more as interchangeable representatives of the social category than as unique individuals within the group. Similarities with other ingroup members are emphasized and differences from those who do not share group membership are accentuated (Haslam, Oakes, McGarty, Turner, Reynolds, & Eggins, 1996).

In line with self-categorization theory and the model of referent informational influence (Turner, 1982; Turner et al., 1987; see also Hogg & Turner, 1987), we proposed that when people self-categorize as group members (a process also referred to as depersonalization) they take on the norms of a group and use these norms to guide self-definition, attitudes, values and behaviours. Here, a social norm is defined as: "a generally accepted way of thinking, feeling or behaving that is endorsed and expected because it is perceived to be the right and proper thing to do. It is a rule, value or standard shared by members of a social group that prescribes appropriate, expected or desirable attitudes and conduct in matters relevant to the group" (Turner, 1991, p. 3; see also Sherif, 1936). It follows that group members are more likely to use norms as a guide when group membership is salient or when the group is an important part of their self-concept (i.e., as for high identifiers) than when group membership is not salient or is less important to define the self (i.e., as for low identifiers).

Importantly, though, the content of group norms gives meaning to a salient identity, and it shapes the form in which depersonalization manifests itself. That is, comparative fit processes (which determine the dimensions that become salient as a basis for self-definition by maximizing intragroup similarity and intergroup difference) cannot be seen as separate from normative fit processes (relating to the match between content of the category and context). For instance, the categorization West versus East may become salient because differences within these categories are perceived to be smaller than the differences between them (see Tajfel & Wilkes, 1964). However, the content of these identities and knowledge about the way the East and West differ informs this process and can potentially reinforce it (e.g., if politicians encourage us to believe that the West is free and democratic but the East is not). Comparative fit and normative fit processes are thus indivisible and their effects have to be considered in conjunction (Turner, Oakes, Haslam, & McGarty, 1994).

But how does this work when the content of group norms is to be collectivist or individualist? When collectivism is the dominant group norm, group members should be more likely to display collectivist behaviours when group identity is salient or identification is high than when salience or identification is low. In a similar vein, but rather more paradoxically, when the group norms prescribe individualism, high salience of the group identity should lead to more individualist behaviour than when group salience is low (see Jetten et al., 2002). Individualist self-definitions can thus be seen as a manifestation of *group* influence: they are the result of conformity to an individualist group norm. Identity salience resulting in depersonalization and perceptions of interchangeability could therefore result in the shared perception that "we are all unique individuals".

Even though it sounds contradictory at first sight that group norms can be individualist, the phenomenon is quite common in everyday life. For instance, Brown and Williams (1984) studied different subgroups' identification within a bakery and found that some groups held relatively individualist attitudes (e.g., wholesale employees) whereas other groups were relatively collectivist (e.g., bakery workers). Interestingly, these researchers found that such individualist orientations did not undermine group identification and that no differences were found in subgroup identification between collectivist and individualist workgroups (see also Moghaddam, Chapter 9 in this volume). Other groups such as artists, work-teams and even academics can also develop highly individualist group norms where differentiation from other group members is demanded and defined as an essential contribution to the group as a whole. Likewise, cultures have been classified as individualist versus collectivist (Hofstede, 1980; Triandis, 1989; see also Markus & Kitayama, 1991) and these cultural orientations can, in addition to being descriptive, also contain strong prescriptive normative components that form the basis of nationalistic and patriotic expressions (see Halloran & Kashima, Chapter 8 in this volume). For instance, not only is the United States one of the most individualist countries in the world (Hofstede, 1980), but American identity is also expressed through displays of individualism and independence and by embracing individual differentiation ideals. Thus, these cultures collectively express individualism and individualism results from and resides in conformity to cultural norms.

Individualism and collectivism as group norms: empirical evidence

In order to test the above ideas we conducted a series of studies to examine the consequences of individualist or collectivist norms for group members. Three studies were conducted to examine how self-definitions were affected by the content of these norms (Jetten et al., 2002). In the first study, it was found that high identifiers defined themselves as less individualist in a collectivist culture (Indonesia) than low identifiers, but that high identifiers were more individualist than low identifiers in an individualist culture (North America). This pattern was replicated in a second study in which group norms of individualism and collectivism were manipulated. Here we found that high identifiers were more likely to internalize salient group norms prescribing individualism or collectivism as an aspect of their self-concept than low identifiers. In a final study, we also showed that high identifiers conformed more strongly to group norms than low identifiers did, and also were more likely to self-stereotype in line with the salient norm when their group was threatened.

Additional studies showed that individualist and collectivist group norms also affected the acceptance of other group members who showed norm-inconsistent behaviour or deviated from majority group opinion and values (McAuliffe, Jetten, Hornsey, & Hogg, 2003; Hornsey, Jetten, McAuliffe, & Hogg, in press). Generally, it was found that collectivist behaviour by another group member was evaluated more positively than individualist behaviour because the former is more beneficial for the group than the latter. However, when group norms prescribed individualism, it was also found that this preference for collectivist behaviour was attenuated because here individualist behaviour represented normative behaviour. Moreover, the finding that group identification moderated the effects of norms (i.e., high identifiers were more likely to show attenuation in their preference for collectivist behaviour over individualist behaviour) provides evidence that supports the idea that it is conformity to group norms that underlies these effects.

A final series of studies showed that collectivist and individualist group norms also affected the way in which intergroup discrimination was expressed (Jetten, McAuliffe, Hornsey, & Hogg, in press). When group identity was salient, members of collectivist groups displayed more intergroup differentiation than did members of individualist ones. In contrast, participants for whom the group was highly salient showed stronger interindividual differentiation when norms endorsed individualism than when they prescribed collectivism (Study 2).

To summarize, these studies indicate that collectivist and individualist group norms affect self-definition, evaluation of other group members and the expression of discrimination. Conformity to individualist group norms led to more individualist self-definitions, greater acceptance of deviance and dissent by other ingroup members, and increased interindividual bias compared to those situations in which group norms prescribed collectivist behaviour. Self-definitions and self-evaluations (i.e., whether they were individualist or collectivist) thus resulted from group processes and occurred when social identity was salient rather than when it was not.

Consequences of individualist and collectivist group norms: a model

In the remainder of this chapter we explore the broader implications and consequences of these ideas and findings. The outcomes of conformity to

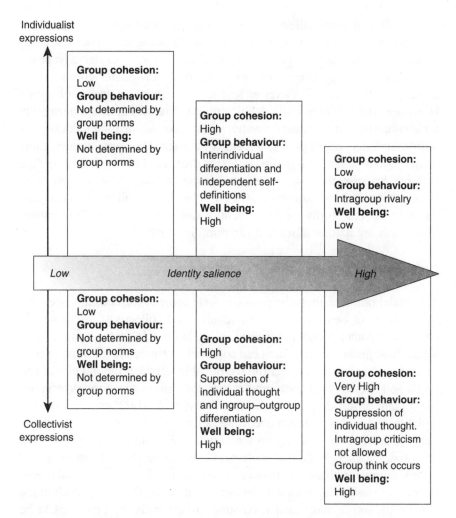

Figure 7.1 **Group processes as a function of identity salience and group norms prescribing collectivism or individualism**

individualist and collectivist group norms as a function of identity salience are modelled in Figure 7.1. In this model, we distinguish three levels of identity salience (low, medium and high) to illustrate that the influence of group identity salience differs at these levels and that norm content determines outcomes differently at each level.

At the core of this model is an assumption that, disregarding the content of identities, there will tend to be a positive correlation between group behaviour that results from social identity salience and collectivist tendencies. This is represented graphically in Figure 7.1 by increased extremity of collectivist expressions when social identity salience increases. In line with comparative fit and meta-contrast principles we argue that the default is for social identity salience to lead to greater uniformity. However, in addition, we propose that this correlation can be strengthened but also over-ridden and even reversed by the content of group norms. Collectivist group norms are generally compatible with this push for greater cohesion and identity salience and will therefore lead to similar types of group behaviour. However, conformity to individualist group norms will enhance intragroup differentiation and increase diversity, which goes against the tendency for uniformity encouraged by social identity salience. The consequence of this is that individualism in a group context is more likely to be moderate than extreme because the salience of the group provides a counterforce to greater cohesion and uniformity. On the other hand, collectivism can take on more extreme forms because identity salience and prioritizing collec-tivist goals are natural allies that can reinforce each other.

Conformity to group norms and well being

The model outlined above helps to illustrate some of the consequences and implications of conformity to individualist and collectivist group norms. One of the outcomes not considered so far, but highly relevant in this con-text, is how group norm content can colour and change the meaning of con-formity and how it can affect the relationship between the individual and social self. For instance, we predict that conformity to norms determines the content of self-definition itself (see Jetten et al., 2002) and the extent to which individual and group needs are perceived as compatible, which is likely to have a direct effect on individual well being. Broadly speaking, we expect higher individual well being the more the content of group norms allows for alignment between group demands and individual needs. In contrast, well being should be negatively affected when, as a result of the content of norms, individual needs and group needs are perceived to be incompatible or even in conflict. We will now examine in greater detail how collectivist and individualist group norms affect self-definition, group behav-iour and well being at different levels of social identity.

When social identity salience is low, group norms should not guide people's behaviour and neither individualist nor collectivist group norms are likely to play a major role in determining behaviour. This should result in low levels of perceived group cohesion and interactions between people that are not motivated by group norms. Level of well being should not be a function of particular group norms.

However, as social identity salience increases, group norms should become an increasingly important guide for group members' behaviour. When collectivist behaviour is normative, perceptions of group cohesion should increase, possibly at the expense of idiosyncratic thought and expressions. Nevertheless, this should have positive effects on wellbeing because giving priority to group goals over individual goals is normatively prescribed and such behaviour is perfectly aligned with individual wishes and desires. The processes underlying the effects of social identity salience on conformity when group norms prescribe individualist behaviour are identical to those that operate when norms prescribe collectivism, but the outcomes are likely to be very different. More specifically, conformity to individualist group norms will also increase perceptions of group cohesion; however, at the same time, this will lead to independent self-definitions and interindividual differentiation within the group. Paradoxically, being individualist and giving priority to personal over group goals is normatively prescribed by such groups and reflects loyalty and conformity to group norms and ideals. Here group members' wellbeing should also be relatively high because individualist group norms allow group members to express their individual self while, at the same time, remaining faithful to important group goals ("I'm loyal to my group and true to myself at the same time"). In addition, the greater latitudes of acceptable behaviour found within these groups have the potential to lead to more effective decision-making and to increase creativity (e.g., Coser, 1962; Nemeth & Owens, 1996; Postmes et al., 2001).

However, the balance between conformity to group norms and the behaviours prescribed by the content of norms may become compromised when social identity salience is very high. When group norms prescribe collectivism, very high social identity salience may exert pressure for group cohesion, homogeneity and conformity. These pressures are likely to interfere with independent self-expressions and diminish tolerance for dissent and intragroup differentiation in the manner outlined by Janis (1972). However, we do not expect that this will have a detrimental effect on wellbeing when behaving in a selfless manner is normatively prescribed. This idea is consistent with work by Lois (1999) examining heroism among a very collectivist volunteer search and rescue organization in the western United States. She described how group goals helped individuals to achieve a balance between the individual and collective self and how core members of the group subscribed to the values and norms of the group and put the group's interest above their own because this was personally gratifying. Lois (1999) states: "The group and the community recognized them as selflessly devoted communitarians, and for that, they were recognized as exceptional individuals" (p. 133). This shows that subsuming the self within the group and the subsequent denial of individual goals occasionally affords prestigious individual status within the group, which preserves and respects individual self-definitions (see Baray, Postmes, & Jetten, 2005, for a similar argument).

Yet while individualist norms may encourage more creativity and flexibility by increasing latitudes of acceptable behaviour within a group, there are downsides to individualism when conformity to these norms is pushed too far (McAuliffe et al., 2003). For instance, extreme individualism may promote callousness and insensitivity to other ingroup members' well being, and it may encourage disloyalty, intolerance for conformity, and increased intragroup competition, all of which harm well being. Ironically too, prioritizing personal goals over group goals may ultimately undermine the *raison d'être* of the group itself: conforming to the individualist ideal becomes incompatible with being a group member and, as a result, the group is likely to suffer from internal ruptures and friction.

Group norms and optimal distinctiveness theory

Comparing and contrasting our reasoning with other models that examine the interplay between collective and individualist self-expressions, it appears that our reasoning differs from these in a number of ways. We focus here on the way in which our reasoning differs from ODT, arguably the dominant theoretical framework in the field. Two differences are particularly pronounced. First, ODT assumes that distinctiveness and assimilation needs are opposing needs that cannot be satisfied at the same level of abstraction. Distinctiveness needs are seen as needs that are satisfied through intergroup comparisons, and needs for assimilation are thought to be personal identity needs that are satisfied through intragroup comparisons (Pickett & Brewer, 2001). We differ from this line of reasoning in assuming that rather than standing in opposition, group identification and individualization may actually be compatible (cf. Pickett & Leonardelli, Chapter 4 in this volume) and that they can both be achieved simultaneously by conforming to group norms that prescribe individual self-expressions. In our view, self-expressions of individuality do not necessarily diminish the relevance or salience of group identity, but can be compatible with a salient group identity, and even strengthen and inform it (see also Postmes, Baray, Haslam, Morton, & Swaab, Chapter 12 in this volume). In this sense, we argue for a *social* individual self and against a disjunction between social and individual self.

Second, in line with ODT (Brewer, 1991, 1993) and uniqueness theory (Snyder & Fromkin, 1980), we propose that well being will be highest when group identification and people's needs to be true to their individual self are simultaneously satisfied. When group salience is low, a meaningful sense of belonging is absent and this should negatively affect well being (Baumeister & Leary, 1995; Manstead, 1997). In line with ODT, we propose that a more balanced situation arises when identity salience is moderate, allowing for individual expressions when norms prescribe collectivism and collective expressions of individual identity when norms prescribe individualism. In contrast to ODT, however, we propose that well being can also be compatible with strong conformity to group norms and that the needs for distinctiveness and assimilation are not necessarily opposite forces: the satisfaction of one need is not necessarily achieved at the expense of the other. Just as individuality can be collectively expressed and experienced (e.g., through the celebration of diversity), so too can collectively abstaining from individualist expressions lead to high levels of well being. The reason for this is that conforming to collectivist norms aligns the self more closely to the group which proves gratifying at the individual or personal level. However, we predict that when group norms prescribe individualism, wellbeing will be lower at either end of the social identity salience spectrum because individualist group norms can undermine a sense of belongingness when social identity salience is very high.

Note that although we arrive at the same predicted relationship between well being and identity salience as ODT in the case of individualist group norms, our rationale is very different. Rather than social and individual self being antagonistic at high levels of social identity salience, we assume that although individual group norms align the social and individual self, extreme levels of individualism are predicted to be dysfunctional for the group, and will therefore indirectly have a negative impact on well being. In other words, there is not one optimum, rather there are different optima determined by processes other than antagonism between individual and social self. Precisely because conformity to individualist group norms encompasses individual and group interests, the individual self is predicted to be damaged when the group embarks on a negative downward spiral because of extreme individualism.

Group socialization and group norms

One issue that requires further exploration concerns the question of when exactly norms of collectivism and individualism have their impact. Does conformity to individualist and collectivist group norms take a different form in the initial stages of group life than in later stages when group identities are better established? The focus on temporal changes in the group should be seen as an attempt to acknowledge the fact that groups generally have a past and a future, and that they are not static entities operating in a time vacuum. Although this is generally acknowledged in small group research (e.g., for instance in group socialization and group development models: Moreland & Levine, 1982; Moreland, Levine, & Cini, 1993; Worchel, Coutant-Sassic, & Grossman, 1992; Worchel, 1998), it has rarely been the focus of empirical research on intergroup relations (but see e.g., Reicher, 1996).

Considering the question of when group norms have an effect, research seems to suggest that group norms are important at different stages of group life (see Hollander, 1958) and conformity may have a different function depending on the developmental stage of the group. It is argued that there are strong pressures on members to conform in the initial stages of group life, when the group has just formed (Worchel et al., 1992; Worchel, 1998). At this juncture, members may be asked to demonstrate their loyalty to the group, and the very formation of the group implicitly demands that its members conform to group norms. In group socialization research it is assumed that in later stages of group development there is more opportunity for individual behaviour, and group norms become less important in guiding group members' behaviour. While group members are more concerned with similarities that hold them together in the early stages of group life, differences between members are more openly acknowledged and even welcomed at later stages. Thus, it is predicted that conformity to group norms might generally be weaker when the group identity is well established. From this, one could also infer that individualist group norms should sit better with groups in later stages of group life whereas collectivist group norms may be more likely to emerge at the beginning of group life. This also implies that it may be difficult to introduce individualist group norms in newly formed groups and collectivist group norms at later stages because that would go against the natural development of most groups.

The idea that collectivist group definitions are likely to precede individualist expressions is also consistent with theorizing that individualist expressions and behaviour only acquire meaning (and will only be recognized as such) in the context of a broader organizing social structure (Durkheim, 1893/1984; see also Postmes et al., Chapter 12 in this volume; Turner, 2005). That is, individualist behaviour in the sense of being independent and different from others only becomes meaningful if there is a social context in which those differences and independence can be appreciated and recognized. In a similar vein, we propose that individualist behaviour that gives priority to individual goals can only be understood in contrast to group goals. In this view, the individual is the figure and the group is the ground. Some of this rationale lies at the core of Marx's reasoning about the meaning of the emerging individual in eighteenth-century society. He states: "But the period in which this standpoint – that of the isolated individual – became prevalent is the one in which the social relations of society … have reached the highest level of development. Man is in the most literal sense of the word a *zoon politikon*, not only a social animal, but an animal which can develop into an individual only in society" (McLellan, 1977, p. 346). This idea that individualist expressions flow from and are contingent on society or groups is also illustrated by a recent recruitment slogan of the Royal Air Force that states: "It takes real team-work to fly solo". One way to interpret this slogan is that one first has to become part of the team in order for individual differentiation and, indeed, individual excellence, to be possible.

Most socialization models assume that norms will become less important over the course of group life and that the decay of solidarity in a group is the result of the disintegration of group norms (Worchel, 1998). However, it is not clear why group norms would necessarily lose their identity-defining potency over time. Instead, we propose not that group norms cease to exert influence over time, but rather that the content of group norms is transformed over time to reflect that the functions of a group change over time, as the demands placed on it become different ones. While group norms are likely to be collectivist at early "start-up" stages of group life when group members explore commonalties, shape their shared identity, and define common goals, procedures and responsibilities, collectivist group norms may transform and become more individualist at later stages in a group's life. Indeed, such development would be functional for group performance.

This idea is consistent with Durkheim's reasoning that it is not decay of social solidarity that marks the transition from simple to more complex societies, but a change in the nature of solidarity (Durkheim, 1893/1984). He proposed that as societies develop and become more complex, mechanic undifferentiated solidarity transforms into organic solidarity where individual autonomy is compatible with social solidarity. Thus, we suggest another explanation for Worchel, Coutant-Sassic, & Wong's (1993) finding that over a six-week period, group members' initial preference for cooperating with an ingroup and competing with an outgroup reversed. On the one hand, this could be a result of group norms becoming less important over time, as Worchel et al. (1993) argued, but, on the other hand, it could be the results of the changing *content* of group norms – such that, over time, the importance of collectivist group norms declined at the expense of individualist group norms. Jetten et al.'s (in press) observation that interindividual differentiation increased while intergroup differentiation decreased as a result of conformity to individualist group norms provides evidence for this alternative explanation. This indicates that the way salient identities are expressed shifts as a function of the content of norms, at the same time that conformity to norms still drives group behaviour.

Extending this reasoning, at the final stages of a group's life cycle, it may not necessarily be a shift from social identity to personal identity that brings about the decay of the group. Conformity to emerging individualist group norms can also herald the break-up of a group. It is conceivable that individualist group norms become so strong that they undermine group cohesion but also that the group implodes as a result of an (implicit) collective decision to dissolve the group. Group break-up may thus emerge not only because group norms lose their power, but because individuals embrace an emergent norm that change is desirable and that it is best for the group if each individual group member goes "their own way". For instance, in the case of the break-up of pop bands, it appears that it is implicitly understood from the beginning, not only by the band but also by their fans, that there will come a time that these bands split up ("This is what bands do"). This goes some way towards explaining the often consensual and orderly nature of the break-up process – indeed, the fact that individuals' actions are still determined by group norms and judged in the framework of a salient shared identity.

We propose that it is not only changes in intragroup processes such as the changing functions of a group that lead to changes in the content of group norms over time. In addition to such intragroup forces, the content of group norms may change as a function of constantly changing intergroup dynamics and the position of the group in the broader social structure. For instance, minority groups that successfully engage in collective action and improve the fate of their group may, over time, abandon their collective orientation that paved the way for increased group status, in favour of a more individualist culture (e.g., women's rights movements).

Group–individual interaction

The study of individualist and collectivist group norms has not only shed light on how conformity to group norms can result in more or less individualist self-definitions, but also speaks more generally to the relation between the content of social identities and the content of personal identities, and how the two may influence each other (Simon, 2004). Figure 7.2 illustrates this. In line with traditional social identity theory research, we start from the assumption that social identities can be expressed by conformity to the content of salient group norms (Hogg & Turner, 1987). For instance, norms to cheer for one's team, to wear team colours, or even to paint one's face in the colour of the team are all ways of expressing team identification and they allow for the definition of the content of the collective identity.

Yet, in some social contexts it is the content of group norms itself that informs us directly about the relation between the individual and the collective. The content of group norms may facilitate or hinder interaction between individual and collective self. For instance, norms can convey the idea either that collective and individual identities are distinct and unrelated (e.g., when group norms prescribe collectivist behaviour) or that they are related and interdependent. This opens up the possibility that social identities determine individual expression and possibly even personal identities (see

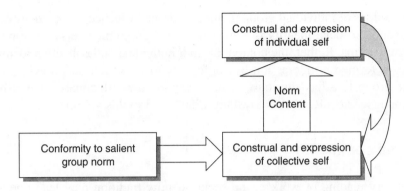

Figure 7.2   **The interaction between individual self and collective self as determined, facilitated or hindered by the content of social norms**

Postmes et al., Chapter 12; Reicher & Haslam, Chapter 13; Turner et al., Chapter 2 in this volume; see also Simon, 2004). The latter process may occur not only when group norms prescribe individualism, but also when salient group norms encourage individual competitiveness within groups or a critical stance towards group actions ("I'm expressing my loyalty to the group by competing with fellow ingroup members" or "I'm expressing my loyalty to the group by questioning its actions"). It follows that those who are more strongly committed to the group are more likely to conform to these salient group norms by standing out as individuals, by voicing their individual criticism and more generally by adhering to idiosyncratic views in the service of the collective. It is in such cases that a strong collective self can be realized and articulated by emphasizing individuality and personal identity. In such situations it thus appears that the content of social identity serves not to differentiate from personal identity, but to inform and shape it (Simon, 2004). We would argue that even though initially it is the social self that informs the personal self, over time there is likely to be mutual influence and reinforcement between the content of the individual and collective self. This point highlights the way in which individual identities can become just as social as collective identities (Simon, 2004; Turner et al., 1987).

In sum, Figure 7.2 illustrates how conformity to group norms can inform not only the collective self, but also the personal self. We propose that it is the content of group norms that determines the degree of interaction between individual and collective self. The content of these norms can align these two self-definitions or highlight the incompatibility of the goals associated with both levels. Importantly, if we are open to the possibility of mutual influence between the two levels of self-definition, we can also easily explain how social change in groups occurs as a result of the actions of individual group members. Group influence is not a one-way street once social identity is made salient and group members conform to group norms. Rather, the content of both individual and collective identities is formed in interaction by conformity to group norms, allowing for the group to affect the individual, as well as the individual to steer the group (see also Reicher & Haslam, Chapter 13 in this volume).

Final comments

Cursory reading of work in the social identity tradition may lead one to conclude that this perspective is ill-equipped to deal with displays of individuality within the group. The interpersonal–intergroup continuum proposed by social identity theory (Tajfel & Turner, 1979) and the hierarchical organization of self-categorizations proposed by self-categorization theory (Turner et al., 1987) is usually taken as evidence for the fundamental antagonism between the individual and social self. Yet, by going beyond issues of perceptual salience, and examining the *content* of the identity, we have shown in this chapter that individual and group expressions can be reconciled at the social level.

This idea is compatible with the suggestion that the difference between personal and social identities does not lie in the level of inclusiveness of the categories that define the self (Turner et al., 1994). Indeed, personal and social identities can be expressed in identical ways. What matters is the content of the personal or social identity and the self-categorization that is salient. For instance, a Dutch person can define him/herself as individualist in comparison to other Dutch people but can also perceive "Dutchness" as essentially individualist. When Dutch identity is salient, the collective self (i.e., expressing Dutch identity) would be realized through adherence to individualist orientations and norms. Thus, we conclude that individualist behaviours and self-definitions are valid and meaningful self-expressions not only at the level of one's personal identity but also at the level of the social self.

By being open to this possibility, we effectively move away from the idea that the individual self and social self relate to each other in an antagonistic way. Moreover, it allows us to think of the ways in which individualist expression can be part of the social self instead of perceiving these self-expressions as operating exclusively at the individual level. Indeed, rather than looking for "the individual in the group", it may be more fruitful to search for "the group in the individual" (Reicher, 2001; see also Spears et al., Chapter 10 in this volume). In this sense, the quote by Asch (1951) cited at the beginning of this chapter describing the "pull" towards the group as identities become salient should perhaps be understood not as meaning that the self becomes identical to, and interchangeable with, other group members. Rather, the "pull" to the group means that precisely because the shared nature of identity becomes salient, the content of that identity also becomes evident. This ultimately determines how personal and social identities are mutually construed.

NOTES

This research was supported by a large ESRC grant and a Leverhulme grant. We would like to thank Alex Haslam for his useful feedback on a previous draft of this chapter.

1 Note that Rabelais believed that people should be encouraged to act as they saw fit because he was convinced of the goodness of human nature. This motivation may in some conditions be different from the motivation to conform to the rule of conformity, which we assume can underlie promoting individual autonomy.

REFERENCES

Asch, S. E. (1951). Effects of group pressures upon the modification and distortion of judgments. In H. Guetzkow (Ed.), *Groups, leadership, and men*. Pittsburgh: Carnegie Press.

Baray, G., Postmes, T., & Jetten, J. (2005). Self-defining groups and the relation between personal and social identity. Manuscript in preparation, University of Exeter.

Baumeister, R. F., & Leary, M. R. (1995). The need to belong: Desire for interpersonal attachments as a fundamental human motivation. *Psychological Bulletin, 117*, 497–529.

Bettencourt, B. A., & Sheldon, K. (2001). Social roles as mechanisms for psychological need satisfaction within social groups. *Journal of Personality and Social Psychology, 81*, 1131–1143.

Breakwell, G. M. (1987). Identity. In H. Beloff & A. Coleman (Eds.), *Psychological Survey 6* (pp. 94–114). Leicester: British Psychological Society.

Brewer, M. (1991). The social self: On being the same and different at the same time. *Personality and Social Psychology Bulletin, 17*, 475–482.

Brewer, M. (1993). Social identity, distinctiveness, and in-group homogeneity. *Social Cognition, 11*, 150–164.

Brown, R. J., & Turner, J. C. (1981). Interpersonal and intergroup behaviour. In J. C. Turner & H. Giles (Eds.), *Intergroup behaviour* (pp. 33–65). Oxford: Blackwell.

Brown, R., & Williams, J. (1984). Group identification: The same thing to all people? *Human Relations, 37*, 547–564.

Cartwright, D., & Zander, A. (1953). Group dynamics, research and theory. Evanston, IL: Row Peterson.

Codol, J. -P. (1975). On the so-called "superior conformity of the self" behavior: Twenty experimental investigations. *European Journal of Social Psychology, 5*, 457–501.

Codol, J. -P. (1984). Social differentiation and non-differentiation. In H. Tajfel (Ed.), *The social dimension: European developments in social psychology* (vol. 1, pp. 314–337). Cambridge: Cambridge University Press.

Coser, L. A. (1962). Some functions of deviant behavior and normative flexibility. *American Journal of Sociology*, *68*, 172–181.

Durkheim, E. (1893/1984). *The division of labour in society*. London: Macmillan (original work published in 1893).

Haslam, S. A. (2004). *Psychology in organizations: The social identity approach* (2nd ed.). London: Sage.

Haslam, S. A., Oakes, P. J., McGarty, C., Turner, J. C., Reynolds, K. J., & Eggins, R. A. (1996). Stereotyping and social influence: The mediation of stereotype applicability and sharedness by the views of ingroup and outgroup members. *British Journal of Social psychology*, *35*, 369–397.

Hewitt, J. (1989). *Dilemmas of the American self*. Philadelphia: Temple University Press.

Hofstede, G. (1980). *Culture's consequences*. Beverley Hills, CA: Sage.

Hogg, M. A., & Turner, J. C. (1987). Social identity and conformity: A theory of referent informational influence. In W. Doise & S. Moscovici (Eds.), *Current issues in European social psychology* (vol. 2, pp. 139–182). Cambridge: Cambridge University Press.

Hollander, E. P. (1958). Conformity, status, and idiosyncrasy credit. *Psychological Review*, *65*, 117–127.

Hornsey, M. J., & Jetten, J. (2004). Balancing the need for group belonging and the need for distinctiveness. *Personality and Social Psychology Review*, *8*, 248–264.

Hornsey, M. J., & Jetten, J. (2005). Loyalty without conformity: Tailoring perception as a means of balancing belonging and differentiation. *Self and Identity*, *4*, 81–95.

Hornsey, M. J., Jetten, J., McAuliffe, B. J., & Hogg, M. A. (in press). The impact of individualist and collectivist group norms on evaluations of dissenting group members. *Journal of Experimental and Social Psychology*.

Hutchison, P., Jetten, J., Christian, J., & Haycraft, E. (2005). Protecting threatened identity: Sticking with one's group by emphasising ingroup heterogeneity. Manuscript submitted for publication.

Janis, I. L. (1972). *Victims of groupthink*. Boston: Houghton Mifflin.

Jetten, J., McAuliffe, B. J., Hornsey, M. J., & Hogg, M. A. (in press). Differentiation between and within groups: The influence of individualist and collectivist group norms. *European Journal of Social Psychology*.

Jetten, J., Postmes, T., & McAuliffe, B. J. (2002). "We're all individuals": Group norms of individualism and collectivism, levels of identification, and identity threat. *European Journal of Social Psychology*, *32*, 189–207.

Kampmeier, C., & Simon, B. (2001). Individuality and group formation: The role of independence and differentiation. *Journal of Personality and Social Psychology*, *81*, 448–462.

Lois, J. (1999). Socialization to heroism: Individualism and collectivism in a voluntary search and rescue group. *Social Psychology Quarterly*, *62*, 117–135.

Manstead, A.S.R. (1997). Situations, belongingness, attitudes, and culture: Four lessons learned from social psychology. In C. McGarty and S. A. Haslam (Eds.), *The message of social psychology* (pp. 238–251). Cambridge, MA: Blackwell.

Markus, H. R., & Kitayama, S. (1991). Culture and the self: Implications for cognition, emotion, and motivation. *Psychological Review*, *98*, 224–253.

McAuliffe, B. J., Jetten, J., Hornsey, M. J., & Hogg, M. A. (2003). Individualist and collectivist group norms: When it's OK to go your own way. *European Journal of Social Psychology*, *33*, 57–70.

McLellan, D. (1977). *Karl Marx: Selected writings*. Oxford: Oxford University Press.

Moreland, R. L., & Levine, J. M. (1982). Socialization in small groups: Temporal changes in individual–group relations. *Advances in Experimental Social Psychology*, *15*, 137–192.

Moreland, R. L., Levine, J. M., & Cini, M. (1993). Group socialization: The role of commitment. In M. A. Hogg & D. Abrams (Eds.), *Group motivation: Social psychological perspectives* (pp. 105–129). New York: Wheatsheaf.

Nemeth, C., & Owens, P. (1996). Making work groups more effective: The value of minority dissent. In M. A. West (Ed.), *The handbook of workgroup psychology* (pp. 125–141). Chichester: Wiley.

Pickett, C. L., & Brewer, M. B. (2001). Assimilation and differentiation needs as motivational determinants of perceived ingroup and outgroup homogeneity. *Journal of Experimental Social Psychology, 37*, 341–348.

Postmes, T., Spears, R., & Cihangir, S. (2001). Quality of decision making and group norms. *Journal of Personality and Social Psychology, 80*, 918–930.

Rabelais, F. (1553). *The works of Mr. Francis Rabelais*. London: Grant Richards, 1904.

Reicher, S. (1996). "The Battle of Westminster": Developing the social identity model of crowd behaviour in order to explain the initiation and development of collective conflict. *European Journal of Social Psychology, 26*, 115–134.

Reicher, S. (2001). Social identity definition and enactment: A broad SIDE against irrationalism and relativism. In T. Postmes, R. Spears, M. Lea, and S. Reicher (Eds.), *SIDE issues centre stage: Recent developments in studies of de-individuation in groups* (pp. 175–190). Amsterdam: Koninklijke Nederlandse Akademie van Wetenschappen Verhandelingen.

Sedikides, C., Campbell, W. K., Reeder, G., & Elliot, A. J. (2002). The self in relationships: Whether, how, and when close others put the self "in its place". In W. Stroebe & M. Hewstone (Eds.), *European Review of Social Psychology* (vol.12, pp. 237–265). Chichester: Wiley.

Sedikides, C., Gaertner, L., & Toguchi, Y. (2003). Pancultural self-enhancement. *Journal of Personality and Social Psychology, 84*, 60–79.

Sedikides, C., Gaertner, L., & Vevea, J.L. (2005). Pancultural self-enahancement reloaded: A meta-analytic reply to Heine. *Journal of Personality and Social Psychology, 89*, 539–551.

Sherif, M. (1936). *The psychology of social norms*. New York: Harper.

Simon, B. (2004). *Identity in modern society: A social psychological perspective*. Oxford: Blackwell.

Snyder, C. R., & Fromkin, H. L. (1980). *Uniqueness: The human pursuit of difference*. New York: Plenum.

Tajfel, H. (1978). Interindividual behaviour and intergroup behaviour. In H. Tajfel (Ed.), *Differentiation between groups: Studies in the social psychology of intergroup relations* (pp. 27–60). London: Academic.

Tajfel, H., & Turner, J. C. (1979). An integrative theory of intergroup conflict. In W. G. Austin & S. Worchel (Eds.), *The social psychology of intergroup relations* (pp. 33–48). Monterey, CA: Brooks/Cole.

Tajfel, H., & Wilkes, A. L. (1964). Salience of attributes and commitments to extreme judgements in the perception of people. *British Journal of Social and Clinical Psychology, 2*, 40–49.

Triandis, H. C. (1989). The self and social behavior in differing cultural contexts. *Psychological Review, 96*, 506–520.

Turner, J. C. (1982). Towards a cognitive redefinition of the social group. In H. Tajfel (Ed.), *Social identity and intergroup relations* (pp. 15–40). Cambridge: Cambridge University Press.

Turner, J. C. (1991). *Social influence*. Buckingham: Open University Press.

Turner, J. C. (2005). Explaining the nature of power: A three-process theory. *European Journal of Social Psychology, 35*, 1–22.

Turner, J. C., Hogg, M. A., Oakes, P. J., Reicher, S. D., & Wetherell, M. S. (1987). *Rediscovering the social group: A self-categorization theory*. Oxford: Blackwell.

Turner, J. C., Oakes, P. J., Haslam, S. A., & McGarty, C. A. (1994). Self and collective: Cognition and social context. *Personality & Social Psychology Bulletin, 20*, 454–463.

Vignoles, V. L., Chryssochoou, X., & Breakwell, G. M. (2000). The distinctiveness principle: Identity, meaning, and the bounds of cultural relativity. *Personality and Social Psychology Review, 4*, 337–354.

Worchel, S. (1998). A developmental view of the search for group identity. In S. Worchel, J. F. Morales, D. Páez, & J.-C. Deschamps (Eds.), *Social identity: International perspectives* (pp. 53–74). London: Sage.

Worchel, S., Coutant-Sassic, D., & Grossman, M. (1992). A developmental approach to group dynamics: A model and illustrative research. In S. Worchel, W. Wood, & J. A. Simpson (Eds.), *Group process and productivity* (pp. 181–202). Newbury Park, CA: Sage.

Worchel, S., Coutant-Sassic, D., & Wong, F. (1993). Towards a more balanced view of conflict: There is a positive side. In S. Worchel & J. A. Simpson (Eds.), *Conflict between people and groups*. Chicago: Nelson-Hall.

Ziller, R. (1964). Individuation and socialization: A theory of assimilation in large organisations. *Human Relations, 17*, 341–360.

8

Culture, Social Identity and the Individual

Michael J. Halloran and
Emiko S. Kashima

Introduction and overview

Culture is a dynamic system of collectively held meanings and practices that are maintained and modified over time. Nevertheless, individuals who contribute to the maintenance of culture do not share all available cultural knowledge with everyone else. Culture is the sum of what various people share with others within a society with whom they also share common social identities. People with a common social identity may further share certain aspects of cultural knowledge, including beliefs about their social contexts (such as stereotypes and implicit assumptions), values, attitudes, social norms and practical skills, as part of their group life, in dealing with their common fate, or simply through sharing space and time together. For instance, distinct aspects of the available cultural knowledge can be sampled by student, religious, work, and sports groups as a function of the specific group goals and priorities. Looking at it this way, it may be suggested that cultural knowledge at a collective level is correlated with social groupings within society. At an individual level, further, cultural knowledge is loosely organized into different spheres, each involving a common identity, and its cognitive associates. We advance the idea in this chapter that cultural knowledge held by the individual is partly organized around his or her social identities, forming clusters of knowledge that are to some extent independent and distinguishable from one another.

We propose a model of culture and social identity here that has several theoretical implications regarding how culture and identity influence individuals dynamically across contexts. First, the model suggests that social identity constrains the aspects of culture that exert influences in the immediate social context. Second, and diametrically opposite to the first, cultural knowledge is highlighted as the regulator of social identity and the group processes that ensue. Our model thus suggests culture and identity have a reciprocal relationship, or they make up each other to some degree. Third, the assumed tie between social identity and culture means that a host of psychological threats that have an effect on social identity processes exert their influence on cultural knowledge as well. In other words, the effects of threats on cultural knowledge are regulated by identities. We will elaborate on these ideas in subsequent sections of the chapter, following a brief review of literatures on culture and social identity that form the background of our theorizing.

Culture and cultural knowledge

Culture can be thought of as a complex and diverse system of shared knowledge, practices and signifiers of a society, providing structure and significance to groups within that society and ultimately an individual's experience of his or her social world (e.g., Clark, 1996; Fiske, Kitayama, Markus, & Nisbett, 1998; Kashima, 2001; Poortinga, 1992). Mental representations of culture, or *cultural knowledge*, are held by the individual as categories or cognitive units that are the building blocks of cultural values, attitudes, norms, beliefs, and self-representations (Triandis, 1972), developing through the processes of learning, reinforcement, and categorization of experience.

Research on culture and psychology has focused on broad configurations of cultural knowledge, or *cultural dimensions*, which distinguish human behaviour across different societies. For example, there is good evidence to demonstrate cross-societal variability in people's emphasis on individualism and collectivism (Hofstede, 1980; Triandis, 1995), analytical and holistic thinking (Nisbett, 2003), the independent and interdependent view of self (Markus & Kitayama, 1991), and universal values (Schwartz & Bilsky, 1987). Yet, investigations of cross-societal differences in individualism and collectivism have been the mainstay of cultural comparative research in the last two decades. According to a recent meta-analysis (Oyserman, Coon, & Kemmelmeier, 2002), the individualistic worldview, which is relatively strong in Western English-speaking nations, has an emphasis on individual autonomy and uniqueness, personal goals, competition, and self-knowledge, whereas collectivism, comparably stronger in Asian cultures, emphasizes ingroup duty, relatedness, and group belonging. Research also shows that distinct configurations of attribution biases (e.g., Choi, Nisbett, & Norenzayan, 1999; Miller, 1984), values (e.g., Hofstede, 2001), group cognitions (Chiu, Morris, Hong, & Menon,

2000; Yuki, 2003), and self-views (e.g., Heine, Lehman, Markus, & Kitayama, 1999) of Westerners and Asians reflect their differential emphasis on an individualistic or a collectivistic worldview.

The use of individualism and collectivism to describe the social psychologies of different societies has translated into a form of "cultural typecasting", which has been extensively criticized in the literature (see Kagitçibasi, 1994; Moghaddam, Chapter 9 in this volume; Takano & Osaka, 1999). The main conceptual concern, however, is that reliable cross-cultural differences in individualism and collectivism are interpreted as if they generalize across individuals and situations within a society, presenting a fixed and unchangeable relationship between cultures, societies, and individuals. This overly mechanistic view of culture's effects resonates with similar theoretical critiques made in this volume concerning social identity theory (e.g., Hornsey, Chapter 5; Jetten & Postmes, Chapter 7; Prentice, Chapter 3) and is challenged by recent research that highlighted the contextualized nature of cultural effects.

The research has demonstrated, for instance, the pivotal effects of priming a value, worldview, or self-view on the self-perceptions and other cognitions reported by people. In a study by Gardner, Gabriel, and Lee (1999), priming American and Chinese students with an independent self-view, or alternatively with an interdependent self-view, led both groups of students to more strongly support individualistic and collectivistic values, respectively (see also Trafimow, Triandis, & Goto, 1991). Hong, Chiu, and Kung (1997) found that having bicultural Hong Kong Chinese (acculturated to both China and the US) think about Chinese cultural icons (e.g., Chinese dragon, Stone Monkey, the Great Wall), or alternatively about American cultural icons (e.g., the American flag, Superman, the Statue of Liberty), led them to make culture-specific causal attributions: the American cultural prime led to greater use of internal attribution and the Chinese cultural prime to external attribution. Other studies also drew attention to the effects of group primes on the cultural values endorsed. Matsumoto, Wessman, Reston, Brown, and Kupperbusch (1997) reported that Koreans, Russians, Japanese, and North Americans each showed varying degrees of support for collectivistic values when primed with several different relationships, including family, close friends, colleagues, and strangers. A group that showed the highest degree of collectivism with one ingroup did not show the same degrees of collectivism with different ingroups. In another study, Rhee, Uleman, and Lee (1996) found that measures of collectivistic tendencies were differentially endorsed according to whether people were primed with either their kin or their non-kin relationships. Finally, experimental research by Jetten, Postmes, and McAuliffe (2002) with Indonesians and Americans has shown that individualistic and collectivistic values can also operate as group norms.

Culture, context, and social identity

Socio-cultural theories that have emerged in the recent literature emphasize the dynamic, context-sensitive and domain-specific conceptualization of culture (e.g., Fiske et al., 1998; Hong et al., 1997; Kashima, 2001; Miller, 1997). In these approaches, culture is not only a system of meanings but also a "signification process" whereby meanings are perpetually produced and reproduced through concrete practices and activities of individuals in particular situations (see Kashima, 2001, for the contrast between the system-oriented view and the practice-oriented view of culture). An activity performed within a context, often involving certain other people, and the deployment of certain tools and objects, may activate a specific domain of meaning. As such an activity is routinely repeated across time, the representations of context, activity, social identity, and the knowledge itself may become bound together as a cognitive network, or a cluster of knowledge. Subsequently, they become activated together as some elements of the cluster become accessible and applicable in a new context. We assume knowledge clusters are flexible and dynamic because they are constantly updated by new experiences as they prepare themselves for future use (Moghaddam, Chapter 9 in this volume). Such a conceptualization of culture as a dynamic process is consistent with the perspectives of connectionism (see Kashima, Kashima, & Aldridge, 2001; Quinn & Strauss, 1993; Smith, 1996, for connectionist modelling of self in its context) and of situated cognition (e.g., Hutchins & Hazelhurst, 1993).

The model we advance here takes advantage of the dynamic and flexible conceptualization of culture, and proposes that social identities that people repeatedly activate while engaging in activities with other people become part of the cultural knowledge network. In other words, repeated social interactions, involving particular activities in contexts, tools and objects, and with people who assume similar social identities due to their shared position within the society, develop shared clusters of cultural knowledge. This cultural knowledge will be chronically accessible and applicable for those people, yet its content may change gradually through shared social experiences that unfold *in situ*.

A concrete example of this model is found in an anthropological report by Jordan (1989), who described the situated learning of Maya girls in Yucatan who are gradually socialized into midwifery through participation in that practice. As an apprentice accompanied by female, senior members of their families, girls engage in routine activities which provide them with skills, practical knowledge, various meanings, and the identity associated with this practice. We argue that the network of knowledge shared amongst nurses, members of a religious congregation, asthma suffers, or social psychologists is maintained via processes comparable in essence to the one experienced by Yucatan midwives.

Our view suggests that, at the collective level, cultural knowledge is differentially distributed amongst people within a society. Further, people with a common social identity, who share similar societal positions, may share certain aspects of the available cultural knowledge more intensely as a part of group life, including cultural values, beliefs, and attitudes. At the individual level of analysis, people can hold discrete aspects of the available cultural knowledge by virtue of their belonging to distinct groups. In other words, an individual's representation of cultural knowledge may be loosely associated with, or organized around, his or her social identities. To the extent that people belong to different groups that subscribe to distinct aspects of culture, individuals may develop clusters of cultural knowledge that are attuned to contexts in which they assume a relevant group identity. By implication, a person who adopts a particular social identity may activate a specific cluster of knowledge held by the relevant group, including the collective goals and normative interaction patterns that they may pursue. In short, cultural effects on social cognitive processes are mediated by the social identity that people adopt across contexts.

Nonetheless, culture is not equal to the sum of knowledge associated with common identities that exist within a society. Many of the behavioural practices and cognitive activities that individuals perform on a daily basis may not be tied directly to a particular shared social identity, or even consciously maintained as *shared* knowledge. Examples may include the language use of pronoun drop where people omit subject pronouns such as "I" and "you" from interpersonal communication (Kashima & Kashima, 1998), the cognitive bias known as fundamental attribution error where people overestimate the internal causes of behaviour (Choi et al., 1999; Gilbert & Malone, 1995), analytical and holistic thinking styles (Nisbett, 2003), and subjective wellbeing (Diener & Suh, 2000; Rice & Steele, 2004). These practices and cognitions are shared in the sense that they reveal similarities among a group of people, and their uniqueness when compared to others. Yet, they are transmitted from one generation to the next, perhaps even unknowingly to the holders of the knowledge themselves. It is less likely, therefore, that such aspects of culture are explicitly linked to a common identity, activated with it or used in identity negotiation.

SCT, social identity and culture

Thus far, our model of the relationship between social identity and culture assumed that people's cultural knowledge may be organized into different domains that are loosely associated with their distinct group memberships.

By implication, the effects of cultural knowledge on social cognitive processes are mediated, to a certain degree, by social identity salience.

Self-categorization theory (Turner, 1985; Turner et al., Chapter 2 in this volume) proposes that the cognitive process of categorizing oneself as a group member is the antecedent condition for various ingroup and inter-group phenomena, such as stereotyping (Oakes, Haslam, & Turner, 1994), social influence (Turner, 1991), ingroup conformity, and prejudice (Turner, 1999). SCT assumes that people develop *in situ* a category of the self that reflects knowledge of their distinct group memberships, or social identities. Individuals *self-categorize* with a certain social identity to the extent that the identity is salient in the ongoing social context (Turner, 1985). The salience of a given social category is said to be a function of the *accessibility* of the social category and the *fit* between the stimulus conditions and the assumed characteristics of the relevant social category (Oakes, 1987). A social identity is adopted when people see themselves as similar to other members of the social category, or the ingroup prototype, and different from members of a contrasted social category, or the out-group prototype. When people self-categorize with a given social identity, the theory predicts that perceptions of the self will be judged against the characteristics of the ingroup prototype. Adopting characteristics of the ingroup prototype becomes normative (Turner & Onorato, 1999): those characteristics prescribe what people ought to believe about themselves and how they should behave.

SCT emphasizes that the process of self-categorization and its conse-quences are highly contextualized; the psychological continuity of such self-categories over time is de-emphasized, with the view that "the content and meaning of self-categories are not determined prior to their use" (Onorato & Turner, 2001, p. 159). Yet, the theory does recognize that self-categorization utilizes knowledge that is shared within a larger society and is maintained over time (Turner, Oakes, Haslam, & McGarty, 1994). For instance, the normative fit that determines self-categorization, along with comparative fit, is said to be based on various *implicit assumptions* and *background theories* concerning relevant social categories (Oakes et al., 1994). However, the issue of how those implicit assumptions and theories concerning social categories are collectively maintained, so that they can be used simultaneously and consensually by multiple participants of the self-categorization and intra/intergroup processes, is not fully addressed in SCT (also see Reicher, 1996). In other words, SCT assumes shared understanding of the social environment to be given.

Nevertheless, recent developments in self-categorization theory and particularly research by Haslam and associates (e.g., Haslam, 1997; Haslam, Turner, Oakes, Reynolds, & Doosje, 2002) have highlighted the process of group consensualization which resonates with our thinking about the relationship between social identity and culture. The process of *group consensualization,* whereby ingroup members communicate and coordinate their shared knowledge of the social world to actively reach group consensus, is said to occur because people expect agreement with those who share the same ingroup identity on beliefs about various social categories, especially ingroup and outgroup beliefs. Haslam et al. (2002) also acknowledge that group consensualization is dynamically influenced both by large-scale social changes that determine the relevant frame of reference and by the particular intergroup attitude, ingroup goals and objectives that unfold in the immediate social context. Thus, group consensus may shift as multiple individuals communicate their knowledge about relevant social categories *in situ,* thereby contributing to the shared knowledge and memories concerning the group and the social identity. Subsequently, given relevant stimulus conditions relating to the group, context, activity, or other cognitions that co-occur in such situations, individuals who are involved will reactivate the relevant shared knowledge.

Our model as described here suggests that culture is to some degree regulated by social identity salience. However, as explained in the opening of this chapter, it is not the case that culture is equal to the sum of knowledge associated with common identities that exist within the society. There are a variety of aspects of cultural knowledge and practice that are unrelated or only implicitly associated with social identity processes. In turn, culture and its shared nature seem to have certain implications for the social identification process. One of these relates to the shared nature of culture *per se*, and suggests this nature informs self-categorization and collective process. The other concerns the content of culture in particular, and suggests that certain cultural features correlate with social identification processes and its consequences.

First, as SCT posits, self-categorization as a member of a particular group is a fundamental precursor to collective processes that follow. As previously mentioned, however, multiple individuals who participate in a given social context must share their knowledge about relevant social categories in order to adopt the same ingroup category, and when this is achieved, they are still required to share group prototypes and ingroup norms before they engage in collective behaviours. Of course, sharedness of these knowledge ingredients of the social identification process can be developed through communication in the ongoing interaction context, as Haslam and colleagues highlight in their research (Haslam, Oakes, Reynolds, & Turner, 1999; Haslam, Turner, Oakes, McGarty, & Hayes, 1992). Nevertheless, the emerging communication is also constrained strongly by the participants' shared background knowledge. The lack of such shared categories and beliefs hinders communication (let alone not sharing a common language). Indeed, research shows people to be generally sensitive to the relative distribution of knowledge in their community, and when less knowledge is shared between communicators, effective communication takes longer to construct (e.g., Lau, Lee, & Chiu, 2004). Research also suggests groups have a tendency to ignore unshared information and discuss primarily the information already shared, reducing the chance of reaching an optimal solution (e.g., Stasser, Taylor, & Hanna, 1989). In short, low levels of shared knowledge encumber the process of consensualization and perhaps group formation. This may partly explain why it is particularly difficult to foster communication in situations that involve people with multicultural and/or multilingual backgrounds, or across different academic disciplines that lack common conceptual tools.

Second, with regard to the contents of culture that potentially influence social identification processes, certain dimensions of cultural meanings have been implied in the literature. Triandis (1989) theorized that the cultural dimensions of individualism–collectivism, tightness–looseness, and complexity relate to the relative probabilities in which the private, public, and collective self aspects are sampled within a society. The theory advanced is that the collectivist self is more likely to be sampled in collectivistic and tight societies, rendering greater psychological significance to ingroup memberships and group goals. More recently, literature has also highlighted the culturally shared implicit theories (or folk theories) concerning groups and individuals to be a potential determinant of social identification processes. For example, Hong et al. (2003) have shown that entity theorists, who assume group nature cannot be changed, tend to adopt a collective rather than personal identity and to perceive the social context in more intergroup terms, relative to incremental theorists who assume group nature to be more flexible. Kashima (2004) also suggested that perceived entitativity of various social categories is related to the degrees to which these categories are referenced as causal agents and communicated as such, with implications for both culture and social identification processes. Further, recent research that compared group perception and ingroup interaction across different societies has highlighted that values and norms concerning interdependence among people (e.g., independent vs interdependent values, generalized trust) vary across societies, and that they are related to patterns of ingroup loyalty, within-group behaviour, and preferred levels of group inclusiveness (Brewer & Roccas, 2002; Yamagishi & Yamagishi, 1994; Yuki, 2003). Hence, social identification processes and their consequences may be influenced by these characteristics of cultural knowledge (see also Moghaddam, Chapter 9 in this volume).

All in all, this section sets out our main ideas about the dynamic relationship between culture and social identity. In theory, social identities and cultural knowledge are mutually constitutive; we see that social identities adopted in the ongoing social context determine the relevant aspects of culture to be deployed in that context. At an individual level, repeated social interactions involving a given identity and cultural cognitions, with certain people in context, form a distinct cluster of interrelated knowledge. We will now turn to the question of what influences the likelihood that such networks of knowledge survive and are maintained over time.

Social identity, threat and cultural maintenance

It is likely that a threat to one's self-view strengthens adherence to a socially relevant ingroup and by implication the maintenance of its cultural worldview. Theorists assume a threat to one's self-view can take a number of forms, such as stereotype threat (Steele, Spencer, & Aronson, 2002) and a threat to one's social identity (Branscombe, Ellemers, Spears, & Doosje, 1999). For example, research shows that when the distinctiveness of one's group is undermined (Jetten, Spears, & Manstead, 1997) or the group status is challenged (Spears, Doosje, & Ellemers, 1997), people who identify with the group show stronger social identification. Still, a further class of threat is posited by terror management theorists (TMT: Greenberg, Solomon, & Pyszczynski, 1997) to cause stronger ingroup identification and adherence to a related worldview. According to TMT, when the threat of mortality is made salient, the process of cultural worldview validation and defence ensues. We posit that through a context involving a salient social identity, mortality salience will strengthen the association between the social identity and associated elements of culture.

This hypothesis was tested in two studies involving different cultural groups within the Australian population (Halloran & Kashima, 2004) and by making their different social identities salient. In our first study, we primed two distinct identities of Aboriginal Australians each of which was associated with distinct worldviews, and then manipulated mortality salience. The traditional Aboriginal worldview incorporates a stronger emphasis on collectivism and relationism (or interdependence) relative to the mainstream Australian worldview (Davidson & Reser, 1996; Fogarty & White, 1994). On the other hand, mainstream Australian culture has been found to be comparatively individualistic (Hofstede, 1980; Kashima, Yamaguchi, Kim, Choi, Gelfand, & Yuki, 1995). We also manipulated a threat to participants by inducing mortality salience in the context of a salient social identity. We expected that priming a social identity associated with distinctive cultural values would strengthen support for those values, especially when the notion of own mortality was salient.

The findings provided clear evidence to suggest that social identity determined value endorsement. As expected, collectivism was stronger under the Aboriginal identity than under the no-prime and the Australian

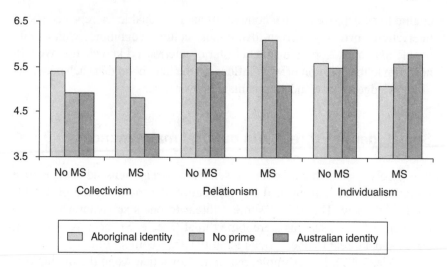

Figure 8.1 **Value support as a function of social identity and mortality salience, first study**

identity conditions. Participants endorsed relationism equally under the Aboriginal identity and no-prime conditions, and more strongly under these than under the Australian identity condition. Analysis also showed individualism was strongest under the Australian identity condition. However, the effect of a primed social identity was qualified by its significant interaction with mortality salience (see Figure 8.1). Contrary to our expectation that mortality salience would enhance the values most relevant to the social identity, analysis showed that it in fact *reduced* support for values contrary to them, that is, collectivism under the Australian identity condition, and individualism under the Aboriginal identity condition. Apparently, mortality salience and the presence of an outgroup experimenter in these conditions triggered a rejection of values associated with that outgroup. What was noteworthy, however, was that in the absence of an outgroup experimenter in the no-prime condition, mortality salience significantly *increased* relationism as expected.

In our second study, we manipulated social identity and mortality salience with three identities that are prominent within an Anglo-Australian university student sample. Two of them, Australian identity and student identity, were believed to be associated with distinct cultural values. According to previous findings, we expected individualism (Hofstede, 1980; Kashima et al., 1995), egalitarianism and· straightforwardness (Feather, 1994; Haslam et al., 1999) to be associated with Australian identity, and achievement values to be linked with student identity (e.g., Winfield & Harvey,

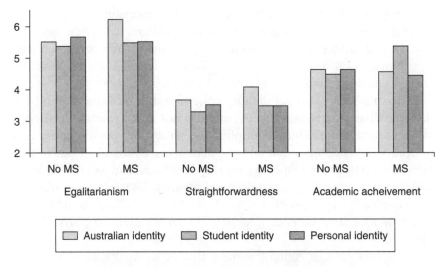

Figure 8.2 **Value support as a function of social identity and mortality salience, second study; the score range was 1–7 for all values except straightforwardness which was 1–5**

1996). In contrast, the third identity we selected, personal identity, was believed to not be associated with any particular value, as personal identity is defined by the attributes that differentiate the self from another individual; personal identity salience is assumed to not involve shared ingroup values (Brewer, 1991; Deaux, 1993; Turner, 1985). From this viewpoint, we expected that highlighting Australian, student, and personal identity across different conditions would enhance support for distinct values or no particular value at all. We further anticipated that mortality salience would strengthen the support for those specific values.

The results showed the effect of a salient Australian identity on support for egalitarianism and straightforwardness, as expected, but not individualism, contrary to our prediction. Support for both egalitarianism and straightforwardness was strongest under the condition that manipulated Australian identity, and mortality salience strengthened this effect (see Figure 8.2). Mortality salience also enhanced support for academic achievement exclusively under the student identity condition. It deserves clarification here that values responded to identity and mortality salience in two patterns. Straightforwardness was strong under Australian identity in the absence of a mortality salience manipulation, but it was made stronger by higher mortality salience. In contrast, both egalitarianism and academic achievement gained their momentum only when mortality was highlighted under the specific identity condition. Thus, it appears as if mortality salience provided the latter with an opportunity to express itself. The notion that mortality thoughts make accessible certain concepts associated with the cultural worldview has been documented in the recent literature (e.g., Arndt, Greenberg, Schimel, Pyszczynski, & Solomon, 2002). Social identity may regulate the particular concepts made accessible in the context by thoughts of death.

In contrast, the personal identity condition did not show support for individualism or any other value, and did not allow mortality salience to accentuate them. Thus, multiplicative effects of social identity and mortality salience on value endorsement were confined to the world-views associated with respective ingroup identities, and were not evident under a condition that primed personal identity. These findings demonstrated clearly that the direction of worldview validation under the threat of mortality salience is dependent on a salient, socially shared identity.

It deserves some attention that the activation of Australian identity did not entail support for individualism, nor did mortality salience accentuate it. Although individualism is thought to be a relatively strong cultural orientation in Australia, and a recent finding has suggested that Anglo-Australians' endorsement of individualistic worldviews is enhanced when thoughts of personal death are activated (Kashima, Halloran, Yuki, & Kashima, 2004), it is possible that individualistic values are not associated with Anglo-Australians' Australian identity. In other words, Anglo-Australians may support individualistic worldviews but not particularly when their national identity has been activated. Indeed, Haslam et al.'s (1999) investigations on Australian self-stereotypes, conducted in the national capital city with student samples, has not found individualism as a consensual Australian characteristic in recent years. Thus, a characteristic of a given culture that emerges from cross-societal comparisons may not necessarily be associated with the national identity.

Taken together, the findings showed that manipulated social identities led to differential cultural value support; thus, lending weight to the first implication of our model of culture and social identity that distinct cultural meanings and identities form a psychological set that may be activated together. We also contend that networks of identity-specific cultural knowledge are likely to crystallize, as it were, under conditions of high threat, as demonstrated in these findings and consistent with the third implication of our model. Whilst we have shown that the threat of personal mortality salience produces identity-specific support for cultural values, in Kashima et al. (2004) we have also reported that collective mortality salience affects greater support for collectivist behaviours amongst Japanese. No doubt, research that tests the effects of other potential threats on social identity and cultural maintenance, such as cognitive uncertainty (Hogg & Mullin, 1998) or direct threats to social identity (see Branscombe et al., 1999), would be worthy.

Culture, the individual and the group

The SCT and cultural perspectives on collective processes together provide a fruitful avenue for investigating and understanding the central question posed in this book: namely, the seemingly paradoxical phenomenon that a person's ingroups can sanction, and sometimes promote, his or her expression of individuality (see Hornsey & Jetten, 2004). A limited appraisal of SCT would suggest that personal identity salience is the only route to expressions of individuality, and that a salient social identity would promote adherence to the collective goals of the group to the exclusion of individual expression. Yet, SCT is clear that group views become normative when a particular social identity is salient (Turner & Onorato, 1999), and as shown by Jetten et al. (2002), group members may endorse individualist behaviour when it represents a normative orientation of the group. Our model of culture and social identity concurs that, depending upon the cultural worldview in question, social, rather than personal, identity salience may promote expressions of individuality.

Our present view assumes that knowledge maintained within the society correlates with social groupings. People may identify at one time with a group that upholds conformity as its strongest norm and at another time with a group that insists on expressions of rugged individualism. Consistent with this view, indigenous Australians were found to endorse individualistic values when they saw themselves as Australians but to endorse collectivistic values when they saw themselves as Aboriginals, as we reviewed earlier. As a result, individuals can hold competing worldviews by virtue of their multiple social identities and deploy them to cope with the ever-changing demands of their social environment. In short, through the cognitive process of self-categorizing as a member of one of these groups, a person is, paradoxically, able to activate cognitions and behaviours that reflect his or her individuality as a manifestation of the shared group norm.

Thus, our perspective on culture and social identity allows certain claims to be made about the relationship between the individual and the group. For one thing, because particular social groups within a society endorse individualistic cultural worldviews, social identity salience can regulate the importance of individual expression within the group. In other words, depending on the ingroup worldview, self-categorization with a particular social identity may activate an individualistic orientation to the social environment. There are two caveats, however. First, although the cross-cultural literature suggests that groups that endorse individualistic values may be more pervasive in modern, industrial, Western societies, this does not automatically translate into an expectation that ingroups in less individualistic societies all inhibit expressions of individuality. We do not know yet whether the degree and nature of individualism prescribed by ingroups are similar or different across societies. Second, while we have emphasized that expressions of individuality may be regulated through an ingroup norm, we do not mean to suggest that all expressions of individuality, or of any culturally shared cognitions for that matter, are regulated exclusively through social identity processes. As we mentioned earlier, there would be aspects of culture that are not directly tied to particular social identity within a society, and those elements of culture may be shared and maintained through some means unrelated to or only implicitly associated with identity processes. Further, the possibility remains that such alternative paths of cultural maintenance lend themselves to maintain parts of culture associated with social identities, such as individualism, egalitarianism, and collectivism. More research is needed to clarify those processes.

Concluding comments

In conclusion, this chapter presented a model of the relationship between culture and social identity. We argued that culture and social identity have a reciprocal relationship: culture enables and influences social identity processes whereas social identity salience regulates the aspects of cultural knowledge that are emphasized in the context. Put in terms of individual cognitive processes, we maintain that distinct social identities and cultural cognitions form a psychological set that may be activated together within a social episode, influencing a person's perception of the social world. We further argue that differing conditions of threat may enhance the likelihood that such networks of cultural knowledge are maintained or diminished over time and space. These arguments also provide one likely explanation for the observation of individual expression within groups: depending on the cultural knowledge held by a group in a particular society, social identity salience may indeed activate thoughts that reflect an individual's distinctiveness as a manifestation of his or her group membership. Finally, we submit that the cultural and SCT approaches together provide a fruitful theoretical and empirical avenue for investigating and understanding the link between culture, society and the individual.

NOTE

The authors of this chapter were co-contributors. Communications should be sent to Michael Halloran (m.halloran@latrobe.edu.au) or Emiko Kashima (e.kashima@latrobe. edu.au).

REFERENCES

Arndt, J., Greenberg, J., Schimel, J., Pyszczynski, T., & Solomon, S. (2002). "To belong or not to belong, that is the question": Terror management and identification with gender and ethnicity. *Journal of Personality and Social Psychology, 83,* 26–43.

Branscombe, N. R., Ellemers, N., Spears, R., & Doosje, B. (1999). The context and content of social identity threat. In N. Ellemers, R. Spears, & B. Doosje (Eds.), *Social identity: Context, commitment, content* (pp. 35–58). Oxford: Blackwell.

Brewer, M. B. (1991). The social self: On being the same and different at the same time. *Personality and Social Psychology Bulletin, 17,* 475–482.

Brewer, M. B., and Roccas, S. (2002). Individual values, social identity, and optimal distinctiveness. In C. Sedikides & M. B. Brewer (Eds.), *Individual self, relational self, collective self* (pp. 219–237). Philadelphia: Psychology Press.

Chiu, C., Morris, M. W., Hong, Y., & Menon, T. (2000). Motivated cultural cognition: The impact of implicit cultural theories on dispositional attribution varies as a function of need for closure. *Journal of Personality and Social Psychology, 78,* 247–259.

Choi, I., Nisbett, R. E., & Norenzayan, A. (1999). Causal attribution across cultures: Variation and universality. *Psychological Bulletin, 125,* 47–63.

Clark, H. H. (1996). *Using language.* Cambridge: Cambridge University Press.

Davidson, G. & Reser, J. (1996). Construing and constructs: Personal and cultural? In B. M. Walker, J. Costigan, L. L. Viney, & B. Warren (Eds.), *Personal construct theory: A psychology for the future.* Carlton South, VIC: Australian Psychological Society.

Deaux, K. (1993). Reconstructing social identity. *Personality and Social Psychology Bulletin, 19,* 4–12.

Diener, E., & Suh, E. M. (Eds.) (2000). *Culture and subjective well-being.* Cambridge, MA: MIT Press.

Feather, N. T. (1994). Attitudes toward high achievers. In M. P. Zanna (Ed.), *Advances in experimental social psychology* (vol. 26, pp. 1–73). San Diego: Academic.

Fiske, A. P., Kitayama, S., Markus, H. R., & Nisbett, R. E. (1998). The cultural matrix of social psychology. In D. T. Gilbert, S. T. Fiske, & G. Lindzey (Eds.), *The handbook of social psychology* (4th ed., vol. II, pp. 915–981). Boston: McGraw-Hill.

Fogarty, G. J., & White, C. (1994). Differences between values of Australian Aboriginal and non-Aboriginal students. *Journal of Cross-Cultural Psychology, 25,* 394–408.

Gardner, W. L., Gabriel, S., & Lee, A. Y. (1999). "I" value freedom, but "we" value relationships: Self-construal priming mirrors cultural differences in judgment. *Psychological Science, 10,* 321–326.

Gilbert, D. T., & Malone, P. S. (1995). The correspondence bias. *Psychological Bulletin, 117,* 21–38.

Greenberg, J., Solomon, S., & Pyszczynski, T. (1997). Terror management theory of self-esteem and cultural worldview: Empirical assessments and conceptual refinements. In M. P. Zanna (Ed.), *Advances in experimental social psychology* (pp. 61–139). New York: Academic.

Halloran, M. J. & Kashima, E. S. (2004). Social identity and worldview validation: The effects of ingroup identity primes and mortality salience on value endorsement. *Personality and Social Psychology Bulletin, 30,* 915–925.

Haslam, S. A. (1997). Stereotyping and influence: Foundations of stereotype consensus. In R. Spears, P. J. Oakes, N. Ellemers, & S. A. Haslam (Eds.), *The social psychology of stereotyping and group life* (pp. 119–143). Oxford: Blackwell.

Haslam, S. A., Oakes, P. J., Reynolds, K. J., & Turner, J. C. (1999). Social identity salience and the emergence of stereotype consensus. *Personality & Social Psychology Bulletin, 25,* 809–818.

Haslam, S. A., Turner, J.C., Oakes, P. J., McGarty, C., & Hayes, B. K. (1992). Context-dependent variation in social stereotyping. 1: The effects of intergroup relations as mediated by social groups and frame of reference. *European Journal of Social Psychology, 22,* 3–20.

Haslam, S.A., Turner, J.C., Oakes, P. J., Reynolds, K. J., & Doosje, B. (2002). From personal pictures in the head to collective tools in the world: how shared stereotypes allow groups to represent and change social reality. In C. McGarty, V.Y. Yzerbyt, & R. Spears (Eds.), *Stereotypes as explanations: The formation of meaningful beliefs about social groups* (pp. 157–185). Cambridge: Cambridge University Press.

Heine, S. J., Lehman, S. J., Markus, H. R., & Kitayama, S. (1999). Is there a universal need for positive self-regard? *Psychological Review, 106,* 766–794.

Hofstede, G. (1980). *Culture's consequences: International differences in work-related values.* Beverly Hills, CA: Sage.

Hofstede, G. (2001). *Culture's consequences: Comparing values, behaviours, institutions, and organizations across nations.* Thousand Oaks, CA: Sage.

Hogg, M. A. & Mullin, B. A. (1998). Joining groups to reduce uncertainty: Subjective uncertainty reduction and group identification. In D. Abrams & M. A. Hogg (Eds.), *Social identity and social cognition* (pp. 249–279). Oxford: Blackwell.

Hong, Y., Chan, G., Chiu, C., Wong, R., Hansen, I., Lee, S., Tong, Y., & Fu, H. (2003). How are social identities linked to self-conception and intergroup orientation? The moderating effect of implicit theories. *Journal of Personality and Social Psychology, 85,* 1147–1160.

Hong, Y., Chiu, C., & Kung, T. M. (1997). Bringing culture out in front: Effects of cultural meaning activation on social cognition. In K. Leung, Y. Kashima, U. Kim, & S. Yamaguchi (Eds.), *Progress in Asian social psychology* (vol. 1, pp. 135–146). Singapore: Wiley.

Hornsey, M. J., & Jetten, J. (2004). The individual within the group: Balancing the need to belong with the need to be different. *Personality and Social Psychology Review, 8,* 248–264.

Hutchins, E., & Hazelhurst, B. (1993). *How to invent a lexicon: The development of shared symbols in interaction.* University of California, San Diego, Department of Cognitive Science.

Jetten, J., Postmes, T., & McAuliffe, B. J. (2002). "We're all individuals": Group norms of individualism and collectivism, levels of identification, and identity threat. *European Journal of Social Psychology, 32,* 189–207.

Jetten, J., Spears, R., & Manstead, A. R. (1997). Distinctiveness threat and prototypicality: Combined effects on intergroup discrimination and collective self-esteem. *European Journal of Social Psychology, 27,* 635–657.

Jordan, B. (1989). Cosmopolitical obstetrics: Some insights from the training of traditional midwives. *Social Science and Medicine, 28,* 925–944.

Kagitçibasi, C. (1994). A critical appraisal of individualism and collectivism: Toward a new formulation. In U. Kim, H.C. Triandis, C. Kagitçibasi, S.-C. Choi, & T. Yoon (Eds.), *Individualism and collectivism: Theory, method and applications* (pp. 52–65). Thousand Oaks, CA: Sage.

Kashima, E. S., Halloran, M. J., Yuki, M., & Kashima, Y. (2004). The effects of personal and collective mortality salience on individualism: Comparing Australians and Japanese with higher and lower self-esteem. *Journal of Experimental Social Psychology, 40,* 398–392.

Kashima, E. S., & Kashima, Y. (1998). Culture and language: The case of cultural dimensions and personal pronoun use. *Journal of Cross-Cultural Psychology, 29,* 461–486.

Kashima, Y. (2001). Culture and social cognition: Towards a social psychology of cultural dynamics. In D. Matsumoto (Ed.), *Handbook of culture and psychology* (pp. 325–360). Oxford: Oxford University Press.

Kashima, Y. (2004). Culture, communication, and entitativity: A social psychological investigation of social reality. In V. Yzerbyt, C.M. Judd, & O. Corneille (Eds.), *The psychology of group perception: Perceived variability, entitativity, and essentialism* (pp. 257–274). New York: Psychology Press.

Kashima, Y., Kashima, E. S., & Aldridge, J. (2001). Toward cultural dynamics of self-conceptions. In C. Sedikides & M. B. Brewer (Eds.), *Individual self, relational self, and collective self* (pp. 277–298). Philadelphia: Psychology Press.

Kashima, Y., Yamaguchi, S., Kim, U., Choi, S., Gelfand, M. J., & Yuki, M. (1995). Culture, gender, and self: A perspective from individualism–collectivism research. *Journal of Personality and Social Psychology, 69,* 925–937.

Lau, I.Y.-M., Lee, S.-L., & Chiu, C.-Y. (2004). Language, cognition, and reality: Constructing shared meanings through communication. In M. Schaller & C. Crandall (Eds.), *The psychological foundations of culture* (pp. 77–100). Mahwah, NJ: Erlbaum.

Markus, H. R., & Kitayama, S. (1991). Culture and the self: Implications for cognition, emotion, and motivation. *Psychological Review, 98,* 224–253.

Matsumoto, D., Wessman, M.D., Reston, K., Brown, B.R., & Kupperbusch, C. (1997). Context-specific measurement of individualism–collectivism on the individual level. *Journal of Cross-Cultural Psychology, 28,* 743–767.

Miller, J. G. (1984). Culture and the development of everyday social explanation. *Journal of Personality and Social Psychology, 46,* 961–978.

Miller, J. G. (1997). Theoretical issues in cultural psychology. In J. W. Berry, Y. H. Poortinga, & J. Pandey (Eds.), *Handbook of cross-cultural psychology* (2nd ed., vol. 1, pp. 85–128). Boston: Allyn & Bacon.

Nisbett, R. E. (2003). *The geography of thought.* London: Brealey.

Oakes, P. J. (1987). The salience of social categories. In J. C. Turner, M. A. Hogg, P. J. Oakes, S. D. Reicher, & M. S. Wetherell (Eds.), *Rediscovering the social group: A self-categorization theory* (pp. 147–161). Oxford: Blackwell.

Oakes, P. J., Haslam, S. A., & Turner, J. C. (1994). *Stereotyping and social reality.* Oxford: Blackwell.

Onorato, R. S., & Turner, J. C. (2001). The "I", the "me", and the "us": The psychological group and self-concept maintenance and change. In C. Sedikides & M. B. Brewer (Eds.), *Individual self, relational self, collective self* (pp. 147–170). Philadelphia: Psychology Press.

Oyserman, D., Coon, H. M., & Kemmelmeier, M. (2002). Rethinking individualism and collectivism: Evaluation of theoretical assumptions and meta-analyses. *Psychological Bulletin, 128,* 3–72.

Poortinga, Y. H. (1992). Towards a conceptualization of culture for psychology. In S. Iwawaki, Y. Kashima, & K. Leung (Eds.), Innovations in cross-cultural psychology: Selected papers from the 10th International Conference of the International Association for Cross-cultural Psychology (pp. 3–17). Amsterdam: Swets & Zeitlinger.

Quinn, N., & Strauss, C. (1993). *A cognitive framework for a unified theory of culture.* Durham, NC: Duke University, Department of Anthropology.

Reicher, S. D. (1996). Social identity and social change: Rethinking the context of social psychology. In W. P. Robinson (Ed.), *Social groups and identities: Developing the legacy of Henri Tajfel* (pp. 317–336). Oxford: Butterworth-Heinemann.

Rhee, E., Uleman, J. S., & Lee, H. K. (1996). Variations in collectivism and individualism by ingroup and culture: Confirmatory factor analyses. *Journal of Personality and Social Psychology, 71,* 1037–1054.

Rice, T. W. & Steele, B. J. (2004). Subjective well-being and culture across time and space. *Journal of Cross-Cultural Psychology, 35,* 633–647.

Schwartz, S. H., & Bilsky, W. (1987). Toward a psychological structure of human values. *Journal of Personality and Social Psychology, 53,* 550–562.

Smith, E. R. (1996). What do connectionism and social psychology offer each other? *Journal of Personality and Social Psychology, 70,* 893–912.

Spears, R., Doosje, B., & Ellemers, N. (1997). Self-stereotyping in the face of threats to group status and distinctiveness: The role of group identification. *Personality and Social Psychology Bulletin, 23,* 538–553.

Stasser, G., Taylor, L.A., & Hanna, C. (1989). Information sampling in structured and unstructured discussions of three- and six-person groups. *Journal of Personality and Social Psychology, 57,* 67–78.

Steele, C. M., Spencer, S. J., & Aronson, J. (2002). Contending with group image: The psychology of stereotype and social identity threat. In M. P. Zanna (Ed.), *Advances in experimental social psychology* (pp. 379–440). San Diego: Academic.

Takano, Y., & Osaka, E. (1999). An unsupported common view: Comparing Japan and the U.S. on individualism/collectivism. *Asian Journal of Social Psychology, 2,* 311–342.

Trafimow, D., Triandis, H. C., & Goto, G. G. (1991). Some tests of the distinction between the private self and the collective self. *Journal of Personality and Social Psychology, 60,* 649–655.

Triandis, H. C. (1972). *The analysis of subjective culture.* New York: Wiley.

Triandis, H.C. (1989). The self and social behaviour in different cultural contexts. *Psychological Review, 96,* 506–520.

Triandis, H. C. (1995). *Individualism and collectivism.* Boulder, CO: Westview.

Turner, J. C. (1985). Social categorization and the self-concept: A social cognitive theory of group behaviour. In E. J. Lawler (Ed.), *Advances in group processes: Theory and research* (vol. 2, pp. 77–122). Greenwich, CT: JAI.

Turner, J. C. (1991). *Social influence.* Buckingham: Open University Press.

Turner, J. C. (1999). Some current themes in research on social identity and self-categorization theories. In N. Ellemers, R. Spears, & B. Doosje (Eds.), *Social identity: Context, commitment, content* (pp. 6–34). Oxford: Blackwell.

Turner, J. C., Oakes, P. J., Haslam, S. A., & McGarty, C. (1994). Self and collective: Cognition and social context. *Personality and Social Psychology Bulletin, 20,* 454–463.

Turner, J. C. & Onorato, R. S. (1999). Social identity, personality, and the self-concept: A self-categorizing perspective. In T. R. Tyler, R. M. Kramer, & O. P. John (Eds.), *The psychology of the social self: Applied social research* (pp. 11–46). Mahwah, NJ: Erlbaum.

Winfield, H. R., & Harvey, E. J. (1996). Psychological maturity in early adulthood: Relationships between social development and identity. *Journal of Genetic Psychology, 157,* 93–103.

Yamagishi, T., & Yamagishi, M. (1994). Trust and commitment in the United States and Japan. *Motivation and Emotion, 18,* 9–66.

Yuki, M. (2003). Intergroup comparison versus intragroup relationships: A cross-cultural examination of social identity theory in North American and East Asian cultural contexts. *Social Psychological Quarterly, 66,* 166–183.

9

Interobjectivity: The Collective Roots of Individual Consciousness and Social Identity

Fathali M. Moghaddam

The Mind of the universe is social. (Marcus Aurelius, 180/1964, p. 88)

The three arguments developed in this chapter are related through their common support for a more social approach in psychology. By "more social" I mean an approach that reflects the collective processes associated with the collaboratively constructed and mutually upheld nature of social reality (following Bruner, 1986; Harré, 2002; see also Postmes, Baray, Haslam, Morton, & Swaab, Chapter 12 in this volume). First, I argue that social identity theory (Tajfel & Turner, 1979) is compatible with a cultural account of behavior. Second, I contend that the conception of the individual central to social identity theory entails assumptions that leave sufficient room for cultural variations. Third, I articulate an example of how a cultural perspective suggests new directions in which social identity theory and research could further develop.

Social identity theory emerged as part of a larger movement toward achieving a non-reductionist psychology (the wider historical and ideological background to the theory is reflected in Israel & Tajfel, 1972; Sampson, 1977). The theory has stimulated an impressive body of research that comes under the broad umbrella of "the social identity tradition" (e.g., see Ellemers, Spears, & Doosje, 1999; Robinson, 1996; Worchel, Morales, Páez, & Deschamps, 1998) as well as self-categorization theory (Turner, Hogg, Oakes, Reicher, & Wetherell, 1987) and other theoretical offshoots (some of them reflected in the chapters of this text, e.g., Pickett & Leonardelli, Chapter 4). However, because of space limitations I address mainly the original theory of intergroup conflict and change.

I begin by clarifying what I mean by "a cultural perspective". This clarification is necessary because of considerable divergence in cultural perspectives in recent years (Moghaddam & Studer, 1997). In the second section, I explore the compatibility of social identity theory with the cultural perspective I adopt. The third section, the longest in the chapter, examines assumptions underlying the concept of the individual within social identity theory and how these assumptions allow for cultural variations. Finally, I discuss how a cultural perspective on rights and duties suggests extensions to social identity theory and research in the domain of social change and stability.

The cultural perspective of this chapter

The central feature of the cultural perspective that guides this discussion is the adoption of a normative rather than a causal account of human thought and action. Thus, my position stands in sharp contrast to both traditional psychology and traditional cross-cultural psychology (Moghaddam & Studer, 1997), which share the search for assumed causes (operationalized as independent variables) and their assumed effects (operationalized as dependent variables) on social behavior. The shift from behaviorism to cognition as the dominant paradigm in psychology has moved the search for "causes" from solely the stimuli in the environment to also include cognitive mechanisms assumed to function in the mind. But common to both behaviorism and cognitive psychology is the insistence that thought and action are causally determined. The limitations of such positivist cause–effect accounts have been convincingly articulated elsewhere (e.g., Harré, 2002), and need not be repeated here. Suffice to say that the positivist cause–effect account leaves no room for personal agency and intentionality.

An alternative normative account entails an understanding of individual choice not as an "effect" causally determined by assumed "underlying cognitive mechanisms" or by external factors, but as regulated by the norms, rules, and other aspects of the normative system that a person interprets to be appropriate in cultural context (see Moghaddam, 1998). In any given context the individual has available various normative systems within which to think and act correctly or incorrectly. For example, an individual who wants to position herself as a rebel in a Western society has a variety of choices, such as in terms of what to rebel against (e.g., classical music) and what "rebel" cause to take up (e.g., post-punk rock). Individual choices are made within constraints, and different degrees of freedom are present in different situations, so that more choices are available in some contexts than in others.

According to this normative account, regularity and predictability in behavior arise because most people most of the time consciously or unconsciously behave correctly according to the normative system dominant in their culture. For example, when participants enter an experimental laboratory, they search for guides as to how they should behave (often participants enter a laboratory and ask "What am I supposed to do?", as a way of seeking information about correct behavior). Most participants interpret the situation and "how they should behave" in a similar way to others who share their culture, and these are the participants whose behavior is used as data to yield "significant results". The other participants, usually a minority, who interpret the situation differently and behave in other ways (such as by deciding that they do not want to be in the experiment) contribute to error or variance in experimental results. Thus, culture guides behavior in the laboratory context, but does not "cause" individuals to behave in particular ways.

The cultural perspective that I am advocating does not negate the utility and value of the laboratory experiment as a research method in psychology. The laboratory has served a highly useful and, indeed, essential role in psychological research. It is the causal interpretation of findings rather than the laboratory method that is faulty (for a more in-depth discussion of the utility of the laboratory method in psychology, see Moghaddam & Harré, 1992).

Is social identity theory compatible with a cultural perspective?

Social identity theory is compatible with the cultural perspective advocated in this discussion, although mechanistic interpretations of the theory that have become dominant in the social identity tradition are not compatible with this cultural perspective. The theory has identified a series of preferences individuals tend to show in social life. From a cultural perspective, these preferences are regulated by belief structures and other important components of normative systems.

The point of departure for certain readings of social identity theory (e.g., Hogg & Abrams, 1988) is that individuals are assumed to have a preference for group membership that supports their proposed need for a positive and distinct identity. My interpretation is that this preference is learned through socialization processes, as individuals are taught that belonging to groups with positive and distinct identities is more rewarding, both in direct material ways and in less direct ways related to emotional support and social acceptance. For example, as a child enters school and moves in and out of different groups, she learns that membership in some groups (e.g., the advanced math class, the winning swim team) brings with it far more positive reactions from her parents, teachers, friends, and so on, than membership in other groups (e.g., the "C" math class, the losing swim team).

Similarly, the child learns the "correct" way to think as a member of different types of groups, including sex, ethnic, and religious groups. This comes about through often subtle but powerful *carriers* – vehicles through which cultural values and "ways of doing things" are sustained, propagated, and moved forward from generation to generation (Moghaddam, 2002). Examples of symbolic carriers are national flags, team mascots, tribal colors and costumes. Other carriers include various scripted practices and rituals, such as initiation ceremonies and the like, and rules about how an individual can correctly enter into and exit from different groups.

From a cultural perspective, social identity theory has postulated certain preferences individuals show in different intergroup contexts. That is, for example, if individuals are members of a group that already enjoys positive and distinct identity they will prefer one kind of strategy (i.e., to try to maintain the *status quo*), but if their group membership leads to inadequate social identity they will prefer other behavioral options (e.g., try to exit from the group). Again, such preferences are acquired during the course of socialization and are dependent on cultural conditions, training, and dominant belief structures. This interpretation is more in line with Tajfel's broader writings than an interpretation based on genetic factors or inheritance more broadly (for a more in-depth discussion of Tajfel's broader approach, see Billig, 1996). From a cultural perspective, a key research question concerns the extent to which the identified preferences actually are consistent across cultures, a topic on which there is as yet little serious research (for an exception, see Wetherell, 1982).

Thus, the general approach adopted by social identity theory is compatible with the cultural approach advocated in this chapter. Next, I turn to consider more specifically the fit between the conception of the individual central to social identity theory and this cultural perspective.

The individual within the social identity tradition and SIT

The conception of the individual central to SIT entails five main sets of assumptions that are particularly noteworthy from a cultural perspective. In this section, I identify these assumptions and show how they leave room for cultural variations in conceptions of the individual.

Positive and distinct identity

A first assumption is that the individual is motivated to achieve a positive and distinct identity. The theory does not postulate the particular criteria according to which the positiveness and distinctiveness of identity are evaluated.

Cultural research suggests that "positive and distinct identity" is not a fixed idea in an individual's head, but should be viewed as a set of collaborative social practices that vary depending on the context and interlocutors. Such practices are used to try to position oneself in relation to others, to achieve particular presentations of oneself, as more or less like others for example, depending on who the interlocutors are and what the context is (see discussions in Harré & Moghaddam, 2003). For example, in supposedly "more conformist" societies such as Germany and Japan, individuals showed less conformity than Americans (a supposedly "low conformist" society) in the standard Asch-type experimental situations (see Moghaddam, 1998, Chapter. 7). A plausible explanation for this finding is that although Germans and Japanese may be more conformist than Americans within certain ingroups (such as family, close friends, and work colleagues), they are less conformist when interacting with strangers (as is the case in the typical psychology experiment). Such processes suggest that motivation, to conform for example, is not something fixed within an individual, but is manifested in ongoing social practices that vary across contexts (see the related discussion by Halloran and Kashima, Chapter 8 in this volume, on how culture moderates the ways in which identities are being expressed). By implication, how motivated an American, German, Japanese, or any other person is to achieve a positive and distinct identity is context dependent. So too are the attributes or "criteria" of the positive and distinct identity.

Of course, a complicating factor is that the context itself changes. I am writing the final draft of this chapter in China, where rapid change has been the most salient feature of society for the last half century. The cultural revolution of the late 1960s and the "perpetual revolution" launched by Chairman Mao Zedong have been overtaken by a state-sponsored market economy and the emergence of a super-rich capitalist elite in the "New China" of the twenty-first century. A "positive and distinct" identity in the context of the cultural revolution meant something completely different from a "positive and distinct" identity in the context of the New China, characterized as it is in many ways by unbridled "wild west" capitalism.

As regards the criteria according to which individuals evaluate positiveness and distinctiveness, enormous variations are suggested by cultural research. Consider, for example, the range of physical characteristics that have been selected to serve as criteria. The most pervasive in Western societies is skin color, on the basis of which the social world is divided into "black" and "white". However, such criteria are "arbitrary", in the sense that they are not objectively selected, and infinite other possibilities are also available. Consider, for example, the division of the social world in Rwanda on the basis of height (Maquet, 1961), and the even more intriguing division between "long-ears" and "short-ears" on ancient Easter Island (Heyerdahl, 1989). In all such cases, social categorization is based on objectively measurable differences, which are transformed into social criteria by the majority group wielding power. For example, the "one drop" rule as practiced by whites in the United States defined "black" as any individual with even "one drop" of "black blood". Such a rule was clearly designed to maximize the size of the population who could be defined as slaves, and later as "colored" (and thus be disenfranchised).

By implication, through the manufacture and manipulation of different criteria for evaluating positive and distinct identity, the majority group can determine *rights*, demands placed on others by the person who possesses them, and *duties*, demands placed by others on the person who owes them, with respect to how the members of different groups will assess their social identity.

Social identity integral to personal identity

Social identity is defined as "that part of an individual's self-concept which derives from his knowledge of his membership in a social group (or groups) together with the value and emotional significance attached to that membership" (Tajfel, 1978, p. 63). There are at least two key issues left open: first, the question of how many groups a person belongs to; second, how strong are the value and emotional significance attached to membership(s) (these issues are to some degree addressed in self-categorization theory and research, where it is assumed people have networks of identities they draw from). Enormous cultural variations exist in both of these areas.

First, on the matter of how many groups an individual belongs to, consider the range of possibilities between the extremes of *mono-group societies*, where membership in one group dominates life and fundamentally influences the behavior of all or most individuals in that society in all domains, and *multi-group societies*, where the influence of membership in many different groups with diverse characteristics has different levels of influence on the behavior of different individuals. An example of a society closer to the mono-group extreme is the Islamic Republic of Iran, where for Shi'i Muslims the importance of membership in the group "Shi'i Muslim" is in practice by far the most important group membership (see

Moghaddam, 2004a). This is because the rules and practices of Shi'i Islam are used to regulate official Iranian government policy, as well as the minute details of everyday social life, such as the clothing people are allowed to wear, the names they are allowed to give to their children, what they are permitted to eat, who they can shake hands with, who they can socialize with, how many wives a man can have at one time and whether he can have "permanent" or "temporary" wives. Even though an individual in the Islamic Republic of Iran can be a member of many different groups, membership in the group "Shi'i Muslim" in practice dominates all other memberships. An example of a society closer to the multi-group end of the continuum is the United States, where conformity is no less than in most other major societies (Moghaddam, 1998, Chapter 7), but membership in no one group has a dominating influence on all or most individuals in that society. In the United States, there are a greater variety of subcultures with different normative systems, such as those relating to sexual orientation, than in Iran, but conformity is *not necessarily weaker* (1998, pp. 240–241).

There is also diversity in the sheer number of groups individuals belong to in different cultures. In most large modern societies multiple group membership is the norm, with family, social, professional, recreational, political, religious, cultural, and other group affiliations competing to influence the individual. However, at the other extreme are examples of much smaller societies where individuals belong to far fewer groups. The clearest cases of this are isolated smaller societies, contemporary examples being the Tibetan Nyinba in the Himalayan mountains (Levine, 1988), the Old Order Amish of Pennsylvania (USA) (Hostetler, 1980), and the Yanomamo who live in the Amazon jungle in Brazil and Venezuela (Chagnon, 1992); but there are even more numerous historical examples, such as the Tiwi of northern Australia (Hart, Pilling, & Goodale, 2001).

By implication, in mono-group societies individuals have a duty to follow the normative practices of one or two groups in all areas of life, and social identity is based in important ways on just those one or two groups; whereas in multi-group societies individuals have the right to practice different lifestyles and develop a social identity that is founded on multiple diverse groups. This has important implications for the range of options available for expressing individuality and personal freedoms within a cultural context.

Second, on the issue of the value and emotional significance attached to group membership, on the surface it would seem that higher individualism should be associated with lower value and emotional significance to group attachment. After all, Hofstede (1991) defines individualism as pertaining to "societies in which the ties between individuals are loose: everyone is expected to look after himself or herself and his or her immediate family" (p. 51). By contrast, collectivism pertains to societies "in which people from birth onwards are integrated into strong, cohesive in-groups" (p. 51). Accordingly, we should find that in more individualistic societies, individuals have weaker attachments to groups. This seems to be in line with arguments from communitarians warning of weakening social ties in the United States and other "individualistic" Western societies (e.g., see Etzioni, 1993), as well as empirical evidence from Putnam (2000) and other political scientists in support of the argument that in the United States, the epitome of an individualistic society, more people are "bowling alone" and refraining from affiliation with all kinds of groups. However, the actual cross-cultural picture is more complicated.

Part of the complexity arises out of the processes of increasing specialization associated with modernization (Moghaddam, 1997). Increasing divisions of labor lead to a paradoxical situation, in the sense that more specialized individuals are more dependent on others to complete "whole" tasks and to function effectively. The United States and other industrially advanced societies are individualistic, yet they pursue a goal of "collective actualization" to try to maximize "how each person can most effectively develop specialized talents specifically in the narrow domains needed for group functioning. In the pursuit of this collective ideal, the criterion for development becomes the requirement on individuals to function effectively in the integrated dynamic structures of the collectivity ... The main objective of socialization ... is to develop individual talents to better meet market demands" (Moghaddam, 1997, pp. 4–5). An implication of this argument is that we should differentiate between individualism–collectivism at the level of the individual and at the level of the larger society, and this is in line with other recent interpretations (see Oyserman, Coon, & Kemmelmeier, 2002): increasing individualism at the individual level need not translate to individualism at the cultural level, and vice versa.

An implication for social identity theory is that increased individualism, at least at the level of the individual, need not translate into weaker value and emotional significance attached to group membership. This idea receives tentative empirical support from a recent correlational study that assessed the relationship between individualism–collectivism and indices of group affiliation across the different states of the United States, as well as across 42 different countries around the world (Allik & Realo, 2004). The results support the view that as individuals become more individualistic, they also become more dependent on others. This seemingly paradoxical relationship reflects the "plight of the individual in the age of individualism" (Moghaddam, 1997), and should be a rewarding area of social identity research in the future (see also the related discussion on individualism and identification in Jetten & Postmes, Chapter 7 in this volume).

Social comparisons determine adequacy of identity

The theory assumes that individuals in making intergroup comparisons come to an idea about the positiveness and distinctiveness of the groups to which they belong. Presumably, through "social creativity" groups can reconstruct the basis and dimensions of social comparisons. However, in the social identity tradition too little consideration is given to local normative systems that guide the individual to make some types of inter-group comparisons and not others.

Each culture guides individuals to make some types of intergroup comparisons rather than others. There is considerable cultural diversity with respect to the targets that are identified as "correct". Consider, for example, comparisons across gender groups. In many Western societies, women are encouraged (particularly by some feminists) to compete with men and to compare their status and rewards not only with other women but also with men (of course, not all women make comparisons across gender lines, and even those who do also make many other types of comparisons). Thus, there are annual publications reporting the average earnings of women and men in different professions, and statistics reporting scholastic achievements of women and men from elementary school to graduate programs. In contrast, women in Islamic societies are encouraged (particularly by government authorities) to see themselves as having a complementary rather than a competitive relationship with men ("like the two wings of a bird, men and women complement one another"). There is an absence of debates about issues such as "same salary for same work" and the like. The same kind of within-gender (rather than cross-gender) social comparisons are normative in many smaller traditional societies, such as the Old Order Amish, the Yanomamo, the Tiwi, and the Tibetan Nyinba.

A closer examination of some traditional societies reveals more subtle cultural variations in comparison targets. For example, in both modern Western societies and in traditional Tiwi culture, it is not proper for young men to compare themselves with old men on the criterion of how much access they have to young women (as girlfriends, companions, wives). But this similarity hides a subtle difference. In Western societies young men have greater access to young women than do old men. In traditional Tiwi society, however, young men have far less access to young women than do old men. This is because in traditional Tiwi society men can only attain a wife after achieving a high level of status and resources, which typically only comes about in the early 30s. Moreover, the first wife of a "young" man is typically a much older widow. However, as a man works his way up the status hierarchy and gains greater resources, he marries younger and younger wives (men can have many wives, and every woman is married all of her life, from birth to death). The Tiwi normative system favors older men; while there is little possibility of a man marrying in his 20s, he typically acquires many young wives when he reaches his 50s. Thus, social comparison targets for both young Western males and young Tiwi males is other young rather than older males, but for very different reasons.

By implication, individual group members have rights and duties to make some types of social comparisons, and not others. Such rights and duties reflect majority group interests, such as "old men" in traditional Tiwi society.

Perceived stability and legitimacy determine availability of cognitive alternatives

Whether or not an individual perceives alterative ways of organizing intergroup relations is postulated by SIT as being dependent on the perceived legitimacy and stability of the present situation. The bases for evaluating stability and legitimacy are not specified, nor is the extent to which instability and illegitimacy would have to be perceived for cognitive alternatives to arise. Finally, the priorities given to different cognitive alternatives remain open.

Considerable cultural variation exists with respect to the basis used to evaluate stability and legitimacy in society. In contemporary Western societies, democratic ideals suggest that stability and legitimacy rest on representative government. In theory, those who win elections govern on behalf of the people, and stability is ensured through smooth transitions from one election to the next. In practice, there is variation as to how such ideals are put into practice, as evident in the United States Presidential elections of 2000 that brought George W. Bush to power. Thus, even within Western democracies, there are considerable differences in how stability and legitimacy play out. Consider now a dramatically different system, that of the Islamic Republic of Iran, where the constitution stipulates that a "supreme Islamic leader", or a council of "Islamic leaders", will oversee all government laws and actions, to ensure that there is no deviation from "true Islam". In this case, representatives elected by popular vote are subordinate to, and only gain legitimacy through, religious authorities.

But to appreciate the deeper difference between legitimacy in Iran and in Western societies, we must consider in greater detail the concept of leadership in each context (Moghaddam, 2004a). In Iran, every practicing

Shi'i Muslim is obligated to select a *marja-i-taqlid*, "a source of emulation", a religious leader who literally will act as an example and guide for how to live, including every detail of daily life. For the Shi'i faithful, the legitimacy and stability of the world are defined by the *marja-i-taqlid*, from the realm of macro social and political events, to the details of how to wash and eat. Even those Iranians who do not routinely practice Shi'i Islam are nevertheless influenced by the normative system put into place by major religious leaders in their society. This leads to complex and subtle points about continuity of cultural systems, and the issue of how much *perceptions* of stability and legitimacy can be influential (see also the discussions of individual/group perceptions by Reicher and Haslam, Chapter 13 in this volume).

SIT gives considerable importance to perceptions of stability and legitimacy, but evidence from studies of revolutions suggests that social practices may continue despite changed perceptions (Moghaddam & Crystal, 1997). These include detailed analysis of revolutions, from the great French revolution (Schama, 1989) to more recent ones in Iran and elsewhere (see Moghaddam, 2004a). Middlebrook (1995) termed this the "paradox of revolution" – the continuity of the "same old" social practices after a major revolution, so that "the more things change, the more they stay the same". This continuity is sustained by carriers, discussed earlier in this chapter. Carriers such as flags, traditions, status symbols, informal norms and rules, act as "conveyers" of social practices; carriers inform people about "what to do", "when to do", and "how to do", in everyday contexts (Moghaddam, 2002). They sustain belief structures and the "mundane" everyday social practices that act as a break and as a limitation on revolutionary programs.

By implication, local cultural carriers can effectively maintain traditional social practices in intergroup relations, despite perceptions of instability and illegitimacy, and even after major revolutions. The social identity tradition should give more attention to continuity and what remains the same at the individual and interpersonal levels in informal life, despite changes in formal macro political and economic systems (the issue of change and continuity is further discussed in the final section of this chapter).

Change-seeking strategies

SIT articulates a range of strategies individuals adopt in order to try to maintain or improve a positive and distinct identity. Depending on the characteristics of the intergroup situation (for example, whether exit from a minority group is possible and whether cognitive alternatives to the present intergroup situation are perceived), such strategies range from the normative and individualistic, as in the case of making intragroup comparisons, to the non-normative and collective, as in the case of directly and collectively challenging the majority group. The theory assumes causal relations between belief structures and the strategies preferred by individuals, and this leaves the door wide open for cultural variations.

Clearly the strategies given priority by an individual are influenced by the belief structures dominant in society. For example, the theory postulates that when the situation is perceived as unstable and illegitimate, the individual will select one of the following strategies: individual mobility, social creativity (which has three dimensions: finding a new dimension of comparison, changing values assigned to attributes of the ingroup, and engaging in comparison with a different outgroup), and social competition. The choice of strategy is not made by the individual in isolation, as is suggested by the image of the lone participant calculating the "best strategy" in paper-and-pencil laboratory tests. Rather, both what are understood to be available strategies, and selection from among them, are achieved though social interactions, collective discourse, and collaborative negotiation. The outcome of these processes is fundamentally influenced by the narratives pervasive in society, as reflected by the emphasis on belief structures in social identity theory. For example, in the United States the "American dream" narrative is particularly pervasive, involving the idea that "anyone can make it in America", that through self-help and personal responsibility any individual can rise to the top positions in society. Associated with this emphasis on individual social mobility are campaigns by powerful economic interest groups against labor unions, government intervention, and social welfare generally, leading to what has been described as a "winner-takes-all society" (Frank & Cook, 1995). The individual, then, comes to appropriate a strategy through participation in collective social life, and through the unequal influence of various minority and majority groups.

By implication, then, in order to understand the actual preferences an individual shows between strategies, it is necessary to consider the shared understandings both within and between groups that typically enjoy unequal power and influence, and this is what I turn to next.

Interobjectivity and change: an example of a cultural extension to social identity theory

There is a fundamental difference between social identity theory, a theory of intergroup conflict and social *change processes*, and the social identity tradition, a body of literature that has tended to neglect social change specifically and collective processes of meaning-making more broadly. From the cultural perspective adopted in this chapter, a vital and invaluable feature of social identity theory is the concern with changing intergroup situations and the preferences individuals show, through the influence of belief structures, for different behavioral options in the context of such changes. The fusion of social identity theory and a cultural perspective can help shift the focus back onto change processes and *collective meaning-making*, and indeed suggest ways in which further theory development could take place in the domain of change and stability.

In several ways social identity theory does address the "puzzle of change", related to the often repeated observation that "the more things change, the more they stay the same" (for a broader discussion of this puzzle, see Moghaddam, 2002, particularly Chapters 1–3 and 15). First, the theory posits that in cases where individuals are content with their social identity, they will make behavioral choices that serve to maintain the present intergroup situation. Presumably, in such contexts a great deal could change in terms of cultural, technological, and even economic and political facets of life, without necessarily changing the intergroup situation and the status and power hierarchy of groups. Second, from among the broad array of behavioral options identified as available to individuals who perceive themselves to have inadequate social identity, only one (collective action) has the potential to lead to social change, and it is the less likely option.

Thus, social identity theory suggests part of a solution to the puzzle of change to be the tendency of individuals to avoid collective action and to prefer individualistic strategies that sustain the *status quo*. But another part of a solution to the puzzle of change is suggested when we consider the role of multiple identities in the change processes.

Multiple social identities

Social identity theory presents a view of individuals as members of multiple groups and having multiple social identities. This is in agreement with the cultural perspective adopted in this chapter, where the emphasis is on choices made by individuals between competing normative systems associated with different groups within the same context (in contrast to traditional cross-cultural psychology, which typically presents a picture of a homogeneous culture acting as a cause of behavior). The social identity perspective of multiple social identities provides another possible solution to "the puzzle of change": change impacting on social identities at one level (e.g., the "macro" national level) need not impact on social identities at another level (e.g., the "micro" local level). For example, a revolution that creates disruptions at the macro level of national identity need not change social identities at the micro level of social relations within families.

Similarly, social identities might change at the level of an individual's intrafamily relations, without social identities at the national level being affected.

It may also be that social identities at the micro or macro levels are transformed, without disrupting other social identities at the same level but in a different sphere. For example, the feminist movement and transformations in gender roles may change Jane's social identity based on her being a woman, but not change her social identity based on her nationality (gender and nationality both being at the macro level, but in different spheres). But there are also cases where social identity based on membership in one group will influence changes in many other social identities, at different levels and in different spheres. Such cases are particularly instructive with respect to the sources of individual consciousness. Consider the case of Shi'i Islam in Iran, discussed earlier in this chapter. For Muslims in Iran, Shi'i Islam has become a *superordinate social identity*, one that embraces and impacts on all other social identities available in a context.

This has come about through the influence of the majority group, Islamic fundamentalists, who hold the reigns of power in Iran. The key point here is that social reality within all groups, particularly minority groups, is in major ways shaped by a majority group that monopolizes power (see also Postmes et al., Chapter 12; Reicher & Haslam, Chapter 13 in this volume).

How are power inequalities perpetuated?

The cultural perspective advocated here leads to an emphasis on *change processes* in intergroup relations and belief structures dominant within groups, and the question of how power inequalities are often perpetuated despite changes in the relative status of particular groups. The "paradox of revolution" is pervasive (although not inevitable): revolutionary groups often come to power only to perpetuate former inequalities (Moghaddam, 2002). Social identity theory already does provide some answers to this riddle, such as through the idea of multiple social identities (above), but another avenue for future research is to explore how belief structures dominant in minorities and majorities lead them to adopt particular rights and duties as priorities.

It is useful to begin a normative account of intergroup relations with two basic ideas. First, culture and the normative system precede the arrival of the individual and help shape individual consciousness. All individuals, no matter how powerful they later become as adults, begin life as helpless infants within the all-embracing normative system of a culture. More specifically, the groups into which individuals are born (e.g., woman, man;

black, white; Christian, Jew, Muslim) have a profound impact on the social constructions individuals acquire. Second, the cultures within which individuals are born vary in some important ways, including with respect to assumptions about the characteristics of individuals. Such differences are reflected in the literature on individualism–collectivism and elaborations such as the "horizontal–vertical" distinction (Nelson & Shavitt, 2002), but a more dynamic account is needed of the *processes* through which individuals come to share certain social constructions, such as those relating to justice, and more broadly the very conception of an individual.

In order to help explain the processes through which individuals become integrated into culture, and culture in individuals, I have introduced the concept of *interobjectivity*, the understandings that are shared within and between cultures about social reality (Moghaddam, 2003). Through socialization processes, individuals arrive at objectifications of the world based on the normative system of their cultures. They come to see their version of social reality as the correct one. But in many ways such understandings are not unique to their culture, nor are they shaped solely by the ingroup. In the case of minority groups, in particular, interobjectivity is shaped by powerful outgroups.

Interobjectivity highlights a fundamentally important feature of understandings shared within and across groups: such understandings arise out of *unequal* intergroup power relations. Some groups have more power than others, and are able to shape in important ways the understandings held by less powerful groups – a tendency discussed in various traditions under titles such as "false consciousness" (e.g., see Moghaddam, 1998, pp. 424–425; and the distinction between "groups-for-themselves" and "groups-in-themselves" in Billig, 1976). This process of unequal intergroup influence is reflected, for example, in understandings shared within and across groups with respect to rights and duties. Despite the centrality of rights and duties in relationships within and between groups, rights and duties remain almost completely neglected in research on groups (e.g., see contents of Brown & Gaertner, 2001; Ellemers et al., 1999).

Beliefs about what constitutes an individual are in large part based on the rights and duties ascribed to an individual (Moghaddam, 2000; Moghaddam & Riley, 2004; Moghaddam, Slocum, Finkel, Mor, & Harré, 2000). In practice, rights and duties are ascribed not just on the basis of individual characteristics, but also on the basis of group memberships. That is, the concept of an "abstract individual" with universal rights is severely tested by cultural variations. Consider, for example, cultural variations in rights reflected in polyandry and polygamy: among the Tibetan Nyinba a woman has the right to practice fraternal polyandry (i.e., marry several husbands who are brothers); in contrast, Shi'i Muslim men have the right to practice a particular form of polygamy (to have up to four "permanent" wives and countless "temporary" wives).

The preferences identified by social identity theory are reflections of perceived rights and duties: for example, an individual perceiving it as her right to attempt individual mobility to try to exit from a lower status group in order to gain entrance to a higher status group, and the same individual perceiving it to be her duty to refrain from the "radical" path of collective action. In general, authorities maintain political stability by teaching individuals it is their right and their duty to "work within the existing system" rather than to take up collective action that might overturn the existing order. Revolutionaries, on the other hand, attempt to persuade people to adopt a redefinition of rights and duties, so that collective action takes priority over individual mobility. But what happens when revolutionaries do succeed and people do adopt collective action with the result that the majority group is toppled?

The reappearance of intergroup inequalities

On the surface, at least, it seems that cultural variations prevent us from proclaiming any universals with respect to rights and duties. However, a closer examination suggests a different picture. Ideas about rights and duties reflect intergroup inequalities: majority rather than minority groups define rights and duties as understood and shared across groups. For example, at the international level, Western conceptions of individual rights rather than alternative conceptions emphasizing collective rights have become influential (Finkel & Moghaddam, 2004). Historically, Western powers have defined rights and duties for all humankind, the economically rich for the economically poor, men for both men and women, whites for both whites and blacks, and so on.

However, rights and duties are not static, just as the concept of the individual and social relations are not static. Consider, for example, the rights and duties ascribed to children in contemporary Western societies. As the child develops and acquires notions of "rights" and "fairness", she makes demands such as "It's only fair that I go to the cinema with my friends". But her parents give priority to duties, as in "You can only go to the cinema after you've finished all your homework". When the child becomes an adult and has children of her own, the cycle of rights and duties resumes, and she now gives priority to duties when interacting with her own children. Thus, the concept of what the person is and what rights and duties she has changes, both in the larger society and in her own mind.

This has implications for intergroup relations that supplement the strategies identified by social identity theory. Specifically, the priority a group gives to rights and/or duties can change across situations, particularly depending on changes in the relative power status of the group. A cycle of rights and duties has been identified: in situations of conflict and/or change, minority groups give priority to rights and majority groups give priority to duties (Moghaddam, 2003, 2004b). For example, since the 1960s a number of minorities have mobilized using slogans such as "women's rights", "Black rights", "gay rights" (rather than "women's duties", "Black duties", "gay duties"). Countering these minority movements, representatives of established majority group authority have emphasized duties, as in the duties of women, Blacks, and gays to abide by long established traditions ("family values", and the like). Similarly, revolutionaries attempting to seize power do so by appealing to rights, "the right to free speech", "the right to power sharing", and the like; while those in power evoke the "duties of citizens to obey the law" and maintain the status quo. However, when a minority group manages to come to power and achieve majority status, it shifts from giving priority to rights to giving priority to duties; just as the adult who once gave priority to rights as a child interacting with her parents now gives priority to duties as a parent interacting with her children.

Thus, the cultural perspective adopted here suggests several avenues through which the social identity tradition could constructively be expanded to provide a better solution to the "puzzle of change". A first avenue of future research is the relationship between multiple group memberships and change: change at one level and in one sphere of social identity need not influence change at other levels and spheres. Indeed, in some contexts change at macro levels of social identity may be resisted by stability in social identities at micro levels, helping to create the "paradox of revolution". A second avenue for future research is in the realm of rights and duties: the majority group is often able to define rights and duties for both majority and minority groups, but in times of conflict there is a tendency for majorities to give priority to duties and for minorities to give priority to rights. After revolutions, there is often a tendency for the new majority to shift from a priority of rights to one of duties, and for a minority (who still sees itself in a situation of conflict) to give priority to rights. This "cycle" is another part of the solution to the "paradox of revolution".

Concluding comment

SIT depicts individual thought and action as guided by belief structures, and this view is in line with the cultural perspective presented here. Belief structures are collaboratively constructed and collectively upheld; they arise out of social interactions, although they reside in individual persons. Moreover, belief structures are shaped by inequalities in the power of different groups. The cultural perspective advocated here leads to a greater focus on interobjectivity and the question of how individual minority group members are often influenced by belief structures that reflect the interests of majority groups, particularly in relation to social change and perceived rights and duties.

NOTE

I am grateful to Rom Harré for comments made on an earlier draft of this chapter.

REFERENCES

Allik, J., & Realo, A. (2004). Individualism–collectivism and social capital. *Journal of Cross-Cultural Psychology*, *35*, 29–49.

Aurelius, M. (180/1964). *Meditations*. Harmondsworth: Penguin.

Billig, M. G. (1976). *Social psychology and intergroup relations*. London: Academic.

Billig, M. G. (1996). Remembering the particular background of social identity theory. In E. P. Robinson (Ed.), *Social groups and identities* (pp. 337–357). Oxford: Butterworth-Heinemann.

Brown, R., & Gaertner, S. L. (Eds.) (2001). *Blackwell handbook of social psychology: Intergroup processes*. Oxford: Blackwell.

Bruner, J. (1986). *Actual minds, possible worlds*. Cambridge, MA: Harvard University Press.

Chagnon, N. A. (1992). *Yanomamo*. New York: Harcourt Brace.

Ellemers, N., Spears, R., & Doosje, B. (Eds.) (1999). *Social identity: Context, commitment, content*. Oxford: Blackwell.

Etzioni, A. (1993). *The spirit of community: The reinvention of American society*. New York: Simon & Schuster.

Finkel, N., & Moghaddam, F. M. (Eds.) (2004). *The psychology of rights and duties: Empirical contributions and normative commentaries*. Washington, DC: American Psychological Association Press.

Frank, R., & Cook, P. (1995). *The winner-takes-all society*. New York: Simon & Schuster.

Harré, R. (2002). *Cognitive science*. London: Sage.

Harré, R., & Moghaddam, F. M. (Eds.) (2003). *The self and others: Positioning individuals and groups in personal, political, and cultural contexts*. Westport, CT: Praeger.

Hart, C. W. M., Pilling, A. R., & Goodale, J. C. (2001). *The Tiwi of Northern Australia*. Belmont, CA.: Wadsworth/Thompson.

Heyerdahl, T. (1989). *Easter Island: The mystery solved*. New York: Random House.

Hofstede, G. (1991). *Cultures and organizations: Software of the mind*. London: McGraw-Hill.

Hogg, M. A., & Abrams, D. (1988). *Social identifications: A social psychology of intergroup relations and group processes*. London: Routledge.

Hostetler, J. A. (1980). *Amish society*. Baltimore: Johns Hopkins University Press.

Israel, J., & Tajfel, H. (Eds.) (1972). *The context of social psychology*. London: Academic.

Levine, N. (1988). *The dynamics of polyandry: Kinship, domesticity, and population on the Tibetan border*. Chicago: University of Chicago Press.

Maquet, J. J. (1961). *The premise of inequality in Rwanda: A study of political relations in a Central African kingdom.* London: Oxford University Press.

Middlebrook, K. J. (1995). *The paradox of revolution: Labor, state, and authoritarianism in Mexico.* Baltimore: Johns Hopkins University Press.

Moghaddam, F. M. (1997). *The specialized society: The plight of the individual in an age of individualism.* Westport, CT: Praeger.

Moghaddam, F. M. (1998). *Social psychology: Exploring universals across cultures.* New York: Freeman.

Moghaddam, F. M. (2000). Toward a cultural theory of human rights. *Theory & Psychology, 10,* 291–312.

Moghaddam, F. M. (2002). *The individual and society: A cultural integration.* New York: Worth.

Moghaddam, F. M. (2003). Interobjectivity and culture. *Culture & Psychology, 9,* 221–232.

Moghaddam, F. M. (2004a). Cultural continuities beneath the conflict between radical Islam and pro-Western forces: The case of Iran. In Y. T. Lee, C. McCauley, F. M. Moghaddam, & S. Worchel (Eds.), *The psychology of ethnic and cultural conflict* (pp. 115–132). Westport, CT: Praeger.

Moghaddam, F. M. (2004b). The cycle of rights and duties in intergroup relations: Interobjectivity and perceived justice re-assessed. *New Review of Social Psychology, 3,* 125–130.

Moghaddam, F. M., & Crystal, D. (1997). Revolutions, Samurai, and reductions: Change and continuity in Iran and Japan. *Journal of Political Psychology, 18,* 355–384.

Moghaddam, F. M., & Harré, R. (1992). Rethinking the laboratory experiment. *American Behavioral Scientist, 36,* 22–38.

Moghaddam, F. M., & Riley, C. J. (2004). Toward a cultural theory of human rights and duties in human development. In N. Finkel & F. M. Moghaddam (Eds.), *The psychology of rights and duties: Empirical contributions and normative commentaries* (pp. 75–104). Washington, DC: American Psychological Association Press.

Moghaddam, F. M., Slocum, N. R., Finkel, N., Mor, T., & Harré, R. (2000). Toward a cultural theory of duties. *Culture & Psychology, 6,* 275–302.

Moghaddam, F. M., & Studer, C. (1997). Cross-cultural psychology: The frustrated gadfly's promises, potentialities, and failures. In D. Fox & I. Prilleltensky (Eds.), *Critical psychology: An introduction* (pp. 185–201). Thousand Oaks, CA.: Sage.

Nelson, M. R., & Shavitt, S. (2002). Horizontal and vertical individualism and achievement values: A multimethod examination of Denmark and the United States. *Journal of Cross-Cultural Psychology, 33,* 439–458.

Oyserman, D., Coon, H. M., & Kemmelmeier, M. (2002). Rethinking individualism and collectivism: Evaluation of theoretical assumptions and meta-analyses. *Psychological Bulletin, 128,* 3–72.

Putnam, R. D. (2000). *Bowling alone: The collapse and revival of American community.* New York: Simon & Schuster.

Robinson, W. P. (Ed.) (1996). *Social groups and identities: Developing the legacy of Henri Tajfel.* Oxford: Butterworth-Heinemann.

Sampson, E. E. (1977). Psychology and the American ideal. *Journal of Personality and Social Psychology, 35,* 767–782.

Schama, S. (1989). *Citizens: A chronicle of the French Revolution.* New York: Vintage.

Tajfel, H. (1978). Social categorization, social identity, and social comparison. In H. Tajfel (Ed.), *Differentiation between social groups: Studies in the social psychology of intergroup relations* (pp. 61–76). London: Academic.

Tajfel, H., & Turner, J. C. (1979). An integrative theory of intergroup conflict. In W. G. Austin & S. Worchel (Eds.), *The social psychology of intergroup relations* (pp. 33–47). Monterey, CA: Brooks/Cole.

Turner, J. C., Hogg, M. A., Oakes, P. J., Reicher, S. D., & Wetherell, M. S. (1987). *Rediscovering the social groups: A self-categorization theory*. Oxford: Blackwell.

Wetherell, M. (1982). Cross-cultural studies of minimal groups: Implications for the social identity theory of intergroup relations. In H. Tajfel (Ed.), *Social identity and intergroup relations*. Cambridge: Cambridge University Press.

Worchel, S., Morales, J. F., Páez, D., & Deschamps, J. C. (Eds.) (1998). *Social identity: International perspectives*. London: Sage.

PART 3

The Individual–Group Dynamic

10

The Individual within the Group: Respect!

Russell Spears, Naomi Ellemers, Bertjan Doosje and Nyla R. Branscombe

Respect (Ali G.)
I don't get no respect (R. Dangerfield)

In this chapter we use the concept of respect to address questions of the "individual within the group", and reveal its intrinsic relation to the "group within the individual". In the process we try to demonstrate the group basis for the fundamental need to belong (Baumeister & Leary, 1995). We use this issue to address the major (meta)theoretical themes of this volume and argue that the (relative) failure of the social identity tradition to tackle the question of the individual within the group is ironically partly a legacy of its success in addressing the group within the individual. We propose that research on respect is one important front on which a theoretical integration of these two crucial components can be developed.

From a social identity perspective, the central theme of this volume "individuality and the group" sounds slightly provocative, perhaps even an oxymoron. The motive of Tajfel and others, in developing social identity theory, was a critique of the individualism inherent in much mainstream social psychology. Although strong traditions in group research already existed, these tended to conceive of groups as comprising individuals *qua* individuals – the group as the sum of its parts (Allport, 1924) – or the individual within the group, so to speak. Part of the anti-dote to this was to develop a new meta-theory, which showed that being a part of a group, can transform identity, and thus "social identity" was born. This idea of the "group within the individual" has been further developed within self-categorization theory. This meta-theory has proven tremendously heuristic in helping us understand the truly group nature of social behaviour. With this tradition in mind, considering individuality in the group might sound to some like a backwards step.

However, as the title of this volume suggests, the social identity approach also gives us a new perspective on individualism, not just as meta-theory or even ideology, but as something that can be subsumed within the social iden-tity account, as a norm, as the content of group identity (Barreto & Ellemers, 2000; Jetten & Postmes, Chapter 7 in this volume; Jetten, Postmes, & McAuliffe, 2002; Spears, 2001). However, another perhaps more fundamental way to consider the complex relation of the individual to the group is to recon-sider the issue of the "individual within the group", but armed with theoretical advances of the social identity approach (Reicher, 2001: see also Postmes et al., Chapter 12; and Reicher & Haslam, Chapter 13 in this volume). This is our goal here. In Turner's (1982) seminal paper on the cognitive redefinition of the group, the "group within the individual" was seen as a critical counter to the individualistic, interdependence-based, research that focused on the individual within the group. However, with this pendulum swing it can now, 20 years later, be plausibly argued that there is a parallel danger in an exclusive focus on group identity, if we thereby neglect issues of interaction and interdependence within the group (see also Postmes, Spears, Lee, & Novak, in press).

By focusing on identity, the social identity approach might be (falsely) accused of idealism. Precisely because the social approach never consid-ered identity to be a replacement for more materialist analyses based on realistic conflict for example, issues of individual and group interest (e.g., interdependence) remain important. More fundamentally, Tajfel (1978) in his early writings saw identity (and identification) not just as a purely sub-jective psychological outcome, but as implicating real and objective inputs, and indeed as a motor for social change. We cannot simply assume the identities we like without costs on both sides of the intergroup bound-ary (the case of Michael Jackson comes readily to mind).

Although objective external correlates of identity seem obvious and taken for granted, the implications have rarely been worked through in the social identity approach. Typically when we do our social identity research, especially where this is experimental, we assign social identities, although we might check this by measuring degree of identification.

However, this is all about the identity (albeit imposed or assumed) "looking out" from the individual as it were, the subjective side of the equation. Very little research (but see below) considers the more objective or socially valid issue of whether the person in question is accepted as a group member (the objective side if you like), and the perception of this acceptance as a group member (the subjective impact of the objective). Such reflections recall the conceptual basis of symbolic interactionism (e.g., Mead, 1934): the idea that our perceptions of ourselves are filtered through meta-perceptions of how we perceive others to perceive us.

This emphasis on the individual looking out stems partly from a focus on identity, rather than say interests and interaction, but it also arguably reflects a methodological route of least resistance. It is easy to take the perceiver's perspective as primary, as a starting point, and a true reflection of their psychology at any one point in time. However this neglects the interactive work going on behind the scenes, and over time, that contributes to group identity. To understand this, much more complex representations of networks and mutual perceptions and evaluations over time may be necessary. Such considerations raise many complex questions of interdependence, and level of analysis, which help explain why more simple experimental approaches have been preferred. Social network approaches (e.g., Monge & Contractor, 2003) and the social relations model (Kenny, 1994) are two ways of addressing this issue, but these have yet to be widely applied in social identity research.

Another reason why the group within the individual has not fed back to inform our understanding of the "individual within the group" has a theoretical basis. As we have already suggested, the "individual within the group" conjures up for many in the social identity tradition a rather individualistic and interdependence-based notion of the group, typically viewed as antithetical to the social identity project (Reicher, 2001). This is unfortunate and misleading. Compounding this problem has been the mistaken assumption (not supported by a more refined reading of SIT and SCT) that "when in a group, people will act as group members". A crude reading of the interpersonal–intergroup continuum might seem to suggest this conclusion (Turner et al., Chapter 2 in this volume). However, this is not the case, and the behaviour of any given individual depends on a range of factors including salience and identification, and how these combine.

The salience of group identity is typically determined by social contextual factors, namely the intergroup nature of the situation for social identity theory (e.g. intergroup conflict, group threat), and accessibility and fit for self-categorization theory. However, responses to such conditions are unlikely to be the same for all people, and prior group identification is a critical variable in determining whether people respond as group members or as "individuals" (Ellemers, Spears, & Doosje, 2002; Spears, Doosje, & Ellemers, 1999). Indeed many studies conducted by the present authors have shown that threats to group identity, and group salience manipulated directly or more subtly, lead to group level responses for high identifiers, but more individualistic distancing strategies for low identifiers. This is evident on measures of group homogeneity (Doosje, Ellemers, & Spears, 1995), self-stereotyping (Spears, Doosje, & Ellemers, 1997), social mobility (Ellemers, Spears, & Doosje, 1997), group effort and productivity (Barreto & Ellemers, 2000; Ouwerkerk, de Gilder, & De Vries, 2000), and outgroup discrimination (Branscombe & Wann, 1994).

A further theoretical impediment to the "individual within the group" agenda concerns the "functional antagonism" principle within self-categorization theory. This principle states that the salience of particular levels of identity tends to inhibit other levels of identity (see also Postmes et al., Chapter 12; Turner et al., Chapter 2 in this volume). This seems to preclude the interaction of different levels of identity (e.g., individual and group) within the individual at any given time. One could then conclude that the "individual in the group" is *either* the individual *or* a group member within the group (or in the case of SIT, some position between the two but not both). Once again this amounts to a question of identity salience, rather than intragroup dynamics that involve interaction between group members. The important role of social interaction has been neglected in two important senses: (1) potential interactions stemming from competing identities within the individual, and (2) interactions between group members who are operating at different levels of identity.

None of these ideas justify neglecting a more systematic understanding of the nature of the individual in the group, but they do help us to understand why this theme has received less attention than it might. However, as the research and theoretical frameworks in this book demonstrate, the time has come to consider more fully the "individual within the group", as informed by, and not contrasted to, the identity implications of the "group within the individual". There are a number of encouraging reasons to think that such a shift may be taking place.

First, the theoretical obstacles to this are more illusory than real. As we have seen, the external objective inputs and constraints on identity have always been there. These include issues of interdependence, and researchers are looking increasingly at how identity and interdependence interact rather than seeing these as either/or questions (e.g., Scheepers, Spears, Doosje, & Manstead, 2002; Stroebe, Lodewijkx, & Spears, 2005). Interdependence explanations have perhaps too often been associated with notions of individual self-interests, in contrast to social identity. However, even when perceived interdependence is shown to be important within the ingroup, it is often still necessary to explain the group-bounded nature of such perceptions (Stroebe et al., 2005).

This points to the value of an intragroup level of analysis, nestled between the interpersonal and the intergroup level, in order to give scope to the role of the individual within the group and in relation to the group. The idea of an intragroup level is present in principle with self-categorization theory (although the interpersonal and the intragroup are sometimes used interchangeably), but rarely has the distinctively intra-group level of analysis been studied empirically from a social identity per-spective. This is beginning to change. For example, there is emerging evidence for a uniquely intragroup dimension to social comparisons (Vliek, Leach, Spears, & Wigboldus, 2005).

Second, as we suggested above, there is greater acknowledgement of individual variations (e.g., group identification) as moderators that can explain differential responses in group contexts (Ellemers, Spears, & Doosje, 2002). Third, in terms of functional antagonism, there has been some recognition that activation of identities does not preclude more strategic and conscious management of identities (Reicher, Spears, & Postmes, 1995; Spears & Lea, 1994). This keeps the door open to the possibility of interactions between identities within, as well as between, individuals (Spears, 2001). Furthermore, approaches to social identity have been pro-posed that challenge some of the more determinist cognitivist/perceptualist readings of social identity and self-categorization theory that inhibit the role of interactive and constructive processes within the group (Reicher, Hopkins, & Condor, 1997).

However, most of these developments continue to address the individual within the group from the perspective of the individual "looking out" into the group. To be sure, many experimental approaches do consider the effect of independent variables on the individuals within the group through (false) feedback about performance, prototypicality, and so forth. However, in many cases this does not reflect the evaluation of other group members and is therefore less concerned with how the individual and group relate to each other (but see Noel, Wann, & Branscombe, 1995; Jetten, Branscombe, Spears, & McKimmie, 2003, for notable exceptions). Perhaps the most critical development to take research beyond this "first-order" perspective is the work on "respect". This forms the basis for the research programme considered in this chapter.

Respect: breaking away from the first-order perspective

Respect is the imputed worth accorded to one person by one or more others. There are many dimensions to respect, as we shall see. Respect can involve, but is not necessarily reducible to, liking by others (here termed liking-based respect), feelings of competence (competence-based respect), and also a sense of positive treatment (treatment-based respect). In short, respect involves some sort of positive worth being communicated by others – in our case, other group members. One construct that taps in to this sense of group worth is "membership esteem" – the sense of one's value to the group (Luhtanen & Crocker, 1992), and we have used this measure extensively in the research we describe. A lack of respect is generally likely to be painful, whereas its presence can enhance a sense of inclusion, and standing within the group (see Sleebos, Ellemers, & De Gilder, 2004a; Simon & Stürmer, 2003). Although we examine the effects of respect as an independent variable here, it can also be viewed as a valued outcome, to which group members aspire, and which they strategically emphasize (Jetten, Schmitt, Branscombe, & McKimmie, 2005).

Research on the importance of respect was pioneered by Tom Tyler and Heather Smith, specifically in the group-value model approach to justice issues (Smith & Tyler, 1997; Tyler, 1999; Tyler, Degoey, & Smith, 1996). This approach focuses on the importance of procedural justice, which has tended to inform how respect is conceptualized and operationalized (i.e., as treatment-based respect). The importance of this approach was that they considered not just the perspective of the "individual looking out at the group" (i.e., group identification or "pride") but also the "group looking in on the individual" ("respect"). Respect was proposed as a key predictor of the acceptance of justice outcomes.

In other words this identity-based, relational, approach to justice concerns both sides of the individual-group relation: the individual relation to the group and the group relation to the individual. It is neglect of this second factor within the social identity tradition that has, we argue, hampered understanding of the individual within the group. It was therefore logical for us to consider respect as a key route to understanding the individual within the group. It is important to note at this stage that Smith and Tyler see their work as perfectly compatible with, if not inspired by, social identity theory, which is after all a relational and identity-based approach to group behaviour. Our research extends theirs by moving beyond the justice context, by expanding the concept of respect from the primarily procedural dimension of treatment-based respect and an emphasis on the treatment by authority figures that has been their main focus (but see Smith & Tyler, 1997).

Respect is a central construct in our attempt to reinvigorate the understanding of the individual within the group because it makes clear the *psychological* relation of the group to the individual as well as vice versa.

Respect introduces the theme of interaction within the group, in the two senses that we have been considering. First, it points to the importance of the interaction among group members as a means of deriving their position within the group (and shows how the subjective is grounded in the objective). Second, it raises the possibility of interactions between levels of identity within the individual in relation to this external interaction (How do we manage identity agendas in relation to how we are evaluated and treated within the group? How does respect change identity and identification?). In short, considering the issue of respect from others provides a means of integrating research on the individual within the group with a theoretical perspective on the group within the individual.

Of course we are not claiming that previous research has ignored these issues. For example, early work on the *primus inter pares* effect (PIP, "first among equals": Codol, 1975) examined the relation of the individual to the group, as does work on prototypicality and on intragroup structure and leadership. However, much of this work stems from a "first-order" perspective in so far as it does not always implicate feedback from (or interaction with) fellow group members. Notable exceptions are the pioneering work of Williams on ostracism, and research on the phenomenology of peripheral group status by Branscombe, Jetten, and co-workers. Williams, Cheung, and Choi (2000) have shown the deleterious psychological consequences of social exclusion from the group, and indeed that this can activate the same brain substrates involved in the experience of physical pain (Eisenberger, Lieberman, & Williams, 2003). Research within the social identity tradition has also demonstrated how threatening it is to find oneself on the periphery of the group and it has identified the factors that motivate attempts at inclusion (Jetten et al., 2003; Jetten, Branscombe, & Spears, in press; Noel et al., 1995; Postmes & Branscombe, 2002). In short, there are good grounds for thinking not only that respect may be valued and enhance group commitment, but that its absence may be painful, especially where commitment to the group is high.

These research programmes stress how aversive rejection from the group can be, which in more positive terms highlights our "need to belong" (Baumeister & Leary, 1995). A central point of our research on respect is that there is a fundamental (intra)group dimension to this need. But what is the evidence for this claim? A key aim of our research has been to show the group basis of respect and explore the implications in terms of emotional and behavioural reactions. Let us therefore briefly step back to consider more general issues of self-evaluation and self-worth and consider the case for a group dimension.

Evidence that people prefer a positive identity and will welcome opportunities to enhance the self, or defend it when threatened, are well known to self researchers (e.g., Sedikides & Strube, 1997). Similarly, researchers of self-esteem have argued that the "need to belong" is a universal human motive (Baumeister & Leary, 1995). These research traditions confirm the assumption that to receive respect from others is likely to be welcome, and the resultant self-esteem is a marker of our belonging among those who value us (the sociometer theory of self-esteem: Leary & MacDonald, 2003).

But is this a group process or one based around individual identity and self-worth? Is it perhaps grounded in interpersonal networks rather than having an intragroup basis as such? This question might also be directed at some of the research on respect conducted within the group-value model. How do we know that the positive value of this respect in how we are treated derives from our group identity rather than the reward value associated with high status individuals in positions of authority? We can also turn this question around and ask: should not respect from any source, and not just the ingroup, be a good thing, and enhance the individual?

This question would seem to return us to the spectre of individualism, which prompted the quest by social identity theorists to provide a more group structured account of social life. A major challenge for our research programme therefore is to consider the case for the group-based nature of respect as a test case for how the individual in the group is shaped by the group within the individual. We aim to show that the effects of respect relate to the group context in which people find themselves. We are not saying that respect from the group is always more valued or consequential than respect from others as individuals, but simply that we need to take both aspects of the relation (individual to group and group to individual) into account in order to understand the effects respect may have.

In the remainder of this chapter we present empirical evidence addressing a number of key questions concerning group-based respect. These questions can be briefly described as follows:

1   What are the consequences of group-based respect for perceptions, feelings, and intra- and intergroup behaviour, and how are these affected by aspects of the intergroup context (e.g., identity threats)?
2   If group-based respect is something more than respect from others *per se*, can we establish different consequences of respect from ingroups and outgroups in terms of feelings and behaviour? If respect is bounded by group identity, we might expect respect from an outgroup to be less valued or even aversive compared to ingroup respect.
3   To what extent is the *dimension* on which respect is forthcoming from the group important in terms of feelings and behaviour? We distinguish between liking-based and competence-based respect to argue that liking-based respect may be primary.

The group basis of group-based respect

In our first study on this topic (Branscombe, Spears, Ellemers, & Doosje, 2002) we were concerned with establishing the effects of being respected by one's own group. Prior to this study, most research on respect had concentrated on treatment-based respect, primarily from authority figures (e.g., Tyler et al., 1996). We were interested in assessing the effects of liking-based respect from ingroup members when the group was high or low in status. We expected that people who were respected by their ingroup would be positively affected by the received respect, particularly when their group was devalued. We were especially interested in the consequences of such respect for their subsequent intergroup behaviour. The most straightforward prediction was that those who were valued by their group would in turn tend to value the group more in the behaviour and be more group serving in their responses.

We also considered a second factor which previous research has shown to moderate group responses, namely threat to group identity. As noted earlier, research has consistently shown that group-based responses are exacerbated under threats to social identity, primarily among high identifiers. In the present research we were interested in assessing whether respect might function in a similar way, such that those who were most respected by the group would show the most group-serving responses when their group identity was threatened. We reasoned that respected members would also be those most likely to stand up for the group when it was threatened, even at the expense of individual interest.

We categorized participants into (bogus) quasi-minimal groups ostensibly on the basis of an association task (Doosje, Spears, & Koomen, 1995). Participants were then required to report one favourable and one unfavourable recent behaviour, purportedly as a way for fellow group members to get to know each other. Participants were then asked to judge ingroup and outgroup members ostensibly on the basis of the behaviours they had generated. The feedback received constituted both the intragroup respect and the group identity threat manipulations. In terms of intragroup respect, participants learnt that the other ingroup members rated them either positively or negatively. In terms of group identity threat, participants received feedback that their group was rated either relatively positively, or negatively (threat) by outgroup members.

The main measures of interest in this study assessed: (1) reward allocations for the ingroup versus outgroup, and (2) the amount of time devoted to a voluntary group-based activity in which participants could allocate their time either to improving their image within the ingroup or to improving the image of their ingroup in the eyes of the outgroup. These tasks were designed respectively to assess the degree of group favouring behaviour, and to set this against a more self-serving task where a real time commitment was implied.

For the reward allocation task, the respect manipulation resulted in more ingroup allocations by those high in respect (a main effect). For the out-group reward allocations, however, there was a main effect of the inter-group identity threat manipulation with the identity threatened group withholding more allocations than the no threat group. There was also an interaction between group threat and intragroup respect, such that outgroup rewards were clearly lowest in the high-respect/identity-threat condition.

In sum, the ingroup reward allocations seem to be driven by intragroup concerns (i.e. respect), whereas the outgroup reward allocations seem to be driven by a combination of respect and threat, with respected group members in the threatened group condition showing the most competitive intergroup responses. This is analogous to the findings in other studies in which high identifiers respond to group identity threats in more group defensive terms.

The work commitment measure revealed conceptually similar results. Times devoted to improve self-image and group image were broadly com-parable for both respected and disrespected group members in the non-threatened group (albeit greater for disrespected group members). However, in the threatened group, respected group members promised to devote the most time to the group and the disrespected group members the least. Once again the combination of high respect and identity threat produces the greatest group-serving response (Ouwerkerk et al., 2000).

The (group-based) source of respect

In the previous study we provided evidence that respect forthcoming from the group can operate rather like group commitment, at least in response to identity threat. However, it may be premature to conclude that the effects of respect were "group-based" because there was no baseline comparison with respect forthcoming from a source other than the ingroup. To provide a strong test of the effect of respect as a group-based phenomenon it is therefore necessary to examine the effects of respect coming from sources other than the ingroup – notably the outgroup.

In the next series of studies (Ellemers, Doosje, & Spears, 2004) we therefore considered the (group) source of respect. A weak form of our hypothesis concerning group-based respect was that respect forthcoming from ingroup members would be more important or consequential than respect coming from an outgroup. A stronger form of this hypothesis, in keeping with the idea that groups may often try to differentiate themselves from outgroups, was that respect from an outgroup might even be problematic or compromise one's position within the ingroup.

In the first study in this series we simply crossed the level of respect (high versus low) with the source of respect (ingroup versus outgroup) in a between-participants design. This study used a scenario methodology in which participants imagined they had criticized a boy on a tram for not giving his seat to an elderly woman. Some bystanders who were present – students from either the ingroup (University of Amsterdam) or a rival outgroup (Free University) – either commended or criticized their intervention (high versus low respect manipulation).

In this and subsequent studies we measured the emotional reactions and effects on membership esteem as a result of the respect-relevant information, as well as a measure of willingness to work to improve one's personal image within the group. Participants reported more pride and less shame in response to high respect irrespective of group source, but only ingroup respect increased membership esteem. That is, whereas the immediate affective responses were the same regardless of source, only the comments by the ingroup source had an impact on membership esteem. Moreover, low respect motivated participants to work to improve their image in the group, but only in the ingroup source condition.

In a second study we examined the effects of respect from both the ingroup and the outgroup (high vs low in both cases), allowing us to examine the consequences of different combinations of respect. We were therefore able to assess conditions where respect from an outgroup source might be most compromising. We thought that receiving low liking-based respect from the ingroup but high liking-based respect from the outgroup would be most undermining of one's position in the group and lead to the most discomfort. A similar scenario procedure to the previous study, in which bystander students from both their own or a rival university were present, allowed for the different combinations of respect from the two groups.

Again, membership esteem was primarily enhanced by ingroup respect, but it was unaffected by outgroup respect. Willingness to invest effort working for the group was also only affected by ingroup respect. As expected, high ingroup respect elicited more positive emotional reactions (more pride and less shame), although this was also true of outgroup respect. However there was also an interaction such that the greater shame at receiving low respect from the ingroup was actually accentuated under conditions of *high* outgroup respect. In other words, when ingroup respect is not forthcoming, respect from the outgroup seems to intensify the negative reaction in line with the idea that being liked by the outgroup compromised one's position in the ingroup further.

In a third study, we attempted to gather further evidence that rather than respect being additive, respect from an outgroup might be problematic and exacerbate insecurity when the ingroup provides low respect. We moved away from the scenario methodology in this case, and returned to the paradigm in which participants were members of experimental groups as in our original study (Branscombe et al., 2002). We crossed high versus low respect with its source – the ingroup and outgroup source.

In addition to straightforward main effects of the respect manipulations on emotional reactions, a similar interactive pattern emerged as in the previous study: participants reported least pride and greatest envy towards other ingroup members when low ingroup respect was combined with *high* outgroup respect. The membership esteem measure also revealed a similar interaction: whereas high outgroup respect enhanced membership esteem when ingroup respect was high, when ingroup respect was low there was no enhancement effect of high outgroup respect. Once again, those with low ingroup respect seem vulnerable to, rather than saved by, high outgroup respect. This vulnerability seemed to be also reinforced by the findings on an effort measure. Those who were low in ingroup respect, but high in outgroup respect, felt the greatest need to improve their self-image within the group (see Ellemers et al., 2004, for further details).

To summarize, the results of these studies provide clear evidence that liking-based respect is not an unequivocal asset, but depends on the group source of respect. We even have evidence that being liked by the outgroup can compromise one's position in the group, albeit only when this position is already vulnerable due to lack of ingroup respect. What is notable, however, is that despite the lack of liking from the ingroup, rather than distancing themselves from this group, members experience negative emotions, suggesting that they are still emotionally attached to the ingroup. Taken together we have established evidence that respect is group-based: the group source is consequential for the effects of ingroup respect.

The dimension of respect

An important theme in the previous set of studies was to show that liking-based respect is not an unconditional positive, but can depend to some extent on the source of that respect. Indeed, liking-based respect from an outgroup can even be compromising. In this section we ask whether all respect from fellow ingroup members is unconditionally positive and therefore adds to the group members' feeling of self-worth and group commitment. Although this might sound straightforward, following on from the previous studies, interesting questions arise when we start to distinguish different dimensions of respect and the ways in which these might interact in producing particular experiences, emotions and behaviours.

So far we have concentrated on liking-based respect. However, many researchers in this field would question whether this was the only component of respect, and might not even regard it as essential or defining. Phrases such as "I respect my boss but I don't like him/her" may be familiar to many of us. That we can respect people without liking them suggests broader and potentially multiple dimensions of respect. This example of the boss is not accidental because we may often have respect without warmth for those in positions of power or status, or more generally people perceived to have competence, leadership qualities, and the like (Fiske, Xu, Cuddy, & Glick, 1999).

In the current set of studies we were therefore particularly interested in distinguishing competence-based respect from liking-based respect. These two dimensions seem to us important because they are the central dimensions of evaluation of others (Rosenberg, Nelson, & Vivekanathan, 1968; Skowronksi & Carlston, 1989).

Perhaps the most straightforward prediction here is that different components of respect from within the ingroup should simply be additive with one form of respect compensating for the absence of another. Clearly, to be both liked and thought competent by one's group is a good thing, and might even signal potential for a leadership role. To be disliked and thought incompetent is clearly a bad thing and may motivate social mobility if possible (see Sleebos, Ellemers, & De Gilder, 2004b). If commitment to the group is high and maintained, negative respect on these two central dimensions may be all the more painful, especially if "exit" does not seem possible. Such considerations underline the plausibility of an additive "more is better" approach to how respect within the group could combine. However, this approach does not take into consideration qualitative differences between different components of respect, and the meaning that particular combinations might convey.

There are good reasons to suppose that liking by the ingroup may be more important or primary than perceived competence. There are limits to this of course: we may consider competence more important during an argument, and competence may be more important to those whose role or position in the group depends on it, but other things being equal, liking is likely to be primary. This issue may be particularly consequential when we consider the combination of respect levels on these two dimensions. In particular, low liking-based respect combined with high competence-based respect may be psychologically problematic for group members seen in this way. While liking from other ingroup members confers belonging, in the group context, the "high flyer" may be seen as less prototypical of the group, perhaps even "too good for us" (the "tall poppy syndrome": Feather, 1994). Someone who is disliked but seen as highly competent could evoke envy (Fiske et al., 1999; Smith, Turner, Garonzik, Leach, Urch, & Weston,

1996) and be seen as a threat, compared to someone who is disliked but not overly competent.

This idea is already evident from research in the leadership literature: leaders seen to deviate from the group average can be less liked and less effective as a result (Duck & Fielding, 2003; Haslam & Platow, 2001; Hollander, 1964). It is the combination of low evaluation but high potency (Osgood, Suci, & Tannenbaum, 1957) that makes an ostensibly positive skill potentially problematic where others are concerned. Ability also confers the possibility of social mobility that may cause people to further question their position in the group (Ellemers, van Knippenberg, & Wilke, 1990; Seta & Seta, 1996).

The point here, from the perspective of the recipient of respect, is that they may share other group members' doubts about fitting into the group as a result of high competence-based respect. Assuming recipients pick up on the implications of this, we would expect them to experience more negative emotions. Paradoxically they might even experience more shame despite (because of) their competence when this is accompanied by being disliked. By contrast, being liked but seen as incompetent carries fewer negative implications for one's relation to others and the group because of the low potency, implying that the person is relatively harmless ("nice but dim": Peeters, 2002; Vonk, 1999). Implicit in this assumption is the idea that liking is to some extent primary and frames the interpretation of competence-based respect rather than vice versa (Asch, 1946). We refer to this alternative to the additive principle as the "compromised" hypothesis: the notion that high competence-based respect when combined with lack of liking can actually undermine one's position in the group from the recipient's perspective.

We set out to evaluate the compensation and compromised hypotheses in a set of studies (Spears, Ellemers, & Doosje, 2005). In a preliminary study we simply tested our assumption that receiving competence-based respect from the ingroup had some psychological and emotional impact, comparable in principle to the receipt of liking-based respect. We used a scenario design in which participants were asked to imagine that, having finished a course assignment before other students on the course, they offered to help them. Competence-based respect was manipulated in terms of the feedback the other students gave about the judged quality of this assignment (i.e., positive vs negative). Ratings on both membership esteem and emotions (pride and shame) confirmed the expected pattern: recipients of low competence-based respect exhibited reduced membership esteem and less pride and more shame. These results confirmed that competence-based respect generates the kind of affective response associated with liking-based respect.

The next question was how different forms of respect might combine and potentially interact, in line with our two competing hypotheses. In the second study we therefore manipulated liking-based respect and competence-based respect independently. We used a similar scenario-based design as in the previous study. The competence-based respect manipulation was similar to before, with recipients receiving either complimentary or critical feedback on the quality of their assignment. In terms of liking-based respect, participants also learned that the other students either appreciated the help with the assignment (high liking-based respect) or did not, seeing it as "showing off" (low liking-based respect).

We found main effects on the self-esteem and emotion measures for both forms of respect but no evidence of either compensation or compromise (i.e., no interactions). However, a measure of the relative importance of the respect dimensions confirmed our assumption that liking-based respect was more important, and only liking-based respect produced a more positive evaluation of the ingroup. Measures of effort to improve one's image within the group were also only affected by liking-based respect, with those low in liking-based respect being less motivated to improve their competence-based image. Although these results provide no direct evidence of compromise in terms of the two forms of respect, they do provide indirect evidence against compensation: participants were less likely to invest in competence to compensate for low liking-based respect.

We thought that we might be able to find more evidence for compromise in a setting where there was more direct involvement in the groups, and where the feedback on both respect dimensions mattered more and was more consequential. This was the aim of the third study where we employed the same design in which liking-based and competence-based respect were manipulated independently. Using the quasi-minimal group paradigm, we first categorized people into groups, ostensibly based on a pre-test in which they received feedback about the types of respect other group members had for them.

Although the respect manipulations only had main effects on membership esteem, a main effect of liking-based respect on emotional reactions (more positive emotions for higher respect) was qualified by an interaction between both forms of respect. In line with the compromised hypothesis, emotions were most negative when low liking-based respect was combined with high competence-based respect. Interestingly, measures of commitment to the group also produced a main effect of liking-based respect (more commitment for high respect) and an interaction: commitment was lowest when both forms of respect were low. In other words, although the low-liking/high-competence cell revealed evidence of being compromised in terms of emotional reactions, it is still associated with some commitment to the group (i.e., as high as other conditions). Indeed, this commitment helps to explain why rejection from the group in terms of liking-based respect is painful, and apparently exacerbated by positive views of one's competence. Overall, the data from this study provide some evidence that being perceived as competent by one's fellow group members does not necessarily compensate for the lack of liking, and may actually compromise this.

Summary of respect research

Our research on respect confirms that evaluation by other group members can have fundamental implications for how we subsequently relate to the group in terms of both emotional and behavioural responses. Moreover, this research shows that the source of respect is crucial and is group-bounded, which supports our contention that respect can stimulate a uniquely intragroup process. Finally, the findings of both the source and dimension studies remind us that positive evaluation is not always *experienced* positively but again depends on the group context, and the overall meaning conveyed by the respect received. We now broaden the discussion in order to relate this work to the central themes with which we started, and which define this volume.

Concluding remarks

The main message of this chapter is that it is crucial to take into account the position of the individual within the group in order to understand the impact of the group within the individual (and the relation between the two). As we stated at the outset, for a range of historical, theoretical, and methodological reasons, work in the social identity tradition has tended to neglect the relation of the group to the individual as a factor in how the individual relates to the group. Research has tended to focus on a first-order perspective, looking out from the individual perceiver, and has neglected the second-order perspective of the group looking in on the individual. Research on respect makes clearer the interactive relation between group and individual, and that the evaluations are mutual and have recursive consequences.

This work complements other recent research suggesting that there is a uniquely "intragroup" dimension to group life situated between the interpersonal and intergroup poles. Self-categorization theory routinely refers to the intragroup level in theoretical terms, but this has rarely been fully worked out or been tested empirically (Vliek et al., 2005). Although research in the group dynamics tradition has addressed intragroup contexts, the absence of a social identity perspective means that these findings often tend to be reduced to individualistic forms of interaction and interdependence.

Our programme of research on respect is situated precisely at this intra-group nexus: the intergroup context is relevant to make group identity salient and meaningful, but the focus is clearly on the relation of the individual to the group. Thus, issues of individual functioning and evaluation are clearly a central concern, not as absolutes or as abstractions, but framed in relation to the ingroup audience. In other words individual functioning is formed in terms of the group and intrinsically linked to it.

Our respect research provided a context in which to address the more general principles around the self, such as self-enhancement, and self-protection, and to question how generic these really are. What our studies seem to show is that positive evaluations of the self are not universally positive (as judged in the famous social vacuum) but also seem to be embedded in, and framed by, the group context. Whereas positive evaluation might seem to be a bonus judged in general and individual terms, it turns out to be much more "contingent" when the individual–group relation is taken into account. Crucially it depends on the group source of the evaluation, and even the dimension of evaluation cannot be judged in a vacuum but can change meaning when combined with other dimensions. In short, examining the intragroup dynamics of the individual within the group provides one source of explanation about how group identification (the group within the individual) forms and develops. Once again this puts the social context, here the intragroup context, centre stage, and demonstrates the fundamentally social character of self-evaluation and motivation.

In developing our thesis about the individual in the group, there is always the danger of swinging back with the pendulum to the individualism that the social identity approach set out to contest. We hope we have shown however that the "individual in the group" agenda is quite different from the individual *instead* of the group (see also Jetten & Postmes, Chapter 7; Reicher & Haslam, Chapter 13; Turner et al., Chapter 2 in this volume). Real emergent properties and reciprocal relations come to light when we start to consider how the group relates to the individual, how this is in turn perceived, and how this in turn affects intragroup dynamics.

Once we enter this cycle we also get much better insights into the group basis of the need to belong. Anecdotal illustrations of this are often the most vivid. Thus the processes and principles explored here help to explain why people who have been extremely successful on the world stage, singers and superstars like Tom Jones, Anthony Hopkins, Richard Burton, despite their fame and fortune, indeed their international respect, still hanker after their first home in the Welsh valleys. If these roots are cultural, then it is a culture peopled and personified by "their" group. A familiar old slogan runs along the lines that you can take the individual out of the group but you can't take the group out of the individual. This idea reinforces the dualism, set up by the European social identity project, to make the case for the group in the individual. Our analysis has been to argue that these two elements, rather than being opposed, actually go together, and that putting the individual back into the group, actually helps to put the group back into the individual.

REFERENCES

Allport, F. H. (1924). *Social psychology*. New York: Houghton Mifflin.

Asch, S. E. (1946). Forming impressions of personality. *Journal of Abnormal and Social Psychology, 41*, 258–290.

Barreto, M. & Ellemers, N. (2000). You can't always do what you want: Social identity and self-presentational determinants of the choice to work for a low status group. *Personality and Social Psychology Bulletin, 26*, 891–906.

Baumeister, R. F., & Leary, M. R. (1995). The need to belong: Desire for interpersonal attachment as a fundamental human motivation. *Psychological Bulletin, 117*, 497–529.

Branscombe, N. R., Spears, R., Ellemers, N., & Doosje, B. (2002). Intragroup and inter-group evaluation effects on group behavior. *Personality and Social Psychology Bulletin, 28*, 744–753.

Branscombe, N. R., & Wann, D. L. (1994). Collective self-esteem consequences of out-group derogation when a valued social identity is on trial. *European Journal of Social Psychology, 24*, 641–658.

Codol, J. -P. (1975). On the so-called "superior conformity of the self" behaviour: Twenty experimental investigations. *European Journal of Social Psychology, 5*, 457–501.

Doosje, B., Ellemers, N., & Spears, R. (1995). Perceived intragroup variability as a function of status and identification. *Journal of Experimental Social Psychology, 31*, 410–436.

Doosje, B., Spears, R., & Koomen, W. (1995). When bad isn't all bad: The strategic use of sample information in generalization and stereotyping. *Journal of Personality and Social Psychology, 69*, 642–655.

Duck, J. M., & Fielding, K. S. (2003). Leaders and their treatment of subgroups: Implications for evaluations of the leader and the superordinate group. *European Journal of Social Psychology, 33*, 387–401.

Eisenberger, N. I., Lieberman, M. D., & Williams, K. D. (2003). Does rejection hurt? An fMRI study of social exclusion. *Science, 302*, 290–292.

Ellemers, N., Doosje, B., & Spears, R. (2004). Sources of respect: The effects of being liked by ingroups and outgroups. *European Journal of Social Psychology, 34*, 155–172.

Ellemers, N., Spears, R., & Doosje, B. (1997). Sticking together or falling apart: Ingroup identification as a psychological determinant of group commitment versus individual mobility. *Journal of Personality and Social Psychology, 72*, 617–626.

Ellemers, N., Spears, R., & Doosje, B. (2002). Self and social identity. *Annual Review of Psychology, 53*, 161–186.

Ellemers, N., van Knippenberg, A., & Wilke, H. (1990). The influence of permeability of group boundaries and stability of group status on strategies of individual mobility and social change. *British Journal of Social Psychology, 29*, 233–246.

Feather, N. T. (1994). Attitudes toward high achievers and reactions to their fall: Theory and research concerning tall poppies. *Advances in Experimental Social Psychology, 26*, 1–73.

Fiske, S. T., Xu, J., Cuddy, A. C., & Glick, P. (1999). (Dis)respecting versus (dis)liking: Status and interdependence predict ambivalent stereotypes of competence and warmth. *Journal of Social Issues, 55*, 473–489.

Haslam, S. A., & Platow, M. J. (2001). The link between leadership and followership: How affirming social identity translates vision into action. *Personality and Social Psychology Bulletin, 27*, 1469–1479.

Hollander, E. P. (1964). *Leaders, groups and influence.* New York: Oxford University Press.

Jetten, J., Branscombe, N. R., & Spears, R. (in press). Living on the edge: Dynamics of intragroup and intergroup rejection experiences. In R. Brown & D. Capozza (Eds.), *Social identities: Motivational, emotional and cultural influences.* London: Sage.

Jetten, J., Branscombe, N. R., Spears, R., & McKimmie, B. (2003). Predicting the paths of peripherals: The interaction of identification and future possibilities. *Personality and Social Psychology Bulletin, 29*, 130–140.

Jetten, J., Postmes, T., & McAuliffe, B. J. (2002). "We're all individuals": Group norms of individualism and collectivism, levels of identification, and identity threat. *European Journal of Social Psychology, 32*, 189–207.

Jetten, J., Schmitt, M. T., Branscombe, N. R., & McKimmie, B. M. (2005). Suppressing the negative effect of devaluation on group identification: The role of intergroup differentiation and intragroup respect. *Journal of Experimental Social Psychology, 41*, 208–215.

Kenny, D. A. (1994). *Interpersonal perception: A social relations analysis.* New York: Guilford.

Leary, M. R., & MacDonald, G. (2003). Individual differences in self-esteem: A review and theoretical integration. In M. R. Leary & J. P. Tangney (Eds.), *Handbook of self and identity* (pp. 401–418). New York: Guilford.

Luhtanen, R. & Crocker, J. (1992). A collective self-esteem scale: Self-evaluation of one's social identity. *Personality and Social Psychology Bulletin, 18*, 302–318.

Mead, G. H. (1934). *Mind, self and society.* Chicago: Chicago University Press.

Monge, P. R., & Contractor, N. S. (2003). *Theories of communication networks.* Oxford: Oxford University Press.

Noel, J. G., Wann, D. L., & Branscombe, N. R. (1995). Peripheral ingroup membership status and public negativity toward outgroups. *Journal of Personality and Social Psychology, 68*, 127–137.

Osgood, C. E., Suci, G. J., & Tannenbaum, P. H. (1957). *The measurement of meaning.* Urbana: University of Illinois Press.

Ouwerkerk, J. W., de Gilder, D., & de Vries, N. K. (2000). When the going gets tough, the tough get going: Social identification and individual effort in intergroup competition. *Personality and Social Psychology Bulletin, 26*, 1550–1559.

Peeters, G. (2002). From good and bad to can and must: subjective necessity of acts associated with positively and negatively valued stimuli. *European Journal of Social Psychology, 32*, 125–136.

Postmes, T., & Branscombe, N. R. (2002). Influence of long-term racial environmental composition on subjective well-being in African Americans. *Journal of Personality and Social Psychology, 83*, 735–751.

Postmes, T., Spears, R., Lee, A. T., & Novak, R. J. (in press). Individuality and social influence in groups: Inductive and deductive routes to group identity. *Journal of Personality and Social Psychology.*

Reicher, S. D. (2001). Social identity definition and enactment: A broad SIDE against irrationalism and relativism. In T. Postmes, R. Spears, M. Lea, & S. D. Reicher (Eds.), *SIDE issues centre stage: Recent developments of de-individuation in groups* (pp. 175–190). Amsterdam: Proceedings of the Dutch Royal Academy of Arts and Sciences.

Reicher, S. D., Hopkins, N., & Condor, S. (1997). Stereotype construction as a strategy of influence? In R. Spears, P. J. Oakes, N. Ellemers, & S. A. Haslam (Eds.), *The social psychology of stereotyping and group life* (pp. 94–118). Oxford: Blackwell.

Reicher, S. D., Spears, R., & Postmes, T. (1995). A social identity model of deindividuation phenomena. *European Review of Social Psychology, 6*, 161–198.

Rosenberg, S., Nelson, S., & Vivekanathan, P. S. (1968). A multi-dimensional approach to the study of personality impressions. *Journal of Personality and Social Psychology, 9*, 238–294.

Scheepers, D., Spears, R., Doosje, B., & Manstead, A. S. R. (2002). Integrating identity and instrumental approaches to intergroup differentiation: Different contexts, different motives. *Personality and Social Psychology Bulletin, 28*, 1455–1467.

Sedikides, C., & Strube, M. J. (1997). Self-evaluation: to thine own self be good, to thine own self be sure, to thine own self be true, and to thine own self better. *Advances in Experimental Social Psychology, 29*, 209–269.

Seta, J. J., & Seta, C. E. (1996). Big fish in small ponds: A social hierarchy analysis of intergroup bias. *Journal of Personality and Social Psychology, 71,* 1210–1221.

Simon, B., & Stürmer, S. (2003). Respect for group members: Intragroup determinants of collective identification and group-serving behavior. *Personality and Social Psychology Bulletin, 29*, 183–193.

Skowronski, J. J., & Carlston, D. E. (1989). Negativity and extremity biases in impression formation: A review of explanations. *Psychological Bulletin, 105*, 131–142.

Sleebos, E., Ellemers, N., & De Gilder, D. (2004a). Being in or out: The effects of respect on perceived standing and inclusion in the group. Manuscript submitted for publication, Leiden University.

Sleebos, E., Ellemers, N., & De Gilder, D. (2004b). The carrot or the stick: Disrespected group members' engagement in group serving effort. Manuscript submitted for publication, Leiden University.

Smith, H. J., & Tyler, T. R. (1997). Choosing the right pond: The impact of group membership on self-esteem and group-oriented behavior. *Journal of Experimental Social Psychology, 33*, 146–170.

Smith, R. H., Turner, T. J., Garonzik, R., Leach, C. W., Urch, V., & Weston, C. (1996). Envy and *Schadenfreude. Personality and Social Psychology Bulletin, 22*, 158–168.

Spears, R. (2001). The interaction between the individual and the collective self: Self-categorization in context. In C. Sedikides & M. B. Brewer (Eds.), *Individual self, relational self, and collective self: Partners, opponents or strangers?* (pp. 171–198). Philadelphia: Psychology Press.

Spears, R., Doosje, B., & Ellemers, N. (1997). Self-stereotyping in the face of threats to group status and distinctiveness: The role of group identification. *Personality and Social Psychology Bulletin, 23,* 538–553.

Spears, R., Doosje, B. & Ellemers, N. (1999). Commitment and the context of social perception. In N. Ellemers, R. Spears and B. Doosje (Eds.), *Social identity: Context, commitment, content* (pp. 59–83). Oxford: Blackwell.

Spears, R., Ellemers, N., & Doosje, B. (2005). Let me count the ways in which I respect thee: Does competence-based respect compensate or compromise liking-based respect? *European Journal of Social Psychology, 35*, 263–279.

Spears, R., & Lea, M. (1994). Panacea or panopticon? The hidden power in computer-mediated communication. *Communication Research, 21*, 427–459.

Stroebe, K. E., Lodewijkx, H. F. M., & Spears, R. (2005). Do unto others as they do unto you: Reciprocity and social identification as determinants of in-group favoritism. *Personality and Social Psychology Bulletin, 31*, 831–846.

Tajfel, H. (Ed.) (1978). *Differentiation between social groups: Studies in the social psychology of intergroup relations.* London: Academic.

Turner, J. C. (1982). Towards a cognitive redefinition of the group. In H. Tajfel (Ed.), *Social identity and intergroup relations* (pp. 15–40). Cambridge: Cambridge University Press.

Tyler, T. R. (1999). Why people cooperate with organizations: An identity-based perspective. *Research in Organizational Behavior, 21,* 201–246.

Tyler, T. R., Degoey, P., & Smith, H. J. (1996). Understanding why the justice of group procedures matters: a test of the psychological dynamics of the group value model. *Journal of Personality and Social Psychology, 70,* 913–930.

Vliek, M. L. W., Leach, C. W., Spears, R., & Wigboldus, D. H. J. (2005). No worse than average: Shifting the in-group average as protection against an unflattering upward comparison. Manuscript submitted for publication, University of Amsterdam.

Vonk, R. (1999). Effects of other-profitability and self-profitability on evaluative judgements of behaviours. *European Journal of Social Psychology, 29,* 833–842.

Williams, K. D., Cheung, C. K. T., & Choi, W. (2000). Cyber-ostracism: Effects of being ignored over the Internet. *Journal of Personality and Social Psychology, 79,* 748–762.

11

Psychological Need Satisfaction through Social Roles

B. Ann Bettencourt, Lisa Molix, Amelia E. Talley, and Kennon M. Sheldon

Many theoretical traditions in social psychology are predicated upon the assumption that there is a fundamental conflict between the individual and the group – an idea that can be traced to Thomas Hobbes (1650/1931). For example, much research on social dilemmas assumes that individuals face a difficult choice between either serving their own interests or serving their group's interests (e.g., Komorita & Parks, 1995). Similarly in the intergroup literature, optimal distinctiveness theory (Brewer, 1991; also see Picket & Leonardelli, Chapter 4 in this volume) proposes an inherent conflict between needs for distinctiveness and needs for inclusion. Brewer (1991) suggests that the need for uniqueness and the need for affiliation are opponent processes, and thus the satisfaction of one tends to come at the expense of the other. Also, in the cross-cultural literature (e.g., Triandis, 1994), a dichotomy is drawn between societies that are collectivistic and those that are individualistic. That is, cultures are characterized as either valuing the collective or valuing the individual.

Along with other theorists (Blatt & Shichman, 1983; Cochran & Peplau, 1985; Deci & Ryan, 1991; Guisinger & Blatt, 1994; Hodgins, Koestner, & Duncan, 1996; Schwartz, 1990), we question (Bettencourt & Sheldon, 2001; Bettencourt, Sheldon, & Hawley, 1998; Sheldon & Bettencourt, 2002) the validity of a necessary conflict between the self and the other. In doing so, we argue that self-based needs and socially based needs can be *mutually* satisfied within the context of group membership.

Our view is consistent with Deci and Ryan's (1991, 2000) self-determination theory, which provides an account of the motivational processes by which individuals seek self-expression within the context of social relationships. Self-determination theory posits that humans have both socially oriented and self-oriented basic psychological needs; among these are needs for relatedness and autonomy. Relatedness involves the "desire to feel connected to others" (Deci & Ryan, 2000, p. 231) – to have a sense of communion (Bakan, 1966) or closeness with others (Baumeister & Leary, 1995). Autonomy involves the desire to "self-organize experience and behavior, and to have activity be concordant with one's integrated sense of self" (Deci & Ryan, 2000, p. 231). Noteworthy is that fact that Deci and Ryan elucidate a distinction between the concept of autonomy and that of independence. Whereas independence involves separating one's self from others, autonomy involves wholehearted volition and authentic self-expression (e.g., Deci & Ryan, 1991; Hodgins et al., 1996). That is, authentic or autonomous self-expression is phenomenally experienced as behavior that is authored by the self (e.g., internally caused).[1]

Importantly, self-determination theory does not assume an opponent process or conflicting relation between needs for autonomy and relatedness. Although autonomy and relatedness motives may manifest in ways that engender conflict, especially in earlier developmental stages (Ryan, 1995), mature autonomy and relatedness motives are viewed as highly compatible and even complementary (Guisinger & Blatt, 1994; Koestner & Losier, 1996; Ryan & Lynch, 1989).

Studies reveal that needs for relatedness and autonomy can be met simultaneously in a variety of intimate relationships (Harter, 1997; Hodgins et al., 1996; Ryan & Lynch, 1989). For example, spouses' feelings of autonomy in their marital relationships are positively correlated with their feelings of marital closeness (Rankin-Esquer, Burnett, Baucom, & Epstein, 1997). Moreover, adult intimate relationships that engender feelings of both autonomy and relatedness are associated with higher levels of relationship satisfaction (e.g., Harter, 1997; Rankin-Esquer et al., 1997).

Although past research in the self-determination theory tradition has focused on interpersonal rather than group processes, we believed that the postulates of self-determination theory could be profitably extended to the group context. We purport that as with interpersonal relationships, needs for authentic self-expression and relatedness can be mutually met within the context of group life (Bettencourt & Sheldon, 2001; Bettencourt et al., 1998; Sheldon & Bettencourt, 2002). Moreover, we argue that social roles in particular, which guide behaviors and interactions between members, are likely mechanisms through which psychological needs are satisfied. In the following sections, we define terms, articulate our approach, and present related empirical work. In addition, we consider the ways in which social identity perspectives can inform our further articulations of the social-role processes and discuss how our approach may inform social identity perspectives.

Distinctions and definitions

Perspectives on social identity have distinguished between personal and social identities (Ellemers, Spears, & Doosje, 2002; Hogg & Abrams, 1999; Turner, 1999). Moreover, in their theorizing, Deaux (1993) and Turner and colleagues (e.g., Turner, Hogg, Oakes, Reicher, & Wetherell, 1987) have subsumed social roles and group categorizations into the single class of social identity. It is worth noting that the work of Deaux has emphasized social roles and that of Turner has emphasized group categorizations. Nevertheless, Thoits and Virshup (1997) argue that equating these two types of social identities unnecessarily limits our understanding of each. Likewise, Tajfel (1972) viewed role identities and group identities as quite different phenomena. We believe that to distinguish between only social identity and personal identity is to ignore the specific consequences that social-role identities have for the lives of individual members of groups. That is, social roles are important means by which individuals and groups intersect. As such, in our work, we delineate role identity from both personal identity and group identity. This is not to say that we fail to consider that a "role identity" is an inherently social identity; rather we use the term "role identity" to distinguish it from "group identity". A social role is conceptualized as "a behavioral repertoire characteristic of a person or a position; a set of standards, descriptions, norms, or concepts held for the behaviors of a person or social position" (Biddle, 1979, p. 9). A social group "constitutes a set of two or more persons who are linked through interaction" (p. 233).

In our research, we focus on social roles that are relatively well defined and formalized. Moreover, under consideration are social roles and groups that are relatively enduring. Finally, we are referring to groups that require interactions among the respective members. One example of this type of group is a psychology department. Some of the roles within the department might include chair of the department, chair of the curriculum committee, and secretary (Thoits & Virshup, 1997). An example of a group not considered in our analysis is people at a dance club, some of whom may be taking on the "role" of either dancer or spectator.

Our emphasis on groups that involve interacting members is narrower than is that of social identity theory (Tajfel & Turner, 1979), which theorizes about both groups that do and groups that do not require interactions. Also different from social identity theory, but not from social categorization theory (Turner, 1985; Turner et al., 1987), our social-role approach concerns processes within groups, mostly to the exclusion of those between groups. This approach is consistent with Tajfel's (1972) acknowledgment that intragroup processes are a greater part of people's everyday lives, compared to intergroup processes. Like social identity theory, our approach articulates the ways that needs are met through group memberships. However, unlike social identity theory, we consider the psychological needs (e.g., authentic self-expression and connectedness) that Deci and Ryan (2000) have identified as the most basic for human functioning.

Social roles as mechanisms for psychological need fulfillment

We (Bettencourt et al., 1998) propose that social roles, fulfilled within groups, have the capacity to satisfy needs for connectedness and authentic self-expression, ultimately leading to healthy functioning (e.g., positive wellbeing). As an indicator of healthy functioning, we use the construct of subjective wellbeing, following the lead of other theorists (Baumeister & Leary, 1995; Ryan, 1995; Sheldon, Elliot, Kim, & Kasser, 2001) who argue that wellbeing indices (e.g., life satisfaction, positive affect) are among the best available criterion variables for determining which experiences are necessary for humans (i.e., psychological needs).

How might needs for connectedness be met through social roles? Social roles require group members to interact, and as such, roles can facilitate positive relations between role players (McCall & Simmons, 1978; Sarbin & Allen, 1969). Specifically, as individuals contribute to the group through the roles that they play, they may experience a sense of being valued by, and connected to, the group. Consistent with this perspective, Stryker (1987) argues that people are motivated to carry out role-related duties because respective roles provide rewarding social interactions and mutual exchanges of support (McCall & Simmons, 1978; Sarbin & Allen, 1969; Stryker, 1987). Researchers focusing on the psychological benefits of group memberships typically have neither studied social roles nor measured need satisfaction directly. However, their research shows that higher levels of collective self-esteem are associated with enhanced psychological wellbeing (Bettencourt & Dorr, 1997; Bettencourt, Charlton, Eubanks, Kernahan, & Fuller, 1999; Blaine & Crocker, 1995; Crocker, Luhtanen, Blaine, & Broadnax, 1994) and strength of group identity is related to psychological adjustment (Jetten, O'Brien, & Trindall, 2002; Postmes & Branscombe, 2002). Though not directly addressing social roles within groups, these findings are consistent with the idea that aspects of the relations between individual and group are predictive of wellbeing, but they do not directly assess social roles within groups.

How might social roles within groups meet needs for autonomy or authentic self-expression? In part, social roles are defined by duties, norms, and expectations (Biddle, 1979; Donahue, Robins, Roberts, &

John, 1993; Goffman, 1950; Stryker, 1987). Because social roles can be dictated by norms and expectations, some early theorists (Laing, 1967; Perls, 1947) speculated that social-role performances were considered inauthentic, non-autonomous behavior. By contrast, we propose that whether a person feels a sense of authentic self-expression in a social role depends upon the degree of correspondence between the self and the specific dictates of the role. More recent sociological perspectives theorize that congruence between personal characteristics and role expectations should be associated with adjustment (Biddle, 1979; Horton & Hunt, 1984; Rodgers, 1959; Sarbin & Allen, 1969). It is also consistent with psychosocial personality theory (Erikson, 1964; Marcia, 2002), which suggests that part of increasing maturity involves achieving greater identification with and commitment to social roles. Moreover, extending from both self-determination theory and social identity theory (Tajfel, 1981), if a social identity is internalized then one would feel authentic in behaving consistently with the social identity.

Perhaps because groups have often been contrived as suppressing the needs of individuals, little research to date supports our hypothesis that autonomy needs may be satisfied within group life. However, consistent with our theoretical perspective, research shows that people vary in the degree of authentic self-expression that they feel in their social roles and that such variations are associated with wellbeing within those roles (Sheldon, Ryan, Rawsthorne, & Ilardi, 1997). Also, supporting our contention that the specific correspondence between the person and the role is important, Roberts and Donahue (1994) showed that the degree of similarity between trait ratings made concerning a role and trait ratings made concerning the self was positively associated with role satisfaction.

It should be noted that the idea that people's characteristics should match social-role requirements need not imply that individuals have no influence in designing the ways in which they carry out their roles. Rather, we assume that, when carrying out the broad dictates of social roles, people can improvise and personalize some of the ways in which they fulfill their roles (Biddle, 1979; McCall & Simmons, 1978; Sarbin & Allen, 1969). Indeed, under these circumstances, persons are more likely to feel authentic (Sheldon et al., 1997), personally expressive (Waterman, 1990), and self-determined (Deci & Ryan, 1991). In contrast, social roles that stifle authenticity and autonomy tend to foster maladjustment and distress (Biddle, 1979; Ryan, Sheldon, Kasser, & Deci, 1996; Sheldon et al., 1997).

Returning to the example of the psychology department: in the role of department chair, a person may feel a sense of authentic self-expression in fulfilling the expectations associated with the role. Or obviously, a person may feel inadequate for or overburdened by associated expectations and norms. If, for example, the role of chair requires that one be well organized, a good listener, and a shrewd negotiator, then whether a person feels authentic in this role should be influenced by the extent to which these expectations are consistent with the person's core skills, values, and self-concept. Assuming that the skills required are part of the person's repertoire, an individual will be more likely to feel a sense of authentic self-expression in this role. Moreover, in enacting the role, the department chair engages in structured interactions with the members of the department (i.e., group members). Through these interactions, and as a consequence of being embedded within the group, feelings of connectedness may be engendered. In this way, as a consequence of fulfilling this social role, needs for both autonomy and relatedness can be met within the context of the group. Finally, needs for competency – a topic we address in subsequent sections – can also be met through role fulfillment.

Related empirical evidence

In our first effort (Sheldon & Bettencourt, 2002) to test our premise that needs for authentic self-expression and connectedness could be met simultaneously within a single group context, we focused on group memberships. Most importantly for the current work, one of the purposes of the study was to examine associations among the two need-related constructs and wellbeing. For this study, university students received a questionnaire and were asked to think of a formal and an informal campus group to which they belonged. After indicating which type of group they had in mind (formal or informal), participants answered questions that assessed feelings of authentic self-expression, feelings of relatedness with other members, and feelings of inclusion in the group. Measures of positive and negative affect were used as indices of subjective wellbeing. First, our findings showed that feelings of authentic self-expression within the group were correlated with both feelings of relatedness and group inclusion. Moreover, simultaneous regression analyses showed that greater feelings of autonomy, group inclusion, and relatedness mutually and independently predicted positive affect. Also the findings suggested that the more members felt included and autonomous in their group, the lower their negative affect. These findings suggest that needs for autonomy and relatedness can be met mutually within the context of group memberships and that levels of fulfillment of each independently influence wellbeing.

Next, we (Bettencourt & Sheldon, 2001) conducted a series of five studies designed to test more specific hypotheses about social-role fulfillment within groups. For these studies, we predicted that in the context of group memberships, (a) feelings of authentic self-expression in fulfilling one's social roles would be positively correlated with feelings of connectedness with the social group, (b) feelings of authentic self-expression in one's social roles would be associated with positive well-being, and (c) feelings of connectedness would be associated with positive wellbeing. Furthermore, given our assumption that autonomy and relatedness in social roles are independent and equally important needs, we predicted that (d) both types of experiences would contribute independently to subjective wellbeing.

For example, in one study, we examined whether feelings of authentic self-expression derived from fulfilling social roles within groups, and feelings of connectedness garnered in these contexts, were mutually and independently associated with subjective wellbeing. Consistent with this, participants answered measures assessing each of these constructs (i.e., authentic self-expression, social-group connectedness, life satisfaction, positive and negative affect). In addition, one friend of each participant was asked to complete the subjective wellbeing measures with respect to the friend's perception of the participant. This latter assessment allowed us to determine whether positive relationships among wellbeing and both social-role authenticity and connectedness could be confirmed via peer reports of the participants' wellbeing. These peer reports were a means of establishing the construct validity of the participants' reports.

Consistent with our hypotheses, the results revealed that feelings of authentic self-expression and feelings of connectedness experienced while fulfilling social roles within group contexts were positively correlated, suggesting that these experiences are not opponent processes. Moreover, greater feelings of authentic self-expression and connectedness were each positively and independently predictive of both self-reports and peer reports of participants' subjective wellbeing. These results suggest that self-related and socially related needs can be mutually met when people fulfill social roles in the context of groups. These results confirmed the findings of two other studies using only participants' self-reports (Bettencourt & Sheldon, 2001, Studies 1 and 3).

In most of our studies, we have used survey methods. In these studies, participants were asked to think about their group memberships and the social roles they fulfilled within them. Participants responded to a given set of three specified social groups and respective social roles as well as to two additional groups and roles of their choosing. To complement these studies, we have also conducted an experimental study in which we randomly assigned individuals to a single group membership as well as to a specific social role to fulfill within the group. We began with the assumption that the degree of correspondence between the person and the assigned role was likely to vary across the participants. Early in a semester, college students completed a survey to assess their own personal traits (e.g., responsible, cooperative, outgoing). Later in the semester and just prior to the experimental session, the instructor of the course assigned a set of readings on violence in the media. On the day of the experimental session, students were randomly assigned to groups via a slip of paper with a number written on it and were directed to sit in a set of chairs labeled with the same group number. Further, participants were told that during the session they would complete a group task related to the assigned readings on violence in the media. Next, participants within each group were randomly assigned to one of the five specific social roles – ideas person, devil's advocate, moderator, secretary, and announcer – and were given a brief description of each role. The idea person's job was to generate ideas for answering the question; the devil's advocate's job was to argue against the idea person's ideas; the moderator's job was to try to help the idea person and the devil's advocate find a compromise position; the secretary's job was to sum up the compromise answer and write it down on the group's answer sheet; the announcer's job was to stand up in front of the classroom and to read the group's written answer to the entire class. Each role player was restricted to her or his assigned role, and was not to join in with any of the other tasks involved in the completion of the group assignment.

Before and after the group task, participants were asked to complete brief questionnaires. More specifically, just prior to the group task, participants answered a questionnaire that included items regarding a set of traits needed for performing the specific role (the same traits responded to in the beginning of the semester), how much the assigned role fits with their own personality, and mood (as a proxy for wellbeing). Subsequent to the group task, participants were asked to complete a survey that assessed their mood as well as feelings of role authenticity and connectedness. Consistent with the results of our previous survey studies, the results showed that participants' feelings of authentic self-expression and group connectedness experienced in the randomly assigned social roles positively predicted wellbeing. Moreover, in accord with our role fit hypotheses, the results revealed that the smaller the discrepancy between the participant's own traits and the traits that the sample, as a whole, agreed were required for the role, the greater the wellbeing. These results suggest that need satisfaction and optimal functioning within a role are influenced by the degree to which a role requires, or is flexible enough to avail, an individual's characteristics.

Meeting the needs for competency in social roles

Deci and Ryan (1991) identify competence as the third basic psychological need. As such, fulfillment of competency needs should be associated with subjective wellbeing. Supporting this proposal, studies from a variety of perspectives accord with the notion that feelings of goal attainment (Brunstein, 1993) and task competence (Elliot, Faler, McGregor, Campbell, Sedikides, & Harackiewicz, 2000) are associated with enhanced mood and satisfaction. In our model of social roles and need fulfillment, we have proposed that the process of fulfilling one's social roles within group memberships is likely to provide important opportunities for meeting competency needs. Further, we have hypothesized that people are most likely to derive feelings of competency from social roles when the roles meet needs for both authentic self-expression and social connectedness.

We reason that one's ability to perform a role competently should be partially a function of how authentic one feels in the role, that is, whether the dictates of the role are consistent with the self. When there is consistency, the social role should draw upon an individual's actual skills and strengths. As a consequence, he or she is more likely to perform well and in turn derive feelings of competency from role performance. Supporting this idea, Scott and Stumpf (1984) argue that a sense of competency develops as a consequence of positive self-evaluated role performances, particularly in roles the person considers central to the self-concept. Moreover, research shows that, compared to those in self-role incongruent situations, participants assigned to roles that are congruent with self-characteristics are more satisfied with their performances (Benoit-Smullyan, 1944; Bunker, 1967) and perform better in group problem-solving tasks (Borgatta, 1960).

We also reasoned that people are most likely to derive feelings of competence from roles that are associated with feelings of social connectedness. This relationship is likely because social roles that provide such feelings should evoke a greater sense of responsibility in role players and motivate stronger effort on their part. In addition, individuals learn about their effectiveness in social roles from others related to the role (e.g., relevant group members: McCall & Simmons, 1978; Stryker, 1987). Feelings of social role competency can arise from the reflected appraisals (Mead, 1934; Sarbin & Allen, 1969) and support of others associated with the fulfillment of social-role (McCall & Simmons, 1978; Scott & Stumpf, 1984; Stryker, 1987; Thoits & Virshup, 1997). Consistent with this theorizing, role players who feel more connected with other group members are likely to receive more social support from those members, which aids them in their performance. Furthermore, underlying the feeling of group connectedness is the experience that, through one's social-role enactments, one is contributing to the group as a whole (e.g., Bettencourt & Hume, 1999; Guisinger & Blatt, 1994; Sarbin & Allen, 1969). This too should induce a sense of competency.

To test our ideas, we conducted a short-term longitudinal study. We proposed that social-role authenticity and social-group connectedness would predict feelings of social-role competency over time, and accumulated feelings of social-role competency should be manifested by enhanced subjective and psychosocial wellbeing over time. For this study, at the beginning of one semester, participants (i.e., college students) were asked to identify a social role that they anticipated fulfilling throughout the semester and to complete measures of social-role authenticity and social-group connectedness. Next, at four points during the semester, participants recalled the social role they had previously identified and responded to items measuring feelings of competency in that role. Finally, at the very end of the semester, participants filled out a survey that assessed their subjective and psychosocial wellbeing. In accord with our hypotheses, the results revealed that social-role authenticity and social-group connectedness were associated with feelings of competency in the respective social roles. Moreover, feelings of social-role competency accumulated over time were associated with enhanced subjective and psychosocial wellbeing at the end of the semester.

In our work, we draw from psychological and sociological theorizing to explain the ways in which basic psychological needs might be met within the context of social groups (see also Hogg, Terry, & White, 1995). Our research findings illustrate the value of bringing together the literatures on group memberships, social roles, and motivation, for a fuller understanding of wellbeing and the "fully functioning individual". Also, our studies highlight that group life does not necessarily present an inherent conflict between the self and others. Instead, our research suggests that, through social-role enactments, needs for autonomy and relatedness as well as competency can be mutually satisfied within social groups. Finally, one of our studies offered preliminary evidence that meeting a particular psychological need (e.g., competency) may in part be contingent on the satisfaction of other needs (Maslow, 1954).

Social identity perspectives and our social-role perspective

Our emphasis on social roles as mechanisms for satisfying basic psychological needs within groups is inherently contextual. We do not merely hypothesize that group memberships, level of group identifications, or even social roles alone benefit the lives of group members. Rather we predict that, under particular situations, social roles within groups have the potential to meet basic psychological needs. We argue that roles will only be beneficial to the extent that there is a fit between the expectations/demands of the role and the skills/strengths of the person fulfilling the role. Moreover, we assume that need satisfaction within roles is partly a function of interactions between role players within the group (i.e., other group members). Despite our contextual approach, we have yet to articulate additional moderators that may influence dynamic role interactions within groups. In what follows, we discuss socio-structural features specified by social identity theory (Tajfel & Turner, 1979) that may inform our further theorizing.

Central to the power of social identity theory for explaining intergroup attitudes and behavior is its emphasis on the comparative status of groups and the perceptual elements of the status structure (Abrams & Hogg, 1999; Oakes, Haslam, & Reynolds, 1999; Turner, 1999). In particular, social identity theory (Tajfel & Turner, 1979) articulates the ways in which perceptions of stability, legitimacy, and group permeability influence group-related attitudes and behaviors. It is likely that the relative status of a particular group as well as structural variables have some influence on the extent to which psychological needs are met via social roles. For instance, depending on the relative status of the group, a given social role may take a somewhat different meaning for role players and role partners. It may be that playing a role within membership of a high status group increases the likelihood that the role confers heightened feelings of competency. Also, that role may be perceived as more important if it is fulfilled within a high status group. However, we believe that the reflection of group status on a respective role is most likely when intergroup comparisons between high and low status groups are salient. In contrast, the comparative status of a role *vis-à-vis* other roles within a group is likely to have a greater influence on the psychological need satisfaction derived from social roles. Greater influence of role status on need satisfaction is tenable, because in the day-to-day fulfillment of roles within groups, social-role comparisons are more likely than intergroup comparisons.

Before we speculate about the ways in which social-role status influences the fulfillment of needs for authentic self-expression, connectedness, and competency, it is important to restate that we believe that the satisfaction of these needs depends upon the degree of correspondence between the characteristics and skills of an individual and the expectations and demands of the social role. That is, even if a person is in a high status role, the person's basic psychological needs will not be optimally satisfied if there is little role–person fit. With that said, in the instance of high role–person fit (i.e., congruence) it may be that there is a greater capacity that a high status role would meet the three basic psychological needs specified by Deci and Ryan (1991). In high status roles, other role players may value the role in such a way as to induce greater feelings of connectedness for the role player. Also in this instance, feelings of competency may be more readily derived from high status roles. Perhaps, persons in high status roles may be more motivated to learn the skills necessary for the role or to adjust the role in such a way as to capitalize on their own authentic talents, thereby enhancing feelings of authentic self-expression. Some of our speculations here are consistent with research that shows that group members who feel respected have higher levels of collective identification and express greater willingness to engage in group-serving behavior (Simon & Stuermer, 2003; also see Branscombe, Spears, Ellemers, & Doosje, 2002; Jetten, Branscombe, Spears, and McKimmie, 2003; Smith, Tyler, Huo, Ortiz, & Lind, 1998).

As with the relative status of groups, the relative status of social roles is likely to vary in stability. The relative status of some roles is likely to be highly stable. For example, the chair of a department is structurally and culturally defined as higher status than a secretary; this status difference is likely to be highly stable. However, the relative statuses of many roles within groups are likely to depend on the demands of the immediate situation. That is, one role may be better suited than others for meeting a particular situational demand and thereby have higher status in the socio-structural context. Over time, under varying situational demands, many roles are likely to be revered as important as persons make role-specific contributions to the group. During such opportunities to fulfill one's role in relevant situations, people may derive psychological need satisfaction. It is likely that feelings of competency and relatedness come from realizing one's particular contribution to the group. Interestingly, in the context of role fulfillments not only the needs of the individual are being met, but also the needs of the group.

At the level of the group, the stability of status is related to the concept of legitimacy of status (Tajfel, 1981). Research shows that status legitimacy has substantial influence on the intergroup attitudes and behaviors of high and low status groups (see Bettencourt, Dorr, Charlton, & Hume, 2001 for a meta-analysis of this literature). The influence of the legitimacy of the social-role status on need fulfillment is less clear. It may be that if a role has high status but the role player or the role partners perceive the status as illegitimately high or illegitimately achieved, the role will have less potential for meeting basic psychological needs. If there is any effect of role status legitimacy, it might most likely influence the satisfaction of needs for relatedness and competency. If a particular role has illegitimate status, the role player and the role partners may be less likely to engage in mutually reinforcing and positive interactions, thereby reducing a feeling of connectedness. Furthermore, if group members devalue the status of the role, positive feedback to the role player is less likely and as a result there may be less capacity for the role to meet needs for competency. When the status of a role is illegitimate these outcomes may be possible because of the discrepancy between the supposed status of the role and others' valuation of it.

Although most roles are relatively permeable, the permeability of a social role is often dependent on the characteristics and skills required for the role. Within a particular group membership, some roles are associated with few expectations and require few skills; thus these roles are likely to be highly permeable. Some roles will be associated with an elaborate set of expectations and thus require a full complement of skills; these roles are likely to be less permeable. Also, those roles involving such expectations and skills may be deemed higher in status. Thus, it is possible that role status and role permeability are often confounded. Because of the likelihood of this confound, we are reluctant to treat role permeability as separate from role status. Moreover, all else being equal, we do not believe role permeability *per se* is as influential as role congruence on psychological need fulfillment. Nevertheless, if the status is equivalent across two roles, it may be that role players and role partners value persons who are in roles that are less permeable, which might engender greater need satisfaction.

Because we focus on social-role fulfillment, particularly within the context of group memberships, social identity perspectives inform our thinking about need satisfaction. However, there are many ideas offered by social identity theory that we have yet to explore. For example, we have focused on intragroup processes to the exclusion of intergroup processes. Future theorizing should specify the ways in which salient intergroup comparisons might influence social-role functioning within groups. Perhaps social identity perspectives may need to consider more fully the importance of social roles within group processes. We provide a few concluding comments about how our integration of social psychological, sociological, and motivational perspectives may inform social identity theory.

Perhaps the most obvious argument we bring to bear is that a distinction should be made between personal identity and social-role identity on the one hand and social-role identity and social-group identity on the other. Some social identity theorists (e.g., Abrams, 1999; Hogg et al., 1995) have equated social-role identity with personal identity (e.g., parent with self) and others (e.g., Deaux, 1993; Turner et al., 1987) have equated social-role identity with social-group identity. From our perspective, greater explanatory accuracy can be derived from keeping in mind these three levels of the self. That social roles and social groups have been cast in a single category is understandable given that a social role and a social group can overlap. For example, the role of doctor and the group membership of doctor have the same label (Deaux, Reid, Mizrahi, & Ethier, 1995). Consider the doctor fulfilling a role in a hospital and interacting with a nurse. The role is doctor, the role partner is the nurse, and the group is hospital staff. Nevertheless, depending on the relative context, it is possible that the doctor and the nurse can be engaging in a social-role interaction (between a doctor and a nurse) or an intergroup interaction (between members of two groups). For example, the latter may occur if nurses in a hospital go on strike for higher wages and make comparisons between the wages of nurses and doctors. Also, sometimes a role such as "role as group member" may be so diffuse, requiring few skills and having few expectations, that the social-role identity and the social-group identity are largely indistinguishable.

In specifying a continuum between personal and social-group identities, social identity theorists (Oakes et al., 1999; Turner et al., 1987) suggest that either the personal or the social identity is likely to be salient (but see Turner, 1999). Of course, in keeping with our approach this continuum should include social-role identity. With that said, we suspect that the general principles of the meta-contrast ratio (Turner, 1985; Turner et al., 1987) can be usefully applied toward understanding when social-role identities are more or less salient compared to social-group identities. Nevertheless, we entertain the notion that it may be possible, in some instances, that when a role identity is salient both personal identity and social identity may be relatively salient. For example, when playing the role of the department chair, the role player may be aware of personal strengths and values associated with the role as well as being aware of the membership in and relationship to the respective group.

Finally, our approach suggests that social identity perspectives may need to consider the importance of social roles in predicting group processes. In our own work we have focused on the influence of psychological need satisfaction, but also social roles may influence group processes such as ingroup identity, group conflict, and group norms and group commitment. For example, those who fulfill social-role memberships in ways that lead to need satisfaction may be more highly identified with their respective groups. Also, given that our research shows that such individual needs as authentic self-expression and competency can be satisfied through role fulfillments in groups, social identity perspectives may consider a broader set of psychological needs than have heretofore been considered (but see

Haslam, Powell, & Turner, 2000). In articulating the ways in which needs may be met though group life, a variety of mechanisms should be considered. Originally, social identity theory specified that social comparisons between groups, upward mobility across groups, and social creativity are means by which group members meet needs for positive social identity. Related perspectives have theorized that needs for inclusion (Brewer, 1991; Pickett & Leonardelli, Chapter 4 in this volume) and needs for subjective certainty (Hogg & Abrams, 1993) can be met through intragroup processes. Our approach suggests that social roles are additional mechanisms by which needs for connectedness, authentic self-expression, and competency can be met. We have concentrated on these three latter needs because influential theorists in the area of motivation (i.e., Deci & Ryan, 2000) specify that these are the most basic of psychological needs. The larger motivation literature may prove fruitful for understanding which needs are present in group life and through what mechanisms they are likely to be met.

NOTE

1 To avoid confusion between the terms "independence" and "autonomy", in the current work we refer to autonomy as authentic self-expression. Also, we use the word "connectedness" because we are interested in feelings of relatedness not only to other group members but also to the group as a whole. Nevertheless, in using these terms, we are linking them to Deci and Ryan's (2000) concepts of autonomy and relatedness.

REFERENCES

Abrams, D. (1999). Social identity, social cognition, and the self: The flexibility and stability of self-categorization. In D. Abrams & M. A. Hogg (Eds.), *Social identity and social cognition* (pp. 197–229). Malden, MA: Blackwell.

Abrams, D., & Hogg, M. A. (Eds.) (1999). *Social identity and social cognition*. Malden, MA: Blackwell.

Bakan, D. (1966). *The duality of existence*. Boston: Beacon.

Baumeister, R. F., & Leary, M. R. (1995). The need to belong: Desire for interpersonal attachments as a fundamental human motivation. *Psychological Bulletin, 17*, 497–529.

Benoit-Smullyan, E. (1944). Status, status types, and status interrelations. *American Sociological Review, 59*, 235–242.

Bettencourt, B. A., Charlton, K., Eubanks, J., Kernahan, C., & Fuller, B. (1999). Development of collective self-esteem among students: Predicting adjustment to college. *Basic and Applied Social Psychology, 21*, 213–222.

Bettencourt, B. A., & Dorr, N. (1997). Collective self-esteem as a mediator of the relationship between allocentrism and subjective well-being. *Personality and Social Psychology Bulletin, 23*, 963–972.

Bettencourt, B. A., Dorr, N., Charlton, K., & Hume, D. L. (2001). Status differences in in-group bias: A meta-analytic examination of the effects of status stability, status legitimacy, and group permeability. *Psychological Bulletin, 127*, 520–542.

Bettencourt, B. A., & Hume, D. (1999). The cognitive contents of social-group identity: Values, emotions, and relationships. *European Journal of Social Psychology, 29*, 113–121.

Bettencourt, B. A., & Sheldon, K. (2001). Social roles as mechanisms for psychological need satisfaction within social groups. *Journal of Personality and Social Psychology, 81*, 1131–1143.

Bettencourt, B. A., Sheldon, K., & Hawley, J. (1998). Social roles: Mechanisms for optimal distinctiveness and well-being. Paper presented at the meeting of the American Psychological Society Convention, Washington DC.

Biddle, B. J. (1979). *Role theory: Expectations, identities, and behaviors.* New York: Academic.

Blaine, B., & Crocker, J. (1995). Religiousness, race, and psychological well-being: Exploring social psychological mediators. *Personality and Social Psychology Bulletin, 21*, 1031–1041.

Blatt, S. J., & Shichman, S. (1983). Two primary configurations of psychopathology. *Psychoanalysis and Contemporary Thought, 6*, 187–254.

Borgatta, E. F. (1960). Role and reference group theory, pp. 16–25. In L. Logan (Ed.), *Social science theory and social work research.* New York: National Association of Social Workers.

Branscombe, N. R., Spears, R., Ellemers, N., & Doosje, B. (2002). Intragroup and intergroup evaluation effects on group behavior. *Personality and Social Psychology Bulletin, 28*, 744–753.

Brewer, M. B. (1991). The social self: On being the same and different at the same time. *Personality and Social Psychology Bulletin, 17*, 475–482.

Brunstein, J. (1993). Personal goals and subjective well-being: A longitudinal study. *Journal of Personality and Social Psychology, 65*, 1061–1070.

Bunker, G. (1967). *Self-role congruence and status congruence as interacting variables in dyadic behavior.* Doctoral dissertation, University of California, Berkeley.

Cochran, S. D., & Peplau, L. A. (1985). Value orientations in heterosexual relationships. *Psychology of Women Quarterly, 9*, 477–488.

Crocker, J., Luhtanen, R., Blaine, B., & Broadnax, S. (1994). Collective self-esteem and psychological well-being among White, Black, and Asian college students. *Personality & Social Psychology Bulletin, 20*, 503–513.

Deci, E. L., & Ryan, R. M. (2000). The "what" and "why" of goal pursuits: Human needs and the self-determination of behavior. *Psychological Inquiry, 11*, 227–268.

Deaux, K. (1993). Reconstructing social identity. *Personality and Social Psychology Bulletin, 19*, 4–12.

Deaux, K., Reid, A., Mizrahi, K., & Ethier, K. A. (1995). Parameters of social identity. *Journal of Personality and Social Psychology, 68*, 280–291.

Deci, E. L., & Ryan, R. M. (1991). A motivational approach to self: Integration in personality. In R. Dienstbier (Ed.), *Nebraska Symposium on Motivation. Vol. 38: Perspectives on motivation* (pp. 237–288). Lincoln, NE: University of Nebraska Press.

Donahue, E. M., Robins, R. W., Roberts, B. W., & John, O. P. (1993). The divided self: Concurrent and longitudinal effects of psychological adjustment and social roles on self-concept differentiation. *Journal of Personality and Social Psychology, 64*, 834–846.

Ellemers, N., Spears, R., & Doosje, B. (2002). Self and social identity. *Annual Review of Psychology*, *53*(1), 161–186.

Elliot, A. J., Faler, J., McGregor, H. A., Campbell, W. K., Sedikides, C., & Harackiewicz, J. M. (2000). Competence valuation as a strategic intrinsic motivation process. *Personality & Social Psychology Bulletin*, *26*, 780–794.

Erikson, E. H. (1964). *Childhood and society* (2nd ed.). Oxford: Norton.

Goffman, E. (1950). *The presentation of self in everyday life*. New York: Doubleday.

Guisinger, S., & Blatt, S. J. (1994). Individuality and relatedness: Evolution of a fundamental dialectic. *American Psychologist*, *49*, 104–111.

Harter, S. (1997). The personal self in social context: Barriers to authenticity. In R. D. Ashmore & L. J. Jussim (Eds.), *Self and identity: Fundamental issues.* (pp. 81–105). New York: Oxford University Press.

Haslam, S. A., Powell, C., & Turner, J. C. (2000). Social identity, self-categorization, and work motivation: Rethinking the contribution of the group to positive and sustainable organisational outcomes. *Applied Psychology*, *49*, 319–339.

Hobbes, T. (1650/1931). *Leviathan*. New York: Dutton (originally published London, 1650).

Hodgins, H. S., Koestner, R., & Duncan, N. (1996). On the compatibility of autonomy and relatedness. *Personality and Social Psychology Bulletin*, *22*, 227–237.

Hogg, M. A., & Abrams, D. (1993). Towards a single-process uncertainty-reduction model of social motivation in groups. In M. A. Hogg & D. Abrams (Eds.), *Group motivation: Social psychological perspectives* (pp. 173–190). Hemel Hempstead: Harvester Wheatsheaf.

Hogg, M. A., & Abrams, D. (1999). Social identity and social cognition: Historical background and current trends. In D. Abrams & M. A. Hogg (Eds.), *Social identity and social cognition* (pp. 1–25). Malden, MA: Blackwell.

Hogg, M. A., Terry, D. J., & White, K. M. (1995). A tale of two theories: A critical comparison of identity theory with social identity theory. *Social Psychology Quarterly*, *58*(4), 255–269.

Horton, P. B., & Hunt, C. L. (1984). *Sociology*. New York: McGraw-Hill.

Jetten, J., Branscombe, N. R., Spears, R., & McKimmie, B. M. (2003). Predicting the paths of peripherals: The interaction of identification and future possibilities. *Personality and Social Psychology Bulletin*, *29*, 130–140.

Jetten, J., O'Brien, A., & Trindall, N. (2002). Changing identity: Predicting adjustment to organizational restructure as a function of subgroup and superordinate identification. *British Journal of Social Psychology*, *41*, 281–298.

Koestner, R., & Losier, G. (1996). Distinguishing reactive vs. reflective autonomy. *Journal of Personality*, *64*, 465–494.

Komorita, S. S., & Parks, C. D. (1995). Interpersonal relations: Mixed-motive interaction. *Annual Review of Psychology*, *46*, 183–207.

Laing, R. D. (1967). *The politics of experience*. New York: Ballantine.

Marcia, J. E. (2002). Identity in psychosocial development in adulthood. *Identity, 2*, 7–28.

Maslow, A. (1954). *Motivation and personality*. New York: Harper & Row.

McCall, G. J., & Simmons, J. L. (1978). *Identities and interactions*. New York: Free Press.

Mead, G. H. (1934). *Mind, self, and society* (C.W. Morris, Ed.), Chicago: University of Chicago Press.

Oakes, P. J., Haslam, S. A., & Reynolds, K. J. (1999). Social categorization and social context: Is stereotype change a matter of information or of meaning? In D. Abrams & M. A. Hogg (Eds.), *Social identity and social cognition* (pp. 55–79). Malden, MA: Blackwell.

Perls, F. S. (1947). *Ego, hunger, and aggression*. New York: Random House.

Postmes, T., & Branscombe, N. R. (2002). Influence of long-term racial environmental composition on subjective well-being in African Americans. *Journal of Personality and Social Psychology*, *83*, 735–751.

Rankin-Esquer, L. A., Burnett, C. K., Baucom, D. H., & Epstein, N. (1997). Autonomy and relatedness in marital functioning. *Journal of Marital & Family Therapy, 23,* 175–190.

Roberts, B. W., & Donahue, E. M. (1994). One personality, multiple selves: Integrating personality and social roles. *Journal of Personality, 62,* 199–218.

Rodgers, D. A. (1959). Spontaneity and specificity in social role relationships. *Journal of Personality, 27,* 300–310.

Ryan, R. M. (1995). Psychological needs and the facilitation of integrative processes. *Journal of Personality, 63,* 397–427.

Ryan, R. M., & Lynch, M. (1989). Emotional autonomy vs. detachment: Revisiting the vicissitudes of adolescence and young adult development. *Child Development, 60,* 340–356.

Ryan, R. M., Sheldon, K. M., Kasser, T., & Deci, E. L. (1996). All goals are not created equal: An organismic perspective on the nature of goals and their regulation. In R. M. Gollwitzer & J. A. Bargh (Eds.), *The psychology of action: Linking cognition and motivation to behavior* (pp. 7–26). New York: Guilford.

Sarbin, T. R., & Allen, V. L. (1969). Role theory. In *Handbook of social psychology* (vol. 1, pp. 488–567). Reading, MA: Addison-Wesley.

Schwartz, S. H. (1990). Individualism–collectivism: Critique and proposed refinements. *Journal of Cross-Cultural Psychology, 29,* 139–157.

Scott, W. A., & Stumpf, J. (1984). Personal satisfaction and role performance: Subjective and social aspects of adaptation. *Journal of Personality and Social Psychology, 47,* 812–827.

Sheldon, K. M., & Bettencourt, B. A. (2002). Psychological need-satisfaction and subjective well-being within social groups. *British Journal of Social Psychology, 41,* 25–38.

Sheldon, K. M., Elliot, A. J., Kim, Y., & Kasser, T. (2001). What is satisfying about satisfying events? Testing 10 candidate psychological needs. *Journal of Personality and Social Psychology, 80,* 325–339.

Sheldon, K. M., Ryan, R. M., Rawsthorne, L. J., & Ilardi, B. (1997). Trait self and true self: Cross-role variation in the Big Five personality traits and its relations with psychological authenticity and subjective well-being. *Journal of Personality and Social Psychology, 73,* 1380–1393.

Simon, B., & Stuermer, S. (2003). Respect for group members: Intragroup determinants of collective identification and group-serving behavior. *Personality and Social Psychology Bulletin, 29,* 183–193.

Smith, H. J., Tyler, T. R., Huo, Y. J., Ortiz, D. J., & Lind, E. (1998). The self-relevant implications of the group-value model: Group membership, self-worth, and treatment quality. *Journal of Experimental Social Psychology, 34,* 470–493.

Stryker, S. (1987). *Symbolic interactionism.* Menlo Park, CA: Cummings.

Tajfel, H. (1972). Some developments in European social psychology. *European Journal of Social Psychology, 2,* 307–321.

Tajfel, H. (1981). *Human groups and social categories.* Cambridge: Cambridge University Press.

Tajfel, H., & Turner, J. C. (1979). An integrative theory of intergroup conflict. In W. G. Austin & S. Worchel (Eds.), *The social psychology of intergroup relations* (pp. 33–47). Monterey, CA: Brooks-Cole.

Thoits, P. A., & Virshup, L. K. (1997). Me's and we's: Forms and functions of social identities. In R. D. Ashmore & L. J. Jussim (Eds.), *Self and identity: Fundamental issues.* (pp. 106–133). New York: Oxford University Press.

Triandis, H. C. (1994). Theoretical and methodological approaches to the study of collectivism and individualism. In Y. Kin, et al. (Eds.), *Individualism and collectivism: Theory, method and applications.* Thousand Oaks, CA: Sage.

Turner, J. C. (1985). Social categorization and the self-concept: A social cognitive theory of group behavior. In E. J. Lawler (Ed.), *Advances in group processes: Theory and research* (vol. 2, pp. 77–122). Greenwich, CT: JAI.

Turner, J. C. (1999). Some current issues in research on social identity and self-categorization theories. In N. Ellemers, R. Spears, & B. Doosje (Eds.), *Social identity: Context, commitment, content* (pp. 6–34). Malden, MA: Blackwell.

Turner, J. C., Hogg, M. A., Oakes, P. J., Reicher, S. D., & Wetherell, M. S. (1987). *Rediscovering the social group: A self-categorization theory.* Oxford: Blackwell.

Waterman, A. S. (1990). Personal expressiveness as a defining dimension of psychosocial identity. In C. Vandenplas-Holper & B. P. Campos (Eds.), *Interpersonal and identity development: New directions. Psychological development* (pp. 103–112). Porto, Portugal: Instituto De Consulta Psicologia.

12

The Dynamics of Personal and Social Identity Formation

Tom Postmes, Gamze Baray, S. Alexander Haslam, Thomas A. Morton, and Roderick I. Swaab

Each one of us has two heritages, a "vertical" one that comes to us from our ancestors, our religious community and our popular traditions, and a "horizontal" one transmitted to us by our contemporaries and by the age we live in. It seems to me that the latter is the more influential of the two, and that it becomes more so every day. Yet this fact is not reflected in our perception of ourselves, and the inheritance we invoke most frequently is the vertical one. (Maalouf, 2000, p. 102)

To many in the West, Islamic religious fundamentalism appears regressive, conservative and destructive. How is it that scores of people are converted by a rhetoric that would seem to place them and their family at risk, and bring their community mostly misery? Historically, this is hardly an isolated phenomenon. During the Reformation in sixteenth and seventeenth century Europe, heated debates over Christianity unleashed carnage and destruction, prompting some religious extremists to found American colonies (MacCulloch, 2003). Much earlier in Christian history, Pope Urban II lit the fuse of the First Crusade in his address to the Council of Clermont (1095). Although he initially addressed only hundreds, his message reached millions throughout Europe. Masses marched on the Orient. None of these movements was simply led from "above": in the First Crusade, for instance, the "leaders" spent most of the time trying to control what they had unleashed (Runciman, 1951). The real question is: what made the *messages* so powerful that they swept the mass of people along?

Some have suggested the power of these movements lies partly (in the terminology of this volume) in the absence of *individuality* within the group. These groups would exert a strong and paradoxical control on individuals precisely because their cause rises above individual people and their day-to-day concerns. Indeed, part of the power of the message behind these movements is the sense of destiny they provide their followers with.[1] In psychological terms, this is consistent with a self-categorization account: people's social identity (as Christian, Protestant, Muslim) becomes salient, and subsequently channels their actions and thoughts. Consistent with this, it has been argued that the power and influence of Islamic fundamentalism lie in the provision of an identity that unites Muslims in opposition and contrast to Western modernity (Maalouf, 2000). Such self-categorization analyses have become the dominant framework for the experimental study of social identity, and research confirms that these processes play a considerable part in group processes (see also Prentice, Chapter 3 in this volume).

However, there is a social counterpart to this cognitive process of self-categorization. A sense of collective destiny does not arise in a social vacuum (Tajfel, 1972); it emerges through interaction and debate with other relevant parties (within the group and outside it). Group members need to develop a common language or ideology that helps them *construct* a collective understanding of social reality, grievance, and shared destiny. In the above examples, the prime vehicles for the development of this common language were mass communication (pamphlets, books), preaching, singing, and debate. We argue that these communications harbour a process of social identity formation that not only underlies mass movements or large social categories, but is also found in much smaller groups. As we shall elaborate below, individuality plays a key role in this process.

Self-categorization theory (or SCT for short) has hitherto not devoted much attention to the role of internal dynamics of groups as a factor either in identity formation or in social influence (see Reicher, 1984; Turner, 1982, for exceptions). In the present chapter we wish to redress this imbalance, arguing that interaction is important not just as a medium to study the influence of self-categorization processes (i.e., as dependent variable), but also as a theoretical process in self-categorization (e.g., Antaki, Condor, & Levine, 1996; Billig, 1987). This is partly (a) because self-categorization depends on *social* consensus, (b) because interaction is pivotal to the mutual formation of personal and social identity in relation to each other, and (c) because interaction informs the *content* of those identities.

Before elaborating this argument, however, we need to devote some more attention to the idea that individuality plays a role even in social movements. The quotation at the start of this chapter makes a distinction between vertical and horizontal influences on (Islamic fundamentalist) identity. The vertical influence is that of heritage; it assumes a firmly established social identity which exists independently (and outside) of the self. Yet, as Maalouf (2000) argues, despite the strong claims of Islamic fundamentalists to tradition and historical consistency, it is very much a new phenomenon, a social identity "under construction". Like Maalouf, we believe that the construction of social identities is, partly, a horizontal or bottom-up process in which individuality plays a key role.

In order to address these issues of identity formation in small groups and social movements, the first section in the chapter explores whether there are any fundamental differences between groups in which individuality appears to be more or less visible. The second section then examines SCT and its ability to account for phenomena in small and large groups alike. The final sections turn to the question of how social identities and personal identities are formed through interaction, and what this implies.

Distinguishing different group types: interactive groups and social categories

Typologies of "the group" are popular in social psychology today. These typologies bear witness to an impressive variety of human forms of aggregation. People can identify meaningful groupings in culture, language, nation, race, wealth, age, religion, gender, organization, sports, city, village, sexuality, neighbourhood, friendship, family, and even the size of ears. Human groupings may vary in terms of their sense of common fate, clarity of goal or purpose, size, degree of interaction, group composition, and so on. Typologies have attempted to impose some structure on this variety by identifying kinds. Lickel, Hamilton, Wieczorkowska, Lewis, Sherman, and Uhles (2000), for example, differentiated between intimacy groups (family and friends), task groups (teams at work), social categories (race, gender), and loose associations (neighbourhoods, people with similar interests). Along different lines, Deaux, Reid, Mizrahi, and Ethier (1995) proposed five types of identities: those based on relationship, vocation/avocation, stigma, political affiliation, and ethnicity/nationality.

The relevance of these typologies to the present volume lies in the clear distinction that runs through them between groups in which the individuality of members is central, and groups in which individuality is peripheral – that is, interactive vs categorical groups (e.g., Deaux & Martin, 2003; Lewin, 1948; Lickel, Hamilton, & Sherman, 2001; Prentice, Miller, & Lightdale, 1994; Wilder & Simon, 1998). Elsewhere, we have referred to these as "interpersonal" groups, which are made up of an identifiable number of individuals, and "categorical" groups, in which individuals other than self are either absent, invisible or "expendable" (Postmes, Haslam, & Swaab, 2005; Postmes, Spears, Lee, & Novak, in press).

The obvious and useful question raised by such distinctions is whether general theories of the group (e.g., self-categorization theory) are equally applicable to each type of group. Implicit in these typologies is an assumption that the kind of processes specified by SCT can only be found in categorical social groups and social movements (e.g., Islamic fundamentalism), and that they are less relevant to smaller interactive groups and intimacy groups within which individuality is centre-stage. This would suggest, of course, that whenever individuality raises its head, whether in small groups, interpersonal relations, or the family, there can be no social movement or social-categorical process (see also Fiske, 1993). Margaret Thatcher seemed to subscribe to this view when she argued in 1987 that "there is no such thing as society. There are individual men and women and there are families."

So let us investigate the assumption that interpersonal and categorical groups are fundamentally different. Do we need different psychologies for different groups?

Group typologies and group psychologies

What is perhaps most revealing about the variety of groups that play a role in our lives is that they are all psychologically significant. Indeed, use of the term "group" when referring to diverse forms of aggregation (a social movement such as Islamic fundamentalism, a social category such as race, or small interactive teams in organizations) is not simply a terminological inaccuracy. On the contrary, it is an accurate reflection of the fact that, in the right circumstances, any one of a bewildering diversity of groupings can become psychologically relevant and consequential – influencing our understanding of the world and the way we act upon it through a powerful emotional significance attached to membership. In this respect, typologies are a helpful reminder of the variety of bases upon which humans may create the social reality of "groupness" (Campbell, 1958).

The study of the formation of a psychological group (and social identity) should certainly take this variety into account. Indeed, we should acknowledge the flexibility of social organization as an essentially human ability. One can contrast this to some studies of human groups from biological and evolutionary perspectives, which assume that human survival depends on small interactive face-to-face groups (Caporael, 2001, p. 255). For example, to identify the "archetypal" social groupings that humans have evolved in and with, Dunbar (1993) infers from brain sizes of different species that the human mind can cope with groups up to about 150 members. This is inferred from the maximum number of concurrent interpersonal relations that we can juggle in our mind. Slightly inconsistent with this, anthropological research suggests that the earliest human hunter-gatherer groups were probably family-dominated bands of about 20–60 people, but also notes that "groups could fragment and coalesce to exploit diverse and variable resources" (Johnson & Earle, 2000, p. 87). Whatever the precise number, though, this kind of work would suggest that the human brain is evolutionarily prepared to cope with small interpersonal groups, not with more abstract social categories. This has led to suggestions that the flexibility of groupings and social organizations witnessed today (and throughout history, in fact) is an adaptation of stone-age minds to a modern world, with people "extending" small group characteristics to larger social categories (cf. Caporael, 2001, p. 255).

From our perspective, the problem with such analyses is that they favour one conception of groups over others. They assume that groups must be a physical entity whose members meet regularly. As a result, they ignore the point that hunter-gatherer societies shared their language and customs not just with their family or band, but with at least several thousands (Johnson & Earle, 2000). In other words, some form of social categories almost certainly existed even then. Moreover, it is not the size of groups or the prevalent form of interaction that ultimately matters, it is their psychological representation. Even a small band of hunter-gatherers may at times operate as an interpersonal network of social support (e.g., when going on a joint hunting expedition), and at different times operate as a social category (e.g., when engaged in conflict with a neighbouring band or clan). The ubiquity and power of social categorization processes today make it very unlikely that this is a modern adaptation. Indeed, far from being an abnormality, the flexibility of conceiving the same groups in terms of different forms of social organization seems to be a distinctively human capacity (see also Dupré, 2001).

However, to say that a capacity for flexible social organization is "normal" does not bring us any closer to explaining how humans manage to found shared (consensual) perceptions of meaningful social groups on such different associations. To explain this capacity for creating social structure is a fundamental challenge to social psychology. To some extent, typologies are helpful in making us realize the magnitude of this challenge. At the same time, however, typologies risk setting an agenda for group psychology that puts us on the wrong path.

Limitations of group typologies

There are at least three potential problems with typologies in general, and with the distinction between interpersonal and categorical groups in particular. First, typologies imply that there are different psychologies for different kinds of groups. The problem with this is that if there were clear differences between the characteristics of groups (see below for some caveats) this does not mean that the psychological consequences of group membership need be any different. The same sense of profound purpose and involvement that characterizes the crowd, for example, can also occur in newly assembled teams at work, or in an amateur choir. Of course, there might be variations in the intensity, generality, and duration of these psychological responses, but what should interest social psychologists is the potential for such fundamentally different social relations to evoke even proximately similar responses.

The second limitation of typologies is that they set an agenda by concentrating on social groupings that are ordinarily encountered in everyday middle-class life (family, work groups, sports teams, religion, and so on). Part of the problem here is that the extraordinary cases (online communities, crowds, social movements) might be the most informative, for they most loudly and clearly contradict some established social psychological theories of groups. For example, consider the anti-globalization protests in Seattle, Genoa, and elsewhere. The very possibility for a fragmented body of individuals and subgroups to coalesce into a crowd acting in unison, with all the psychological conviction of those who take part in its mass movement, raises thorny questions for group theories based on social exchange principles (Kelly & Breinlinger, 1996). The crowd phenomenon forces us to consider the flexible and dynamic nature of social organization in action (Drury & Reicher, 2000; Reicher, 1996). Similarly, the capacity for humans to find psychological meaning in virtual groups (e.g., for social support) challenges some of the physical conceptions of the group as grounded in physical presence or physical similarity (Postmes & Baym, 2005; Spears, Postmes, Lea, & Wolbert, 2002). If we are serious about putting social psychological theory to the test, these extraordinary groups matter.

In contemporary group typologies the crowd or virtual community does not make an entry (cf. Lickel et al., 2001). Indeed, this is ensured by the methodologies and samples of the studies validating them. If participants are asked what social groups they belong to, that question already favours permanent groups over transient ones such as the crowd. Moreover, if one asks this question of Midwestern university students, then the composition of that group can explain why race and gender are perceived as being of low "social identity value" (Lickel et al., 2000, p. 234). Finally, it is likely that these participants do not realize just how important certain groups are to them; after all, the significance of being American, white or Christian only becomes apparent when one is exposed to a different culture. Typologies risk narrowing our understanding of the group by restricting the analysis to common and typical groups such as family and friends.

A final problem is with the validity of the characterization of types itself. Any typology should meet two assumptions: one of homogeneity within types, and one of distinctiveness between types. In the case of group typologies, both assumptions are questionable. Reflecting on the homogeneity assumption, it is apparent that a social grouping assumes a different character across time and context. For example, on different occasions a family may operate as a network of personal relations, or as a categorical entity which gives its members a social identity that guides their behaviour (e.g., through the provision of group norms) and that of other people (e.g., through stereotyping). One does not need examples as extreme as the royal family, the mafia or the British National Party to appreciate this point: any social grouping can function *both* as a set of individuals *and* as a social category, depending on what its activities are, what other groups are involved, and what it is attempting to achieve. This contextual variability raises theoretical and practical doubts about the homogeneity of "types".

Further concerns can be raised about the distinctiveness assumption. There is a remarkable interdependence that cuts across boundaries between interactive and categorical groups. The writing on a postcard from Waco, Texas (1916), may illustrate the point. The writer refers to the picture on the front: "This is the barbecue we had last night. My picture is to the left with a cross over it. Your son, Joe" (Allen, Als, Lewis, Litwack, & Litwack, 2000). On its own this sounds like innocent family banter – love and affection at work, clearly a process found in interactive groups. But the picture on the front is not so innocent: it is a graphic photograph of a gruesome lynching, with a cross to identify one of the proud perpetrators. The nature of this "barbeque" reveals that this family's intimate personal relations are grounded in a shared social-categorical positioning that most people would consider racist and criminal today. Indeed, far from being divorced from social categories, the intimate relationships with family and friends are the primary context within which our understanding of categories is shaped and changed. Thus, it is not entirely obvious that the functions of, say, family and friendship groups can be understood separately from the social categories in which they are grounded, or vice versa.

The challenge for a psychology of groups, then, is not to carve up group life into neat little subdomains, each with its own set of processes and principles which structure human interaction. Rather, the challenge is to find one general theory from which we can better understand the human capacity for forming groups in a wide variety of ways. SCT aims to provide just such a theory.

Interpersonal groups, intragroup dynamics and self-categorization processes

Building on pioneering work by Henri Tajfel, SCT aimed to resolve the individual–group dualism (Turner, 1982; Turner & Oakes, 1986). The purpose was to replace the idea that individuality (in here) and group (out there) are two separate forces with the idea that individuals internalize the group and may call on more personal or more social aspects of their own identity (Turner, 1991; Turner, Hogg, Oakes, Reicher, & Wetherell, 1987). By incorporating the group within the individual, SCT is able to account for the fact that while humans are perpetually under the implicit or explicit influence of groups, they tend to experience this group behaviour as profoundly authentic and self-authored (i.e., as stemming from individuality). Moreover, because SCT conceives of the group as a psychological, not just a physical or sociological, entity, its ideas can be applied to any kind of social relationship which can be represented as a group; the influence of social identity can therefore be found in anonymous dyads collaborating over the Internet (Tanis & Postmes, 2005) as well as in the midst of the crowd (Reicher, 1984).

Self-categorization in all groups great and small

From its inception, a core assumption of self-categorization theory has been that social identity processes are as central to the internal dynamics of small groups as to those of large social categories. Indeed, Tajfel (1978) observed that "the three aspects of group membership ... – the cognitive, the evaluative and the emotional – can be made to apply equally well to small groups and to large social categories" (p. 29). SCT was even more explicit about this (Turner, 1982, 1985; Turner et al., 1987). In fact, its initial emphasis was on polarization in small groups as the testing ground for self-categorization theory's meta-theoretical assumptions (e.g., Turner et al., 1987, p. 88). Thus, the theory has provided an ambitious agenda by proposing that it is capable of accounting for social influence as much in small groups as in any other (inter)group setting (Turner, 1991).

Yet, partially as a result of the persistent assumption that we need different psychologies for different groups, SCT's impact on small group research has remained limited, at best. Small group researchers themselves have suggested that SCT is more suited to explaining the way that (out)groups are perceived than the internal dynamics of groups (e.g., Moreland, Argote, & Krishnan, 1996). Similarly, a recent review of decision-making and productivity research contrasted studies of small groups with "approaches popular in European social psychological circles with clear relevance to groups, but with a clear interpersonal (e.g., minority influence) or intergroup (e.g., social identity theory) focus". Somewhat cryptically, it added that "For those interested in intragroup processes, *per se*, this could be viewed as a half-empty glass" (Kerr & Tindale, 2004, p. 641). As such comments indicate, self-categorization principles are typically seen as irrelevant to small group dynamics.

There is one obvious reason why the message of self-categorization theorists has failed to convince the audience of small group researchers. Some notable exceptions notwithstanding, research in the social identity tradition has eschewed the study of small interactive groups (Morton & Postmes, 2005), instead focusing on minimal groups (i.e., without interaction) or perceptions of groups. This may have been part of a general move away from studying interaction in social psychology (Haslam & McGarty, 2001), but it has undoubtedly constrained the ability to provide empirical backing for SCT principles. Fortunately, there is a growing body of research that is starting to address this (Postmes et al., 2005).

However, there are more fundamental factors that help explain why SCT's implications for small groups have been overlooked. One is that SCT has not sufficiently elaborated issues of individuality and diversity within the group, leading to the common misconception that social identity processes inevitably lead to the elimination of intragroup differences or the denial of individuality (Hornsey & Jetten, 2004; see also Jetten & Postmes, Chapter 7; and Spears, Ellemers, Doosje, & Branscombe, Chapter 10 in this volume). There are many different solutions to this problem, and several of them are presented elsewhere in this volume. Suffice it to say that all of them demonstrate, in one way or another, that diversity within groups, the experience of individuality and distinctiveness, and even the encouragement of innovation, creativity and deviance, can all stem from processes of social (not merely personal) identity.

A second issue is that SCT makes a rigid distinction between personal and social identity (see also Turner, Reynolds, Haslam, & Veenstra, Chapter 2 in this volume). Within SCT, the relation between personal and social identity is shaped by several assumptions. One is that social identity is a product of comparisons made in social context, with other comparable groups (driven by the principle of meta-contrast), whereas personal identity is a product of comparison with comparable individuals (Onorato & Turner, 2004; Turner & Onorato, 1999). This is essentially a perceptual phenomenon related to the Gestalt principle that a salient figure invites contrast from the ground (Tajfel & Wilkes, 1963; 1964). Another key assumption is that social and personal identity are functionally antagonistic, meaning that the salience of one will be at the expense of the other. Again this is related to the Gestalt principle that seeing an entity precludes seeing its constituent parts, and vice versa.

In conjunction, these two assumptions appear to imply that small group dynamics are governed by personal identity concerns.[2] This is because in many small group studies there is no apparent or obvious outgroup (as in the case of an orchestra or a theatre group, for example), and group members' actions would have to be based largely on intragroup comparisons and personal identity. Moreover, a strong interpretation of functional antagonism (or Tajfel's interpersonal–group continuum for that matter) implies that there could not be, within a small group, any obvious way of reconciling the acute interpersonal dynamics of interaction between individual members with the *concurrent* salience of a superordinate sense of social identity (but see Haslam, 1997).

The application of SCT to dynamics in interactive groups, then, appears to be obstructed by some of its own core assumptions. The resolution is not particularly complex, we argue, but it does require an elaboration of the key assumptions outlined above. This elaboration needs to address (a) the way in which personal and social identity are constituted or formed, both on their own and in relation to each other, and (b) the capacity for social interaction to transform social cognitive processes into shared cognitive ones.

The formation of social identity

Basic work in the social identity tradition has explored how social identity is grounded in intergroup comparisons and associated dynamics (Oakes, Haslam, & Turner, 1994; Reicher, 1996). Framed by historical and ideological understandings, group members can deduce from these intergroup factors specific properties of social identity – what it means to be a member of this group at a particular junction. As an example, a perceived conflict with Israel and America exerts an undoubted influence on Islamic fundamentalism. In addition to these factors, however, we argue that the behaviour of individual group members (which may be dictated by social identity, but also by *personal* identity) will also exert an influence on the content of social identity (see also Reicher & Haslam, Chapter 13 in this volume). People take note of individual actions by leaders (Khomeini, Arafat or Mahmoud Abbas) and they are in constant dialogue and debate with ordinary ingroup members in order to induce how group membership is to be interpreted and enacted (see Figure 12.1; and see also Postmes, Haslam, & Swaab, in press; Postmes, Spears et al., in press; Turner, 1982). This is the "horizontal" heritage referred to by Maalouf (2000).

The implications of this line of thought are interesting. In particular, it follows that small group dynamics can, in their own right, give rise to the induction of group norms and other aspects of identity. It means that social identity processes are not restricted to categorical groups, but also occur in groups like an amateur choir or theatre company – groups that do not operate in the salient intergroup context that is so characteristic of Islamic fundamentalism. It also implies that social identity processes are likely to

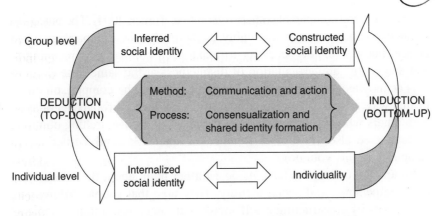

Figure 12.1   An interactive model of (social) identity formation

have played a role in some of the classic social influence studies such as Sherif's (1935) research on norm formation in laboratory groups (see also Turner, 1991).

Moreover, the power of these inductive processes also explains why group members who are driven by their own strategic and selfish concerns (bound up with personal identity) invest so much in attempting to shape ingroup norms. For example, the success of neoconservatism in the US is partly the result of careful management of perceived intergroup relations and actual wars with "evil" empires (e.g., the USSR) and antagonists (e.g., Islamic fundamentalism). It is through the systematic highlighting of these outside threats that neoconservatives come to be perceived as prototypical of national social identity (cf. Reicher & Hopkins, 2001). However, the fact that representations of intergroup relations are the tools for achieving intragroup objectives does not distract from the conclusion that this, ultimately, is also a project of bottom-up social identity construction by individuals. The fact that personal identities can shape the construction of social identity suggests that the two are more closely connected than is often acknowledged.

The formation of personal identity

In addition to a bottom-up process whereby individuals construct social identities, there is the reverse process: the formation of personal identity is also informed by aspects of social identity. As is the case for the outcome of any social comparison process, the feelings of distinctness that give rise to personal identity must, to some degree, be rooted in a contrast between self and comparable others (Onorato & Turner, 2004). The outcomes of such comparisons are inevitably anchored by the comparison other. Hence, because of the necessity to make such comparisons meaningful and diagnostic, any articulation of distinctness at the same time (implicitly) acknowledges similarity and congruence with the comparison other. In this way, a sense of personal identity is achieved through negotiation with others who are, in some sense, members of an overarching common ingroup (see also Haslam & Reicher, Chapter 13; and Turner et al., Chapter 2 in this volume).

Simon and colleagues have made a further point about the relationship between personal and social identity. They note that people differentiate themselves by constructing a self-image that integrates multiple elements drawn from the patchwork of social groups to which they belong (Kampmeier & Simon, 2001; Simon, 2004). Thus, to be a feminist might be a distinctive feature in a group of men, but at a feminist conference one obvious source of distinctiveness would be the simple fact of being male. Although this may appear to be a cognitive process of self-construal, it can only be achieved if members of the overarching group sanction (or at least do not challenge) the results of this process. In that sense, the establishment of personal identity is strongly dependent on the group. What emerges from this is a much more organic model in which individuals construct personal identity by using social group memberships as a resource – a process which is no doubt partly motivated by the desire to seek positive differentiation from others and to establish a meaningful position for self within the group (cf. Pickett & Leonardelli, Chapter 4 in this volume), but which is also likely to be restricted by the kinds of individuality that are permitted by others in the group, and by the boundaries that norms and culture impose on this process of construal (cf. Moghaddam, Chapter 9; and Halloran & Kashima, Chapter 8 in this volume).

As our description of this process of normative guidance implies, we believe that there are also more direct (and profound) influences of social identity on personal identity (Baray, Postmes, & Jetten, 2005). For even when personal identity is made salient within the group, people will necessarily take account of the content of social identity (see also Turner, et al., Chapter 2 in this volume). In fact, we propose that membership of some groups may shape the personal identity of their members, both within the context of the group and outside it. This is particularly true where groups have an ideology, culture and/or philosophy that aims to inform the identity of its members in such a way that it permeates all social contexts, not merely those in which the group's social identity is explicitly made salient. Religious groups are a good example of this. Although religion no doubt varies in salience from context to context, for "true believers" it cannot but pervade all aspects of their life. Thus, in the Bible Jesus says "I am the way, the truth, the light" (John, 14: 6), not "I am the way, the truth, the light, some of the time." The content of religion expressly aims to inform and regulate *all* ways of life. It delineates a set of norms, values, and beliefs whose validity and applicability are assumed and often claimed to be universal. Similar influences can also be exerted by one's culture. A sense of personal identity cannot but emerge from such social identities, and must be congruent with them (Jetten, Postmes, & McAuliffe, 2002).

Recent research examined this proposal in a sample of members of the Turkish Nationalist Action Party (Baray et al., 2005). This is an extreme right-wing party with a nationalist and Islamic agenda. Its unofficial militant arm, the "grey wolves", has a long history of violence and terrorist activities. More than other political parties, it provides an ideology for its followers that encompasses all aspects of their lives, regulating their social interactions with ingroup and outgroup others. Indeed, one of their nine key doctrines is about "character building" (Arikan, 2002). In our research, we discovered that for members of this group, aspects of personal identity and social identity are not negatively correlated or independent of each other. In fact, when we attempted to make personal identity salient, and promote intragroup comparisons in members of these groups, they became *more* willing to let their individual identity and destiny be dictated by their group, and aspects of personal and social identity became strongly and positively associated.

Putting these perspectives on social and personal identity formation together, it would appear that in terms of the construction of identity content, there is an ongoing dynamic between personal and social identity. Moreover, this dynamic interaction between personal and social aspects of identity is not a purely cognitive process. As Marx (1857/1993) pointed out, it is because of "society" *(Gesellschaft)* that individuality exists. The original term *Gesellschaft* used by Marx refers not just to the state or nation, but to a social process. Lost in translation is the point that individuality can only emerge in an enduring and cooperating social group whose members have developed organized patterns of relationships through *interaction* with one another (see also Durkheim, 1893/1984).

Personal identity and social identity in social interaction

The conclusion to be drawn from the above discussion is that social identity and personal identity cannot be constructed entirely independently of each other, and are in fact constrained and informed by each other in important ways. For social identity, the content is socially constructed in interaction: cognitive representations of ingroup stereotypes or social norms need to be grounded in a social consensus before they can be effective guides for ingroup behaviour (Haslam, 1997; Haslam, Turner, Oakes, McGarty, & Reynolds, 1998). Such social constructs inevitably depend on a system of social validation and social interaction to define and perpetuate them (Festinger, 1954; Searle, 1995). In other words, it is because of social interaction that social identities become social realities that we can act upon, rather than mere cognitive and subjective representations of the group (Haslam, Postmes, & Ellemers, 2003; Stott & Drury, 2004).

For personal identity we find a similar process occurs. The degree to which one can successfully differentiate oneself from others (and express personal identity) is as dependent on the tacit consent of the audience as is one's claim to a social identity. In fact, there is a long tradition in social psychology which argues that there is no other way to know the self than through a process of actual and symbolic interaction with others (e.g., Mead, 1934). Even the apparently private sense of personal identity therefore requires some social consensus that allows one to legitimately differentiate oneself from others on particular dimensions.

Thus, social consensus is pivotal to the successful enactment of personal and social identity in our social lives. There are several examples from our research which speak to this. Swaab and colleagues, for example, have conducted a series of studies examining negotiations between multiple parties (Postmes et al., 2005; Swaab, Postmes, Neijens, Kiers, & Dumay, 2002; Swaab, Postmes, Spears, Van Beest, & Neijens, 2005). The success of settlement in these negotiations was a direct function of the interaction within the groups. In the first phase of the experiment, a simple manipulation in which group members circulated information created a sense of shared cognition (e.g., Swaab et al., 2005, Studies 1, 3, 4). In the second phase, when group members sat down to negotiate a thorny issue, this shared cognition provided the basis for the emergence of a sense of social identity, which in turn was powerfully predictive of successful negotiation settlement. In some sense, this process of convergence of individual cognitions through communication is essentially a form of consensualization (Haslam, 1997). Importantly, however, the manipulation itself only created an awareness among group members of each other's cognitions; in itself, it did not resolve any of the tensions or conflicts of interest.

Communication has also been shown to play a key role in the emergence of a sense of shared identity in computer-mediated groups (Postmes, Spears et al., in press; Sassenberg & Postmes, 2002). These studies suggest that in groups that have a sense of shared identity to begin with (either because individuality is not visible, or because groups have been led to develop a shared identity from the outset), communication serves to reinforce the existing identity – with convergent and homogeneous communications predicting the establishment of a clear group norm and polarized group position (much as predicted by self-categorization theory). Communication appears to play a crucial role in social identity processes by translating an abstract common identity, that could *potentially* unite the group, into a concrete shared identity that actually influences and guides their actions in relation to the task at hand.

Quite different communication processes take place when personal identity and interpersonal relations are salient from the start (Postmes, Spears et al., in press; Sassenberg & Postmes, 2002). Here, too, a sense of social identity emerges over the course of interaction, but convergence on a common identity is achieved differently. Under these conditions it is the degree to which groups thoroughly talk through and negotiate the issues they face that predicts whether they succeed in complementing the interpersonal interactions with a superordinate sense of identity. This is direct evidence for a process of induction – the inference of commonalities from the broad range of perspectives expressed by individuals within the group – achieved through interaction.

This process of induction can be fragile in the sense that it may not always result in the establishment of a strong sense of social identity. Nevertheless, to the extent it does occur this has implications for functional antagonism. There may be antagonism at the level of the perceptual salience of personal vs social identity as cognitive constructs (see Turner et al., 1987, pp. 49–50), but the stream of individual actions within the group demands continuous reassessment. Each distinctive act raises a question: is it best assimilated into what counts as "group behaviour" or should it be contrasted as an idiosyncratic individual act? The very fact that social identity is at the same time a product of social consensus and a subjective representation of that consensus means that we can never be entirely sure what our ingroup stands for, and whether each person within our group is representative of it: social identity salience may stimulate the search for consensus within the group (Turner, 1991), but it does not make us blind to intragroup heterogeneity. This is perhaps best illustrated by the crowd. Even when, in the heat of the moment, crowds act apparently single-mindedly, their members still display awareness of individuality – fulfilling individual roles, renegotiating their tactics with each other, and displaying individual initiative even to the point of policing their own actions (Drury & Reicher, 2000; Reicher, 1996; Stott, Hutchison, & Drury, 2001).

Yet, some have suggested that functional antagonism implies that when social identity is salient, any individual differentiation within the group becomes impossible (Hogg, 1996; Swann, Kwan, Polzer, & Milton,

Figure 12.2   Rubin's vase

2003). This strong interpretation of functional antagonism can be illustrated with the well-known image of "Rubin's vase" (Figure 12.2). In this image, one can see either a vase or two faces, but not both at the same time; seeing one as figure relegates the other to ground. However, the dynamic interaction between individuals does not follow such perceptual laws. In the first instance this is because interaction is an ongoing process. Although at any specific moment it may be cognitively difficult or impossible to "see" figure and ground (personal and social identity), one only needs to take a slightly longer look at the figure to realize that figure and ground are there, and that they are dependent on each other. Moreover, interaction is based on language, and within language (unlike perception) it is possible to acknowledge both faces and vase. Finally, such an interpretation of functional antagonism assumes that personal and social identity exist as concrete cognitive *entities* that are equivalent and contrastable, but the notion that both are constituted through social interaction entails that they are ongoing social processes that may be more or less complementary or antagonistic.

Beyond these implications for SCT, it is clear from this research that social identity processes do play a role in interactive groups. Even in "personal" groups that have been deliberately constructed around interpersonal relations, the emergence of a social identity can be witnessed over time, just as social identity processes may explain interactions in dyads (Tanis & Postmes, 2005). SCT manages to transcend typologies of groups that exist "out there" by introducing and connecting the core features of those typologies within the psychology of the individual "in here". It explains why group members have the cognitive capacity to engage with others at different levels of social abstraction (individual, group, human) irrespective of the actual physical constraints imposed by group size, proximity and communication channels. Moreover, the fact that social identity and personal identity are products of social consensus provides a crucial link between cognition and interaction.

Implications for a social identity perspective on individuality

In this chapter we have argued that members of groups draw on interaction within the group partly in an effort to develop and change ideas of "who we are" (identity) and "what we are about" (purpose) and that these activities regulate and shape group members' self-conceptions and actions. These ideas, importantly, cannot be reduced to properties of the individual or to properties of the group. They are carried forward and changed by individuals, but can only exist by virtue of some degree of consensualization within the group which creates a "social reality" outside of the individual (Haslam et al., 2003; Searle, 1995). The approach in this chapter has been to define individuality as the perpetually unfinished product of this process: as a sense of identity that emerges within the group, and that is socially constructed through action and cognition, in which elements of both personal and social identity are represented.

There is actually a surprising amount of consensus about this issue among theorists coming from very different perspectives. Many have pointed out that the diachronic and interactive nature of the construction of identity in and from interaction invalidates or qualifies a static cognitive analysis of self and social categorization (Antaki et al., 1996; Billig, 1987; Moghaddam, Chapter 9 in this volume; Moreland, Levine, & McMinn, 2001; Oakes et al., 1994; Reicher & Hopkins, 2001). Whatever forms the analysis of this process may take, it is clear that social psychology needs to return to the study of groups in interaction in order to make progress on this front. Only in this way can we begin to understand the interaction between identities "out there" and "in here". For SCT, the study of small interactive groups remains not just the ultimate testing ground for its meta-theoretical assumptions (cf. Turner et al., 1987, p. 88), but one that can inform future elaboration of the theory.

Elsewhere we have presented a model of how social identities organically emerge through processes of induction, and are mechanically inferred through processes of deduction (Postmes et al., 2005; Postmes et al., in press). In this chapter we elaborated this model, suggesting that personal identity may be constructed in similar ways. The model suggests that the group is not necessarily weakened by individuality (see also Hornsey & Jetten, 2004). In fact, the results discussed above suggest that diversity can be a group's strength, rather than its weakness (e.g., Postmes, Spears, et al., in press). Most obviously, the emergence of interpersonal bonds can shore up the emergence of a superordinate solidarity. Moreover, if shared identity is the very basis for the emergence of individuality (Marx, 1857/1993), then by implication any displays of distinctiveness can be interpreted as signs of (collective) trust and as emblems of ingroup membership (Jetten et al., 2002). In this way too, diversity may strengthen the group's ability for coordinated action, and enhance its efficacy and associated feelings of collective power (Durkheim, 1893/1984).

The model also suggests that the contents of personal and social identity are constructed in relation to each other. This implies that personal and social identity contents are not necessarily antagonistic, but can be mutually reinforcing (Baray et al., 2005). Our research has shown that this antagonism is certainly not an issue in the content of particular identities (which may be more or less congruent and mutually dependent upon each other). Moreover, it is likely that cognitive salience is similarly affected by the processes of social identity construction that interaction continuously enables and requires.

Postscript: theorizing social movements

At the start of this chapter we considered three social movements: Islamic fundamentalism, the Reformation, and the First Crusade. Revolving almost entirely around intergroup conflict, they are dominated by social identity concerns. The question we asked was: does individuality play any role in these movements? The chapter addressed the issue from several angles. We suggested that despite the many distinctions between large social movements, social categories, and small interactive groups, similar processes are found in all of them. We also presented research suggesting that small groups "dominated" by individuality can construct (induce) a social identity. Finally, we have shown that groups "dominated" by powerful social identities inform personal identity and individuality.

Putting these things together, the model of identity formation that we have presented suggests that socio-structural, economic and historical conditions play an important role in producing social movements, but social consensus gives them their influence. The process of achieving consensus is not a mechanical one, and is closely bound up with the way in which social and personal identity are constructed in relation to each other, and with reference to the future. Consensus and identity do not simply exist "out there" (in society) or "in here" (in cognition). They are processes that organically emerge from ongoing interactions within and between groups. Invariably, autonomy and individuality play a key role in such interactions. Thus, our analysis of social movements (or groups in general, for that matter) should not just take into account socio-structural or cognitive processes, or personal or social identities. The key message of this chapter is that we can only understand the group if we study all these factors in conjunction, as they are expressed and formed in social interaction.

NOTES

This research was supported by a research fellowship of the Economic and Social Research Council no. RES-000–27–0050, and a grant from the Leverhulme Trust no. F/00144/V.

1 We have no time to discuss the multitude of other factors involved (but see Reicher & Haslam, Chapter 13 in this volume). Invariably, collective movements are based on a consensus that something is very wrong – often a profound sense of unhappiness with the current reality (either material or social), paired with a sense of urgent threat from outside or inside. Moreover, it helps if some attainable alternative is available (although this should not be exaggerated; many social movements have either no clear purpose, or promise only glory in the afterlife).

2 Issues of functional antagonism have been the subject of considerable debate. We do not have the space to review this literature here. Suffice to say that in its original conception, functional antagonism was much more nuanced than some subsequent interpretations suggest (see Turner et al., Chapter 2 in this volume). This chapter is more concerned with identifying its positive uses than with disentangling past (mis)understandings.

REFERENCES

Allen, J., Als, H., Lewis, J., Litwack, L. F., & Litwack, L. (2000). *Without sanctuary: Lynching photography in America.* Santa Fe, NM: Twin Palms.

Antaki, C., Condor, S., & Levine, M. (1996). Social identities in talk: Speakers' own orientations. *British Journal of Social Psychology, 35,* 473–492.

Arikan, E. B. (2002). The ultra-nationalists under review: A study of the Nationalist Action Party. *Nations and Nationalism, 8,* 357–375.

Baray, G., Postmes, T., & Jetten, J. (2005). Self-defining groups and the relation between personal and social identity. Manuscript in preparation: University of Exeter.

Billig, M. (1987). *Arguing and thinking: A rhetorical approach to social psychology.* Cambridge: Cambridge University Press.

Campbell, D. T. (1958). Common fate, similarity and other indices of the status of aggregates of persons as social entities. *Behavioral Sciences, 3,* 14–25.

Caporael, L. R. (2001). Parts and wholes: The evolutionary importance of groups. In C. Sedikides & M. B. Brewer (Eds.), *Individual self, relational self, collective self* (pp. 241–258). Philadelphia: Psychology Press.

Deaux, K., & Martin, D. (2003). Interpersonal networks and social categories: Specifying levels of context in identity processes. *Social Psychology Quarterly, 66,* 101–117.

Deaux, K., Reid, A., Mizrahi, K., & Ethier, K. A. (1995). Parameters of social identity. *Journal of Personality and Social Psychology, 68*, 280–291.

Drury, J., & Reicher, S. (2000). Collective action and psychological change: The emergence of new social identities. *British Journal of Social Psychology, 39*, 579–604.

Dunbar, R. I. M. (1993). Coevolution of neocortical size, group-size and language in humans. *Behavioral and Brain Sciences, 16*, 681–694.

Dupré, J. (2001). *Human nature and the limits of science.* Oxford: Oxford University Press.

Durkheim, E. (1893/1984). *The division of labour in society.* London: Macmillan (original work published in 1893).

Festinger, L. (1954). A theory of social comparison processes. *Human Relations, 7*, 117–140.

Fiske, S. T. (1993). Controlling other people: The impact of power on stereotyping. *American Psychologist, 48*, 621–628.

Haslam, S. A. (1997). Stereotyping and social influence: Foundations of stereotype consensus. In R. Spears, P. J. Oakes, N. Ellemers, & S. A. Haslam (Eds.), *The social psychology of stereotyping and group life* (pp. 119–143). Oxford: Blackwell.

Haslam, S. A., & McGarty, C. (2001). A 100 years of certitude? Social psychology, the experimental method and the management of scientific uncertainty. *British Journal of Social Psychology, 40*, 1–21.

Haslam, S. A., Postmes, T., & Ellemers, N. (2003). More than a metaphor: Organizational identity makes organizational life possible. *British Journal of Management, 14*, 357–369.

Haslam, S. A., Turner, J. C., Oakes, P. J., McGarty, C., & Reynolds, K. J. (1998). The group as a basis for emergent stereotype consensus. In W. Stroebe & M. Hewstone (Eds.), *European Review of Social Psychology* (vol. 8, pp. 203–239). Chichester: Wiley.

Hogg, M. A. (1996). Intragroup processes, group structure and social identity. In W. P. Robinson (Ed.), *Social groups and identities: Developing the legacy of Henri Tajfel* (pp. 65–94). Oxford: Butterworth-Heinemann.

Hornsey, M. J., & Jetten, J. (2004). The individual within the group: Balancing the need to belong with the need to be different. *Personality and Social Psychology Review, 8*, 248–264.

Jetten, J., Postmes, T., & McAuliffe, B. (2002). "We're *all* individuals": Group norms of individualism and collectivism, levels of identification, and identity threat. *European Journal of Social Psychology, 32*, 189–207.

Johnson, A. W., & Earle, T. (2000). *The evolution of human societies: From foraging groups to agrarian state.* Palo Alto, CA: Stanford University Press.

Kampmeier, C., & Simon, B. (2001). Individuality and group formation: The role of independence and differentiation. *Journal of Personality and Social Psychology, 81*, 448–462.

Kelly, C., & Breinlinger, S. (1996). *The social psychology of collective action: Identity, injustice and gender.* Washington, DC: Taylor & Francis.

Kerr, N. L., & Tindale, R. S. (2004). Group performance and decision making. *Annual Review of Psychology, 55*, 623–655.

Lewin, K. (1948). *Resolving social conflicts.* New York: Harper.

Lickel, B., Hamilton, D. L., & Sherman, S. J. (2001). Elements of a lay theory of groups: Types of groups, relational styles, and the perception of group entitativity. *Personality and Social Psychology Review, 5*, 129–140.

Lickel, B., Hamilton, D. L., Wieczorkowska, G., Lewis, A., Sherman, S. J., & Uhles, A. N. (2000). Varieties of groups and the perception of group entitativity. *Journal of Personality and Social Psychology, 78*, 223–246.

Maalouf, A. (2000). *In the name of identity: Violence and the need to belong.* New York: Penguin.

MacCulloch, D. (2003). *Reformation: Europe's house divided.* London: Penguin.

Marx, K. (1857/1993). *The grundrisse: Foundations of the critique of political economy.* London: Penguin.

Mead, G. H. (1934). *Mind, self and society*. Chicago: University of Chicago Press.

Moreland, R. L., Argote, L., & Krishnan, R. (1996). Socially shared cognition at work: Transactive memory and group performance. In J. Nye & A. Brower (Eds.), *What's social about social cognition? Research on socially shared cognition in small groups* (pp. 57–84). Newbury Park, CA: Sage.

Moreland, R. L., Levine, J. M., & McMinn, J. G. (2001). Self-categorization and work group socialization. In M. A. Hogg & D. Terry (Eds.), *Social identity processes in organizational contexts* (pp. 87–100). Philadelphia: Psychology Press.

Morton, T., & Postmes, T. (2005). Communication and social identity. Manuscript in preparation: University of Exeter.

Oakes, P. J., Haslam, S. A., & Turner, J. C. (1994). *Stereotyping and social reality*. Oxford: Blackwell.

Onorato, R. S., & Turner, J. C. (2004). Fluidity in the self-concept: the shift from personal to social identity. *European Journal of Social Psychology, 34*, 257–278.

Postmes, T., & Baym, N. (2005). Intergroup dimensions of the Internet. In J. Harwood & H. Giles (Eds.), *Intergroup communication: Multiple perspectives* (pp. 213–238). New York: Peter Lang.

Postmes, T., Haslam, S. A., & Swaab, R. (2005). Social influence in small groups: An interactive model of social identity formation. *European Review of Social Psychology, 16*, 1–42.

Postmes, T., Spears, R., Lee, T., & Novak, R. (in press). Individuality and social influence in groups: Inductive and deductive routes to group identity. *Journal of Personality and Social Psychology.*

Prentice, D. A., Miller, D. T., & Lightdale, J. R. (1994). Asymmetries in attachments to groups and to their members: Distinguishing between common-identity and common-bond groups. *Special Issue: The self and the collective, Personality and Social Psychology Bulletin, 20*, 484–493.

Reicher, S. (1984). The St Pauls' riot: An explanation of the limits of crowd action in terms of a social identity model. *European Journal of Social Psychology, 14*, 1–21.

Reicher, S. (1996). "The Battle of Westminster": Developing the social identity model of crowd behaviour in order to explain the initiation and development of collective conflict. *European Journal of Social Psychology, 26*, 115–134.

Reicher, S., & Hopkins, N. (2001). *Self and nation*. London: Sage.

Runciman, S. (1951). *A history of the crusades. 1: The First Crusade*. Cambridge: Cambridge University Press.

Sassenberg, K., & Postmes, T. (2002). Cognitive and strategic processes in small groups: Effects of anonymity of the self and anonymity of the group on social influence. *British Journal of Social Psychology, 41*, 463–480.

Searle, J. R. (1995). *The construction of social reality*. London: Penguin.

Sherif, M. (1935). A study of some social factors in perception. *Archives of Psychology, 187*, 1–60.

Simon, B. (2004). *Identity in modern society: A social psychological perspective*. Oxford: Blackwell.

Spears, R., Postmes, T., Lea, M., & Wolbert, A. (2002). The power of influence and the influence of power in virtual groups: A SIDE look at CMC and the Internet. *Special Issue: Social impact of the Internet, The Journal of Social Issues, 58*, 91–108.

Stott, C., & Drury, J. (2004). The importance of social structure and social interaction in stereotype consensus and content: Is the whole greater than the sum of its parts? *European Journal of Social Psychology, 34*, 11–23.

Stott, C., Hutchison, P., & Drury, J. (2001). "Hooligans" abroad? Inter-group dynamics, social identity and participation in collective "disorder" at the 1998 World Cup Finals. *British Journal of Social Psychology, 40*, 359–384.

Swaab, R. I., Postmes, T., Neijens, P., Kiers, M. H., & Dumay, A. C. M. (2002). Multiparty negotiation support: The role of visualization's influence on the development of shared mental models. *Journal of Management Information Systems, 19,* 129–150.

Swaab, R. I., Postmes, T., Spears, R., Van Beest, I., & Neijens, P. (2005). Shared cognition as a product of, and precursor to, shared social identity: The role of communication in negotiations. Manuscript submitted for publication.

Swann, W. B., Kwan, V. Y. A., Polzer, J. T., & Milton, L. P. (2003). Fostering group identification and creativity in diverse groups: The role of individuation and self-verification. *Personality and Social Psychology Bulletin, 29,* 1396–1406.

Tajfel, H. (1972). Experiments in a vacuum. In J. Israel & H. Tajfel (Eds.), *The context of social psychology* (pp. 69–119). London: Academic.

Tajfel, H. (1978). Interindividual behaviour and intergroup behaviours. In H. Tajfel (Ed.), *Differentiation between social groups: Studies in the social psychology of intergroup relations* (pp. 1–60). London: Academic.

Tajfel, H., & Wilkes, A. L. (1963). Classification and quantitative judgement. *British Journal of Psychology, 54,* 101–114.

Tajfel, H., & Wilkes, A. L. (1964). Salience of attributes and commitments to extreme judgements in the perception of people. *British Journal of Social and Clinical Psychology, 2,* 40–49.

Tanis, M., & Postmes, T. (2005). A social identity approach to trust: Interpersonal perception, group membership and trusting behavior. *European Journal of Social Psychology, 35,* 413–424.

Turner, J. C. (1982). Towards a cognitive redefinition of the group. In H. Tajfel (Ed.), *Social identity and intergroup relations* (pp. 15–40). Cambridge: Cambridge University Press.

Turner, J. C. (1985). Social categorization and the self-concept: A social cognitive theory of group behaviour. In E. J. Lawler (Ed.), *Advances in group processes: Theory and research* (vol. 2, pp. 77–122). Greenwich, CT: JAI.

Turner, J. C. (1991). *Social influence.* Milton Keynes: Open University Press.

Turner, J. C., Hogg, M. A., Oakes, P. J., Reicher, S., & Wetherell, M. S. (1987). *Rediscovering the social group: A self-categorization theory.* Oxford: Blackwell.

Turner, J. C., & Oakes, P. J. (1986). The significance of the social identity concept for social psychology with reference to individualism, interactionism and social influence. *Special Issue: The individual-society interface, British Journal of Social Psychology, 25,* 237–252.

Turner, J. C., & Onorato, R. S. (1999). Social identity, personality, and the self-concept: A self-categorizing perspective. In T. R. Tyler & R. M. Kramer (Eds.), *The psychology of the social self. Applied social research* (pp. 11–46). Mahwah, NJ: Erlbaum.

Wilder, D. A., & Simon, A. F. (1998). Categorical and dynamic groups: Implications for social perception and intergroup behavior. In C. Sedikides, J. Schopler, & C. A. Insko (Eds.), *Intergroup cognition and intergroup behavior* (pp. 27–44). Mahwah, NJ: Erlbaum.

13

On the Agency of Individuals and Groups: Lessons from the BBC Prison Study

Stephen Reicher and S. Alexander Haslam

Introduction: the history, psychology and politics of agency in groups

Social psychology is one of the social sciences that emerged in the nineteenth century, in response to the crisis of order provoked by industrialization. Where once the population lived in small villages, now they were increasingly concentrated in towns and cities. Where once they had been known to the social elite, now they were anonymous. The identifiable labourer had been absorbed into the ranks of unknown workers and had thereby become the stuff of political nightmares. Would the masses rise up and shatter the status quo? In striving to offset this possibility, the individual was clearly preferable to the collective and, accordingly, theorists translated this ideological preference into a psychological hierarchy (Barrows, 1981; Giner, 1976).

This accommodation was achieved by arguing that, when people are submerged in the mass, they both lose their individual identity and gain a sense of invincible power. Since individual identity supplies the grounds for choice and judgement, this means that people have no basis for discriminating between different ideas and messages. As a result, any idea or emotion becomes contagious and those in the mass become incapable of resisting it (Le Bon, 1895). So, not only will people go along with extreme suggestions, but they also have the confidence and the numbers to bring them to fruition. The masses are doubly dangerous.

While these ideas of "group mindlessness" have a long history, they were imported into modern social psychology through deindividuation theory – the term "deindividuation" being a direct translation of the submergence concept. There are a number of variants of this theory (see Reicher, Spears, & Postmes, 1995). However, what they all share is the idea that being immersed in a group leads people to lose their normal standards. At best, they become puppets pulled around by contextual forces; at worst, they express all the antisocial tendencies that they normally hold in check. One of those who has championed the former view particularly forcefully is Philip Zimbardo (1969). Indeed Zimbardo's work has played an important role in promoting the view that group members are helpless victims even when they perpetrate the most extreme acts upon others. Most famously, this is the message associated with his Stanford Prison Experiment (SPE).

According to the version related by Zimbardo in his video and website on the study, and as recounted in numerous introductory textbooks, the SPE shows how individuals in groups become overwhelmed by their roles. Thus, when well-adjusted young men were divided into the roles of guard and prisoner in a simulated prison environment, the guards quickly became tyrants while the prisoners became passive victims and developed associated psychosomatic disorders. Ultimately, a study scheduled to last two weeks had to be terminated after six days when an external observer pointed out to Zimbardo (who had himself become overwhelmed by his own role as prison superintendent) the ethical indefensibility of what was happening. From all this Zimbardo and his colleagues drew the conclusion that: "guard aggression … was emitted simply as a 'natural' consequence of being in the uniform of a 'guard' and asserting the power inherent in that role" (Haney, Banks, & Zimbardo, 1973, p. 12).

Our concerns with the group mindlessness approach in general, and with Zimbardo's work in particular, are empirical, theoretical and political. Empirically, it overplays the ways in which people in groups are dominated by the existing context and underplays the ways in which groups allow people to challenge the world as it is. Theoretically, it portrays the group as destroying individual judgement and agency, and fails even to address issues of collective agency. Politically, it absolves people of responsibility for their collective actions and of choice over the type of world they create.

In so far as the dramatic account of the Stanford Prison Experiment plays a key role in buttressing these views, then any challenge to them ultimately needs to revisit the SPE itself. It is for this reason that, in collaboration with the BBC, we ran another simulated prison study (for a complete account, see Haslam & Reicher, 2002; Reicher & Haslam, in press). As in the SPE, men were randomly divided into groups as prisoners and guards (with the proviso that they were matched on key psychological variables). The prisoners locked up in three cells, each containing

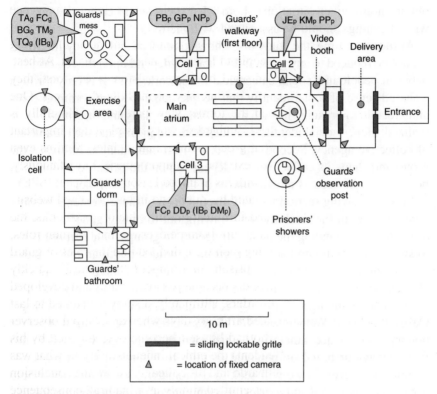

Figure 13.1   Plan of the prison (from Haslam & Reicher, 2002)

three people (see Figure 13.1). Although the setting was obviously not a real prison, the differences between groups were real. The guards had better living conditions; their meals were far superior and they had control over additional resources such as cigarettes, snacks and drinks; they also had unique access to various parts of the prison and special surveillance equipment for viewing the prisoners at all times, even at night in their cells. These inequalities were strongly felt from the very start of the study. Our interest was in the conditions under which the guards would assert their dominance and the conditions under which the prisoners would challenge these intergroup inequalities.

As we shall see, there are a number of ways in which our findings challenge the idea that, in groups, people become mindless and lose agency.[1] First, they show that people do not automatically internalize the roles thrust upon them by others as their own subjective identities (see also Spears, Ellemers, Doosje, & Branscombe, Chapter 10 in this volume). Second, they show that people not only contest whether they should be seen as category members but also contest the very nature of the categories that obtain in any given situation – both what the relevant categories are and what meanings should be associated with them.

At the same time, the study also shows that ideas and agency in groups cannot be reduced to any given individual but depend upon the relationship between people in a social categorical framework. First, it is only through a shared sense of social identity that people come to share common goals and are able to organize in such a way that their plans and priorities can be realized. Hence social identity provides both the means and the parameters of collective agency. Second, the ability of an individual to influence the group and shape its collective fate depends upon the extent to which their position can be seen as representative of the group as a whole.

In the following section we will discuss each of these elements in more detail before, in the final section, drawing out the more general implications for understanding the nature of agency in groups. Our purpose is not to swing the pendulum back from group mindlessness to an individualistic account but rather to transcend the very terms of the debate. As may already be clear, we start from the perspective of social identity and self-categorization theories (Tajfel, 1982; Tajfel & Turner, 1979; Turner, Hogg, Oakes, Reicher, & Wetherell, 1987). More specifically, we assume that people neither lose nor accentuate individual identity in groups, but rather shift from behaviour based on personal identity to behaviour based on social identity. However, as we will seek to demonstrate, social identity should not be seen as a rigid and *a priori* determinant of group behaviour. Rather, it should be understood as an enabling framework within which people act as agents. This conceptualization has important implications for our understanding of agency. It also has important implications for our understanding of social identity processes.

Four findings concerning agency in groups

Identifying with the social group

From a social identity perspective, it is hardly news to argue that people do not passively accept the social positions ascribed to them. From the outset, one of the major preoccupations of social identity theory was to explore the conditions under which members of subordinated groups come to see themselves collectively and act collectively to challenge perceived inequalities. Tajfel and Turner (1979; see also Tajfel, 1978) argued that critical variables that shape such outcomes are (a) whether people experience group boundaries as permeable (that is, whether they can progress as individuals despite their group membership or will inevitably be disadvantaged because of it), (b) whether they perceive group inequalities as legitimate and (c) whether they can envision the status quo being changed. Only with impermeability will there be collective action; only with illegitimacy and cognitive alternatives will there be an explicit challenge to the dominant group.

These predictions were supported in our study. On day 1, we told our participants that they had been divided into groups on the basis of psychometric tests which they had completed and which had revealed that some had the qualities to be guards while others did not. However, we also told them that because certain people might have qualities not revealed on the tests, the participants would be observed for three days and that a promotion from prisoner to guard might occur on the fourth day. Hence, at the start of the study the intergroup divide was legitimated, it was permeable and there were no clear alternatives to it. On day 4 a promotion was made, after which we stated that it was no longer practical to make further changes, so that, whatever their qualities, people would have to stay in their current groups. As a result, the system was rendered impermeable and illegitimate. Moreover, by this time it was clear that the guards were uncomfortable with their power and unwilling to exercise it (a point we shall return to shortly). This led to a sense that the system was weak and open to challenge – a sense that was further increased when a new prisoner, DM_p,[2] with a background as a trade union organizer, was introduced to the study. In short, there was also an emerging sense of cognitive alternatives and hence all the conditions to bring about collective action for social change were in place – and change is precisely what occurred.

In the first three days, the prisoners were divided. Some worked hard, were compliant and sought to gain the privileges of the guards through promotion. Others rejected the system from the start but, lacking collective support, were in no position to challenge it. Immediately after the promotion (i.e., once the prisoners' position was made impermeable and illegitimate), there was a dramatic change in prisoner behaviour and intergroup relations. Within half an hour all the prisoners in cell 2 (two of whom had, only minutes before, been obedient and polite to the guards) sat down and started to plot how, together, they could turn the tables on the guards by trapping them in a room and barricading them in. These observations were backed up by psychometric data collected every day. Over time, and especially after the promotion, the level of social identification of the prisoners increased significantly as did their sense of cognitive alternatives. Clearly, then, the prisoners did not immediately and passively accept their group position. It was only when they experienced the social structure as ruling out any alternative form of social organization that they started to organize themselves as prisoners. However, even then, they adopted the category as a way of challenging rather than acceding to the status quo.

What then of the guards? Our initial expectation was that they would identify with their assigned group from the start. After all, it was a positive identification in every respect. We had told the guards that they had been selected because of laudable qualities such as trustworthiness and reliability. They had higher status in the study and also had superior resources. In spite of this, though, they were reluctant to identify with their group (and in fact their level of identification decreased, albeit non-significantly, over the course of the study). The reason for their reluctance became clear from a conversation that occurred the first time the guards got together in their common room. As they started discussing how they should treat the prisoners – whether to be harsh or whether to be lenient – a number of the guards started to express the fear of acting–and, perhaps more to the point, being seen to act – tyrannically. Whatever the positive value placed on being a guard within the context of the simulated prison, participants could imagine the negative ways in which guard identity and guard behaviour would be viewed in other contexts at other points in time and space.

In part, of course, this sensitivity was a consequence of the fact that the guards (like the prisoners) knew that their behaviour was being recorded and would be shown on national television. However, to see this as diminishing the significance of the study is to miss the point. On the one hand, one of the fundamental aspects of being human is that we have imaginations and that our understandings are not simply rooted in the here-and-now but oriented towards the future. Once this point is acknowledged then the extreme situational determinism of Zimbardo's role account becomes untenable. Context may well affect behaviour, but context should not be taken as a simple given. Certainly, the here-and-now is often the context that concerns us, but because we have imaginative capacities it needn't always be so. Put the other way round, to assume that context is restricted to the immediate situation involves viewing human beings as lacking all imagination.

On the other hand, while it is obviously rare to be faced with the prospect of one's behaviour being observed by millions of people, human beings constantly live under conditions of surveillance. Sometimes this involves technology (e.g., use of surveillance cameras: Lyon & Zuriek, 1996). Sometimes it involves those who are with us in one context talking about our behaviour in another context (Emler, 1994). Overall, our awareness of surveillance in any given context is likely to guide our imaginations and to determine the contexts and the audiences which we consider when determining how to act. By the same token, the nature of surveillance determines the extent to which, when acting in terms of any given identity, we can ignore the values and understandings of other identities in our lives. Where the behaviours expressed in terms of one group membership will become known to members of another of the groups with which one identifies, then it becomes difficult to act – and even to sustain both social identities – if the norms of the two groups are in tension (Emler & Reicher, 1995).

In order to know whether, in a given situation, an individual will assume a social identity and act in terms of it, we therefore need to know about (a) the full range of group memberships which are significant to that individual and (b) the social relations of visibility between these various groups. So of course there will be individual differences in social identification, but these have more to do with the fact that every individual has a unique structure of social relations and a unique combination of social identities than with some primordial individual characteristic (see also Turner, Reynolds, Haslam, & Veenstra, Chapter 2 in this volume).

To take just one example from our study, the one guard, TQ_g, who was least willing to assert his authority and who was most conflicted about his position was someone who, in his job, was most used to leadership and control. He ran a successful IT company. However, that also meant he was more publicly visible and accountable to a variety of audiences (including employees and customers) than many other participants. Given that TQ_g's company had a liberal and egalitarian culture, then to be seen acting tyrannically could have ruinous consequences. Whatever he did to fulfil his requirements in the study would have undermined his position outside the study and vice versa – so this presented an ultimately insoluble conflict (see also Bettencourt, Molix, Talley, & Sheldon, Chapter 11 in this volume).

We are now in a position to bring together the two sides of our argument thus far, drawing on evidence of the identification patterns of prisoners and guards. From these it is clear that people define their identities in relation to the social structuring of action and, more particularly, partly as a function of social constraints that determine what they can and cannot do. The prisoners began to identify and act as a group to the extent that they were constrained in their ability to be treated as individuals and to advance as individuals. Yet such constraints are imagined as well as immediate. The guards were reluctant to identify and act as a group to the extent that they could envisage the constraints imposed by their other identities beyond the immediate context of the study.

However, imagination does not only serve to invoke existing identities and increase constraint. Imagination can also lead us to invoke novel identities in order to overcome constraint. In this way, imagination does not simply bind us in the present, it opens up the possibility of new futures. This takes us to the next phase of our study and the next point in our argument.

Shaping social identities

On the fifth day – a day after the promotion – we introduced a new prisoner, DM_p, to the study. DM_p was as naïve about the study's aims as other participants, but, as we have noted above, he had a history as a senior trade unionist. This led us to expect that he would offer a new perspective on the prison system and thereby provoke new forms of challenge to it. Indeed, his entry into the study was delayed to allow us to investigate how cognitive alternatives can develop and be promoted.

A few hours after arriving, DM_p started discussing with his cellmates FC_p and DD_p what they were wearing: baggy orange trousers and an orange singlet. He suggested that they looked like the uniforms of local council manual workers. The others picked up on this and elaborated it: they certainly looked like workers – miners in particular. Shortly afterwards, DM_p started a new conversation concerning how hot it was:

DM_p: Has anyone explained why it is an environment like this?
DD_p: It's a prison.
DM_p: Has anyone explained why it's like this though?
DD_p: Because that's part of the experiment.
FC_p: We just ended up in here.
DM_p: Why put up with this though?
DD_p: [pause] That's really a very good question.
FC_p: Because I signed a form to say I would.
DM_p: No you didn't. I didn't sign a form to say I would put up with, you know, heat like this, and, and – I signed a form to say I would participate in an experiment. I didn't sign a form to say I would put up with this kind of heat.

In this interchange DM_p begins by using imagery that replaces the categories of prisoner and guard with the category of worker (and, by implication, boss). He then invokes an issue which renders those categories both meaningful and contextually relevant. As long as participants see themselves as prisoners, then poor conditions in general, and the heat in particular, are not an issue. They are simply taken for granted as what happens to the prisoners in the study.

This relationship between issues and categories works both ways round. On the one hand, to define the categories is to define the issues. DM_p has to contest the validity of construing the heat within the agreed terms of the study in order to encourage the participants to see it as a problem. On the other hand, to define the issues is to define the categories. In making the heat into a problem, the terms of the study itself become a topic: it is no longer a situation of "prisoners versus guards", it is now one where participants (workers) as a whole are suffering from unfair conditions imposed by the experimenters (bosses).

The broader conceptual point is that we must consider both how reality determines categories and hence social action (Oakes, Haslam, & Turner, 1994; Veenstra & Haslam, 2000) and also how social categories are used to shape the social action that creates social realities (cf. Reicher & Hopkins, 2001). That is, DM_p is not simply describing the social world as he finds it, he is seeking to create a world where the participants challenge experimenters. He does this through his creative use of image, metaphor and analogy and his leadership is effective because this language defines social categories in particular ways (Reicher & Hopkins, 1996a; 1996b).

So far we have examined DM_p's creativity concerning what the categories are. He showed equal creativity concerning the meanings associated with categories. Even as he was beginning to sow the seeds of a participant alliance, DM_p had to confront the fact that, if anything, division and confrontation between prisoners and guards were increasing. That morning, another prisoner, PB_p, had stolen a set of guards' keys and was considering how to use this to humiliate his opponents. As DM_p explained later, before he could unite the two groups he had first to defuse the tension sufficiently to allow them to talk together. If they could establish a dialogue, this would provide a setting in which he could address and promote their common interests and common identity. The opportunity came as the prisoners met in order to decide the terms on which they would return the keys to the guards:

PB_p: What the issue is, they want the fucking keys back and all I am saying is I want to use the keys as a lever to move us forward as a group.

DM_p: Can I make a suggestion? What we should do is, we should suggest to them – and I suggested this to a couple of lads before, and the guards, and they were nodding – we should have a forum that meets once a day between us, all of us, the guards and us, and in the forum we'll discuss the grievances we have.

There are two things to note about this exchange. First, PB_p's language (*I* am saying, *I* want) is individualistic while DM_p's is collectivistic (what *we* should do, *we* should have, *we*'ll discuss). Second, DM_p is advocating a structural demand, the forum, which removes the need for conflictual action, whereas PB_p is not. PB_p wants a specific outcome – getting regular hot drinks for the prisoners – which requires further acts of "terrorism" (the analogy is his), and therefore people prepared to be "terrorists", in order to obtain further concessions. As he puts it, "the only reason we've got this meeting now is because somebody stole the fucking keys". This is not just a contrast between one person (DM_p) promoting the collective good and another (PB_p) promoting the individual good. Both are concerned with improving the lot of the group. What they differ over is how group members should act to achieve such an end. The contrast is between two different versions of the group ethos, the one based on cooperation and dialogue, the other based on individual heroism and sacrifice. The more PB_p advocates his view and seeks to recruit others to it, the more they turn towards DM_p's proposal and embrace his leadership (see Reicher, Haslam, & Hopkins, 2005, for a more detailed treatment of this point).

So, it is by no means self-evident that people will see themselves in terms of a given category (as a prisoner, say), but, even if they do, that is by no means the end of the story. Once again (a) the content is open to contestation (as collective and cooperative vs individual and confrontational), (b) different content is bound up with particular forms of social action (negotiation vs terrorism) and (c) different action in turn creates different social realities (order and unity vs disorder and disunity). As we argued above, being a group member and acting in terms of social identity is not a passive process but rather involves the *active* engagement of group members in the question of how their group identity should be defined.

This leaves the question of why one version wins out over others – why DM_p's forum is preferred to PB_p's heroism. There are many answers to this question. But one critical factor has to do with the inclusive practice of the forum in which everyone can participate and everyone has a say. Individual heroism is necessarily exclusive and requires the weaker and less bold to defer to the stronger and to be dependent upon them. Linked to this is a recognition that an inclusive social identity which ensures that everyone acts together in a mutually supportive manner is a source of collective power and is therefore likely to be effective. The agency of individual group members may be important in creating collective identities, defining collective norms and shaping collective action, but, as we will now argue, individuals are only able to act agentically in and through collective identities.

Social identity and collective efficacy

While the prisoners may have been divided over the precise meaning of their identity, it is important to stress, first, that they still identified with the category and, second, that the differences between them concerned *how*, not *whether*, to challenge the authority of the guards. In fact, at the end of day 5 we withdrew DM_p from the study because we were interested in the influence of his perspective rather than his personal ability to organize. In the short term, the balance then swung back to the more confrontational style of PB_p and the occupants of Cell 2: KM_p, JE_p and PP_p. The broader point, though, has to do with the consequences of the fact that the prisoners shared a social identity whereas the guards did not.

One of the predictions of self-categorization theory in this regard is that members of a common group expect to agree with each other because they share a common perspective on social reality (Turner, 1991; Turner et al., 1987; see also Haslam, Oakes, Turner, McGarty, & Reynolds, 1998). It follows that those who share a social identity assume they can trust other group members to act in ways they would approve of (Kramer & Tyler, 1996) and can expect other group members to support them in their endeavours (Haslam, O'Brien, Jetten, Vormedal, & Penna, in press; Levine,

Cassidy, Brazier, & Reicher, 2002; Schmitt & Branscombe, 2002). Shared social identity creates group coordination, group power and therefore group efficacy (Drury & Reicher, 2005; Drury, Reicher, & Stott, 2003; Haslam, 2004; Postmes & Branscombe, 2002; Turner, 2005). Our findings gave strong support to these ideas. Indeed, one of the most striking features of the whole study was that the guards' lack of a shared social identity rendered them incapable of organizing themselves and hence made them incapable of controlling the prisoners – especially as the prisoners themselves forged a common identity and mounted increasingly coordinated challenges to the guards' authority.

One incident can be used to illustrate the effects of social identification (or lack of it) on the efficacy of the guards and the prisoners, and hence upon the relationship between them. Just after the promotion, the three prisoners in Cell 2 confronted the guards over lunch. First JE_p threw his plate to the ground and complained about the food. As the guards rushed to contain him, KM_p joined in by demanding footwear for his blistered feet. Next PP_p backed up his cellmates and refused to comply until he was allowed a cigarette. As the confrontation developed the cellmates repeatedly backed each other up while the guards bickered and disagreed about what to do. Ultimately one of them, TQ_g, made a unilateral decision to concede to the prisoners' demands and the prisoners agreed to return to their cells. Even as the deal was being made, BG_g, another guard, said bitterly: "That was handled totally wrong". Afterwards the guards were despondent and felt impotent:

TA_g: This is only day 4. They can see what happened today and now they know they can do whatever they want.

BG_g: No, that's wrong.

TA_g: Yes. Anytime they are out of their cells they can start effing and blinding to each other. They can do whatever they want and there's nothing we can do about it. Now, if we really think we have to endure this for the next ten days then we have to seriously consider changing the way we work ...

TQ_g: We won't, we won't.

TA_g: ... the way we act. Now there are issues here, because it's happened! Yeah, I mean, come on. You know what that has done? That has lit the fuse on [PB_p's] arse.

By contrast the prisoners felt empowered and gleeful:

PP_p: That was fucking sweet.

KM_p: You was fucking quality man.
[the participants exchange "high fives"]

PP_p: This is just the start mate, this is the start.

Overall, what we see here is that the guards were disorganized and divided whereas the prisoners were coordinated and united. The actions of the guards cancelled each other out and their numbers served only to weaken them. In contrast, the actions of the prisoners complemented each other and their numbers served to make them stronger. The guards were unable to make their views prevail either individually or collectively. In contrast, the prisoners were entirely successful in achieving their aims and objectives. In this way the asymmetry of identification between the two groups entailed a process whereby power shifted from the guards to the prisoners.

Two further points emerge from this incident. One has to do with the psychological consequences of the interaction. In the case of the guards, inefficacy led to negative mental states, whereas in the case of the prisoners it led to very positive mental states. This observation is backed up by our psychometric data. Over time, the guards became more depressed while the prisoners became less depressed. Unlike the prisoners, the guards also became more burnt-out (see Haslam & Reicher, in press). Likewise, the guards displayed a diminishing sense of collective self-efficacy while, for the prisoners, this sense was progressively enhanced.

The second point flows from this. The fact that our study was conducted over an extended period allows for a much more dynamic view of identity processes than is possible in the case of the standard (e.g., 30 minute) social psychology experiment (Haslam & McGarty, 2001). While our findings show that identity affected coordination and hence increased efficacy, it is equally clear that an enhanced sense of efficacy on the part of the prisoners led to increased collective solidarity and an escalation of collective challenges. On the other hand, decreased efficacy amongst the guards further increased the divisions amongst them and made them less able to resist. Over time, the prisoners in general and those in cell 2 in particular became more daring while the guards became more atomized, until, ultimately, the prisoner–guard system collapsed.

This unfolding process demonstrates that the power needed to turn psychological priorities into actualities is not simply a matter of material resources or general psychological competencies (Turner, 2005). The guards had an abundance of such resources: keys to lock the prisoners up, food, cigarettes and drinks to use as rewards or to withdraw as punishment, surveillance equipment to observe the prisoners and various other things besides. However, they chose not to employ their resources because they did not wish to be seen as guards. Equally, the guards in general had many skills. They had been assessed by clinicians and psychometric tests before the study; they were all intelligent, well-adjusted and articulate. All had responsible positions in the external world – especially TQ_g. As a successful computer entrepreneur he excelled intellectually, he was an adept organizer and motivator. Yet, once again, he was unwilling to apply those skills to the task of being a guard because he did not identify with that position.

The prisoners were similarly skilled, but they lacked resources, apart, that is, from their sheer number. Yet because they were highly identified with their position, they were able to apply all their skills to the collective struggle. Resources and competencies without identity left the guards collectively inept; it made them increasingly reactive and turned them into victims. Identity, even without resources, allowed the prisoners to use their abilities and render them the architects of their own fate. Collective identity allowed individuals to be agents.

Being influential and being representative

After the old system collapsed, the study did not end. Instead, it became more the participants' own study as they were no longer responding to the social system which we, the experimenters, had created but were now creating one of their own devising. At first they attempted to set up a "self-governing, self-disciplining commune" in which all worked together and shared resources as a single group. However, they only implemented half of their project. The commune was self-governing, but members were reluctant to discipline those who flouted the commune's rules. As a result, the system fell into crisis and, despite their efforts, those running the commune could not make it work.

In this context four participants – a combination of ex-guards and ex-prisoners – formulated a plan to take over the prison and impose a harsh and authoritarian regime. Now even those who abhorred such a system and strongly believed in the principles of the commune acknowledged that their support was slipping and that the takeover had some attractions. As one of them put it, it would almost have been a relief since they had invested considerable energy into trying to run the commune but had nothing to show for it. So, a study which began with the rejection of mild imposed inequalities ended with people almost creating a world of tyranny for themselves. The issue that we want to address here concerns the relationship between individual choice and group process in producing this dramatic shift.

In the previous section we argued that the effective agency of individuals in the group depends on the achievement of a shared social identity. Here we argue that the issue of *which* individuals are most able to shape the fate of the group depends upon who is perceived by group members in general as most prototypical of the shared social identity (Turner et al., 1987; Turner, 1991; see also Haslam, 2004; Hogg, 2001; Platow & van Knippenberg, 2001; Hopkins & Reicher, in press). As Haslam (2001) puts it, leadership centres around a partnership with followers in a social self-categorical relationship, and this identity-based partnership makes leadership possible. Leaders and followers are mutually bound together in a shared sense of "we-ness" and the leader is chosen on the basis of who best represents "who we are". The implication of this is that there are no general qualities which make people into leaders (cf. Stogdill, 1948). Nor can one predict from the general features of a situation who will emerge as a leader (Gibb, 1958). Rather, one must look more closely at (a) the precise characteristics of the individual (or, to be more accurate, how they represent themselves to other group members and how they are perceived by their fellows), (b) the specific meanings associated with the group identity and (c) the relationship between them (Haslam, 2001; Reicher & Hopkins 2001; 2004; Turner, 1982, 1991).

With this in mind, let us now return to the issue of leadership in and after the commune – although it is slightly misleading to talk of leadership *in* the commune because the ethos was one of equality and cooperation rather than hierarchy. Anyone who styled himself as a leader in the conventional understanding of the term (as someone who is in charge, who directs others, who has distinct status within the group) would, *ipso facto*, have been rejected as dissonant with the collective identity. In this sense, the rejection of a conventional leader is, in itself, evidence of our broader argument. In another sense, though, there clearly was leadership in that certain people were more prominent in speaking for the group and influencing decisions about how the system should be structured – although it is notable that "communards" used terms like "spokesperson" rather than "leader" to refer to this position.

One person in particular stood out. An ex-prisoner, FC_p, was given the task of proposing the commune system to us, the experimenters, and of negotiating the terms by which it would run. He was then accorded the position of organizer – deciding what tasks were to be performed, by whom and when. For instance, where previously the guards had handed out daily cleaning tasks to the prisoners, now FC_p discussed with people who would do what. FC_p's prominence here contrasted completely with his previous profile. Until the advent of the commune he had been one of the quietest participants: he had hardly spoken in collective discussions, he had not participated in the challenges to the guards and he had little influence on others. If anything, he was one of the clearest examples of a "follower".

In order to understand this shift from follower to leader we must take into account, first of all, FC_p's individual history and social commitments. As an environmentalist and social activist, he was an active member of a number of non-hierarchical organizations and was committed to their principles. Hence he found the conflictual nature of the original system uncongenial. Given the issues of visibility to others that we have already discussed, to have participated in conflict may have undermined his extra-experimental identities. He was not motivated to have influence in the

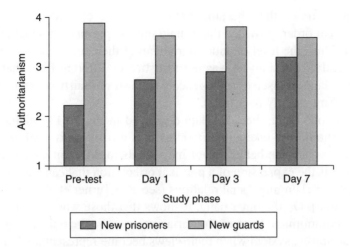

Figure 13.2   Right-wing authoritarianism as a function of self-selected group and time (from Reicher & Haslam, in press)

prisoner–guard system; there were constraints on him even if he had been, and others would have been unlikely to have been influenced by him. By contrast, the commune was not an imposed system at odds with his preferences. It was something that he was motivated to construct precisely in order to affirm those values and beliefs he subscribed to outside the study. Moreover, he was seen by others to represent the type of system they were trying to build. Hence he had the motivation, the lack of external constraint and the existence of internal support to represent the group both symbolically and practically.

What then of leadership *after* the commune as displayed by the four would-be "new guards" who proposed the new tyranny? Our psychometric data, reproduced in Figure 13.2, show that they were the most authoritarian participants. Before the study started, their mean level of authoritarianism was 3.9 (on a seven-point scale) compared to only 2.2 for the rest of the participants. Using these data alone one might argue for a simple personality explanation of tyranny (along the lines suggested by Adorno et al., 1950; Altmeyer, 1996), suggesting that those with authoritarian personalities tend to create and run authoritarian regimes. However, to do so avoids the critical issue of why and when such authoritarians are successful in making an authoritarian world. After all, for much of the study, participants opposed authority structures and, at the start of the commune, the authoritarians were clearly marginalized. They played no part in the creation of the system or in the way it was run. Nor did they have the confidence to challenge it.

It was only when the commune started to fail that a takeover became thinkable. As the communards lost faith in their own ability to create an egalitarian order they became more accepting of any order, even a hierarchical order, provided that it held out the promise of a viable social system. Thus, the level of authoritarianism of the communards rose until, by the end of the study, it was not statistically different from that of the authoritarians themselves (whose scores had stayed fairly constant, if anything falling slightly over time).

On the one hand, then, the data displayed in Figure 13.2 demonstrate that we should not take authoritarianism as a fixed individual difference that can explain the behaviour of individuals in different social settings. Rather, it is the expression of a political orientation that can vary as a consequence of changing social relations (see also Turner et al., Chapter 2 in this volume). On the other hand, it shows that those who are more stable in their commitment to an authoritarian perspective are only able to create an authoritarian system when their views become representative of a consensus that characterizes the position of the group as a whole. A simple "authoritarian personality" explanation will not do.

The changing patterns of leadership in our study and the changing ability of individuals to give practical expression to their ideas show that individuals can only shape group histories when their contribution is recognized by others to be representative of collective identity. In our analysis of findings from the BBC Prison Study, we have sought to show how both sides of the story are equally important: the role of individual agency in defining the group, and the dependence of individuals upon the group in order to be agentic. It is now time to conclude by drawing out the broader implications of these findings for understanding the relationship between individual agency and group process.

Conclusion

The first general point to be made is that the image of group members that comes out of the BBC Prison Study is very different from Zimbardo's image of the deindividuated dupe, helpless and clueless, a somnambulist, a victim of circumstance. Rather, our group members struggle to make sense of the world, to define the categories which constitute their society, sometimes adapting to the world as it is, sometimes seeking to change it, but always doing so in conscious debate with others. The distinction between the solitary individual and the group member is not, therefore, between the active and the passive, the mindful and the mindless.

Yet, while there may be no difference in *whether* people do more thinking in groups than when they are alone, there may be a difference both in *what* they think of – the content of the values and norms that they subscribe to – and in their ability to *act* on those thoughts, to express them in the world and to create a world in their image. Thus, the group neither increases nor decreases thought and debate but rather constitutes a new framework within which these things occur. If groups act on the basis of values and understandings, they are collective values and collective understandings. If they debate over the definition of these values and understandings, it is always at the collective level: what *we* think, what *we* value, what *we* should be doing. One sees few examples of what *I* want or what is good for *me* – and where one does, as in PB_p's debate with DM_p over how to deal with the guards, those who assert their personal identity at the expense of the group tend to be marginalized.

At the same time, it is through the group that individuals are able to act on their thoughts. As long as the prisoners worked as separate individuals they had to exist within a world built by others for the benefit of others. Only collectively were they able to rebuild that world on their own terms. Conversely, the lack of collectivity amongst the guards saw their world unbuilt in favour of one imposed by others. So, cognition is altered through collectivity while agency is enhanced. This is very different to the traditional view that in the group both cognition and agency are lost.

The second general point concerns the two-sided relationship of determination between individuals and the group: individual agents define the nature of groups while individuals become agents through groups (see also Postmes, Baray, Haslam, Morton, & Swaab, Chapter 12 in this volume). We have seen both sides of this relationship in this study. On the one hand, the individual circumstances and characteristics of participants undoubtedly played an important part in the study. Nonetheless, the impact of these individual differences on the history of the study was entirely dependent upon collective factors. First, seemingly stable factors (such as authoritarianism) were altered by the collective dynamics. Second, the significance of individual factors was not straightforward but rather depended upon their meaning within the relations of the study. Thus TQ_g's competence as a liberal entrepreneur outside the study was precisely what undermined his ability to act as a guard inside the study. Third, whatever their characteristics, individuals' capacity to exert influence was dependent on their ability to represent a group position. Thus, as the groups changed so the influence of specific individuals waxed and waned. FC_p was a case in point: quiet before the commune, a leader during the commune, marginalized as the commune failed. Equally, the authoritarian quartet only gained influence at the end because the other participants had shifted towards their position.

This can be rephrased as a matter of leadership. Throughout our study, aspirant leaders sought to shape group behaviour and the social system by actively engaging in the construction of social categories. Whether they worked towards greater equality or greater hierarchy, whether they sought to engage others, or command others, were obviously related to their individual values and skills. However, whether they were successful was dependent upon the extent to which their peers saw them and their pro- posals as representing the social identity of the group. So what then deter- mines which versions of identity are more liable to be accepted?

The answer, we would argue, depends upon seeing categorization in relation to the structure of social action. That is, categories are more than merely perceptual – they are practical-experiential. Such a perspective is inherently dynamic and two-sided. Unlike perception, which is oriented to the present, practice always takes place in the present but is oriented towards the future: it is about the transformation of the social world. Hence cate- gories not only reflect the existing structure of social action but are aimed at creating new forms of social structure. In this sense, individuals can con- strue categories creatively as a function of the structures they aspire to cre- ate. However, they and their categories will only be taken seriously to the extent that such a project seems practically viable. A set of categories that cannot be transformed into actual social organization is, literally, useless. As an illustration of this, we saw that, once it became impractical, the com- munal view of the world began to be abandoned even by its proponents, a hierarchical perspective began to be seen as more viable by comparison, and authoritarian leadership became more attractive as a result.

The key point here is that we cannot create the world at will. We live in a world where existing categories have been sedimented into customs and laws and institutions. Any attempt to change those categories will meet counter-mobilizations seeking to maintain the status quo. In this way, change comes up against the combined weight of the past, the present and the future.

Nonetheless, there are two factors that are critical in maintaining the possibility of change. The first is the human imagination: as humans we are able to envisage different worlds and we are able to imagine the social forces that would bring those worlds about. The second factor is the achieve- ment of a common identity through which individual imaginations can cohere to produce a collective vision and the associated power of groups to translate this collective vision into collective reality.

It is precisely this coherence of individual creativities in the group which ensures that history will never reach a full stop and why we must take responsibility for the histories that we do create. It is precisely because of this that those who have an interest in freezing the status quo and denying our responsibility for its blemishes seek to deny the creativ- ity of individuals in groups both in theory and in practice. As we stated at the outset, the notion of group mindlessness is empirically, theoretically and politically dubious. It is high time that it be laid to rest.

NOTES

We would like to thank the participants as well as the staff of the BBC for their commitment to this research and for comments on the ideas in this chapter. The contribution of Andrew Livingstone, Lucy O'Sullivan and the editors is also gratefully acknowledged. Correspondence to Stephen Reicher, School of Psychology, University of St Andrews, St. Andrews, Fife KY16 9JU, UK, sdr@st-andrews.ac.uk; Alex Haslam, School of Psychology, University of Exeter, Exeter, Devon EX4 4QG, UK, A.Haslam@exeter.ac.uk.

1 There is a long debate over the meaning of the term "agency", let alone how to account for it (e.g., see Barnes, 2000). We simply use the term to refer to participation in a process, either individual or collective, whereby one's mental perspective contributes to the construction of social reality.

2 $_p$ indicates a prisoner, $_g$ indicates a guard.

REFERENCES

Adorno, T. W., Frenkel-Brunswik, E., Levinson, D. J., & Sanford, R. N. (1950). *The authoritarian personality.* New York: Harper.

Altmeyer, B. (1996). *The authoritarian specter.* Cambridge, MA: Harvard University Press.

Barnes, B. (2000). *Understanding agency.* London: Sage.

Barrows, S. (1981). *Distorting mirrors.* New Haven, CT: Yale University Press.

Drury, J., & Reicher, S. (2005). Explaining enduring empowerment: A comparative study of collective action and psychological outcomes. *European Journal of Social Psychology, 35,* 35–58.

Drury, J., Reicher, S., & Stott, C. (2003). Transforming the boundaries of collective identity: from the "local" anti-road campaign to "global" resistance. *Social Movement Studies, 2,* 191–212.

Emler, N. (1994). Gossip, reputation, and social adaptation. In B. F. Goodman & A. Ben-Ze'ev (Eds.), *Good gossip* (pp. 117–138). Lawrence: University of Kansas Press.

Emler, N., & Reicher, S. (1995). *Adolescence and delinquency.* Oxford: Blackwell.

Gibb, C. A. (1958). An interactional view of the emergence of leadership. *Australian Journal of Psychology, 10,* 101–110.

Giner, S. (1976). *Mass society.* London: Robertson.

Haney, C., Banks, C., & Zimbardo, P. (1973). A study of prisoners and guards in a simulated prison. *Naval Research Reviews,* September (pp. 1–17). Washington, DC: Office of Naval Research. Reprinted in E. Aronson (Ed.), *Readings about the social animal* (3rd ed., pp. 52–67). San Francisco: Freeman.

Haslam, S. A. (2001). *Psychology in organizations: The social identity approach.* London: Sage.

Haslam, S. A. (2004). *Psychology in Organizations: The social identity approach* (2nd edn). London: Sage.

Haslam, S. A., & McGarty, C. (2001). A hundred years of certitude? Social psychology, the experimental method and the management of scientific uncertainty. *British Journal of Social Psychology, 40,* 1–21.

Haslam, A., Oakes, P., Turner, J., McGarty, C., & Reynolds, K. (1998). The group as a basis for emergent stereotype consensus. *The European Review of Social Psychology, 8,* 203–239.

Haslam, S. A., O'Brien, A., Jetten, J., Vormedal, K., & Penna, S. (in press). Taking the strain: Social identity, social support and the experience of stress. *British Journal of Social Psychology.*

Haslam, S. A., & Reicher, S. D. (2002). *A user's guide to the experiment: Exploring the psychology of groups and power.* London: BBC Worldwide.

Haslam, S. A., & Reicher, S. D. (in press). Stressing the group: Social identity and the unfolding dynamics of responses to stress. *Journal of Applied Psychology.*

Hogg, M. A. (2001). A social identity theory of leadership. *Personality and Social Psychology Review, 5,* 184–200.

Kramer, R. M., & Tyler, T. R. (Eds.) (1996). *Trust in organizations: Frontiers of theory and research.* Thousand Oaks, CA: Sage.

Le Bon, G. (1895). *The crowd: A study of the popular mind* (trans. 1947). London: Benn.

Levine, R. M., Cassidy, C., Brazier, G., & Reicher, S. D. (2002). Self-categorization and bystander non-intervention: Two experimental studies. *Journal of Applied Social Psychology, 32,* 1452–1463.

Lyon, D., & Zuriek, E. (1996). *Surveillance, computers and privacy.* Minneapolis: University of Minnnesota Press.

Oakes, P. J., Haslam, S. A., & Turner, J. C. (1994). *Stereotyping and social reality.* Oxford: Blackwell.

Platow, M. J., & van Knippenberg, D. (2001). A social identity analysis of leadership endorsement: The effects of leader ingroup prototypicality and distributive intergroup fairness. *Personality and Social Psychology Bulletin, 27,* 1508–1519.

Postmes, T., & Branscombe, N. R. (2002). Influence of long-term racial environmental composition on subjective well-being in African Americans. *Journal of Personality and Social Psychology, 83,* 735–751.

Reicher, S. D., & Haslam, S. A. (in press). Rethinking the psychology of tyranny: The BBC Prison Study. *British Journal of Social Psychology.*

Reicher, S. D., Haslam, S. A., & Hopkins, N. P. (2005). Social identity and the dynamics of leadership: Leaders and followers as collaborative agents in the transformation of social reality. *Leadership Quarterly, 16,* 547–568.

Reicher, S. D., & Hopkins, N. (1996a). Seeking influence through characterising self-categories: An analysis of anti-abortionist rhetoric. *British Journal of Social Psychology, 35,* 297–311.

Reicher, S. D., & Hopkins, N. (1996b). Self-category constructions in political rhetoric: An analysis of Thatcher's and Kinnock's speeches concerning the British Miners' Strike (1984–5). *European Journal of Social Psychology, 26,* 353–372.

Reicher, S. D., & Hopkins, N. (2001). *Self and nation.* London: Sage.

Reicher, S. D., & Hopkins, N. (2004). On the science of the art of leadership. In D. van Knippenberg & M. Hogg (Eds.), *Identity, leadership and power.* Oxford: Blackwell.

Reicher, S. D., Spears, R., & Postmes, T. (1995). A social identity model of deindividuation phenomena. *European Review of Social Psychology, 6,* 161–198.

Schmitt, M. T., & Branscombe, N. R. (2002). The meaning and consequences of perceived discrimination in disadvantaged and privileged social groups. *European Review of Social Psychology, 12,* 167–199.

Stogdill, R. M. (1948). Personality factors associated with leadership: A survey of the literature. *Journal of Psychology, 25,* 35–71.

Tafjel, H. (1978). Interindividual behaviour and intergroup behaviour. In H. Tajfel (Ed.), *Differentiation between social groups: Studies in the social psychology of intergroup relations* (pp. 27–60). London: Academic.

Tajfel, H. (1982). *Social identity and intergroup relations.* Cambridge: Cambridge University Press. Paris: Maison des Sciences de l'Homme.

Tajfel, H., & Turner, J. C. (1979). An integrative theory of intergroup conflict. In W. G. Austin & S. Worchel (Eds.), *The social psychology of intergroup relations* (pp. 33–47). Monterey, CA: Brooks/Cole.

Turner, J. C. (1982). Towards a cognitive redefinition of the social group. In H. Tajfel (Ed.), *Social identity and intergroup relations.* Cambridge: Cambridge University Press.

Turner, J. C. (1991). *Social influence.* Milton Keynes: Open University Press.

Turner, J. C. (2005). Examining the nature of power: A three-process theory. *European Journal of Social Psychology, 35,* 1–22.

Turner, J. C., Hogg, M. A, Oakes, P. J., Reicher, S. D., & Wetherell, M. S. (1987). *Rediscovering the social group: A self-categorization theory.* Oxford: Blackwell.

Veenstra, K., & Haslam, S. A. (2000). Willingness to participate in industrial protest: Exploring social identification in context. *British Journal of Social Psychology, 39,* 153–172.

Zimbardo, P. G. (1969). The human choice: Individuation, reason, and order versus deindividuation, impulse and chaos. In W. J. Arnold & D. Levine (Eds.), *Nebraska Symposium on Motivation.* Lincoln: University of Nebraska Press.

14

Reconciling Individuality and the Group

Tom Postmes and Jolanda Jetten

> I have no grand theory to offer ... and I am nearly convinced that a grand "theory of social behaviour" is not possible. (Tajfel, 1972, p. 115)

There is no doubt that the dual theories of social identity and self-categorization have grown immensely over the past decades. This growth has been the effort not of a single person or research group, but of an increasingly diverse group of scholars. Some of these were students and colleagues of Henri Tajfel or John Turner, many were students of their students, and large numbers (like us) came to the theories from different quarters. It is a testament to the strength of these theories that they were able to accommodate this influx, especially considering that this was coupled with an increasing diversity of applications. In that sense, social identity has been a success. This closing chapter reflects on the broader thrust of the directions taken and elaborations proposed (emergent themes) in this book and comments on the conceptual implications for the direction of social identity theories.

But before we can begin this integrative task, we should acknowledge at least two challenges to such growth. One is that an expanding theory cannot remain static. The other is that it cannot lose its identity. Elaborating social identity is therefore a tricky business. We will say a little more about each of these challenges. First, despite the fact that social identity and self-categorization theory are about social change, there is a pervasive perception that both theories themselves have remained rather static, and that their proponents doggedly oppose any changes. In response to such charges, Steve Reicher, a student of John Turner and Henri Tajfel, has sometimes asked the question: would Tajfel himself have considered social identity theory "finished business"? As most readers will know, Tajfel's life was cut short by his death in 1982, in the midst of a highly productive period, and the question is therefore largely rhetorical.

As illustrated by the quote at the beginning of this chapter, Tajfel was well aware of the limitations imposed by our subject matter, and the theoretical modesty these necessitate. And indeed, just as social identity theory has been elaborated on in many enriching ways, so has self-categorization theory – by Turner and others. This book was grounded in our firm belief that, over the past decade and more, our understanding of social identity processes has advanced enormously. In these developments, our thinking about the individual in the group has changed, sometimes subtly, but with profound theoretical implications. The chapters in this volume make this theorizing explicit and put individuality in the group on the agenda as a core issue.

The second challenge noted above is that of a theory losing its identity. When a theory is rapidly expanding into other domains, being applied to phenomena it was not originally concerned with (and usually modified or elaborated to achieve this), there is an inevitable danger of stretching its core concepts and principles too far. How can we tell if a theoretical modification (necessary or otherwise) is so profound that it does irreparable damage to the structural integrity of the theoretical framework? Does a focus on individuality end up rendering the concept of social identity any weaker, or any less social (see Spears, Ellemers, Doosje, & Branscombe, Chapter 10 in this volume)? In the short space remaining, we are not in a position to provide a systematic analysis of what we believe are the core structures of social identity perpectives. But we can summarize why we feel this volume has strengthened these theories.

First, this is because several chapters in this volume bring social identity into sharper relief by providing a more fine-grained analysis of what personal identity is, and how it stands in relation to social identity. And, as in a marriage, deepening the relationship strengthens both partners.

A further reason why our focus on individuality has strengthened social identity theories is that it has enhanced our understanding of the way in which social identity "speaks to" individuality. Several chapters explored issues of social identity *content*: how this relates to and regulates individuality, diversity and intragroup divisions, and how this is informed by it. Although at least one previous volume has focused on identity content (Ellemers, Spears, & Doosje, 1999), few textbooks acknowledge it as a central feature of the theory, and its role is often marginalized or ignored in empirical research. But it is a key component of both social identity and self-categorization theories for good reason. It is the key factor that channels group actions, connecting the dual aspects of social identity as a structure that defines self and enables the person to realize or enact self. More pragmatically, social identity content allows us to predict what the effects of identification and identity salience will be. Without content, social identity is rudderless.

Finally, this volume has ended up strengthening our understanding of social identity because so many chapters focus on the (dynamic) interaction between individuality and the group. This chimes well with the concerns at the heart of both social identity and self-categorization theories: they were developed to address issues of social change and consequently are fundamentally concerned with changing social identities. As chapters in this volume highlight, the dynamism of social identity entails that it emerges through intra- and intergroup interaction and is thereby constantly revised. We are therefore convinced that, rather than stripping away the theoretical richness of social identity theories by elaborating on individuality in the group, this endeavour strengthens social identity perspectives. It underlines that social identity is not a thing (Tajfel, 1978; Turner, 1999).

Having elaborated what are, to us, the key reasons why this volume has strengthened social identity perspectives, it is time for a closer look at what has been achieved theoretically. We will now identify what we see as the five key themes that emerge from this book.

Socializing the individual

One purpose of this book was to elaborate the ways in which personal identity, a person's unique sense of self, is informed by social identity. The chapters in this book make several points that are relevant to the elaboration of theory. Ideas on the way in which social identity informs personal identity have been developed in the work of Bernd Simon and colleagues (Simon, 2004). Simon's model takes as its starting point the common assumption that personal identity is constituted through intragroup comparisons with other individuals (see also Turner, Reynolds, Haslam, & Veenstra, Chapter 2). Personal identity in that conceptualization is what differentiates the individual from ingroup others. These may be genuinely personal attributes, but Simon observes that more often than not, these differentiating characteristics are derived from social identities.

The chapters in the current volume go beyond this statement in several (non-exclusive) ways. One recurrent feature is the argument that social identities and cultures hand us the building blocks and cognitive instruments with which to characterize the self (Halloran & Kashima, Chapter 8; Jetten & Postmes, Chapter 7; Moghaddam, Chapter 9; Postmes, Baray, Haslam, Morton, & Swaab, Chapter 12; Reicher & Haslam, Chapter 13; Turner et al., Chapter 2). By creating a social consensus that limits the different selves that one can legitimately or possibly assume, social identity provides an important boundary condition for the kinds of individuality which are tolerated. It is important to note these limitations, for they provide the mechanism by which material and social reality (cf. Moghaddam, Chapter 9) restrict the person's identity to freely construct the personal self; not *anything* goes, as has been proposed by postmodern theorists (Turkle, 1995).

However, many of these chapters also point out that the role of social iden- tity is more than a passive (definitional) marker of boundaries. Specifically, the *content* of identities – as determined by material and social-structural relations (Lorenzi-Cioldi, Chapter 6; Reicher & Haslam, Chapter 13) or by group norms (Jetten & Postmes, Chapter 7; Moghaddam, Chapter 9) – is one through which personal identity must be defined; social identity has an *active* influence in shaping personality. This does not mean that social iden- tity will always inform personal identity, but depending on the group there can be a social identity content that actively seeks to guide individuals' exploration or development of their individuality. This is for instance illus- trated in research conducted among people with body piercings (Jetten, Branscombe, Schmitt, & Spears, 2001). For members of this group, identity (and one would assume a sense of individuality) is typically reaffirmed through a contrast with mainstream society. In the realm of creativity, social identity not only delineates the kinds of innovations that will be tolerated within the group, but also informs the particular lines along which individ- uals can develop their own creative urges (Adarves-Yorno, Postmes, & Haslam, in press). Just as "genius cannot be lawless" (Coleridge), the devel- opment of a distinct sense of personal identity depends at least in part on the social validation and recognition of ingroup others.

Finally, various chapters in this volume develop the idea that social identity, through the actions of the group and the actions of oneself within an intragroup context, can transform individuality and personal identity (Postmes et al., Chapter 12; Reicher & Haslam, Chapter 13; Turner et al., Chapter 2). According to Bertrand Russell (1949), partici- pants in the American revolution (1776) and British revolution (1688) were engaged in just this process: they started their revolutions as law- abiding individuals, as ingroup members. It was the opposition to their attempts to effect social change from *within* the ingroup (a lack of "respect": Spears et al., Chapter 10) that transformed their movement and coordinated their actions into a fully fledged rebellion from without (cf. Reicher, 1996; Sani & Todman, 2002). In this process of developing a "rebel" identity, their personal identity transformed as well, and they had to completely rethink their personal relationship to authority, and author- ity itself.

The subjective experience of autonomy

A second theme that runs through this book is that the subjective experi- ence of individuality is rather different than the expression of individuality through action (Prentice, Chapter 3). The subjective experience of autonomy was celebrated by humanists such as Giovanni Pico della Mirandola:

> O great and wonderful happiness of man. It is given to him to have that which he desires, and to be that which he wills. (*Oration on the Dignity of Man*)

Deborah Prentice's point is that this celebration of autonomy and free will is perhaps more a figment of imagination than an actuality. She argues that people's rationalizations for their behaviour are self-serving: people tend to explain their own behaviour in individualistic terms even when it is blatantly under social influence (although they might attempt to claim that their undesirable behaviour were conformity if they wanted to "disown" it). Indeed, one may appreciate the limitations of Mirandola's perspective on autonomy if one were to modernize the translation, and replace "man" with "person" or "woman" (cf. Lorenzi-Cioldi, Chapter 6).

This analysis resonates with the observations of Cynthia Pickett and Geoffrey Leonardelli (Chapter 4) who address the question of *when* distinctiveness vs assimilation will become more or less important. Taking Brewer's (1991) theory of optimal distinctiveness as their starting point, they propose that people's affiliation with groups serves two distinct needs – that for distinctiveness and that for assimilation. The paradoxical result of this is that affiliation with certain groups can, at the same time, satisfy both needs. In other words, identification with certain groups and social contexts can fulfil individual level needs and can make us feel unique through close affiliation with the group.

Both these perspectives (Pickett & Leonardelli's and Prentice's) concur that the experiences of autonomy and actual behaviour have different bearings, and Prentice adds that individual self-perception needs serious calibrating. Bettencourt, Molix, Talley, and Sheldon (Chapter 11) offer a rather different solution to this, taking as their starting point the assumption that needs for connectedness on the one hand, and for autonomy and authentic self-expression on the other, need not be opposites. Far from it, they argue: in intragroup contexts, social roles within groups are perfectly placed to satisfy all these needs simultaneously, and conflict between them need not arise. Thus, individuality within the group is satisfied through acting out roles which, while connecting individuals to the group, simultaneously differentiate them from it.

All these chapters serve as a useful reminder that the experience of individuality (whether in terms of rationalizations or needs) is a topic which has received short shrift in self-categorization and social identity theories. As noted by several authors (e.g., Pickett & Leonardelli) it would be worthwhile to remedy this, for although individuals might well fool themselves about the degree to which they are autonomous (cf. Prentice), people often let their needs dictate their actions, and their myths, self-generated or otherwise, are powerful motives for action.

The group's response to displays of individuality: the autonomous/collective

One of the interesting developments of this focus on individuality in the group has been a marked shift in how we expect ingroup deviants to be treated. The classical prediction (derived from SCT in particular) is that ingroup members who deviate are perceived as black sheep: they are chastised and ousted. This prediction rests on the assumption that, when social identity is salient, group members will do what it takes to preserve the integrity and distinctiveness of their group. No doubt there are conditions under which this kind of response will occur, but the emphasis in the present volume on the functionality of group members acting as individuals in and for the group leads to a rather different prediction. As shown by Matthew Hornsey (Chapter 5), the ingroup critic can be evaluated quite positively, if only their actions are perceived to be for the good of the group.

Hornsey's findings provide an important counterpoint to more mechanical assumptions about the way in which the distinctiveness within social categories is managed by group members (e.g., subjective group dynamics: Marques, Abrams, Paez, & Martinez-Taboada, 1998). As Hornsey's research shows, not all deviance meets the fate of a black sheep. From the present volume's vantage point, the important implication of the endorsement of critics found in Hornsey's studies is that (a) category characteristics and (b) ingroup norms can be changed from within. In practice, this once again reinforces that it is often not safe to treat social categories as "given". Social categories and social identities might be more undisputed in clear-cut cases of intergroup divisions (such as a war) or in an experimental "vacuum" which allows the creation of such ideal circumstances (Tajfel, 1972). But given that the majority of situations are less ideal, in the sense that group members are likely to be willing to question social identities, it may be more fruitful to move beyond the study of individuals in isolation "looking out" on social categories (Spears et al., Chapter 10).

Indeed, such a transition to a more dynamic study of social identity would resonate with conclusions reached in several chapters in this volume: that social identity is not a "thing" isolated from its broader historical and ideological context, but a project populated by individuals, who influence and shape it, and use it as an instrument for personal and social change (Reicher & Haslam, Chapter 13); that social identities are not just deduced from contextual givens, but are also induced from expressions of individuality and intragroup interaction (Postmes et al., Chapter 12); and that intragroup roles do not undermine the unity or homogeneity of the group (threatening its distinctiveness) but strengthen the integrity of the group, and reinforce social identities as a result (Bettencourt et al., Chapter 11). All this suggests a far more organic approach to social identity, wherein group members do not and cannot immediately know social identity from context, but are actively involved in its evaluation and formation. As Turner et al. observe in Chapter 2: "there is no Chinese Wall between the individuality and groupness of people. One cannot be reduced to or subsumed by the other but neither should any false dichotomy be invented to deny the living reality of people in which being an individual and being a group member function collaboratively."

The relation between personal and social identity

The developments described so far are neither piecemeal nor minor. They represent radical innovations and major advances in our thinking about personal and social identity. How do they reflect on some original assumptions of social identity theory and self-categorization theory? As noted by Spears et al., (Chapter 10), there is a danger of reverting back to the individualism which social identity perspectives sought to escape.

The key theoretical assumptions of social identity and self-categorization theory that most chapters in this book speak to are those that differentiate personal and social identity. In social identity theory, Tajfel (1978) differentiated between interpersonal and intergroup behaviour on a continuum, implying that the more interpersonal behaviour became, the less it would be under the influence of social identity. In self-categorization theory there is a similar assumption that personal and social identity are functionally antagonistic – that as one becomes more salient it becomes harder for the other to be salient (see Turner et al., Chapter 2). On the face of it, some chapters in this volume appear to flatly contradict these two principles. Some argue that through the content of social identity, a heightened salience of social identity can make group members more aware of their sense of individuality and individual distinctiveness (Halloran & Kashima, Chapter 8; Jetten & Postmes, Chapter 7; Lorenzi-Cioldi, Chapter 6). Others argue that it is possible for individuals to construct a sense of social identity (Postmes et al., Chapter 12; Turner et al., Chapter 2).

But the fact that there is a reciprocal interaction between personal and social identity does not invalidate the distinction between interpersonal and intergroup behaviour. One way of understanding the effects described in these chapters, we believe, is that *intragroup behaviour* is qualitatively different from these two (see also Spears et al., Chapter 10). In intragroup behaviour (as in interpersonal behaviour) the individual remains a significant factor, but (unlike in interpersonal behaviour) their contribution is evaluated in terms of the framework of a shared identity. Intragroup behaviour is therefore a dialogue between group members concerning the group.

This reciprocal interaction does not invalidate the distinction between personal and social identity either. Quite the reverse. Chapters in this volume have articulated the way in which personal identities within the group are shaped through intragroup comparisons, while at the same time being regularized by the (normative) framework provided by an overarching ingroup identity (see "Socializing the individual" above). This can be contrasted from an elaborated conception of social identity as the product of both inductive and deductive processes (see "The group's response" above). By elaborating the fundamentally distinct pathways through which these two aspects of identity are constituted, this volume underlines once again the functionality of the personal/social identity distinction.

Intra- and intergroup dynamics

As several chapters in this volume acknowledge, the role of individuals in the group only comes into focus when the group is studied as a dynamic system rather than as a static entity. Bettencourt et al. (Chapter 11) emphasize the intragroup process through an analysis of roles and their relation to personal and social identity respectively. Postmes et al. (Chapter 12) focus on the role of communication. Reicher and Haslam (Chapter 13) offer a joint perspective on the interaction between intra- and intergroup dynamics. Rather than reiterate their conclusions in detail here, let us simply conclude that the analysis in these chapters is rather different from the traditional social identity focus. This shift in emphasis does not, however, signal a retreat to a classic group dynamics approach to studying groups or a shift away from categorical groups and toward interactive ones (Postmes et al., Chapter 12). Rather, it signals that we can fruitfully extend our understandings of categorical processes in groups, linking them to the dynamics observed in (smaller) social groups as well.

The possibilities for this cross-fertilization were always acknowledged, especially in self-categorization theory. Reicher (1987; also 1996) discussed at some length the importance of intragroup processes in the formation of a situated social identity. Indeed, this emphasis on the role of intra- and intergroup dynamics in the constitution of social identity is understandable given that the regularities of crowd behaviour are to some extent emergent from the context and interaction (R. H. Turner & Killian, 1972). Similarly, Turner (1982) had already signalled that social identities could not be conceived of as givens, and noted the possibility that they were induced from intragroup dynamics.

But, although their role was occasionally acknowledged, it would be wrong to say that intragroup dynamics have been a central concern of social identity researchers. This is in part due to the pervasiveness of research paradigms which are inherently static – being concerned with the individual cognizing their relationship to the group. But it is also in part due to the research topics with which they have been concerned. With the exception of group polarization (where research exploits have not been an overwhelming success: Postmes, Haslam, & Swaab, 2005), social identity researchers have tended to stick with familiar issues of intergroup relations such as ingroup bias and stereotyping. It is through application to new domains (organizational issues, communication, intragroup dynamics, and so on) that this different side to social identity now comes to be explored.

Once again, we must conclude that for the study of social identity to progress, and for it to be progressive, we need to focus on the ways in which social identities evolve and change, and on the ways in which they enable social change. Tajfel (1972) certainly did not believe that to study social identity as a static structural feature was the way to go: "As soon as anything changes in the environment ... new choices confront the individual. The processes which underlie these choices, and thus constitute the psychological aspects of social change at all levels, are the proper subject matter of social psychology" (p. 115).

Conclusion: the pragmatic utility of social identity

The central concern of this discussion, and indeed of this volume, has been with theoretical advance and innovation. But the advance of theory is not a very useful pursuit in its own right, unless it is accompanied by a greater scope of application. There is no doubt that our focus on individuality in the group has opened up several new fields of research for social identity researchers to explore, and opened up new ways of studying familiar topics. To conclude, we would like to extract some of these new research directions from the chapters in this volume. This is of course an arbitrary and somewhat personal list; other areas exist that may also (and perhaps more fruitfully) be explored. Yet, we believe that our choice reflects the key new areas for future growth in theory and application.

One obvious area for future research opened up by the developments charted above is the study of individuality in its social context. The study of personality and individuality from a social identity perspective would be one interesting avenue. This could entail a focus on the way in which context systematically informs personality and individuality, personality change, and continuity. One could also focus on the way in which intrapersonal categorization affects the structure of self. And one could focus on the way in which personality and individuality are constructed socially, in dynamic interaction with others (see also Antaki, Condor, & Levine, 1996).

Another area for future growth is the systematic study of the way individuality influences (and interacts with) social identity. This would require greater emphasis on intragroup processes and on social identities in small groups because these contexts would allow for the examination of the dynamic ways in which social identities are formed and changed. This opens an array of possibilities for the study of relations between individuality and social identity in areas such as group decision-making, conformity, deviance, productivity, creativity, negotiation, corruption, leadership and roles. We believe that the study of intragroup processes would make researchers more aware of the dynamic and interactive nature in which individuality informs social identity (and vice versa). In that way, it would help to move away from dualist conceptions of the individual and the group and encourage a proper analysis of core assumptions about a link between the self and the group.

A third issue for future consideration is the study of culture and its relations to social identity. One key role for social identity here is to fill the "gap" in cultural analyses – which typically assume a direct and straightforward relationship between culture and individuality. Although cultural psychology is a rich field, its models of social influence are probably not as advanced as those within self-categorization theory (Turner, 1991). Moreover, there is an important issue of the reciprocal relationship between social identity and culture. As Halloran and Kashima discuss in Chapter 8, the relation between social identity and culture is in some ways similar to that between individuality and social identity. Translating insights from this elaborated view of social identity to culture could provide an important stepping stone towards a better understanding of cultural change.

Areas where this new perspective on social identity could be fruitfully (re)applied are conformity, depersonalization and stereotyping research, to name a few. For instance, if individuality is recognized in the group, we may no longer perceive conformity as the absence of individual voice, but view it as emerging from individual group members in relation to and in interaction with a salient identity. In a similar vein, depersonalization may not be about the submergence of the individual to the group, but rather may imply the close alignment of individual and group goals. In stereotyping research, it may be fruitful to pay more attention to intragroup and interindividual dynamics that shape whether outgroup members are perceived in individualist or categorical terms. More generally, we believe that a rigid understanding of the principle of functional antagonism and the interpersonal–intergroup continuum has stood in the way of examining individual–group interaction in areas such as research on the black sheep effect, social influence, and ingroup bias. A more dynamic and interactive approach as advocated by chapters in this volume could benefit our understanding of these issues.

In sum, we believe that this volume has provided not just food for thought, but food for practice. The benefits of focusing on the role of individuality in the group are now clear. They are not just in producing some concrete theoretical advances, such as a novel perspective on personality (Turner et al., Chapter 2). They are also, and perhaps more importantly, in opening a new window on the study of social identity, and the interaction between individual and group. Focusing once again on the individual in the group is therefore not a move away from the core concerns of social identity and self-categorization theories. It is a move towards the core concerns of the social identity project. Pursuing the study of individuality in the group allows us to shine a brighter light on social identity, and on the dynamic processes that give rise to it.

REFERENCES

Adarves-Yorno, I., Postmes, T., & Haslam, S. A. (in press). Social identity and the recognition of creativity in groups. *British Journal of Social Psychology*.

Antaki, C., Condor, S., & Levine, M. (1996). Social identities in talk: Speakers' own orientations. *British Journal of Social Psychology*, *35*, 473–492.

Brewer, M. B. (1991). The social self: On being the same and different at the same time. *Personality and Social Psychology Bulletin*, *17*, 475–482.

Ellemers, N., Spears, R., & Doosje, B. (Eds.) (1999). *Social identity: Context, commitment, content*. Oxford: Blackwell.

Jetten, J., Branscombe, N. R., Schmitt, M. T., & Spears, R. (2001). Rebels with a cause: Group identification as a response to perceived discrimination from the mainstream. *Personality and Social Psychology Bulletin*, *27*, 1204–1213.

Marques, J. M., Abrams, D., Paez, D., & Martinez-Taboada, C. (1998). The role of categorization and in-group norms in judgments of groups and their members. *Journal of Personality and Social Psychology*, *75*, 976–988.

Postmes, T., Haslam, S. A., & Swaab, R. (2005). Social influence in small groups: An interactive model of social identity formation. *European Review of Social Psychology*, *16*, 1–42.

Reicher, S. (1987). Crowd behaviour as social action. In J. C. Turner, M. A. Hogg, P. J. Oakes, S. Reicher, & M. S. Wetherell (Eds.), *Rediscovering the social group: A self-categorization theory* (pp. 171–202). Oxford: Blackwell.

Reicher, S. (1996). "The Battle of Westminster": Developing the social identity model of crowd behaviour in order to explain the initiation and development of collective conflict. *European Journal of Social Psychology*, *26*, 115–134.

Russell, B. (1949). *Authority and the individual*. London: Allen & Unwin.

Sani, F., & Todman, J. (2002). Should we stay or should we go? A social psychological model of schisms in groups. *Personality and Social Psychology Bulletin, 28,* 1647–1655.

Simon, B. (2004). *Identity in modern society: A social psychological perspective.* Oxford: Blackwell.

Tajfel, H. (1972). Experiments in a vacuum. In J. Israel & H. Tajfel (Eds.), *The context of social psychology* (pp. 69–119). London: Academic.

Tajfel, H. (1978). Interindividual behaviour and intergroup behaviour. In H. Tajfel (Ed.), *Differentiation between groups: Studies in the social psychology of intergroup relations* (pp. 27–60). London: Academic.

Turkle, S. (1995). *Life on the screen: Identity in the age of the internet.* New York: Simon & Schuster.

Turner, J. C. (1982). Towards a cognitive redefinition of the group. In H. Tajfel (Ed.), *Social identity and intergroup relations* (pp. 15–40). Cambridge: Cambridge University Press.

Turner, J. C. (1991). *Social influence.* Milton Keynes: Open University Press.

Turner, J. C. (1999). Some current issues in research on social identity and self-categorisation theories. In N. Ellemers, R. Spears, & B. Doosje (Eds.), *Social identity: Context, commitment, content* (pp. 68–89). Oxford: Blackwell.

Turner, R. H., & Killian, L. M. (1972). *Collective behavior* (2nd ed.). Englewood Cliffs, NJ: Prentice-Hall.

Author Index

Lehman, S., 139, 152
Lehmiller, J. J., 21, 26, 27, 29, 34
Leonardelli, G. J., 7, 56–73, 63, 69, 118, 155, 196, 262
Levine, J. M., 74, 79, 90, 91, 127, 134, 135, 231, 235
Levine, M., 216, 231, 233, 267, 268
Levine, N., 161, 172
Levine, R. M., 246, 247, 256
Levinson, D. J., 26, 33, 79, 88, 251, 255
Lewin, K., 93, 112, 217, 234
Lewis, A., 217, 234
Lewis, J., 221, 233
Leyens, J., 80, 90
Lickel, B., 217, 220, 234
Lieberman, M. B., 181, 192
Lightdale, J. R., 43, 54, 109, 114, 217, 235
Limbert, W. M., 102, 110
Lind, E., 207, 213
Litwack, L., 221, 231
Litwack L. F., 221, 231, 233
Lodewijckx, H. F. M., 178, 194
Lois, J., 116, 125, 134
Lorenzi-Cioldi, F., 7, 93–115, 111, 112, 113, 118, 197, 261, 262, 264
Losier, G., 197, 212
Lott, B., 96, 113
Louis, W. R., 30, 34
Luhtanen, R., 180, 193, 199, 211
Lynch, M., 197, 213
Lyon, D., 242, 256

MacCulloch, D., 215, 234
Macdonald, G., 182, 193
Mackie, D. M., 85, 90
Madsen, R., 1, 9
Majka, K., 82, 90
Major, B., 102, 113
Malone, P. S., 101, 111, 141, 151
Manstead, A. R., 152
Manstead, A. S. R., 69, 118, 126, 134, 145, 178, 194
Maquet, J. J., 160, 173
Marcia, J. E., 200, 212
Markus, H., 12, 34
Markus, H. R., 43, 54, 58, 72, 77, 90, 121, 134, 138, 139, 140, 151–153
Marques, J. M., 75, 80, 82, 88, 90, 263
Marques, J., 80, 106, 113
Marshall, T. C., 58, 72
Martin, D., 217, 233
Martinez-Taboda, C., 263, 268
Marx, K., 227, 232, 234
Maslow, A., 205, 212
Maslow, A. H., 57, 72

Matheson, K., 82, 90
Matsumoto, D., 139, 153
Mavor, K., 30, 34
McAdams, D. P., 40, 54
McAuliffe, B. J., 21, 26, 29, 34, 60, 71, 77, 89, 97, 103, 112–3, 119, 120–4, 126, 129, 134, 139, 149, 152, 193
McAuliffe, B., 42, 53, 227, 232, 234
McCall, G. J., 199, 200, 204, 212
McCoy, S. K., 102, 113
McDougall, W., 39, 54
McFarland, C., 48, 50, 51, 54
McGarty, C., 17, 20, 21, 33, 34, 73, 60, 65, 134, 142, 143, 152, 223, 228, 234, 246, 248, 255
McGarty, C. A., 14,16, 22, 24, 36, 120, 132, 136
McGregor, H. A., 204, 212
McHugh, M., 102, 115
McKimmie, B., 179, 181, 193
McKimmie, B. M., 180, 207, 212
McKone, E., 21, 26, 27, 35
McLaughlin-Volpe, T., 109, 110
McLellan, D., 128, 134
McMinn, J. G., 84, 90, 231, 235
Mead, G. H., 177, 193, 204, 212, 228, 235
Medin, D. L., 17, 34
Mein, J., 66, 71
Menon, T., 138, 151
Meyer, G., 99, 111
Middlebrook, K. J., 165, 173
Milgram, S., 74, 90
Miller, D. T., 43, 48–51, 54, 109, 114, 217, 235
Miller, J. B., 102, 113
Miller, J. G., 138, 153, 140
Millett, D., 96, 113
Milton, L. P., 13, 36, 46, 47, 55, 229, 236
Mirandola G. P., 262
Mischel, W., 12, 25, 34
Mizrahi, K., 209, 211, 217, 234
Moghaddam, F. M., 8, 41, 43, 96, 106, 114, 115, 155–174, 156, 172, 173, 174, 226, 260, 261
Molix, L., 9, 47, 196–214, 262, 264, 265
Molouki, S., 47, 49, 50, 54
Monge, P. R., 177, 193
Moore, M., 87
Morales, J. F., 155, 174
Mor, T., 169, 173
Moreland, R. L., 58, 72, 74, 84, 90, 127, 134, 135, 222, 231, 235
Morray, J. P., 79, 90
Morris, M. W., 138, 151
Morrison, D., 84, 90

Reynolds, K. J., 6, 11–36, 33, 35–6, 40–1, 59, 66, 71, 120, 131, 134, 142–3, 146, 148, 152, 177, 178, 191, 206, 209, 212, 223, 226, 228, 233–4, 246, 256, 260–1, 264, 268
Rhee, E., 139, 154
Rice, T. W., 141, 154
Richards, Z., 100, 114
Richeson, J., 51, 55
Riecken, H. W., 102, 114
Riley, C. J., 169, 173
Roberts, B. W., 199, 200, 211, 213
Robins, R. W., 199, 211
Robinson, W. P., 155, 173
Roccas, S., 44, 53, 54, 59, 71, 144, 151
Rodgers, D. A., 200, 213
Rosch, E., 19, 35
Rosenberg, M., 105, 114
Rosenberg, S., 187, 194
Ross, L., 49, 53
Ross, E., 50, 54
Rothbart, M., 101, 114
Rubin, M., 3, 10, 62, 72, 100, 114
Rubini, M., 103, 114
Runciman, S., 215, 235
Russell, B., 1, 10, 261, 268
Ryan, C. S., 101, 114
Ryan, M., 35
Ryan, M. K., 21, 26, 27, 28, 35, 256
Ryan R. M., 57, 71, 196–7, 199–200, 204, 207, 210–1, 213

Sampson, E. E., 155, 173
Sanford, R. N., 26, 33, 79, 88, 251, 255
Sani, F., 21, 35, 76, 77, 91, 261, 269
Sarbin, T. R., 199, 200, 204, 205, 213
Sassenberg, K., 44, 54, 228, 229, 235
Schachter, S., 75, 82, 91
Schama, S., 165, 173
Schatz, R. T., 79, 91
Scheepers, D., 178, 194
Schimel, J., 148, 151
Schmitt, M. T., 21, 26–7, 29, 34–5, 180, 193, 247, 256, 261, 268
Schopler, J., 84, 89
Schreiber, H. J., 61, 69, 72
Schroeder, C. M., 49, 51, 54
Schwartz, S. H., 138, 154, 196, 213
Scott, W. A., 204, 213
Searle, J. R., 228, 231, 235
Sedikides, C., 46, 53, 54, 119, 135, 181, 194, 204, 212
Seixas, E., 106, 113
Sekaquaptewa, D., 98, 114
Sennett, R., 97, 114

Senter, M. S., 103, 105, 112
Seta, C. E., 188, 194
Seta, J. J., 188, 194
Shaver, P. R., 57, 71
Shavitt, S., 169, 173
Sheldon, K. M., 9, 47, 55, 196–214, 213, 262–5
Sheldon, K., 47, 53, 118, 133, 200, 211
Shelton, J. N., 51, 55
Sherif, M., 20, 35, 120, 135, 225, 235
Sherman, S. J., 217, 220, 234
Shichman, S., 196, 211
Shoda, Y., 12, 25, 34
Sidanius, J., 26, 35
Siegel, A. E., 27, 35
Siegel, S., 27, 35
Silver, M. D., 63, 72
Silverman, R. A., 106, 112
Simmons, J. L., 199, 200, 204, 212
Simon, A. F., 217, 226, 236
Simon, B., 15, 35, 40, 41, 42, 45, 53, 55, 63, 72, 97, 103, 114, 116, 130–1, 134–5, 194, 207, 213, 234, 235, 260
Skowronksi, J. J., 187, 194
Sleebos, E., 180, 187, 194
Slocum, N. R., 169, 173
Smith, E. R., 57, 72, 98, 115, 140, 154
Smith, H. J., 99, 114, 180, 183, 194, 195, 207
Smith, R. H., 187, 194
Snodgrass, S. E., 100, 114
Snyder R., 18, 33,
Snyder, C. R., 57, 58, 72, 118, 118, 126, 135
Solomon, S., 145, 148, 151
Sommerville, J., 79, 91
Spears, R., 2, 8, 10, 17, 34, 42–3, 54, 66, 68–9, 71–2, 75, 81, 90–1, 119, 125, 132–5, 145, 149, 151–5, 169, 172, 175–195, 192–195, 198, 207, 211–2, 217, 220, 228–2, 235–6, 238–9, 256, 261, 263–4, 268
Spence, K., 56, 64, 72
Spencer, S. J., 145, 154
Sperber, D., 43, 55
Stasser, G., 144, 154
Statham, A., 12, 35
Staub, E., 79, 91
Steele, B.J., 141, 154
Steele, C. M., 145, 154
Stephenson, G. M., 15, 35, 103, 114
Stewart, T., 101, 113
Stogdill, R. M., 18, 35, 250, 256
Stott, C., 21, 35, 228, 229, 235, 247, 255
Strauss, C., 140, 153
Stroebe, K. E., 178, 194
Strube, M. J., 181, 194

Subject Index

Indices complied by Lucy O'Sullivan